Developmental
Academic
Advising

*Addressing Students' Educational,
Career, and Personal Needs*

Roger B. Winston, Jr.
Theodore K. Miller
Steven C. Ender
Thomas J. Grites
and Associates

Developmental Academic Advising

❧❧❧❧❧❧❧❧

Jossey-Bass Publishers

San Francisco • Washington • London • 1984

DEVELOPMENTAL ACADEMIC ADVISING
Addressing Students' Educational,
Career, and Personal Needs
by Roger B. Winston, Jr., Theodore K. Miller,
Steven C. Ender, Thomas J. Grites, and Associates

Copyright © 1984 by: Jossey-Bass Inc., Publishers
433 California Street
San Francisco, California 94104

&

Jossey-Bass Limited
28 Banner Street
London EC1Y 8QE

Library of Congress Cataloging in Publication Data

Main entry under title:

Developmental academic advising.

(The Jossey-Bass higher education series) The Jossey-
Bass social and behavioral science series
Includes bibliographies and index.
1.   Personnel service in higher education—United
States—Addresses, essays, lectures.   I. Winston,
Roger B.   II. Series.   III. Series: Jossey-Bass social
and behavioral science series.
LB2343.D42   1984   378'.194'0973   84-48001
ISBN 0-87589-633-2

Manufactured in the United States of America

The paper in this book meets the guidelines for
permanence and durability of the Committee on
Production Guidelines for Book Longevity of the
Council on Library Resources.

JACKET DESIGN BY WILLI BAUM

FIRST EDITION

Code 8435

A joint publication in
The Jossey-Bass Higher Education Series
and
The Jossey-Bass
Social and Behavioral Science Series

72411

Preface

As long as there have been colleges, there has been a need for students to receive guidance and assistance as they plan their programs of study, become adjusted to the college environment and its unique academic, social, and psychological demands, and face the rigors of growing up. In the early days of higher education in America, the duty of providing guidance generally was fulfilled by the college president. As institutions became more complex, faculty members joined, and then replaced, the president as "academic advisors." With the gigantic growth in enrollment during the 1960s and early 1970s, academic advising seems to have become one of the victims of the dash to admit greater numbers of students. Much of the personal attention and concern often shown students in an earlier day is lost. As a result, the nature of students' educational experience has been affected profoundly.

Surveys of students and college administrators alike, consequently, reveal general dissatisfaction with both the quality and effectiveness of academic advising on most college campuses. DeCoster and Mable* reported, based on student interviews, that "the

---

*DeCoster, D. A., and Mable, P. "Interpersonal Relationships." In D. A. DeCoster and P. Mable (Eds.), *New Directions for Student Services: Understanding Today's Students*, no. 16. San Francisco: Jossey-Bass, 1981.

very mention of academic advisors would invariably be met with a roar of laughter." At the same time, colleges are faced with the pressures of a changing composition of the population of potential students, limited financial resources, the need to increase the retention of students, and the emergence of student consumerism. Many have argued that a means for solving some of these problems would be to revitalize the academic advising system. College administrators, however, often have been at a loss as to how best to approach the problem. The first response has often been to increase the number of advisors, employ full-time advisors, or threaten faculty advisors if they did not give more attention to their advising chores. Few of these approaches have worked very well as a *primary* intervention.

This book is intended to help academic advisors and institutional decision makers better understand the potential power academic advising has for improving the quality of students' educational experiences and facilitating the intellectual and personality development of students. Quality academic advising is a pragmatic way for college administrators and faculty members to demonstrate they are serious about "educating the whole person," as is often asserted in mission statements. Further, this book is designed to present those who are confronted with organizing, directing, and delivering academic advising with practical strategies and techniques that can be used to strengthen existing programs.

The basic theses of this book are that (1) academic advising is an integral part of the educational process, not just a support service; (2) in order to revitalize academic advising, new models are required; (3) the most appropriate models for academic advising are grounded in human/student development theory and are based on the establishment of a personal relationship between the student and advisor; and (4) effective advising programs offer students greater opportunities to realize more fully their potentials—as persons, citizens, and workers—by taking better advantage of the resources available in the college environment. In other words, academic advising has the potential for being a powerful educational intervention, which can greatly improve the quality of education experienced by students.

This book was conceived to meet three related sets of needs. First, there is a dearth of literature that addresses academic advising in a more than superficial manner. In fact, this book marks the first attempt to present a comprehensive, in-depth treatment of academic advising in higher education. Second, those responsible for academic advising are seeking a source of ideas and practical strategies that can be used on their campuses. Third, there is a need for a well-conceived theoretical framework that practitioners can use to guide them as they develop programs.

Hence, this book is intended for a number of audiences in higher education: It is offered to those who are faced with evaluating their present advising programs and who desire new perspectives and additional information. College presidents, academic vice-presidents, deans, department chairpersons, directors of academic advising, and student affairs professionals will find in it ideas that can help them improve the quality of advising on their campuses. Persons who currently serve as academic advisors should find this book a source of new ideas and alternative approaches for solving problems. Faculty members in graduate programs for students who will go on to leadership roles in academic advising as well as advising coordinators and directors who wish to increase their staff members' effectiveness will find this book valuable.

The book is organized into four parts. Part One, "Academic Advising for Student Development: Foundations and Current Practices," introduces the concept of developmental academic advising and the human/student development theory on which it is based, presents an overview of current advising practices, and proffers an institution-wide perspective of academic advising by a college president. Part Two, "The Advising Process: Strategies and Clientele," deals with specific strategies that can be used to make academic advising an effective educational intervention, namely, educational planning and decision making, integration of advising and career planning, strategies for enhancing the intellectual and personal development of students, specific tools and techniques individual advisors can use with students, and the uses of computers in the advising process. Part Two also deals with the special advising needs of several important undergraduate subpopulations—including academic high-risk, international, part-time, academically gifted, and handicapped students—and graduate students. Part Three, "Organizing and Administering Advising Programs," addresses issues associated with structuring and administering advising programs. The design of delivery systems, daily administrative concerns, legal issues associated with advising, introduction of developmental advising ideas to faculty academic advisors, and training programs for professional and paraprofessional advisors are all addressed. Part Four, "Translating Theory into Practice," describes existing advising programs at fourteen widely varied colleges and universities, focusing on four different delivery approaches: advising centers, decentralized (departmental) advising, student paraprofessional advisors, and advising provided in conjunction with an academic course. Part Four concludes with proposals for improving academic advising and forecasts of challenges and opportunities likely to develop during the coming decade.

A number of people deserve recognition for the assistance they provided during the three years this project has required to reach fruition. Gary Hanson was particularly helpful in the early stages of development of the ideas that ultimately led to the book. His editorial advice also has been valuable.

A special note of appreciation is extended to the chapter authors; they have worked diligently, indulged the editors in style and content preferences, and contributed solid scholarship and creative ideas. And for this they are thanked profusely! This book has been a collaborative effort intended to produce an integrated, comprehensive view of advising; contributors were selected because of their expertise and their commitment to the concept of developmental academic advising. Authors, however, were encouraged to express their own ideas, thereby producing a diversity of opinions, sometimes conflicting.

Finally, we wish to acknowledge especially the persons who provided information about advising programs described herein: Janice Abel, Ronald V. Adkins, Joyce Alberts, Francis L. Battisti, Kitty Corak, Julianne Daffin, John N. Gardner, Linda C. Higginson, Mary Stuart Hunter, David W. King, Margaret A. Landry, Harry M. Langley, Joseph F. Metz, Jr., James Pappas, Bryan D. Smith, G. Robert Standing, Linda A. Syrell, Sharon Van Tuyl,

Kathryn O. Venema, Eric R. White, and Leanne Wolff. Without their cooperation and willingness to share, the touch of reality we sought to maintain throughout this book would have been missing.

August 1984   Roger B. Winston, Jr.
Athens, Georgia   Theodore K. Miller
                                    Steven C. Ender
                                    Thomas J. Grites

Contents

Contents

The Authors

◆◆◆◆◆◆◆◆

Roger B. Winston, Jr., is associate professor in the Student Personnel in Higher Education Program, Department of Counseling and Human Development Services, University of Georgia. He received his A.B. degree (1965) in history and philosophy from Auburn University and his M.A. degree (1970) in philosophy and Ph.D. degree (1973) in counseling and student personnel services from the University of Georgia.

Winston's primary research interests have been in the measurement of student development constructs, investigation of environmental influences on student growth, and academic advising as a student development intervention. When he was a student affairs administrator he coordinated an experimental freshman-year academic advising program; he currently serves as an academic advisor to graduate students. He served as editor of *ACPA Developments* (1975–1977), as a senator in the American Personnel and Guidance Association (1978–1981), and as a member of the executive council of the American College Personnel Association (1978–1981). Currently he is an associate editor of the *College Student Affairs Journal* and serves on the editorial board of the *Journal of College Student Personnel*. Winston's test publications include the *Student Developmental Task Inventory*, 2nd edition, with T. K. Miller and J. S. Prince (1979), and the *Academic Advising Inventory*, with J. A. Sandor (1984). He has edited three books: *Developmental Ap-*

proaches to Academic Advising, with S. C. Ender and T. K. Miller (1982), *Administration and Leadership in Student Affairs,* with T. K. Miller and W. R. Mendenhall (1983), and *Students as Paraprofessional Staff,* with S. C. Ender (1984).

Theodore K. Miller is professor of education in the Department of Counseling and Human Development Services, College of Education, University of Georgia. He earned his B.S. degree (1954) in business and English and M.A. degree (1957) in guidance and counseling from Ball State University. He received his Ed.D. degree (1962) in counseling and student personnel services from the University of Florida.

Miller has been interested in the process of student development in higher education settings and has focused attention on the application of human development theory to work with college students, particularly in the areas of programming and academic advising. He is past president of the American College Personnel Association (1975-76) and was director of the ACPA Tomorrow's Higher Education Project. He has represented ACPA on the board of directors of the American Personnel and Guidance Association, the Council for Accreditation of Counseling and Related Educational Programs (CACREP), and the Council for the Advancement of Standards for Student Services/Development Programs (CAS). He has been president of CAS since its inception in 1980. In 1976, Miller was recipient of the first Mel Hardee Award for Outstanding Achievement and Contribution to the College Personnel Profession presented by the Southern College Personnel Association. He was recipient of the first annual Professional of the Year Award presented by the Georgia College Personnel Association in 1980 and received the ACPA Professional Service Award in 1981. He is author or editor of four books: *The Future of Student Affairs,* with J. S. Prince (1976); *Students Helping Students,* with S. C. Ender and S. S. McCaffrey (1979); *Developmental Approaches to Academic Advising,* with R. B. Winston and S. C. Ender (1982); and *Administration and Leadership in Student Affairs,* with R. B. Winston and W. R. Mendenhall (1983).

Steven C. Ender is assistant professor and counselor, Center for Student Development, Kansas State University. He received his

B.S. degree (1973) in business management from Virginia Common-
wealth University and his M.Ed. degree (1976) in student personnel
in higher education and Ed.D. degree (1981) in counseling and
student personnel services from the University of Georgia.

Ender's primary professional interests include programs for
training student paraprofessionals and developing institutional
programs in learning skills acquisition, retention, academic advising, and assisting academic high-risk athletes. Additionally, he
teaches classes through the Counseling Department at Kansas State
University and provides personal counseling services. He has experience at both the University of Georgia and Kansas State with
programs to improve retention, study skills, and academic advising.
His research includes a nation-wide investigation of undergraduate
paraprofessional utilization in student affairs settings. He is author
or editor of three books: *Students Helping Students,* with S. S.
McCaffrey and T. K. Miller (1979); *Developmental Approaches to
Academic Advising,* with R. B. Winston and T. K. Miller (1982);
and *Students as Paraprofessional Staff,* with R. B. Winston (1984).

Thomas J. Grites is director of academic advising at Stockton
State College in Pomona, New Jersey. He received his B.S. degree
(1966) and his M.S. degree (1967), both in education, from Illinois
State University, and his Ph.D. degree (1974) in college student
personnel administration from the University of Maryland.

Grites's main professional interests have been in writing and
consulting about academic advising and in assisting the development of the National Academic Advising Association. In 1983, he
received an Alumni Achievement Award from Illinois State University. His publications include *Academic Advising: Getting Us
Through the Eighties* (1979) and numerous journal articles.

He has served as chairperson for three National Conferences
on Academic Advising and was president of the National Academic
Advising Association for two years. He also served as chairperson
of the American College Personnel Association's Commission on
the Organization, Administration, and Development of Student
Personnel Services. He currently serves on the academic councils of
two external degree-granting institutions and on his local board of
education.

Arthur W. Chickering is distinguished professor of higher education and director of the Center for the Study of Higher Education at Memphis State University. He received his B.A. degree (1950) in comparative literature from Wesleyan University, his M.A.T. degree (1951) in English from Harvard Graduate School of Education, and his Ph.D. degree (1958) in school psychology from Columbia University.

Chickering's main research and development projects have concerned college influences on student development and systematic efforts to use research to improve educational practices for diverse student populations in colleges and universities. He was founding academic vice-president of Empire State College, a new nontraditional unit of the State University of New York. As director of the center at Memphis State University, he and his colleagues have worked with numerous institutions across the country in developing alternative programs to better serve the educational needs of adult learners. His first book, *Education and Identity,* received the 1969 Book Award of the American Council on Education for its "outstanding contribution to higher education." He received the Outstanding Service Award from the National Association of Student Personnel Administrators in 1972 and the Contribution to Knowledge Award from the American College Personnel Association in 1980. His other major publications are *Commuting Versus Resident Students* (1974) and *The Modern American College* (1981).

Chickering has been chairman of the board of trustees of the American Association for Higher Education and of the Council for the Advancement of Experiential Learning.

David S. Crockett is vice-president for public affairs at American College Testing Program. He received his B.A. degree (1957) in history and physical education from Ohio Wesleyan University and his M.A. degree (1958) in higher education from the University of Maryland.

He has served as editor of two major resource documents designed to assist college personnel in improving the advising process and has contributed to numerous other publications including the second National Survey on Academic Advising (1983). He was the recipient for ACT of the first Research Award for Outstanding Contribution to the Field of Academic Advising from the National Academic Advising Association. He is a nationally recognized authority on the subject of academic advising in colleges and universities and has directed nearly forty national academic advising conferences.

Leroy Ervin is assistant vice-president for academic affairs and director of the Division of Developmental Studies at the University of Georgia. He received his B.S. degree (1963) in science and physical education from Wayne State University, his M.S. degree (1970) in public management from Case Western Reserve University, and his Ph.D. degree (1975) in counselor education from the University of Akron.

Ervin's major research interests focus on the academic performance of nontraditional students. His publications include "The Relationship of Special Studies to the Dropout Rate of Black and White College Students," with S. Brown (1979); "A Comparison in the Prediction of Academic Performance for College Developmental Students and Regularly Admitted Students," with M. Hogrebe, P. Dwinell, and I. Newman (1982); and "Proposal 48: The Right Direction But Short of the Mark," with S. A. Saunders and H. L. Gillis (1984).

Robert E. Gardner is the senior associate director of admissions for Cornell University. He received his B.A. degree (1966) from Linfield College in chemistry and history, his M.S. degree (1969) from Cornell University in history, and his Ph.D. degree (1970) from Cornell University in history, specializing in scientific and European history. Shortly after receiving his doctorate, he worked as an assistant to the dean of the College of Engineering at Cornell. He has served as codirector of the Cornell summer advising workshop, coauthored a number of books and articles on academic advising—including *Advising by Faculty*, 2nd edition, with H. C. Kramer (1983)—and consulted with a variety of two-year and four-year institutions on academic advising programs.

Donald D. Gehring is professor of higher education and university student grievance officer at the University of Louisville.

He received his B.S. degree (1960) in industrial management from Georgia Institute of Technology, his M.Ed. degree (1966) in mathematics education from Emory University, and his Ed.D. degree (1971) in higher education from the University of Georgia.

Gehring's primary research activities center on legal issues in higher education. He serves as state editor for the National Organization for Legal Problems in Education and has written the chapter entitled "Students" in the *NOLPE Yearbook of Higher Education Law*. His books include *The College Student and the Courts*, with D. P. Young (1977), and *Administering College and University Housing: A Legal Perspective*, with others (1983).

Virginia N. Gordon is coordinator for academic and career advising, University College, Ohio State University. She received her B.S. degree (1949) in education and her M.A. degree (1973) and Ph.D. degree (1977), both in counseling and guidance, from Ohio State University. She is an adjunct assistant professor in the College of Education, where she teaches courses in student personnel and counseling.

Gordon's experience in higher education includes teaching, programming, administration, and counseling. She has designed and implemented career development programs for a variety of college populations, including a nationally known program for the undecided student. She serves as a national consultant in the areas of academic advising, career advising and programming, and the undecided student. Her research interests are in the areas of academic and career advising, the returning adult student, and decision making. Among her numerous publications are many journal articles and the book *The Undecided College Student* (1984). She is immediate past president of the National Academic Advising Association.

Janet D. Greenwood is president of Longwood College. She received her B.S. degree (1965) in English and psychology from East Carolina University, her M.Ed. degree (1967) in counseling from East Carolina University, and her Ph.D. degree (1972) in counselor education from Florida State University.

Greenwood is a licensed psychologist in the State of Ohio. She is the first woman president of a state-assisted, four-year and graduate, higher education institution in Virginia. She was vice-provost for student affairs, graduate faculty member, and professor at the University of Cincinnati, and has worked as a self-employed organizational consultant and psychotherapist. She served as a member of Secretary Terrel Bell's National Forum on Excellence in Education. Greenwood is a member of the Association of Governing Boards' Commission on Strengthening the Leadership of the Presidency and the American Council on Education's liaison for the National Identification Program with the American Association of State Colleges and Universities. She has been chairperson of the Policies and Purposes Committee and member of the editorial board and board of directors of the American Association of State Colleges and Universities; chairperson of the 1981 national convention of the American College Personnel Association; editor-in-chief of the ACPA's media board; and member of the board of directors for the Organizational Behavior Teaching Society.

Wesley R. Habley is the director of academic and career advising at the University of Wisconsin at Eau Claire. He received his B.S. degree (1969) in music education from the University of Illinois, his M.S. degree (1970) in student personnel from the University of Illinois, and his Ed.D. degree (1978) in educational administration from Illinois State University.

In addition to serving as a consultant in academic and career advising, Habley has published articles in the *Journal of College Student Personnel* and *NASPA Journal*. Topics of his publications include organizational structures in academic advising, the relationship between academic advising and retention, career and life planning, and peer advising. He has been active in the development of the National Academic Advising Association (NACADA), serving first as a member of the board of directors for the East-Central Region, and later as treasurer.

Edward R. Hines is associate professor of educational administration and acting director of the Center for Higher Education at

xxvi   The Authors

Illinois State University. He received his A.B. degree (1963) in
zoology from Colgate University, his M.A. degree (1969) in higher
education from Teachers College, Columbia University, and his
Ph.D. degree (1974) in educational administration from Ohio State
University.

Hines's main research activities have been in higher educational administration and educational policy making. He has
served as an administrator in the admissions office at Carnegie-
Mellon University (1967–1969) and residence halls at the University
of Cincinnati (1969–1971). He has participated in policy making on
the research staff of the National Educational Governance Project
at Ohio State University (1971–1974) and with the Governor's
Commission on Higher Education in New York State (1976–1977).
He has authored over forty articles and monographs, including
"Academic Advising: More Than a Placebo" in *NACADA Journal*
(1981), "Policy Making for More Effective Academic Advising in
Two-Year Colleges" in *Research in Higher Education* (1981),
Politics of Higher Education, with L. S. Hartmark (1980), and
Higher Education Finance, with J. R. McCarthy (1984).

James C. Hurst is the associate vice-president for academic
affairs and professor of psychology at the University of Wyoming.
He received his B.S. degree (1961) from the University of Utah and
his Ph.D. degree (1966) from Brigham Young University in counseling psychology. He completed his internship in counseling
psychology at Duke University. Hurst also held appointments at
Oregon State University, Colorado State University, and University
of Texas at Austin, where he served as dean of students, assistant
vice-president for student affairs, and professor of counseling
psychology.

Hurst's main research activities have emphasized delivery of
services within the human development framework. He was coau-
thor, with W. H. Morrill, of *Dimensions of Intervention for Student
Development* (1980). In addition he has published over fifty journal
articles, chapters, and technical papers related to psychotherapeutic
and student development intervention strategies. In 1982, Hurst
received the Contribution to Knowledge Award from the American
College Personnel Association for writing and research basic to the

profession. He is also a fellow in the American Psychological Association, Division 17 (Counseling Psychology).

David W. King is associate dean of arts and sciences at the State University of New York at Oswego. He received his B.A. degree (1963) in history and English and his M.A.T. degree (1965) in European history from the University of Rochester. He received his Ph.D. degree (1979) in European intellectual and social history from the State University of New York at Stony Brook. He also pursued graduate study in early modern European and medieval English history at the University of London (1965–1966). He joined the history department faculty at the State University of New York at Oswego in 1966.

King's major research interests, outside the field of nineteenth-century European history, have been in academic and student services, academic advising, and the application of cognitive and student development theory to curriculum design, teaching, professional development, advising, and other areas of higher education.

The State University of New York at Oswego has received national recognition for its differentiated advising delivery system and its advising publications, coedited by King: *Student Advising Handbook* with F. E. Moody and L. A. Syrell (1982–1984), *Mentoring Handbook for Academic Advisors* with F. E. Moody, L. A. Syrell, and R. C. Wheeler (1982), and *Advising Resource Folio*. King has served on the governing board of the National Academic Advising Association.

Gary L. Kramer is an assistant professor of educational psychology and director of academic advising and graduation evaluation at Brigham Young University. He received his B.S. degree (1970) in sociology and M.A. degree (1971) in counseling and guidance from Brigham Young University and his Ph.D. degree (1977) in education from Oregon State University.

Kramer's main research activities have been in computer-assisted advisement and related academic advising practices. He has authored or coauthored numerous articles in the last two to three years on such topics as planning and managing academic advising,

designing and implementing a computer-assisted advisement program, using computers to improve academic advising, peer counseling and orientation, using an accreditation model to evaluate
academic advisement of new students, developing a faculty mentoring program, and using college advising centers to facilitate and revitalize academic advising. Kramer currently serves as vice-president
of programs in the National Academic Advising Association.

Howard C. Kramer is director of research and planning for
the Division of Campus Life at Cornell University. He received his
B.A. degree (1960) in education and M.A. degree (1961) in guidance
and counseling from the University of Northern Colorado and his
Ph.D. degree (1966) in counseling psychology from the University
of Nebraska at Lincoln. He has also done postdoctoral work at the
University of North Carolina at Chapel Hill and at Ohio State
University.

Kramer has served as codirector of the Cornell summer
advising workshop. He has consulted with a number of two- and
four-year colleges regarding advising, has written extensively on the
subject of academic advising, and has been a program presentor at
numerous advising convocations and conferences. He is the author
of *Advising by Faculty*, 2nd edition, with R. E. Gardner (1983).

Randi S. Levitz is assistant director of the ACT National
Center for the Advancement of Educational Practices. She received
her B.A. degree (1970) in history and her M.A. degree (1972) in
educational communications from the State University of New
York at Albany, and her Ph.D. degree (1982) in administration from
the Center for the Study of Higher Education at the University of
Michigan.

As assistant director of the ACT National Center, Levitz has
codirected twenty-eight national conferences that focus on student
retention, the outcomes of general education, and academic advising. Her publications include *How to Succeed with Academically
Underprepared Students*, with Lee Noel (1982); "The Predictability
of Academic Achievement for Nontraditional and Traditional-Age
Freshmen" (1982); and *Attracting and Retaining Adult Learners:
Summary Report of a Nationwide Survey*, with Lee Noel (1980). She

is currently working on a book with Noel concerning student retention.

Erlend D. Peterson is assistant dean of admissions at Brigham Young University. He received his B.S. degree (1967) in business management and his M.S. degree (1971) in sociology from Brigham Young University.

For the past twenty years, Peterson's primary area of involvement has been developing and managing academic advisement and registration systems. He was a leading member of the team that designed and implemented Brigham Young University's on-line, interactive advisement-by-computer program. For three years he served as coordinator of academic advisement at Brigham Young University. His publications include "Legal Responsibilities and Contractual Obligations Imposed on a University by its Catalog" (1982); "Advisement by Computer (ABC): A Tool for Improving Academic Advising," with others (1982); "Utilizing College Advisement Centers to Facilitate and Revitalize Academic Advisement," with others (1982); and "Opportunities in the Eighties: The Impact of Emerging Technologies on Admissions and Records" (1983).

Mark C. Polkosnik is a doctoral candidate in the Department of Counseling and Human Development Services at the University of Georgia. He received his B.S. degree (1978) in economics and his M.Ed. degree (1980) in student personnel in higher education from the University of Georgia.

Polkosnik's research interests are in the area of human development with special emphasis on the relationship between cognitive and psychosocial developmental patterns. He is currently chairperson of the American College Personnel Association Committee on New Professionals. He has been director of financial aid at St. Mary's Dominican College in New Orleans and is presently an intern in the Office of the Vice-President for Student Affairs at the University of Georgia.

Gene A. Pratt is associate professor of botany and director of the Center for Academic Advising at the University of Wyoming. He received his B.S. degree (1955) and M.S. degree (1957) in botany from

Brigham Young University and his Ph.D. degree (1965) in botany
(cytogenetics) from the University of Texas at Austin. He assumed
leadership of the University of Wyoming Center for Academic
Advising in 1982.

Pratt's research interests are primarily in retention and
preparation for college. He also has been instrumental in developing training materials for faculty academic advisors and an advising
program for undeclared majors.

Sue A. Saunders is associate director of the Division of
Developmental Studies at the University of Georgia. She received
her B.S. degree (1972) in journalism and M.Ed. degree (1973) in
counseling from Ohio University and her Ph.D. degree (1979) in
counseling and student personnel services from the University of
Georgia.

Saunders' major research interests include career development processes of undergraduate students, nonintellective factors
related to academic performance, and academic performance of
student athletes. Her publications include *Students Helping Students*, with S. C. Ender and T. K. Miller (1979); "Environmental
Influences on Fraternity Academic Achievement," with R. B. Winston and G. S. Hutson (1980); "Career Maturity of Graduate and
Undergraduate Students," with T. K. Miller and R. B. Winston
(1984).

Robert W. Spencer is dean of admissions and records and an
associate professor of educational psychology at Brigham Young
University. He received his B.S. degree (1963) and M.S. degree
(1965), both in psychology, from Utah State University and his
Ed.D. degree (1971) in educational psychology from Brigham
Young University.

Spencer is the primary designer and implementer of Brigham
Young University's on-line administrative computer system, which
includes academic advisement, admissions, transfer credit evaluation, registration, classroom scheduling, records, graduation clear-
ance, and financial aid. His publications include "Advisement by
Computer (ABC): A Tool for Improving Academic Advising," with
others (1982); "Utilizing College Advising Centers to Facilitate and

Revitalize Academic Advising," with others (1982); "Designing and Implementing a Computer-Assisted Academic Advisement Program," with others (1983); and "A Baker's Dozen: Thirteen Years with On-Line Admissions" (1984). He has served on advisory committees for the American College Testing Program and the College Entrance Examination Board and has lectured and conducted workshops for ACT and the Interuniversity Communications Council, United States (EDUCOM).

Russell E. Thomas is associate professor of counseling and personnel services and a staff member of the Center for the Study of Higher Education at Memphis State University. He earned his B.S. degree (1963) in psychology, his M.S. degree (1965) in counseling and student personnel, and his Ph.D. degree (1970) in counseling from Purdue University.

Thomas has written several articles in the area of student affairs related to organizational issues, developmental theory foundations for mentoring, values development, and effects of college size on student development. He has a long-standing interest in student development theory and its applications. He is also interested in pursuing research efforts related to the personal development of minorities in higher education.

Developmental Academic Advising

Addressing Students' Educational, Career, and Personal Needs

Part One

Academic Advising for Student Development: Foundations and Current Practices

Part One lays a foundation in terms of rationale for developmental advising and grounds it in a theoretical base of student and human development theory. It also addresses the current state of the art by presenting data from a national survey of advising practices and examining a college president's perspective concerning the desirability for a campus-wide developmental advising system.

Specifically, Chapter One, "Academic Advising Reconsidered," evaluates the impact of the significant, widespread changes that have occurred since the mid to late 1950s, as well as the present status of higher education in America. Attention is focused on the "rising tide of mediocrity" within higher education resulting from increased size of student bodies and institutions, characteristics and values of today's students, and students' perceptions of the educational experience. In an attempt to restore confidence in the quality and integrity of the college experience, Steven C. Ender, Roger B. Winston, Jr., and Theodore K. Miller advocate a reconceptualization of the advising process within the context of holistic

1

education. Present-day realities of the advising process are presented and explained, along with a definition of developmental academic advising and explication of the critical factors that must be addressed if the system is to be responsive to individual students. The chapter concludes with an outline of a model advising program.

David S. Crockett and Randi S. Levitz update the findings of a 1979 national study that focused on advising procedures. Chapter Two presents a comprehensive view of the current status of undergraduate academic advising practices in colleges and universities, based on the results of a second survey conducted in the fall of 1982. The survey polled respondents about the structure of advising services, the use of advising centers, the administration of advising programs, training, evaluation procedures, and the like. The study also examined special advising services for selected student populations, personnel utilized to serve as advisors, and the use of information systems in conjunction with advising.

In Chapter Three, "Academic Advising and Institutional Goals: A President's Perspective," Janet D. Greenwood considers the implications of developmental advising from a broad, institutional perspective. She discusses how institutional goals can be addressed directly and accomplished through the advising process and the utilization of systematic planning.

Finally, in Chapter Four, "Foundations for Academic Advising," Russell E. Thomas and Arthur W. Chickering outline the major components of several developmental theories and postulate the impact that advising programs grounded in developmental theory have on both advisors and students. They argue forcefully that advisors need to be cognizant of life cycle theory and relevant developmental tasks of students at different stages in their lives and also be sensitive to their own developmental needs in the advising process. Several vignettes are presented to illustrate these implications.

1

Academic Advising
Reconsidered

꧁ꦽ꧂ ꧁ꦽ꧂ ꧁ꦽ꧂ ꧁ꦽ꧂ ꧁ꦽ꧂ ꧁ꦽ꧂ ꧁ꦽ꧂ ꧁ꦽ꧂

Steven C. Ender, Roger B. Winston, Jr.,
Theodore K. Miller

During the final quarter of the twentieth century, the higher-education enterprise will be faced with paying the consequences for actions taken from the mid-1950s to early 1970s. In this period when the expansion of higher education in America was running rampant, many colleges and universities lost sight of their long-term educational responsibilities to the American public. As a result, the integrity of the higher-education experience has been called into question. Specifically, there are charges of grade inflation, reduced academic requirements, low-quality off-campus programs, false promises by institutions, cheating, vandalism, and defaults on student loans (Carnegie Council on Policy Studies in Higher Education, 1980). Similarly, the National Commission on Excel-

3

lence in Education (1983) has noted that although the American people can take pride in what their schools and colleges have done in the past, the educational foundations of society are presently being eroded by what they refer to as the "rising tide of mediocrity" that threatens the very fate of the nation and its people.

Current Realities in Higher Education

The strong indictments against today's higher-education system are based on such characteristics of that system as (1) the size of student bodies and educational institutions, (2) characteristics and values of today's students, and (3) students' perceptions of their educational experience.

Student Enrollment and Institutional Size. When the post–World War II baby boom population reached young adulthood in the 1960s, colleges and universities opened their arms wide to embrace the increasing number of prospective students seeking admission. As a direct result of this rapid increase in student enrollment, several changes in the process of higher education occurred. Henderson and Henderson (1974) have maintained that higher education in America has emerged from both Judeo-Christian ethics, which emphasized individual uniqueness, and the British tradition of individual rights and freedoms. These qualities describing higher education in America have changed rather drastically as a direct result of the rapid growth in institutional size and complexity during the 1960s. Until the 1950s, colleges had always emphasized the development of intellectual abilities and individual achievement as well as the tradition of building community life on campus, including frequent interpersonal communications between faculty and students. The rapid, extensive change in institutional size altered this environment. Higher education has become a less viable community-building experience and more a dehumanizing one. Computer cards in place of faculty, lectures rather than active participation in class, mass or videotaped lectures rather than small classes with faculty leaders that allow for discussion, routinized laboratory experiments rather than individualized ones, and long lines and milling crowds on campus have raised the question "How can college students become educated in the true sense of the word?" (Henderson and Henderson, 1974). After all, education takes place only as the individual changes, grows, and develops as a result of direct interaction with the environment.

As the number of students seeking a finite number of educational opportunities increases, redundancy results. "Redundancy occurs when increases in the number of inhabitants of a setting lead to decreasing opportunities for participation and satisfaction for each individual" (Chickering, 1969, p. 186). Redundancy promotes increased specialization wherein a hierarchy of prestige and power tends to develop. Such an environment pits student against student rather than encouraging achievement through competition with oneself to meet realistic standards for a particular activity or task. One major result of this redundancy in higher education is pointed out by the Carnegie Council on Policy Studies in Higher Education (1980, p. 43) when analyzing present-day student dropout rates: "The dropout rate in four-year colleges historically has been about 50 percent with many dropouts for financial reasons. It has now fallen to 40 percent, with the major single reason being given as boredom." Is it any wonder that those who value the education of the academy feel uncomfortable with the current educational milieu?

As society has become more complex, with high tech, biomass, and laser-age thinking becoming more apparent, so too have institutions of higher learning been faced with a period of rapid transition. Whereas in the 1960s growth was conspicuously evident, in the 1980s institutions of all types face a decline in the population between the ages of seventeen and twenty-four, the age group from which the student population has traditionally been drawn. Kerr and Gade (1981) indicated that although future enrollment predictions are difficult and risky, the declining birthrate will result in the number of young Americans in that age group dropping by approximately 23 percent between the years 1978 and 1993. Likewise, they suggest that college enrollment among that population will also decrease, possibly to an even greater extent, because of the decreasing economic returns accruing from an investment in a college education. To maintain a reasonable semblance of order and economy of effort and resources, many institutions will seek to admit increasing numbers of nontraditional students, that is, older persons, women, minority students, and foreign students, to keep their classrooms and coffers full. These students, however, are more inclined to study on a part-time basis only and to attend community and comprehensive colleges instead of the more traditional four-year liberal arts colleges and mega-universities. The Carnegie Council on Policy Studies in Higher Education (1980) forecasts that roughly one half of the students in the classroom of the year 2000 would not have been there if the composition of 1960 had been continued. It would appear that sweeping and significant demographic changes are occurring within higher education.

This portends an additional problem for colleges and universities, especially in regard to faculty and staff, for another side of redundancy is that "it occurs when manpower available exceeds the number necessary to do the job" (Chickering, 1969, p. 186). What criteria are used to decide the numbers of faculty and staff necessary to do the job? What specific tasks, skills, and expectations are included? These are critical questions for higher education to address and solve if redundancy is to be minimized.

Student Characteristics and Values. Traditionally, American colleges have evidenced a concern with moral and ethical development. To a great extent, this seems to have diminished with the departure of *in loco parentis.* Students now attribute their moral development and personal values to family interactions, peer friendships, and religious training (DeCoster and Mable, 1981a). Current research also suggests an atmosphere of sexual permissiveness, casual acceptance of marijuana, and a preoccupation with drinking alcoholic beverages on most college campuses. What is of greater significance and concern is the open acknowledgment that academic dishonesty is so widespread that many students consider cheating a necessity in order to remain academically competitive (DeCoster and Mable, 1981a). The unfortunate results are that college graduates tend to be overrepresented among citizens who are divorced, have mental problems, commit suicide, are alcoholics, and commit white-collar crimes (Blimling, 1981). To the extent that college graduates' behavior reflects their higher-education experience, institutions are suspect. To what extent do students use faculty and staff members as social models? Do the institution's policies, procedures, and practices influence the personal as well as the intellectual education of students? It appears that too often higher education fails in its mission to educate the "whole student," primarily because it gives only lip service to the concept but makes no systematic effort to actualize it.

Students' Experiences and Perceptions. Brown (1972) noted that most freshmen begin college with idealistic goals and openness to change, but many become disenchanted by the end of their first year of study because they have learned that they must be committed to academic game playing and grade getting rather than to learning. When students experience the collegiate environment as callous and insensitive to their educational and personal needs, the quality of the educational experience degenerates. A serious indictment against the process of education is reflected in this quote from an interview with an undergraduate student: "I think a lot of their [institutional leaders'] concerns are with the image of the college—how good their programs look on paper—not the practicality of what you're going to get out of it. . . . I hate to have to play these games with people . . . to be successful, you've got to get within the system and beat them at their own games. . . . You have to manipulate the situation around to where you want it. . . . I've been in a lot of systems, and this is really a bullshit game to have to play with adults" (Mable and DeCoster, 1981a, p. 12).

But, one may ask, is this not an aberration? Do not most students believe that the educational experience is a positive, healthy, and intellectually stimulating one? There is mounting evidence that this is not the case (Levine, 1980; DeCoster and Mable, 1981a; Newton, Angle, Schuette, and Ender, 1984). Are there solutions to these present-day indictments? What about the academic support system called advising that nearly all colleges have? Can it help solve the problems of redundancy, rapidly changing students' needs, and student disenchantment? It is our contention that it can! Many changes in both the conceptualization and implementation of present-day advising systems must occur, however, if they are to bring renewed purpose and meaning to students' interaction with institutions of higher education.

Academic Advising as Academic Support

There is little doubt that the traditional advising system has
failed to reach its potential as an intervention that supports and
enhances learning and self-understanding for the majority of students. In a major study of college students' perceptions of the
higher-education experience, DeCoster and Mable (1981c, pp.
43–44) found that "students frequently described the idea of approaching one of their instructors as scary, threatening, or demeaning. . . . At the same time, the very mention of academic advisors
would invariably be met with a roar of laughter." Not a pretty
picture from the students' point of view. But how about the
advising system in general? A student's letter to the editor of a
college newspaper describing her advising experience is illustrative.

When he finally came, I introduced myself and
explained that he was my new advisor. He was surprised that it was that time of the year again, and advised me to visit Calvin 13 where the real advisors are,
and quit bothering the teachers. He gave me a marketing schedule to follow, and told me that if I had any
questions to come visit him the next day, but he would
be just as grouchy.
Would somebody please help me!
We need a system. None of us are happy with
the current system. Teachers are trained for teaching,
not advising. If they wanted to be advisors, they would
have gone to school for that instead of teaching. A lot
of them don't understand the system, and since they
are not interested in advising they don't want to learn
it. Besides they have their own classes to take care of.
Because they do not enjoy advising, they feel negative
when students come for help.
I understand their situation, but in the mean-
time, we need help. Why can't we have professional
advisors who could spend the time with and for the
students [sic]. Something is needed. Help! [Bachelor,
1983, p. 5]

In addition to the students' discontent, the problems with academic advising have not been lost on academic leaders. One of the strongest indictments came from David Riesman (1981, p. 258) when he stated "faculty advising of students, including entering freshmen and those transfer students who are in effect freshmen twice, is at most large institutions, including my own, at best an embarrassment, at worst a disgrace."

It appears that the one area that has a most immediate potential for changing the course of student disenchantment— academic advising—has a long way to go before its proponents can exhibit it as a viable part of the solution to the shortcomings of effective higher education in America. But it does have potential, especially when one examines it in relationship to the purposes of higher education.

Educating the Whole Student

The "tide of mediocrity" that has slowly engulfed higher education has led to educational processes that can be described as academic game playing and the awarding of degrees rather than a systematic educational process designed to help individuals reach their maximum potential as students and human beings. Sadly enough, even though many institutions have mission statements that reflect concern for the total development of students, few colleges have intentionally undertaken the systematic, sustained efforts required to offer total student development programs (Cross, 1980). Intentional student development refers to educational programs and processes that affect the quality of students' learning in human development dimensions such as academic competence, capacity for intimacy, and vocational development (Chickering and Havighurst, 1981). In more general fashion, others have articulated the purposes of higher education (Kerr, 1963; Perkins, 1966; Bok, 1974; Bowen, 1977) and the definitions and processes of student development (Committee on the Student in Higher Education, 1968; Brown, 1972; Miller and Prince, 1976; Creamer, 1980; Morrill and Hurst, 1980). There is little doubt that the positions of most educational authorities have, over the years, increasingly evolved in the direction of concern for the total development of students. This evolution of the conception of the higher-education process has moved increasingly toward the integration of the affective and the practical with the cognitive aspects of the educational experience. Bowen (1977), for instance, identified cognitive learning, affective development, and practical competence as the three broad goals that higher education is seeking to promote. The developmental needs of college students appear to have utility as a rationale for guiding the programs and procedures institutions can follow in attempting to be educationally responsible to both individual students and society as a whole.

Purposes of Higher Education. If the developmental needs of college students can be accepted as the force that guides higher education's purposes, then a logical framework upon which to build is presented by Rippey (1981). He suggests that the developmental needs of college students can be classified into three categories or a combination thereof:

- the development of knowledge, skills, and attitudes
- the development of self-determination
- the development of an ability to control one's environment

From this perspective, the institution must seek to be responsive not only to the intellectual and academic needs of students but also to their personal and social needs. Further, this perspective calls for an integration throughout the educational community of the skills and competencies needed to successfully educate the total student.

As a result, the traditional roles of the teacher, the counselor, and the administrator must be altered. To some extent, these roles must be redefined and become merged in a mutual attempt to enhance the educational experiences of students. Such redefinition calls for a careful re-examination of the various relationships established between members of the educational community and the students who pursue their education therein. Astin's (1977) research clearly indicates that greater amounts of student-faculty interaction promote higher levels of student satisfaction with the college experience than any other involvement variable he studied. This strongly supports the idea of creating an environment wherein students have opportunity to have meaningful interaction with many members of the academic community.

Doonesbury, Copyright, 1976, G. B. Trudeau. Reprinted with permission of Universal Press Syndicate. All rights reserved.

One of the most apparent and viable student-faculty/staff interactions occurs in the academic advising process. Student-advisor relationships, then, have potential for enhancing not only the academic and personal growth of students but also their satisfaction with the educational experience as well. Academic advising relationships can be used to intentionally guide students toward achieving higher levels of academic competence. Additionally, advising programs and systems that are designed to stimulate the students' total development can assist them as they develop the ability to use knowledge effectively, develop meaningful self-understanding and decision-making skills, and make more effective use of campus resources. In effect, academic advising has potential for stimulating and facilitating achievement of the primary goals of higher education defined in terms of human and student development, that is, assuming the academic advising process is reconceptualized. As the Doonesbury cartoon so vividly illustrates, it is totally unrealistic to expect students to take full advantage of the intellectual and personal development opportunities without some assistance from the institution. Such an approach is analogous to giving a computer to a person who knows nothing about computers. Computers have the potential for doing wondrous things, but only if used by a knowledgeable person. A reconceptualized academic advising process should have as its primary goal teaching students how to realize to the utmost their potential and to use fully the resources available in the academic community.

Renewed Interest in Academic Advising. There has been increased interest in the advising process in higher education during the last several years, in part due to the previously cited changes in higher education. Ender, Winston, and Miller (1982) pointed out several issues presently affecting higher education that signal a need for purposeful response by the institution. These include the fact that most, if not all, institutions are failing in their mission of educating the whole student and have as a result lost the public's trust in this all-important area. Additionally, the competition for students among colleges has fueled a renewed sense of consumerism on the part of students—their expectations of the role education should play in their lives are such that they expect institutional representatives to respond directly to them individually, helping to provide the best education possible for them as individuals. Present-day student bodies are increasingly represented by first-generation college students, minorities, and returning adults, and enrollment by these groups is growing steadily (Cross, 1974; Brodzinski, 1980; Chickering and Havighurst, 1981). The needs these students bring to the educational arena are great and will require individual attention by concerned educators if success in college is to be obtained.

Students' satisfaction and retention are two key areas that are also prompting a renewed interest in academic advising. Several researchers (Heath, 1968; Astin, 1977; Bowen, 1977) have found significant relationships between student satisfaction with the institution and their relationship with its faculty. The academic advisor, as institutional representative, should strive to develop relationships with student advisees that have mutual benefits for both of them.

Recently, several studies have pointed to academic advising services as one key to student retention (Glennen, 1976; Noel, 1976; Carstensen and Silberhorn, 1979). In fact, Carstensen and Silberhorn (1979) in a major study of 947 institutions found retention rates increased 25 percent or more for some institutions that improved academic advising programs.

It is apparent that many college leaders and administrators are beginning to look to the advising process as a place to begin to affect the mission of the institution (including total student development) and student satisfaction and retention. There has been an advising movement in the United States for the past several years that culminated in the incorporation of the National Academic Advising Association in 1979. Trombley and Holmes (1981) reported that membership in the organization reached 500 less than one year after incorporation. Membership now approaches 800, with steady annual increases. One important aspect of the interest in advising has been the extensive participation of academic vice-presidents and college presidents on the national level (Trombley and Holmes, 1981).

Changes That Must Occur. If the advising process is to have an impact on students, many changes must occur. The greatest difficulty students cite with the quality of academic experiences is advising (Mable and DeCoster, 1981a). There is going to have to be a reconceptualization of the advising process at most institutions if the developmental issues of students are to be addressed. Perhaps the greatest change must involve institutional leaders and administrators. They must be willing to make a commitment to implement an institutional intervention that will affect the purpose, quality, and educational experience of all attending students. Developmentally oriented academic advising should be the centerpiece of the changes. Mable and DeCoster (1981b) concluded, after an extensive research project focusing on students' personal accounts of their collegiate experience, that urgent needs of higher education are to "establish teaching and learning relationships, to improve the quality of academic advising, and to begin programs that aid students in assessing their current individual development, setting goals for accomplishment, determining learning experiences, evaluating progress, and recording results" (p. 110). The Carnegie Council on Policy Studies in Higher Education (1980) agrees: "We expect that students will be more nearly the center of attention on campus during the next twenty years than in the past ten years. They will be recruited more actively, admitted more readily, retained more assiduously, counseled more attentively, graded more considerately, financed more adequately, taught more conscientiously, placed in jobs more insistently, and the curriculum will be more tailored to their tastes" (p. 53).

Each statement is a clear endorsement for an educational experience highlighted by individuality and concern for the total well-being of each student. Academic advising can provide the process for this type of educational experience.

What Academic Advising Is Not

Occasionally, it is desirable to examine the worst-scenario view of a situation or circumstance to glean from it those factors that may cause the greatest problems. This helps identify some of the pitfalls in thinking. To understand better the nature of what something is, it is equally important to understand what it *is not*. As an introduction to a comprehensive definition of developmental academic advising, then, ten views of academic advising as commonly practiced in higher education are presented.

- *"Academic advisor" is not synonymous with "faculty member."* Not all faculty members are, or should be, advisors. Not all advisors are, or should be, faculty. Some of the best academic advisors are members of the faculty but so are some of the worst. The two positions, therefore, do not automatically go hand in glove. Some student affairs staff members make excellent academic advisors as do some well-trained and supervised paraprofessionals. There are many within the academic community who can carry forward the advising process, but it is dangerous to assume that because an individual is hired to serve one role or function, he or she is automatically qualified to carry out another. Just as some people cannot learn to swim no matter how hard they try, some cannot become competent advisors no matter how much they, or others, wish it to be so.

- *Academic advising is not primarily an administrative function.* Advising's raison d'etre is not to assure a smoothly run organization. Although those who act as advisors do represent the institution and reflect its mission in their activities, advising should not be viewed as a sorting process that will place students in classes in a manner that will assure maximum efficiency of faculty time at the lowest possible costs. Effectiveness and efficiency of advising systems should be measured by how well students' needs are met and the quality of their educational experiences.

- *Academic advising is not a paper relationship.* Although all good advising programs call for a well-organized record keeping system, the records are not an end in themselves. Whether computerized or longhand, advising reports should function as a comprehensive record of the student's personal, educational, and academic experience while in college. This record should reflect the student's progress through the higher-education experience and should include essential information and assessment data, significant experiences and activities, key decisions and plans made, and other important elements of the college-going experience. The record, no matter how accurate and complete, should never be construed as being anything other than an aid to the advising process. Advising is much more than a good set of records.

- *Advising is not a computer printout.* Even when an educational plan has been developed, a list of required courses on a computer printout is not enough. Too often an initial plan is carried to its conclusion without adequate formative assessment. Even a carefully worked-out educational plan requires regular re-examination of the process and outcome goals. One significant danger of a computer-based approach is the tendency of both student and advisor to become complacently dependent upon the computer printout to tell them what to do next. The computer is merely a tool to aid the advising process, not a decision-making instrument.

- *Academic advising is not a conference held once a term.* In too many instances, advising is viewed as little more than a short meeting held once a term between the student and an institutional representative. Winston and Sandor (1984) found that the average advising conference at one university was less than twenty minutes long. If academic advising is to have any significant influence on students' lives, the quality and depth of the interaction between student and advisor require commitment and purpose. Short, limited, and irregular interactions between individuals seldom have lasting impact.

- *Academic advising is not obtaining a signature to schedule classes.* Too often academic advising is seen as being synonymous with class scheduling and course registration. Granted, one outcome of academic advising *may* be the selection of an appropriate class schedule, but advising is much more than this. Without a clearly defined educational plan based upon a number of previously made decisions regarding interests, aptitudes, and career objectives, class scheduling can be at best guesswork, at worst educational malfeasance.

- *Academic advising is not a closed or limiting activity.* Quality advising can take many forms but is invariably "open-ended." Advising depends as much on the educational and academic needs of the student as upon the intention of the advisor to be of help. Although advising centers upon the educational and the academic, all factors that influence these areas of the student's life have potential for consideration. Quality academic advising attends to the total development of the student.

- *Academic advising is not a judgmental process.* The purpose of advising is to facilitate development, not to diagnose students' behavior or judge their values. It is, on the other hand, certainly within the realm of the advising process to aid students in self-assessment and values clarification processes that are essential to both personal and educational growth. Likewise, it is valuable for students to be able to use their advisor as a sounding board to test out new ideas and alternatives. It is even appropriate for the advisor to communicate his or her personal opinions and positions about issues and problems faced by the student within the framework of the advising relationship. It is not, however, the purpose of advising to impose the advisor's values on students or to seek to direct or manage the way students confront the educational process. Advisors must be aware that students may view education differently from an academician and that advisors should not attempt to impose their values.

- *Academic advising is not personal counseling.* Although the outcomes of academic advising may well reflect students who function at high levels of effectiveness in their personal as well as in their academic lives, advising is not another form of counseling. Good human relations skills are essential to both activities, but the advising relationship centers on the individual as a student in search of both academic and personal competence. Shane (1981) has proposed four depths of involvement an advisor may have with a student: (1) informational, where the focus is upon informing the student, providing data, usually about deadlines, procedures, or policies (communication is generally one-way); (2) explanatory, where the focus is upon helping the student understand college expectations, rules, and procedures (communication is two-way); (3) analytic, where the focus is upon the student and is directed at helping the student analyze options available in the college environment and understand himself or herself in relationship to opportunities and options available; and (4) therapeutic or counseling, where the focus is on values, commitments, and emotional preferences (often only marginally connected with college attendance) and may involve unusual or self-defeating kinds of behavior. It seems quite appropriate for advisors to be involved in the first three types of intervention, but the latter type would require experience, knowledge, and skills not possessed by most advisors. Advisors who encounter students who have remedial concerns (requiring the fourth type of intervention), rather than normal developmental concerns, can best assist by referring students to appropriate agencies on the campus that have personnel trained to deal with such concerns. (See Ender and Winston (1982) for a discussion of the distinction between developmental and remedial concerns.)

• *Academic advising is not supplementary to the educational mission.* Although often viewed as something of a "foster child," academic advising is an essential part of the educational process. "To supplement" means to add something to an already finished or complete entity. Academic advising is not supplemental to the educational process because that process is not complete or whole without advising. Too often the advising function is viewed as a necessary evil, even by those responsible for its delivery. The essence of the educational process centers on the relationship between the student as a person, his or her goals and aspirations, and the available resources. To place academic advising in a peripheral or ancillary position is to misconstrue its educational potential and importance. Academic advising is, most essentially, an instructional or teaching function that assists students in finding purpose and personal meaning in their educational experience.

Developmental Advising: A Definition

The academic advising literature now offers many definitions of the advising process that are grounded in a developmental perspective (Crookston, 1972; Crockett, 1978; Mash, 1978; Grites, 1979; Walsh, 1979; Ender, Winston, and Miller, 1982). *Developmen-*

tal academic advising is defined as a systematic process based on a close student-advisor relationship intended to aid students in achieving educational, career, and personal goals through the utilization of the full range of institutional and community resources. It both stimulates and supports students in their quest for an enriched quality of life. Developmental advising relationships focus on identifying and accomplishing life goals, acquiring skills and attitudes that promote intellectual and personal growth, and sharing concerns for each other and for the academic community. Developmental academic advising reflects the institution's mission of total student development and is most likely to be realized when the academic affairs and student affairs divisions collaborate in its implementation.

This definition will be most difficult to implement if assigned exclusively to the faculty, given the present status of relationships between students and faculty. To be successful, it must be a collaborative effort between academic affairs and student affairs.

Seven conditions or principles that are essential in the advising process if the goal of developmental advising is to be achieved have been proposed by Ender, Winston, and Miller (1982). They have proven utility within the context of developmental advising (Ender, 1983).

1. *Academic advising is a continuous process with an accumulation of personal contacts between advisor and student—these contacts have both direction and purpose.* Whether in the context of the group format or a series of individual appointments between advisor and student, the process must be one that is purposeful. Both participants should be aware of the purpose the institution ascribes to the advising process. Outcome objectives of "quality" advising must be established and communicated to administrators, faculty, staff, and students. Each participant in the advising process should have an understanding of what advising can and cannot deliver. Responsibilities of each partner in the process need to be discussed until mutual agreement is reached.

2. *Advising must concern itself with quality-of-life issues, and the advisor has a responsibility to attend to the quality of the*

student's experience in college. This condition is directly
related to the mission of the institution. Are student outcome
goals established by the institution and do they reflect intellectual, personal, physical, and moral/ethical concerns? If so, are
advisors aware of and do they communicate to students the
resources and services available on campus and in the community that are designed to enhance the quality of the student's
educational experience? Are students aware of the objectives of
the institution as they relate to student outcomes as a result of
college participation? Do advisors understand their critical
roles as institutional representatives? These are important
questions that need affirmative responses if the goal of developmental advising is to be achieved.

3. *Advising is goal related. The goals should be established and
    owned by the student and should encompass academic, career,
    and personal development areas.* The formation of student
    goals and objectives must be one outcome of the advising
    process. The advisor should assist in the goal-setting process
    and challenge students to consider the outcomes they are
    seeking as a result of their interaction with the higher-
    education environment. The articulation and recording of
    goals lend direction to the student's matriculation and assist
    in the clarification of both student and advisor roles in the
    process.

4. *Advising requires the establishment of a caring human rela-
    tionship—one in which the advisor must take primary respon-
    sibility for its initial development.* All institutions of higher
    education must communicate to students their regard for them
    as individuals in the learning process. This caring must extend
    beyond the contact with the admissions office and the "wel-
    come" given new students during orientation. It is the advisor's
    role to continue to reinforce the institution's objective of
    offering a humanizing experience. Assisting students as they
    assess their intellectual skill levels, referring students to services
    available to facilitate personal achievement, and listening to
    students as they describe their educational experience will
    enhance the development of a caring relationship. The strength
    of this relationship will illustrate the institution's willingness

to work with students as individuals striving to take full advantage of the resources available to enhance their educational success.

5. *Advisors should be models for students to emulate, specifically demonstrating behaviors that lead to self-responsibility and self-directiveness.* Perhaps the greatest impact a faculty or college staff member can have on students is to demonstrate the types of outcome behaviors the college is attempting to foster in attending students. Sharing decision-making strategies, modeling responsible, self-directed behavior, and in other ways helping students learn basic skills necessary to live and contribute to a democratic society are important advisor roles. The college representatives in the advising process, no matter who fulfills these roles, are models—whether they like it or not. All advisors need to consider the impact they are having on students as a result of the interactions that take place between them and the behaviors they demonstrate in and out of the classroom and advising office.

6. *Advising should seek to integrate the services and expertise of both academic and student affairs professionals.* One strength of any advising system is the attention paid to the area of faculty-staff collaboration. Scarce resources, as well as practical considerations, mandate a symbiotic relationship between student affairs and academic affairs. There is no place within the present-day realities of higher education for either the duplication of services or the lack of attention to cost-efficiency. Professionals in both academic and student affairs have a multitude of skills that can enhance the advising system. Collaboration is essential to the overall success of an advising system concerned with the students' total development.

7. *Advisors should seek to utilize as many campus and community resources as possible.* The collaboration called for should manifest itself through the referral process. Up-to-date information in the areas of academic and student services and the ability to make timely and appropriate referrals are essential for any successful advising program.

This definition and seven conditions challenge the advisor and institution to engage with students in ways that stretch them to their full potential. These challenges should occur in both intellectual and affective areas. Intentional, institutional-designed developmental advising interventions should begin during the freshman year, at the very least, and ideally should be evident during a student's whole academic career. Heath (1968), Chickering (1974), and Astin (1977) have pointed to the freshman year as critical in the educational benefits that the student is open to receive. Educators and advisors must take advantage of students in these teachable moments.

Undergraduate Academic Advising Organizational Structures

It is important to keep in mind that at present even though 80 percent of all academic advising is provided by faculty members (see Chapter Two), there is little evidence that this approach is either more effective or cost-efficient than other approaches. It can be argued that academic advising is too important to the overall quality of education offered to students to be left to any single constituency in the institution but should be shared by faculty, student affairs staff, academic administrators and leaders, and students themselves. It should be a collaborative effort.

"Academic advising" is not synonymous with "advising by faculty"; there are a wide variety of organizational structures or delivery systems that can effectively and efficiently accomplish the goals of developmental academic advising. The faculty, an essential coterie concerned with advising, is not the only stakeholder.

As Crockett (1982) noted, there are a number of documented shortcomings with traditional faculty advisors: (1) they tend to be subject matter oriented and lack institution-wide information; (2) not all faculty members possess an interest in or the temperament for effective advising; (3) they are often inaccessible to students when most needed; (4) they lack necessary skills and often resist systematic training efforts; and (5) they have difficulty in keeping updated on institutional policies, procedures, and rules, and, consequently, dispense inaccurate and untimely information.

The issues of organizational structures, staffing of the organization, and advising techniques often become confused. Organizational structure may be centralized or decentralized. Centralized organizational structures usually have an advising center with a director and a physical location from which advisors make contact with students. Advising may be provided for all students of a particular classification (freshmen, for example) or for all students who fail to fit an administrative classification scheme (for example, undecided majors). Decentralized structures usually have a coordinator whose primary function is to pass information to and/or about students to faculty or staff members located across campus in their departmental offices. Centralized versus decentralized organization is not concerned with who provides the advising; rather it is concerned with the degree of standardization (both services and location), amount of coordination and direction provided, and rewards structure (or lack thereof). Centralized structures can be found campus-wide, in separate colleges or divisions, or individual departments, or even academic programs.

The organization can reflect varied staffing patterns. It may be staffed by (1) faculty members who have advising responsibilities as an additional duty beyond teaching, research, and public service assignments; (2) faculty members who have a specific work assignment of advising (in other words, given release from some teaching, research, or service duties, or given extra compensation); (3) student paraprofessionals who are trained and supervised to perform specific duties, often associated with class scheduling; (4) nonstudent paraprofessionals, usually part-time employees, who function primarily as information providers and class schedulers; or (5) professional advisors who may have backgrounds in student affairs, counseling, or teaching in an academic discipline, who have received in-depth training or education in areas related to counseling, personal management, and educational and career planning, and who work full-time as advisors.

A wide array of advising techniques or service delivery approaches may be employed no matter where the organizational structure falls on the centralization continuum or what staffing patterns are utilized. Potentially effective techniques include one-to-one advising in private sessions, group advising, and advising offered in conjunction with a course. An ideal situation would be for each student to be assigned an advisor who would have multiple personal, in-depth, one-to-one contacts with the student and who would remain assigned to the student for his or her first two years, and even possibly his or her entire academic career. However, the realities of institutional structure, politics, and availability of funds probably preclude this from being implemented. A structure that combines a variety of organizational structures and personnel seems most realistic. No single model delivery system, however, can fit all institutions. Each institution must design a system that best fits its educational mission and goals for academic advising.

Model Advising Structure

Following is a model advising structure that would appear to fit many higher-education institutions.

Principles. Several general principles guided construction of the model: (1) Advising should be offered *only* by personnel who voluntarily choose to advise, who receive systematic skills training, who have advising as a specified job responsibility, whose performance is systematically evaluated, and who are rewarded for skillful performance. (2) Academic advising is an important institutional function that requires the same attention and support given to classroom instruction. (3) Academic advising should be a collaborative effort of academic administrators, faculty members, student affairs staff members, and students. (4) Academic advising serves as a quality control mechanism that helps maintain high academic standards and aids students in satisfying their educational and personal development needs. It relates directly to the mission of the institution. (5) Academic advising helps students understand the institution, its goals, purposes, and policies, and helps students gain personal meaning from the educational experience.

Advising Centers. For most college campuses, an academic advising center that has responsibility for all students until they fulfill the general education or core curriculum requirements is desirable. Advantages of a campus-wide center include:

- easier access for students
- continuity of contact
- better-trained, better-supervised personnel

- student-centered focus, rather than department- or content-centered focus
- more accurate and timely information provided to students
- generally, more complete records and more consistent monitoring of academic progress
- possibility of offering wide range of advising services by specially trained personnel (Crockett, 1982)

One responsibility of the advising center would be to train appropriate personnel and staff the freshman seminar.

Freshman Seminar. Wilson (1981) has correctly pointed out that the first year of college is often filled with anxiety and frustration, no matter whether the student is eighteen or forty. At many colleges, he contends, points of discontent center around (1) orientation to the college and uncertainty about the institution's expectations of students; (2) dissatisfaction with the quantity and quality of faculty-student interaction and academic advising services; (3) ethical and value issues associated with abuse of alcohol and other drugs, sexuality, ecology, academic standards, honesty, and integrity; (4) political and citizenship issues such as leadership and assertive pressure groups; and (5) opportunities to engage in discussion with others different from themselves.

As a means of addressing many of these issues, a year-long freshman seminar is recommended that would include academic advising. This course, offered for academic credit, would have as its goals to help students learn about:

- the purpose of a college education and how to realize personal goals within the existing structure
- the purpose and relationship of the general education component (or a liberal arts education for liberal arts colleges) to citizenship, a democratic society, and postcollege life
- study skills for college success
- personal goal setting and life-management techniques
- career awareness
- educational planning
- locating and using campus and community resources and services

- academic policies and procedures
- adjustment to the college environment, including its stress and demands
- personal developmental processes experienced during college
- contemporary ethical, moral, and value issues, such as capital punishment, environmental policy, race relations, and abortion policy

Class size would be between twelve and fifteen students. The same students and teachers (ideally a team composed of a faculty/staff member and a trained student paraprofessional) would spend the year together. Classes would be taught through lectures and discussions, with greatest emphasis on discussion and sharing of experiences. Students would read assigned material as preparation for discussions and would design and execute projects that would aid them in applying the self-management techniques taught, such as time management, goal setting, test preparation, note taking, and educational planning.

At Emory University, where a similar program was begun in 1981, students generally have responded positively. Samples of comments by students included: "I guess the most important thing I got from the seminar was a better understanding of people and a better understanding of what college can be." "I learned a lot about Emory and that there's so much offered here if you look for it. Other students [not in the seminar] would come to people [in the seminar] if they wanted to know where to find anything or do anything." "Whenever a mixed group of students was seen on campus—blacks, whites, Northerners, Southerners, males, females—they tend to be . . . [students in the seminar]." Students also valued the opportunity to get personally acquainted with a faculty member outside class (Smith, 1982, p. 27).

Sophomore Year. During the students' second year, their advisor would be their teacher of the freshman seminar. Advisors would see students individually to discuss the educational plan formulated at the end of the freshman year and to deal with any problems encountered. (Class scheduling and registration would be done by the student paraprofessional and support staff of the center.) Other services offered by the center likely to be needed by some second-year students include workshops dealing with selecting a major, career exploration, study skills, and decision making. Such workshops could best be developed in consultation with personnel in the student affairs division or the academic assistance center. Many programs will already be offered; through close liaison, advising center personnel can make appropriate referrals. Other workshops and programs can be developed and cosponsored by the center and student affairs departments. For students in junior and community colleges who plan to transfer to senior colleges, advisors must play an important role in helping determine which courses, especially electives, will be accepted by the receiving institution, as well as meet the graduation requirements of the two-year college. These students may also need assistance in selecting the appropriate senior college.

Upperclass Advising Centers. At small liberal arts colleges, it may be feasible to continue advising from a campus-wide center during the last two years as well. At large colleges and universities, however, it is recommended that individual colleges or divisions within the institution form advising centers. It would be staffed by a professional advisor-director, student paraprofessional advisors, support staff, and allied professional (faculty) advisors who are assigned to the center as a part of their work load. Students would be assigned to an allied professional advisor from their major fields of study. The paraprofessional and support staff would provide information and make referrals to other campus agencies, assist with record keeping, provide clerical support, and assist students with class scheduling and registration procedures. A centralized location, staffed by personnel who have specific responsibilities for providing academic advising and who are evaluated and rewarded for supporting the goals of developmental academic advising, offer the best opportunities to meet the needs of students. Other services that could be offered for upperclass students in conjunction with various student affairs departments through such centers include assistance in the job placement process, making applications to graduate or professional schools, or increasing career awareness in fields served by the center.

Is Developmental Academic Advising Workable?

Two important questions remain to be answered about developmental academic advising. Do students want this type of advising, and is the concept of developmental advising a realistic goal for higher education?

Larson and Brown (1983) studied faculty and student perceptions of academic advising. They found that both groups agreed that advisors should be involved in helping students solve personal problems, facilitating students' interaction with the bureaucracy, acting as a referral agent to tools of the academic discipline, financial aid, and part-time employment, assisting in their involvement with campus activities from an informational perspective, and helping plan an academic program consistent with the students' abilities and interests. Winston and Sandor (1984) found that students desired that their advisors teach them: how to register themselves, problem-solving approaches, processes for deciding on an academic major, and goal-setting strategies. They also wanted them to assist with class selection (but not to make decisions for them), form a relationship characterized by warmth and genuine concern, relate the advising process to selection of a major and future careers, and be knowledgeable about all aspects of the institution, not just academic matters. While students wanted advisors to be concerned about them as individuals and to spend time getting to know them, they did not want to return to the days of *in loco parentis.* The majority of students seemed to want interest and support from advisors in regard to academic matters and out-of-class activities but did not want their freedom curtailed. Advisors were seen primarily as persons who teach and support students but allow them maximum freedom of both behavior and decision making. *Students wished to be considered partners in the advising process, not the recipients of advice.* Consequently, the answer to the first question posed in this section is *yes,* students want developmental academic advising.

Is developmental academic advising attainable? Borgard (1983, p. 380) argued that "developmental advising implies regular and fairly intensive contact with students over a long period. . . . Many advising-oriented faculty presently decry the lack of contact that they have with students (let alone the faculty who must advise but don't really want that much interaction). . . . Is it realistic to assume that faculty, besieged by requirements to teach more, while maintaining or increasing current levels of research and service, will subscribe to more demands on their time?"

Borgard is correct to assert that developmental academic advising is not feasible, given the present approach to academic advising as being another burden for already overextended faculty members. Faculty, however, are not the only legitimate providers of academic advising. If academic advising is given priority by institutional leaders, however, and if they desire to see their institutions survive the predicted hard times of the upcoming decade, then they will find the resources to respond to students' legitimate needs and concerns. As Sanford (1981, p. xx) noted, "The hardest thing about educational reform is finding, or arousing, the motivation for it." Increasing student consumerism, a need to improve retention, and a desire to rehabilitate education's role and standing in society should help to provide the motivation. It is in colleges' best interest to seek to implement developmental academic advising concepts because it is in students' best interests.

How to Begin the Process of Change

To move from advising programs that have as their sole function the filling out and signing of registration forms to a system that responds to the student as an individual in the process of change—intellectually, psychologically, physically, socially, and ethically—will take time, thought, and sustained effort by many individuals on the college campus.

Perhaps the most immediate action a college could initiate to begin the change process would be to name an individual who would have responsibility for serving as the institution, college, or departmental advising coordinator. The functions of this advisor coordinator would be substantial. Many chapters in the remainder of this book articulate the roles administrators must fulfill when implementing developmental advising systems.

Perhaps the most immediate role of this person would be to begin a *pilot* developmental advising program along the lines of the model outlined herein. That is, choose a college population that needs extensive advising/developmental services. There are many subpopulations present on all campuses that desperately need this type of programming effort. Then design, implement, and evaluate the program. The results will justify the time, energy, and money required to implement the concepts of developmental academic advising. The challenge is a great one. If higher education is to move beyond the "tide of mediocrity," changes must take place. Academic advising seems to be a wise place to begin.

References

Appleton, S. "The Impact of an Academic Advising Program: A Case Study." *National Academic Advising Association (NAC-ADA) Journal,* 1981, *3* (1), 57–63.

Astin, A. W. *Four Critical Years: Effects of College on Beliefs, Attitudes, and Knowledge.* San Francisco: Jossey-Bass, 1977.

Bachelor, T. "Advisory System Needs to Change" (letter to the editor). Kansas State University, Manhattan, Kans. *Kansas State Collegian,* April 12, 1983, p. 5.

Blimling, G. S. "Residence Halls in Today's Compartmentalized University." In. G. S. Blimling and J. H. Schuh (Eds.), *New Directions for Student Services: Increasing the Educational Role of Residence Halls,* no. 13. San Francisco: Jossey-Bass, 1981.

Bok, D. "On the Purposes of Undergraduate Education." *Daedalus,* Fall 1974, pp. 159–172.

Borgard, J. H. "Review of Developmental Approaches to Academic Advising." *Journal of College Student Personnel,* 1983, *24,* 379–381.

Bowen, H. R. *Investment in Learning: The Individual and Social Value of American Higher Education.* San Francisco: Jossey-Bass, 1977.

Brodzinski, F. R. "Adult Learners—The New Majority: A Demographic Reality." In A. Shriberg (Ed.), *New Directions for Student Services: Providing Student Services for the Adult Learner,* no. 11. San Francisco: Jossey-Bass, 1980.

Brown, R. D. *Student Development in Tomorrow's Higher Education: A Return to the Academy.* Washington, D.C.: American College Personnel Association, 1972.

Carnegie Council on Policy Studies in Higher Education. *Three Thousand Futures: The Next Twenty Years for Higher Education.* San Francisco: Jossey-Bass, 1980.

Carstensen, D. J., and Silberhorn, C. A. *A National Survey of Academic Advising, Final Report.* Iowa City, Iowa: American College Testing Program,1979.

Chickering, A. W. *Education and Identity.* San Francisco: Jossey-Bass, 1969.

Chickering, A. W. *Commuting Versus Resident Students: Overcoming the Educational Inequities of Living Off Campus.* San Francisco: Jossey-Bass, 1974.

Chickering, A. W., and Havighurst, R. J. "The Life Cycle." In A. W. Chickering and Associates, *The Modern American College: Responding to the New Realities of Diverse Students and a Changing Society.* San Francisco: Jossey-Bass, 1981.

Committee on the Student in Higher Education. *The Student in Higher Education.* New Haven, Conn.: Hazen Foundation, 1968.

Creamer, D. G. (Ed.). *Student Development in Higher Education: Theories, Practices and Future Directions.* Washington, D.C.: American College Personnel Association, 1980.

Crockett, D. S. "Academic Advising: A Cornerstone of Student Retention." In L. Noel (Ed.), *New Directions for Student Services: Reducing the Dropout Rate,* no. 3. San Francisco: Jossey-Bass, 1978.

Crockett, D. S. "Academic Advising Delivery Systems." In R. B. Winston, Jr., S. C. Ender, and T. K. Miller (Eds.), *New Directions for Student Services: Developmental Approaches to Academic Advising,* no. 17. San Francisco: Jossey-Bass, 1982.

Crookston, B. B. "A Developmental View of Academic Advising as Teaching." *Journal of College Student Personnel,* 1972, *13*, 12–17.

Cross, K. P. *Beyond the Open Door: New Students to Higher Education.* San Francisco: Jossey-Bass, 1974.

Cross, K. P. "Education for Personal Development." In D. A. DeCoster and P. Mable (Eds.), *Personal Education and Community Development in College Residence Halls.* Washington, D.C.: American College Personnel Association, 1980.

DeCoster, D. A., and Mable, P. "Personal Values, Attitudes and Behavior." In D. A. DeCoster and P. Mable (Eds.), *New Direc-*

tions for Student Services: Understanding Today's Students, no. 16. San Francisco: Jossey-Bass, 1981a.

DeCoster, D. A., and Mable, P. (Eds.). *New Directions for Student Services: Understanding Today's Students*, no. 16. San Francisco: Jossey-Bass, 1981b.

DeCoster, D. A., and Mable, P. "Interpersonal Relationships." In D. A. DeCoster and P. Mable (Eds.), *New Directions for Student Services: Understanding Today's Students*, no. 16. San Francisco: Jossey-Bass, 1981c.

Ender, S. C. "Assisting High Academic Risk Athletes: Recommendations for the Academic Advisor." *National Academic Advising Association (NACADA) Journal*, 1983, *3* (2), 1-10.

Ender, S. C., and Winston, R. B., Jr. "Training Allied Professional Academic Advisors." In R. B. Winston, Jr., S. C. Ender, and T. K. Miller (Eds.), *New Directions for Student Services: Developmental Approaches to Academic Advising*, no. 17. San Francisco: Jossey-Bass, 1982.

Ender, S. C., Winston, R. B., Jr. and Miller, T. K. "Academic Advising as Student Development." In R. B. Winston, Jr., S. C. Ender, and T. K. Miller (Eds.), *New Directions for Student Services: Developmental Approaches to Academic Advising*, no. 17. San Francisco: Jossey-Bass, 1982.

Glennen, R. E. "Intrusive College Counseling." *School Counselor*, 1976, *24*, 48-50.

Grites, T. J. *Academic Advising: Getting Us Through the Eighties.* Washington, D.C.: American Association for Higher Education–Educational Resource Information Center (AAHE-ERIC)/Higher Education Research Report No. 7, 1979.

Heath, D. H. *Growing Up in College: Liberal Education and Maturity.* San Francisco: Jossey-Bass, 1968.

Henderson, A. D., and Henderson, J. G. *Higher Education in America: Problems, Priorities, and Prospects.* San Francisco: Jossey-Bass, 1974.

Kerr, C. *The Uses of the University.* Cambridge, Mass.: Harvard University Press, 1963.

Kerr, C., and Gade, M. "Current and Emerging Issues Facing American Higher Education." In P. G. Altback and R. O. Berdall

(Eds.), *Higher Education in American Society.* Buffalo, N.Y.: Prometheus Books, 1981.

Larson, M. D., and Brown, B. "Student and Faculty Expectations of Academic Advising." *National Academic Advising Association (NACADA) Journal*, 1983, *3* (1), 31–37.

Levine, A. *When Dreams and Heroes Died: A Portrait of Today's College Student.* San Francisco: Jossey-Bass, 1980.

Mable, P., and DeCoster, D. A. "Academic Experiences and Career Orientations." In D. A. DeCoster and P. Mable (Eds.), *New Directions for Student Services: Understanding Today's Students*, no. 16. San Francisco: Jossey-Bass, 1981a.

Mable, P., and DeCoster, D. A. "Postsecondary Education Futures: Implications, Innovations, and Initiatives." In D. A. DeCoster and P. Mable (Eds.), *New Directions for Student Services: Understanding Today's Students*, no. 16. San Francisco: Jossey-Bass, 1981b.

Mash, D. J. "Academic Advising: Too Often Taken for Granted." *College Board Review*, 1978, *107*, 32–36.

Miller, T. K., and Prince, J. S. *The Future of Student Affairs: A Guide to Student Development for Tomorrow's Higher Education.* San Francisco: Jossey-Bass, 1976.

Morrill, W. H., and Hurst, J. C. *Dimensions of Intervention for Student Development.* New York: Wiley, 1980.

National Commission on Excellence in Education. *A Nation at Risk: The Imperative for Educational Reform.* Washington, D.C.: U.S. Government Printing Office, April 1983.

Newton, F. B., Angle, S. S., Schuette, C. G., and Ender, S. C. "The Assessment of College Student Needs: First Steps in a Preventative Response." *Personnel and Guidance Journal*, 1984, *62*, 537–543.

Noel, L. "College Student Retention: A Campus-Wide Responsibility." *Journal of the National Association of College Admissions Counselors*, 1976, *21*, 33–36.

Perkins, J. A. *The University in Transition.* Princeton, N.J.: Princeton University Press, 1966.

Riesman, D. *On Higher Education: The Academic Enterprise in an Era of Rising Student Consumerism.* San Francisco: Jossey-Bass, 1981.

Rippey, D. *What Is Student Development?* Washington, D.C.: American Association of Community and Junior Colleges, 1981.

Sanford, N. "Student Development and the American College." In N. Sanford and J. Axelrod (Eds.), *College and Character.* Berkeley, Calif.: Montaigne, 1979.

Sanford, N. "Forward." In A. W. Chickering (Ed.), *The Modern American College: Responding to the New Realities of Diverse Students and a Changing Society.* San Francisco: Jossey-Bass, 1981.

Shane, D. "Academic Advising in Higher Education: A Developmental Approach for College Students of All Ages." *National Academic Advising Association (NACADA) Journal,* 1981, *1* (2), 12-23.

Smith, J. "A Formula for Contented Freshmen: The Emory College Seminar Program." *Emory Magazine,* 1982, *52* (2), 22-27.

Trombley, T. B., and Holmes, D. "Defining the Role of Academic Advising in the Industrial Setting: The Next Phase." *National Academic Advising Association (NACADA) Journal,* 1981, *1* (2), 1-8.

Walsh, E. M. "Revitalizing Academic Advisement." *Personnel and Guidance Journal,* 1979, *57*, 446-449.

Wilson, M. E. "Facilitating Human Development Through Administrative Leadership." In D. A. DeCoster and P. Mable (Eds.), *New Directions for Student Services: Understanding Today's Students,* no. 16. San Francisco: Jossey-Bass, 1981.

Winston, R. B., Jr., and Sandor, J. A. "Developmental Academic Advising: What Do Students Want?" *National Academic Advising Association (NACADA) Journal,* 1984, *4* (1), 5-13.

2

Current
Advising Practices
in Colleges
and Universities

David S. Crockett, Randi S. Levitz

An increasing number of decision makers view effective advising as an essential educational activity on the campus. These leaders know that good academic advising, like good teaching, is vital to students as they define and develop their interests, abilities, and goals. In many cases, substantive advising is a key factor in student persistence (Beal and Noel, 1980; Forrest, 1982). In recent years, those responsible for the administration and delivery of advising services have expressed interest in information about current practices and trends in academic advising that transcend their respective campuses.

In 1979, with the encouragement and support of the National Academic Advising Association (NACADA), the American College Testing Program (ACT) conducted the first National Survey of Academic Advising. Carstensen and Silberhorn (1979) reported the following conclusions from that study:

1. There are more similarities than differences in the approaches institutions take in the delivery of academic advising services. In general, institutions are traditional in their reliance on faculty to dispense information through the academic advising process.
2. Generally, academic advising has been and still is perceived by administrators to be a low-status function.
3. Those responsible for the delivery of academic advising services see advising as addressing the informational needs of students rather than as an integral part of the students' total development that includes career and life planning. This is reflected not only in the manner in which the service is delivered but also in the materials used and the training provided to those who serve as advisors.
4. There are few effective systems in place for the evaluation of academic advising and little reward or recognition attached to its successful delivery.
5. Generally, institutions have no comprehensive statement of policy regarding the delivery of academic advising. This may indicate a lack of a clear sense of institutional mission in delivering this service.

The results from this national survey have been cited frequently in the literature on advising and used as a catalyst to improve support for academic advising on individual campuses. Because these survey data have been useful to many members of the advising community, it was deemed appropriate to update the study to ascertain what, if any, changes have occurred in the delivery and organization of advising services since 1979.

This chapter presents a comprehensive view of the current status of undergraduate academic advising practices in colleges and universities based on the results of a second National Survey of Academic Advising conducted by ACT in the fall of 1982. The survey instrument focuses on those elements identified in the research on academic advising as important characteristics in the organization and delivery of advising services. It does not, however, address directly the quality of advising provided by individual advisors. Issues of quality and effectiveness are more appropriately assessed through program evaluation efforts on individual campuses.

Methodology

The data in the 1982 National Survey of Academic Advising are based on a random, national sample of 1,095 two- and four-year public and private institutions of higher education. The same institutions, chosen by a random sampling procedure that ensured responses would reflect national trends with a sampling error of less than 5 percent, were included in the sample for the 1979 National Survey of Academic Advising.

Surveys were mailed to the director/coordinator of academic advising at each institution. In institutions in which advising services are provided through individual academic departments only, the questionnaire was to be forwarded to the person overseeing these services campus-wide (for example, vice-president for academic affairs). The questions pertained to the design and delivery of undergraduate advising services, and respondents were asked to answer all items applicable to their campus.

In 1982, 754 institutions responded for a return rate of 69 percent. Table 1 shows the 1982 return rate by type of institution. This response compared favorably with the 1979 survey, which had a return rate of 75 percent. Of the 1982 respondents, 601 or 80 percent had responded to the first survey in 1979, making some comparisons with the results of the earlier survey possible.

The data presented in the tables at the end of this chapter have been weighted to reflect sampling stratification and are tabulated by institutional type. Data from the 754 responding institutions were weighted to reflect responses for 2,593 institutions nationwide, except where noted. Where tables are based on fewer institutions than are included in the total weighted group of respondents, notes appear detailing the actual size of the subgroup on which the weighted percentages were calculated. All numbers appearing in the tables are percentages except where noted.

Advising Goals and Needs

Before proceeding to findings that describe current advising design and delivery strategies, it is important to first consider the

goals of such efforts. NACADA has established a set of goals that
relate to the process of advising as well as to its primary outcome,
student educational growth and development. The goals listed in
Table 2 are obviously all legitimate statements of what should occur
in the interaction between advisors and students. The advising goal
most often reported by survey respondents as being successfully
achieved for the majority of students is that most traditionally
associated with advising efforts—the provision of accurate information about institutional policies, procedures, resources, and programs. Also ranked as satisfactorily achieved are goals related to
assisting students in developing and evaluating progress toward
achievement of an educational plan consistent with life goals and
objectives, as well as other goals related to processing and dissem-
inating information. These represent the traditional advising function of matching information with stated student needs. According
to the achievement ratings assigned, the advising programs are less
successful in helping students to formulate life goals, increase self-
understanding and self-acceptance, and develop decision-making
skills. These developmental goals represent functions only recently
considered as important elements in the advising process on most
campuses.

In conjunction with this rating of the achievements of
advising goals, it is interesting to note what institutions perceive to
be the most important needs associated with their advising programs. As the data in Table 3 indicate, administrative recognition of
the importance of advising takes precedence over all concerns in the
design and delivery of services, *including* the addition of more staff.
Overall, 16 percent of the institutions surveyed felt that greater
administrative recognition is required for faculty to better justify
time spent in advising. This appears to be an even greater problem
among four-year public institutions than others, as 25 percent
indicated that administrative recognition was the top-ranked need
of their advising program. (Current patterns of recognition and
rewards for advising are described in Table 20.) Other priorities
ranked first from the list of nine "needs" were expanded advisor
training program/activities (11 percent), more staff (10 percent), a
different or improved delivery model or organizational framework

(10 percent), and more readily available data on students—abilities, interests, goals, and so on (9 percent).

Structure of Academic Advising Services

While there is probably no "best" administrative structure for advising appropriate to all institutions and situations, Table 4 shows various ways in which institutions have chosen to administratively organize the delivery of this service. Campus-wide determination of advising policies and procedures occurs in 79 percent of two-year private and 69 percent of two-year public institutions. Among four-year institutions, 47 percent of those in the private sector and 20 percent in the public sector centrally determine advising policies and procedures. The more decentralized approach characteristic of four-year public institutions is probably dictated by considerations of organizational size and complexity.

About one third of the institutions indicated an administrative structure was in place combining aspects of both the centralized and decentralized models. These combination structures centralized services for some students (undeclared majors) and decentralized them for others (upperclass students with declared majors). Purely decentralized administration of advising, in which policies and procedures are determined by individual departments or schools, occurs at only 14 percent of the institutions. Totally decentralized administration of advising services may promote inconsistent delivery of information to students and is probably the least desirable delivery mode of those currently in use. Completely centralized systems, on the other hand, provide for consistency but may fail to involve those best equipped to deliver certain aspects of the advising process, that is, faculty. A combination of administrative approaches probably incorporates most of the advantages and few of the disadvantages associated with a purely centralized or decentralized structure.

There are several alternative strategies for assigning students to advisors. Table 5 suggests that the most common practice is to assign entering freshmen directly to schools or departments on the basis of intended major (31 percent). In this case, students without a declared major are also assigned to faculty advisors but receive supplemental advising services. Forty-one percent of the private four-year colleges reported that they assign entering freshmen to selected faculty advisors for their first year but not necessarily on the basis of their intended major. This approach may risk potential "discipline bias" as the advisor assists the student in selecting an appropriate major.

Twelve percent of the institutions assign freshmen to an academic advising center for all academic advising. A combination strategy that uses both the advising center approach for undeclared students and departmental/college advisors for those with stated major preferences has been adopted by 20 percent of the institutions.

Advising Centers. An emerging trend in the delivery of academic advising has been the establishment of advising centers. This may be partially in response to the literature indicating that students with undeclared majors are high attrition risks and that institutions are wise to provide such students with additional support services (Cope and Hannah, 1975; Beal and Noel, 1980). In general, centralized advising centers are academic or student affairs agencies designed to make information accessible to students and to assist them in their academic decision-making process. They are frequently staffed with some full-time professional advisors assisted by faculty on release time and/or peer and paraprofessional advisors. There may be a central, campus-wide center, separate centers in specific colleges or academic units, or centers designated as agencies serving the special advising needs of specific groups of students.

Table 6 reveals that 30 percent of the institutions have implemented the concept of an academic advising center as a primary delivery mechanism for advising. Overall, the number of institutions with advising centers has increased approximately 5 percent since the 1979 survey. As was the case in 1979, more public than private institutions have implemented this delivery model.

Table 6A provides insight into the wide range of functions of advising centers in helping to coordinate advising programs on campus. Primary responsibilities most frequently include working with students with undeclared majors (85 percent), advising students on general education requirements (79 percent), conducting freshman orientation (69 percent), developing and updating advisor handbooks (65 percent), advising transfers (64 percent), and maintaining advising records (61 percent). Because of the number and complexity of tasks performed by such centers, the advisor/student ratio is higher than that generally existing when more traditional faculty advising systems are employed. As the data in Table 7 indicate, in 37 percent of the institutions the advising load exceeds fifty students per advisor. When these data are compared to Table 22, it is evident that this ratio is significantly higher than that experienced by faculty advisors.

Administration of Advising Programs. Effective advising programs, like most worthwhile campus activities, need coordination and direction. When everyone is responsible for advising, no one is generally held accountable. Directors/coordinators of academic advising assist others with delivery by planning and managing the advising program campus-wide or within an academic unit.

A growing recognition of the need for administrative coordination is evidenced by a small increase since 1979 in the prevalence of the position of director/coordinator of academic advising. Today 19 percent of the institutions have a coordinator holding that title, compared to 14 percent in 1979. Generally, however, coordinating this important function is part of the responsibilities of those holding a variety of other positions on campus, as can also be seen in Table 8. Coordination of advising is the responsibility of academic affairs administrators (vice-presidents, deans, and assistants or department chairs) at 34 percent of the institutions and is the responsibility of student affairs or student counseling administrators at 19 percent.

The extent to which this increasing official recognition of the advising coordinator's position is an acknowledgment of a need to systematically manage the advising process is somewhat in question, however. As noted in Table 9, only 10 percent of the directors/coordinators devote full time to this function. This suggests that other duties and responsibilities unrelated to advising compete for their time and energies. Among those with full-time advising coordination duties, Tables 9A to 9C reveal that the "typical" full-time director/coordinator of advising has earned at least a master's degree, makes an annual salary of $24,000 or more, and has a twelve-month appointment.

Basic to the development of a good advising program is a common sense of what the institution wants to achieve through advising. If program design and modifications grow out of a thoughtful discussion of objectives, the program is more likely to meet institutional expectations. Out of this deliberative process should come a written statement on academic advising. Table 10 indicates that 63 percent of the responding institutions had such a document. This is in marked contrast to the 1979 survey in which only 26 percent of the institutions responded affirmatively. Colleges and universities have obviously seen a greater need during the past several years to develop a comprehensive, written statement formulating the purposes and procedures of their advising program.

As indicated in Table 10A, the majority of these written statements deal with responsibilities of advisors (78 percent) and contain references to philosophy (72 percent), goals (81 percent), and delivery strategies (55 percent). More limited attention is paid to other important elements of a good advising program such as selection of advisors (30 percent) and training of advisors (23 percent). Consistent with the often-repeated theme of a lack of recognition and reward for advisors, only 8 percent of these written documents delineate recognition/reward systems for those delivering advising to students.

The freshman year, indeed the first term of that year, represents a critical point in a student's life—for many it is their first opportunity to make independent decisions about their future. Frequency of contact with advisors during this critical period enhances the student's sense of "connectedness" with the institution as well as providing opportunities for advisors to lend decision-making support. Data in Table 11 indicate that there are one to two meetings between freshmen and their advisors during the first term in 43 percent of the institutions, and three to four meetings in another 43 percent of the institutions. Students in two- and four-year private institutions are much more likely to meet with their advisors three to four times the first term than are those in public institutions.

In the past several years there has been increasing support in the advising literature for more intrusive advising strategies (Glennen, 1976). Intrusive advising systems require contact between students and advisors at important points in the student's educational decision-making process. Table 12 indicates the degree of intrusiveness prevalent in advising programs today. Class scheduling/registration (90 percent) and changes in registration (62 percent) remain the most common required contact times. Less than half the institutions reported requiring contact with an advisor prior to changing a major (44 percent), before withdrawing from school (39 percent), following a report of unsatisfactory performance or class attendance (35 percent), or prior to declaring a major (29 percent). Based on their responses to this item, private four-year colleges appear to have the most intrusive advising systems. Overall, comparisons with the 1979 survey data would suggest little change in the degree of intrusiveness evident in advising programs.

Training and Evaluation. The frequency or timing of advising sessions matters little if these encounters fail to produce the desired results. One method of ensuring consistency of results is to provide an effective training program for advisors. Table 13 tends to substantiate the commonly held belief that institutions, by and large, are not doing an adequate job of advisor training. One fourth of the institutions provide no training opportunities whatsoever to those engaged in advising students. Among those that provide some training, the most common activity is an annual orientation meeting at the beginning of the school year (46 percent). While this approach is not intrinsically valueless, too often such meetings focus solely on the mechanics of advising and are limited to a hurried exchange of information regarding policy and procedural changes. Only 26 percent of the institutions surveyed conduct regularly scheduled in-service workshops on campus. Fewer still (7 percent) permit advisors to take advantage of opportunities to attend off-campus advising seminars and workshops.

Advisor training sessions should deal with problems perceived by advisors to be common obstacles to advising students effectively. Table 13A depicts topics commonly included in faculty advisor training activities. Academic regulations, policies, and registration procedures (95 percent), campus referral sources (76 percent), and use of information sources (68 percent) are the most widely featured topics. Just slightly more than half the institutions provide training designed to build advising skills and techniques. It is also of interest that only 14 percent include training on the decision-making skills that in many ways are the essence of the advising process. This lack of training in these critical interactive areas may be reflected in the failure of many institutions to achieve the NACADA goal of developing student decision-making skills.

Tables 14 and 15 reveal that there is clearly a need for the vast majority of colleges and universities to develop a more systematic and regular appraisal of both their advising programs and individual advisor performance. The 1979 National Survey of Academic Advising reported that three fourths of the responding institutions had no formal process for evaluating their advising programs. In 1982, 50 percent of the institutions evaluate advisors but only 24 percent systematically evaluate the overall effectiveness of their advising program. Clearly, this situation has not changed. This apparent lack of concern on the part of institutions with the effectiveness and outcomes of their advising programs is disappointing and difficult to understand. Evaluating the effectiveness of this critical educational activity is crucial to establishing and documenting its contribution to the achievement of both individual and institutional goals.

Specialized Advising. College students can be categorized into campus subpopulations, and their advising needs vary accordingly. It is unlikely that any single advising delivery system or individual advisor can be expected to meet the advising needs of all students. Different advising styles and strategies accommodate individual differences and facilitate student growth and development.

Table 16 provides information on the provision of special advising services for selected student populations. Institutions most commonly provide special advising services for the academically underprepared (45 percent), foreign students (44 percent), and students with undeclared majors (33 percent). The data also suggest that two-year colleges provide fewer special advising opportunities than do four-year institutions. Twenty-eight percent of institutions do not provide advising services for selected student populations that can be distinguished from services available to all students.

Delivery of Advising Services

Academic advising, like most educational programs and services, is being delivered in a variety of ways by colleges and universities. Tables 17 through 27 depict the multiplicity of delivery mechanisms currently in use.

Advisors. The vast majority of institutions continue to rely heavily on faculty as the major providers of academic advising (80 percent). From a historical perspective, predominance of this delivery mode is easily understood when we consider that student/faculty relationships have always been viewed as an integral part of the college experience. Many also use faculty as a support to other delivery systems (33 percent), as noted in Table 17. These findings are consistent with the results of the 1979 survey.

Professional counselors were most frequently mentioned as providing the chief means of support to faculty or other primary advisors, as noted by 57 percent of the institutions. The use of nonfaculty advisors is most prominent in two-year public colleges.

As to other means of supplementing primary advisors, the use of fellow students as peer helpers has had a long tradition in higher education. It was, therefore, not surprising to learn that 27 percent of the institutions continue to use student advisors. No increase was noted in the use of peer advisors between the 1979 and 1982 studies. About one quarter of the institutions used residence hall advisors to supplement other advising staff in 1979 and the same proportion was reported in this study. There was only limited use of other paraprofessional personnel to support the regular advising program (10 percent). Full-time advisors are employed by 14 percent of the institutions to assist others in the delivery of advising.

Group advising is another technique used to supplement regular advising. It may be used as an overload method for dealing with large numbers of students or to provide specific information to students on a particular topic. As shown in Table 18, small group meetings scheduled as part of orientation (73 percent) or during the academic term (34 percent) are the most common group advising efforts.

Faculty Advisors. Table 19 indicates the manner in which faculty members become academic advisors. In 1979, advising was considered to be a "condition of employment" at half the institutions surveyed. Now, all or almost all faculty are expected to serve as advisors in the majority of institutions (64 percent). Only a limited number of institutions (11 percent) are employing any type of selection process in determining those faculty members qualified to advise. Such a system most likely results in the use of some advisors with little interest or skill in advising students and makes training of advisors an especially critical factor. In approximately one half the institutions, more than 75 percent of the faculty have major undergraduate advising responsibilities.

The survey results support the fact that in many institutions advising is an activity that carries little or no recognition or reward. Table 20 reveals that 62 percent of the institutions have no formal recognition or reward system for those involved in academic advising. This percentage has unfortunately increased since 1979. At that time, 56 percent indicated there was no formal recognition or reward system in place. Of those institutions who recognize in a tangible way the contributions made by advisors, 25 percent consider this contribution in making tenure or promotion decisions. There was no significant difference on this particular item between the 1979 and 1982 surveys. Thus, it is clear that most colleges fail to recognize that good advising—like good teaching, publication, and research—needs to be rewarded in some manner.

Advisors must expend an adequate amount of time on their advising responsibilities if they are to achieve the desired results. The amount of time committed to advising varies, depending on such factors as expectations, student load, and competing priorities. Table 21 shows the approximate proportion of time faculty advisors are expected to commit to their advising responsibilities. The fact that 22 percent of institutions have no specific time expectations for faculty advising is perhaps another indicator of a failure to recognize the importance of the advising function.

To perform satisfactorily, advisors must be assigned a reasonable student load. Too large a load of students will inevitably result in inaccessible advisors, hurried advising sessions, failure to get to know students on a personal basis, and, in general, poor advising experiences for students.

Table 22 indicates that the most typical ratio of faculty advisors to students at all types of institutions is one advisor to nineteen or fewer students (44 percent). Sixty-four percent of the four-year private colleges reported this favorable ratio of advisor to students, while about one third of two- and four-year public institutions reported advisor loads of thirty or more students.

Peer Advisors. Perhaps the single most persuasive argument for the use of peer advising is that it works. The literature on this delivery mechanism strongly supports the assumption that peer advising can be as effective as that provided by professionals and faculty in many advising situations.

Tables 23, 23A, and 24 provide information on the selection and training of peer advisors. Overall, 42 percent of the institutions reported using peer advisors in their advising program. Peer advising is employed by about half of the four-year institutions and by about one third of the two-year institutions. This difference is probably attributable to the fact that it is more difficult to select and train peer advisors in two-year colleges because students are generally enrolled for a shorter time.

Few institutions simply accept all who apply to become peer advisors (2 percent). Most use some criteria in selecting those to perform this function. Academic performance as measured by grade point average (GPA) is the most common selection criterion for peer advisors (55 percent). About one third of the institutions require peer advisors to have participated in campus and extracurricular activities. Academic regulations, policies, and registration procedures (65 percent), campus referral sources (61 percent), and advising/counseling skills (56 percent) are the most common topics included in training programs for peer advisors.

Advising Information. Quality advising is based on good information systems. Individual students' educational/career decisions are enhanced by the ready availability and use of relevant information by both the advisor and the student. Tables 25 to 27 address the type of support or reference materials institutions routinely provide to advisors and students. Academic planning worksheets (70 percent), advising handbooks (62 percent), computerized student academic progress records (56 percent), and directory of campus referral sources (49 percent) are the most common support and reference materials provided to academic advisors. In comparing these findings to those of the 1979 survey, it is interesting to note that there has been an increase in the percentage of institutions providing advising handbooks, computerized student records, and campus referral directories. Advisors most frequently have access to college transcript/grade reports (80 percent) and admissions test—ACT, Scholastic Aptitude Test (SAT)—results (72 percent). Approximately half the institutions routinely provide advisors with copies of the high school transcript and the results of locally administered interest/placement test results. Students most often are provided with a catalogue (90 percent), class scheduling guide (85 percent), and a student handbook (81 percent). Only about one third of the institutions provide students with a campus referral directory.

Conclusions

The following statements highlight the results of the second National Survey on Academic Advising.

- With the exception of student development goals, institutions perceive that they are by and large successfully meeting the advising goals established by the National Academic Advising Association.
- Respondents cite greater administrative support and recognition for advising and expanded training for advisors as their greatest needs.
- On half the campuses, advising policies and procedures are determined centrally for the entire institution.
- The most common method of assigning students to advisors is to make assignments directly to academic units on the basis of intended major. Students without a declared major receive supplemental advising services.
- Advising centers are more frequently employed in the delivery of advising at public rather than private colleges. Since 1979,

there has been an increase of approximately 5 percent in the number of advising centers established by postsecondary institutions.

- There is a director/coordinator of academic advising at about one fifth of the institutions. Most persons holding this title are not assigned these responsibilities on a full-time basis.
- There appears to have been a significant increase in the percentage of institutions that have developed a comprehensive, written statement on the purposes and procedures of their advising programs. However, many of these statements still exclude important elements such as the selection, training, and rewarding of advisors.
- The degree of intrusiveness, as measured by requiring students to contact advisors at critical decision junctures, did not increase during the three years between 1979 and 1982. Further, students continue to experience one to four contacts with their academic advisor during the first term of their freshman year.
- Less than half the institutions indicate that they provide special advising services for selected groups of students distinguishable from services available to all students.
- Faculty advising continues to be the predominant delivery mode for academic advising at all types of institutions. Typically between one and nineteen students are assigned to each faculty advisor. The majority of institutions have no formal recognition/reward system for those engaged in advising students. Approximately three fourths of the colleges do not consider advising effectiveness in making promotion/tenure decisions.
- Many institutions are providing less than adequate training to those involved in the advising process.
- The vast majority of institutions have not implemented a systematic and periodic appraisal of either their advising programs or individual advisor performance.
- Group advising, except during freshman orientation, appears to be an underutilized advising strategy.
- Peer advisors are used to supplement the regular advising program in nearly half the institutions.
- Six out of ten institutions have developed advising handbooks. Advisors routinely have available college grade reports and

admissions test data for use in advising and are provided with material and resources necessary to the course selection and registration process.

As colleges and universities move toward the goal of providing effective advising services for all students, it is important that they continue to review and evaluate their efforts in the context of current advising practices. It is hoped that results from the second National Survey on Academic Advising will prompt self-assessment and promote improvement and innovation.

TABLE 1

DEGREE LEVEL AND AFFILIATION OF INSTITUTIONS SURVEYED

	Sample Number	Respondents*	
		Number	% of N Sampled
Two-Year Public	320	241	75 %
Two-Year Private	73	28	38 %
Four-Year Public	286	198	69 %
Four-Year Private	406	279	69 %
Other	10	8	80 %
	1,095	754	69 %

*Responses were weighted to reflect 2,593 institutions nationally.

TABLE 2

GOALS OF ADVISING PROGRAM SUCCESSFULLY ACHIEVED FOR MOST STUDENTS
(Mean rating scale appears below.)

	Two-Year Public	Two-Year Private	Four-Year Public	Four-Year Private	Total[b]
ing accurate information about institutional policies, procedures, ces, and programs	3.96	4.00	3.95	4.04	3.99
ng students in developing an educational plan consistent with life and objectives (alternative course of action, alternate career erations, and selection of courses)	3.40	3.50	3.12	3.41	3.35
ng students in evaluation or reevaluation of progress toward shed goals and educational plans	3.34	3.42	3.18	3.40	3.33
g referrals to other institutional or community support services	3.30	3.23	3.15	3.38	3.30
ing information about students to the institution, colleges, and/or mic departments	3.08	3.77	3.18	3.42	3.25
ng students in their consideration of life goals by relating ts, skills, abilities, and values to careers, the world of work, and ture and purpose of higher education	2.99	3.58	2.79	3.07	3.01
ng students in self-understanding and self-acceptance (value ation, understanding abilities, interests, and limitations)	2.71	3.07	2.50	2.83	2.73
ng students in developing decision-making skills	2.55	2.61	2.32	2.65	2.55

 based on scale of 1 to 5, where:
es not apply, no services have been implemented to address this goal
hievement not very satisfactory
hievement somewhat satisfactory
hievement satisfactory
hievement very satisfactory

are presented in rank order according to the percentage of responses in the "Total" column.

TABLE 3

ADVISING PROGRAM NEEDS[a]

(Response ranked first in list of 9 needs)
(in percentages)

	Two-Year Public	Two-Year Private	Four-Year Public	Four-Year Private
Greater administrative recognition of the importance of advising so that faculty can better justify time spent in advising (Based on 455 institutions)	15	7	25	15
Expanded advisor training program/activities (Based on 501 institutions)	7	11	7	17
More staff (Based on 390 institutions)	15	7	10	7
A different or improved delivery model or organizational framework (Based on 403 institutions)	14	7	10	7
More readily available data on students (e.g., abilities, interests, goals, etc.) (Based on 449 institutions)	11	11	5	8
More effective evaluation of advisors and advising services (Based on 477 institutions)	4	18	5	9
Assignment of responsibility and accountability for advising services campus-wide (Based on 395 institutions)	5	—	11	5
More effective advisor selection process (Based on 397 institutions)	2	4	4	3
Alternate delivery systems (Based on 360 institutions)	3	—	2	<1

[a]Multiple responses possible; percentages will not total 100%.

[b]Data are presented in rank order according to the percentage of responses in the "Total" column.

TABLE 4

ADMINISTRATIVE STRUCTURE OF ADVISING SERVICES ON CAMPUS

(in percentages)

	Two-Year Public	Two-Year Private	Four-Year Public	Four-Year Private
Centralized, campus-wide advising services (advising policies and procedures are determined centrally for the whole institution)	69	79	20	47
Centralized/decentralized advising services—centralized for some students (e.g., freshmen, those without majors) and decentralized for others (e.g., upperclassmen, students with declared majors)	19	7	52	36
Decentralized advising services (advising policies and procedures are determined by individual departments or schools)	8	14	25	12
Other	3	—	3	2
Blank	1	—	1	2

[b]Data are presented in rank order according to the percentage of responses in the "Total" column.

TABLE 5   53

ASSIGNMENT OF RESPONSIBILITY FOR ADVISING OF FRESHMEN
(in percentages)

	Two-Year Public	Two-Year Private	Four-Year Public	Four-Year Private	Total[b]
ng freshmen are assigned directly to colleges and departments on sis of intended major; students without a declared major are ed to faculty advisors, but receive supplemental special advising es	30	29	32	30	31
ng freshmen are assigned to selected faculty advisors for their an year, but not necessarily on the basis of intended major	7	32	10	41	22
ng freshmen without a declared major are assigned to an mic advising center for general education advising and special advising; those with a declared major are assigned to tmental/college advisors	21	18	37	11	20
shmen are assigned to an academic advising center for all mic advising	20	7	10	6	12
	18	14	5	8	11
	4	—	7	4	4

are presented in rank order according to the percentage of responses in the "Total" column.

TABLE 6

ACADEMIC ADVISING CENTER ESTABLISHED
(in percentages)

	Two-Year Public	Two-Year Private	Four-Year Public	Four-Year Private	Total
Yes	36	25	39	22	30
No	62	71	58	77	68
Blank	2	4	3	1	2

TABLE 6A

PRIMARY RESPONSIBILITIES OF THE ADVISING CENTER[a]
(Based on 232 institutions with an established Advising Center)
(in percentages)

	Two-Year Public	Two-Year Private	Four-Year Public	Four-Year Private	Total[b]
ing undecided/undeclared/exploratory students	91	71	91	73	85
ing students on general education requirements	85	71	81	66	79
ucting freshman orientation	71	71	64	71	69
oping and updating advising handbook	60	57	70	68	65
ing transfer students	83	71	47	49	64
taining advising records	55	57	59	69	61
ating advising services	58	14	51	50	53
ing advisors campus-wide	33	29	44	53	42
aring registration instructions and materials	38	43	26	38	35
ating transfer credit	40	29	17	26	30
ing veterans	54	14	14	8	29
taining and publishing degree requirements	30	43	22	13	23
ying graduation clearance	28	29	8	21	21
ing Educational Opportunity Program students	20	—	16	10	15

ple responses possible; percentages will not total 100%.

are presented in rank order according to the percentage of responses in the "Total" column.

54

TABLE 7

RATIO OF ADVISORS TO STUDENTS IN ADVISING CENTER
(Based on 232 institutions with an Advising Center)
(in percentages)

	Two-Year Public	Two-Year Private	Four-Year Public	Four-Year Private	Total
1 advisor to fewer than 50 students	11	57	18	55	27
1 advisor to 50-75 students	8	29	8	8	8
1 advisor to 76-100 students	3	—	6	8	5
1 advisor to more than 100 students	29	14	30	9	24
Students are not assigned to individual advisors	35	—	30	14	27
Blank	14	—	7	5	9

TABLE 8

TITLE OF INDIVIDUAL RESPONSIBLE FOR COORDINATING ADVISING ON CAMPUS
(in percentages)

	Two-Year Public	Two-Year Private	Four-Year Public	Four-Year Private	Total
Director/Coordinator of Advising	12	7	32	22	19
Director of Student Counseling	24	4	3	4	11
Vice President/Dean of Academic Affairs	10	39	17	19	16
Assistant Vice President/Dean of Academic Affairs	2	4	6	9	6
Vice President/Dean of Student Affairs	11	7	2	3	6
Assistant Vice President/Dean of Student Affairs	3	—	1	1	2
College Dean or Department Chairperson	10	11	12	14	12
Other	22	7	15	22	20
No one responsible	3	4	7	2	3
Blank	4	18	6	5	6

TABLE 9

PROPORTION OF TIME DESIGNATED INDIVIDUAL SPENDS
COORDINATING ADVISING ON CAMPUS
(in percentages)

	Two-Year Public	Two-Year Private	Four-Year Public	Four-Year Private	Total
Less than one-quarter time	52	57	42	52	51
One-quarter time	21	11	10	17	17
Half time	11	11	11	14	12
Three-quarters time	3	7	5	3	3
Full time	7	7	22	8	10
Blank	6	7	10	6	7

CHARACTERISTICS OF FULL-TIME ADVISING COORDINATOR'S POSITION
(Based on N of 84 institutions with a full-time Coordinator)
(in percentages)

	Two-Year Public	Two-Year Private	Four-Year Public	Four-Year Private	Total
BLE 9A—HIGHEST DEGREE HELD BY COORDINATOR					
BA or BS	—	—	—	9	3
MA or MS	67	50	50	55	55
PhD or EdD	13	50	45	32	34
Other	—	—	3	—	1
Blank	20	—	2	5	7
BLE 9B—AVERAGE YEARLY SALARY OF COORDINATOR					
$15,001 - 18,000	—	—	7	9	5
$18,001 - 21,000	13	—	7	23	14
$21,001 - 24,000	6	—	7	9	7
>$24,000	44	100	55	41	49
Other	—	—	2	—	1
Blank	38	—	22	18	24
BLE 9C—TERM OF COORDINATOR'S CONTRACT					
9-month	6	—	7	5	6
12-month	63	100	87	91	83
Other	13	—	7	5	7
Blank	19	—	—	—	5

TABLE 10

WRITTEN INSTITUTIONAL STATEMENT ON ADVISING AVAILABLE
(in percentages)

	Two-Year Public	Two-Year Private	Four-Year Public	Four-Year Private	Total
Yes	63	57	62	66	63
No	36	43	36	31	35
Blank	1	—	2	3	2

TABLE 10A

ELEMENTS DETAILED IN WRITTEN INSTITUTIONAL STATEMENT ON ADVISING[a]
(Based on 471 institutions with written statements on advising)
(in percentages)

	Two-Year Public	Two-Year Private	Four-Year Public	Four-Year Private	Total[b]
Goals of advising	82	81	80	81	81
Responsibilities of advisors	72	100	71	83	78
Philosophy of advising	73	76	68	73	72
Delivery strategies	54	56	59	53	55
Selection of advisors	28	38	29	31	30
Training of advisors	22	18	28	21	23
Recognition/reward for advisors	9	6	11	7	8

[a]Multiple responses possible; percentages will not total 100%.

[b]Data are presented in rank order according to the percentage of responses in the "Total" column.

56

TABLE 11

**ESTIMATED FREQUENCY OF ADVISOR/STUDENT CONTACT
DURING THE FIRST TERM OF THE FRESHMAN YEAR**
(in percentages)

	Two-Year Public	Two-Year Private	Four-Year Public	Four-Year Private	Total
1-2 times	61	14	54	24	43
3-4 times	33	68	38	51	43
5-7 times	4	14	5	14	8
8-10 times	—	4	1	2	1
More than 10 times	—	—	2	7	3
Blank	2	—	1	2	2

TABLE 12

OCCASIONS WHEN STUDENTS ARE REQUIRED TO CONTACT THEIR ADVISORS[a]
(in percentages)

	Two-Year Public	Two-Year Private	Four-Year Public	Four-Year Private	To
Class scheduling/registration	84	89	87	98	9
Prior to any change in class registration	50	68	54	76	6
Prior to changing a major	28	43	50	58	4
Prior to withdrawal from school	38	36	39	41	3
Following a report of unsatisfactory performance or class attendance	29	50	24	44	3
Prior to declaring a major	8	14	36	49	2
On completion of graduation requirements	28	22	30	23	2
Other	9	14	13	9	1
No contact is ever required	10	4	7	<1	

[a]Multiple responses possible; percentages will not total 100%.

[b]Data are presented in rank order according to the percentage of responses in the "Total" column.

TABLE 13

TYPES OF TRAINING ACTIVITIES PROVIDED FOR FACULTY ADVISORS[a]
(in percentages)

	Two-Year Public	Two-Year Private	Four-Year Public	Four-Year Private	To
Annual advisor orientation meeting	42	64	34	55	
Regularly scheduled in-service workshops on campus	27	28	30	22	
No training provided	27	25	32	22	
Other	14	11	23	25	
Off-campus training (seminars and workshops)	8	4	7	6	

TABLE 13A

TOPICS INCLUDED IN TRAINING ACTIVITIES FOR FACULTY ADVISORS[a]
(Based on 530 institutions that provide training activities)
(in percentages)

	Two-Year Public	Two-Year Private	Four-Year Public	Four-Year Private	Total[b]
demic regulations, policies, and registration procedures	95	100	94	95	95
pus referral sources	75	71	78	78	76
of information sources (admissions test results, scripts)	70	67	61	69	68
sing/counseling skills	57	52	55	55	56
er and employment information	32	43	33	39	36
sion-making skills	10	5	18	17	14

tiple responses possible; percentages will not total 100%.

a are presented in rank order according to the percentage of responses in the "Total" column.

TABLE 14

METHODS OF EVALUATING ACADEMIC ADVISORS[a]
(in percentages)

	Two-Year Public	Two-Year Private	Four-Year Public	Four-Year Private	Total[b]
isors not evaluated	47	57	52	51	50
ual advisor performance review by supervisor	27	22	26	14	22
dent evaluation of the advisor	20	11	15	26	20
isor self-evaluation	14	18	10	11	12
er	6	7	6	5	6

tiple responses possible; percentages will not total 100%.

a are presented in rank order according to the percentage of responses in the "Total" column.

TABLE 15

SYSTEMATIC EVALUATION OF THE OVERALL EFFECTIVENESS
OF THE ADVISING PROGRAM
(in percentages)

	Two-Year Public	Two-Year Private	Four-Year Public	Four-Year Private	Total
Yes	22	7	17	23	21
No	75	89	80	74	76
Blank	4	4	3	3	3

58

TABLE 16

PROVISION OF SPECIAL ADVISING SERVICES FOR SELECTED STUDENT POPULAT

(in percentages)

	Two-Year Public	Two-Year Private	Four-Year Public	Four-Year Private
Academically underprepared students	44	39	49	46
Foreign students	32	46	52	51
Students with undeclared majors	26	21	53	30
Transfer students	23	22	34	38
Handicapped students	41	21	46	14
Same advising services are available to all students	37	36	19	23
Adult students	15	14	29	33
Pre-professional students	5	4	38	32
Educational Opportunity Program students	20	—	39	15
Athletes	9	14	30	10

[a]Multiple responses possible; percentages will not total 100%.

[b]Data are presented in rank order according to the percentage of responses in the "Total" column.

TABLE 17

OTHER PERSONNEL PROVIDING ADVISING SUPPORT[a]

(in percentages)

	Two-Year Public	Two-Year Private	Four-Year Public	Four-Year Private	Total[b]
Professional counselors	66	53	57	50	57
Faculty advisors	37	28	36	26	33
Peer advisors	16	18	39	32	27
Residence hall advisors	2	32	26	42	24
Professional advisors	7	11	25	15	14
Paraprofessional advisors	11	11	14	7	10
Other	3	14	8	15	9

[a]Multiple responses possible; percentages will not total 100%.

[b]Data are presented in rank order according to the percentage of responses in the "Total" column.

TABLE 18

GROUP ADVISING FORMATS AVAILABLE[a]

(in percentages)

	Two-Year Public	Two-Year Private	Four-Year Public	Four-Year Private	Total
Small group meetings during orientation	69	71	78	76	73
Small group meetings during academic term	26	46	40	38	34
Credit or non-credit courses	37	32	27	18	27
Workshops or seminars	27	25	27	28	27
Group advising not available	14	14	10	12	13

[a]Multiple responses possible; percentages will not total 100%.

[b]Data are presented in rank order according to the percentage of responses in the "Total" column.

TABLE 19

FACULTY ADVISOR SELECTION PROCESS
(in percentages)

	Two-Year Public	Two-Year Private	Four-Year Public	Four-Year Private	Total[b]
˃r almost all faculty are expected to serve as advisors	58	75	65	66	64
ˈulty who meet certain advisor selection criteria serve as ˈsors (voluntary or non-voluntary appointments)	10	14	10	12	11
ˈ faculty member may volunteer to serve as an advisor	10	7	8	6	8
ˈulty advisors are not used in undergraduate advising	13	—	—	3	5
ˈer	4	—	7	3	4
ˈk	5	4	10	12	9

ˈta are presented in rank order according to the percentage of responses in the "Total" column.

TABLE 19A

PROPORTION OF THE FACULTY WITH MAJOR ADVISING RESPONSIBILITIES
(Based on 721 institutions that use faculty as undergraduate advisors)
(in percentages)

	Two-Year Public	Two-Year Private	Four-Year Public	Four-Year Private	Total
ˈs than 25%	29	11	24	11	20
ˈ50%	13	22	9	15	13
ˈ5%	7	11	18	24	16
ˈre than 75%	50	57	46	48	49
ˈnk	1	—	3	2	2

TABLE 20

WAYS IN WHICH FACULTY ARE RECOGNIZED/REWARDED FOR THEIR ADVISING ACTIVITIES[a]
(Based on 721 institutions that use faculty in undergraduate advising)
(in percentages)

	Two-Year Public	Two-Year Private	Four-Year Public	Four-Year Private	Total[b]
ˈrmal recognition or reward for advising	71	75	51	58	62
ˈderation in tenure and promotion decisions	11	14	30	36	25
ˈsed time from instruction	7	11	17	9	10
ˈy increments for time spent in advising	4	7	11	7	7
ˈsed time from other faculty responsibilities	4	—	11	6	6
	7	4	5	3	5
ˈds for excellence in advising	2	—	7	3	3

ˈple responses possible; percentages will not total 100%.

ˈare presented in rank order according to the percentage of responses in the "Total" column.

TABLE 21

PROPORTION OF TIME FACULTY ADVISORS ARE EXPECTED TO COMMIT TO ADVISING RESPONSIBILITIES

(Based on 721 institutions that use faculty in undergraduate advising)
(in percentages)

	Two-Year Public	Two-Year Private	Four-Year Public	Four-Year Private	Total
Less than 10%	49	43	37	39	42
10-20%	25	36	30	32	29
21-30%	3	—	2	2	2
31-40%	—	—	—	—	—
More than 40%	2	—	1	1	1
No specific time expectation	19	22	23	23	22
Blank	3	—	8	3	4

TABLE 22

APPROXIMATE RATIO OF FACULTY ADVISORS TO STUDENTS

(Based on 721 institutions that use faculty in undergraduate advising)
(in percentages)

	Two-Year Public	Two-Year Private	Four-Year Public	Four-Year Private	Total
1 advisor to 1-19 students	25	71	28	64	44
1 advisor to 20-29 students	30	22	27	24	26
1 advisor to 30-39 students	14	4	11	5	9
1 advisor to 40 or more students	24	4	21	2	13
Blank	8	—	13	5	8

TABLE 23

WAYS STUDENTS ENTER THE SELECTION PROCESS FOR PEER ADVISORS[a]

(in percentages)

	Two-Year Public	Two-Year Private	Four-Year Public	Four-Year Private
Peer advisors not used	67	68	47	53
Formal application by students	13	11	33	22
Recommendations from faculty/staff	10	18	21	27
Recommendations from the advising staff	10	4	11	13
Other	4	—	8	5

TABLE 23A

CRITERIA USED IN SELECTION OF PEER ADVISORS[a]
(Based on 325 institutions that use peer advisors)
(in percentages)

	Two-Year Public	Two-Year Private	Four-Year Public	Four-Year Private	Total[b]
demic performance (GPA)	37	78	64	61	55
ain level of participation in campus/extracurricular ities	19	34	39	44	35
r	31	11	39	18	26
nitory residence	—	44	10	18	12
pplicants accepted	—	—	3	2	2

tiple responses possible; percentages will not total 100%.

a are presented in rank order according to the percentage of responses in the "Total" column.

TABLE 24

TOPICS TYPICALLY INCLUDED IN THE TRAINING PROGRAM FOR PEER ADVISORS[a]
(Based on 325 institutions that use peer advisors)
(in percentages)

	Two-Year Public	Two-Year Private	Four-Year Public	Four-Year Private	Total[b]
emic regulations, policies, and registration procedures	52	66	77	69	65
us referral sources	48	67	73	64	61
ng/counseling skills	49	66	61	59	56
f information sources (admissions test results, cripts)	28	23	45	32	33
r and employment information	26	—	33	27	27
r decision-making skills	27	10	19	24	23

ole responses possible; percentages will not total 100%.

are presented in rank order according to the percentage of responses in the "Total" column.

TABLE 25

SUPPORT OR REFERENCE MATERIALS ROUTINELY PROVIDED TO ACADEMIC ADVISORS[a]

(in percentages)

	Two-Year Public	Two-Year Private	Four-Year Public	Four-Year Private
Academic planning worksheets	70	68	64	75
Advising handbook	62	53	62	66
Computerized student academic progress records	56	50	58	58
Directory of campus referral sources	49	39	60	46
Systematically collected data on student abilities, goals, retention, etc.	33	61	35	40
Articulation worksheets or agreements between institutions	51	22	18	10
Forms for anecdotal records or contracts	19	25	27	27
Employment outlook projections	26	14	18	13
No materials provided	3	4	3	3

[a]Multiple responses possible; percentages will not total 100%.

[b]Data are presented in rank order according to the percentage of responses in the "Total" column.

TABLE 26

STUDENT INFORMATION ROUTINELY PROVIDED TO ACADEMIC ADVISORS[a]

(in percentages)

	Two-Year Public	Two-Year Private	Four-Year Public	Four-Year Private
College transcript/grade reports	73	86	79	88
Admissions test results (ACT, SAT, other)	62	71	75	81
High school transcript	51	68	41	60
Locally administered interest/placement test results	60	61	42	49
Admissions application	41	39	30	47

[a]Multiple responses possible; percentages will not total 100%.

[b]Data are presented in rank order according to the percentage of responses in the "Total" column.

TABLE 27

SUPPORT OR REFERENCE MATERIALS PROVIDED TO STUDENTS FOR ADVISING PURPOSES[a]

(in percentages)

	Two-Year Public	Two-Year Private	Four-Year Public	Four-Year Private
Institutional handbook or catalog	87	93	89	93
Class scheduling guide	85	86	83	88
Student handbook	76	89	79	87
Admissions test results (ACT, SAT, other)	54	36	48	37
Computerized student academic progress record	42	43	45	47
Referral service information (directory)	30	36	45	40
No materials are provided	—	—	1	1

[a]Multiple responses possible; percentages will not total 100%.

[b]Data are presented in rank order according to the percentage of responses in the "Total" column.

References

Beal, P. E., and Noel, L. *What Works in Student Retention*. Iowa City, Iowa: American College Testing Program and National Center for Higher Education Management Systems, 1980.

Carstensen, D. J., and Silberhorn, C. *A National Survey of Academic Advising, Final Report*. Iowa City, Iowa: American College Testing Program, 1979.

Cope, R., and Hannah, W. *Revolving College Doors: The Causes and Consequences of Dropping Out, Stopping Out, and Transferring*. New York: Wiley, 1975.

Forrest, A. *Increasing Student Competence and Persistence: The Best Case for General Education*. Iowa City, Iowa: American College Testing Program National Center for the Advancement of Educational Practices, 1982.

Glennen, R. E. "Intrusive College Counseling." *School Counselor*, 1976, *24*, 48–50.

3

Academic Advising and Institutional Goals: A President's Perspective

꧁ꯥ꧂ ꧁ꯥ꧂ ꧁ꯥ꧂ ꧁ꯥ꧂ ꧁ꯥ꧂ ꧁ꯥ꧂ ꧁ꯥ꧂ ꧁ꯥ꧂

Janet D. Greenwood

The reasons are numerous and compelling for an institution to establish an effective academic advising system that is responsive to student needs. Quality academic advising promotes the creation of a caring environment, builds a positive public image, enhances students' development, fosters a better understanding of academic and administrative processes, rewards advisors for their work, and produces primary and secondary benefits to society. From the perspective of a chief administrative officer, the academic advising program can be one of the most important and influential components of a higher-education institution. Academic advising has the capacity, latent if not evident, to become the primary integrating factor that brings students, faculty, student affairs staff, academic disciplines, and curriculum together into a truly meaningful educational whole. Academic advising is probably the single most important educational activity that *all* students experience as they move through college.

Much research on college students substantiates the contention that positive rewards can accrue from effective advising. Walsh (1979) asserted that developmental advising, which requires a redefinition of the traditional role for advisors, can enhance achievement of the academic goals of an institution. His research supports the position that "(1) higher education should have as one goal helping students explore and synthesize academic, career, and life goals, (2) academic advisement can help provide this synthesis, and (3) the concept of developmental advisement—while new—is indeed workable" (pp. 448-449). Astin and Kent (1983) compared students' life goals as expressed by two generations of students a decade apart. They found that students expressed increased goal orientation in the areas of (a) influencing the political structure, (b) influencing social values, (c) being well off financially, (d) becoming a community leader, and (e) succeeding in a self-owned business. Interestingly, men evidenced an increase in the importance of raising a family while women expressed a decrease. Astin and Kent concluded that women need more leadership experiences as undergraduates if they are to emerge from college feeling strong, independent, self-assured, and well prepared.

To create campus environments in which such important learning can take place, faculty members' behaviors, attitudes, and approaches must be altered. For example, faculty members need to spend greater amounts of time socializing with students and participating in faculty development programs designed to teach helping skills, attitudes, and behaviors. Systematic staff development programs are essential on most campuses if developmental academic advising is to become a reality. Campus leaders cannot rely on normal evolutionary processes alone to bring about desired change. Rather, they must take the risks necessary to precipitate it.

Weissberg and others (1982) found that students' career development needs are expressed strongly, especially the practical and realistic concerns related to work experience, job opportunities, and job-seeking skills. They also found that most students expressed a need for improving their basic skills in reading, writing, and mathematics. However, the selection and scheduling of classes were ranked as a low advising need when compared with career and academic needs. The research of Weissberg and his associates provides information worthy of consideration in determining the types of advising activities that deserve high priority. The low rankings given to selecting and scheduling courses reflects the need for academic advisors to pay greater attention to the important personal developmental needs of students.

The impact of faculty-student interaction on students' achievement and college satisfaction is well documented (Astin, 1977). Terenzini, Pascarella, and Lorgan (1982) reported that freshman-year achievement is highly influenced by the frequency of informal student-faculty contacts that focus on career as well as intellectual matters. Also, it is apparent that the quality of students' experiences with faculty and staff has a positive influence on both academic achievement and general intellectual growth and competence. To a great extent, the "hidden curriculum" reflected in a healthy and stimulating interaction between students and college staff members directly influences the quality of the students' education and personal growth. Student-faculty dialogue and interaction, whether in or out of the classroom, and teaching techniques that facilitate personal development in students must be considered as integral parts of advising systems.

Student academic advising, when broadly defined, supported by technology, and involving faculty, staff, paraprofessionals, and a coordinated system, can become a major asset for an institution of higher education. Ignoring the potential influence of academic advising does not appear to be in the best interests of students, faculty, staff, or the institution as a whole. Systems of academic advising can be built that are cost-effective and efficient and that promote positive attitudes about the institution. Institutional leaders have a responsibility to assure a quality educational experience to every student admitted. In an attempt to achieve this important goal, the college president can make a major contribution by marshaling institutional resources, establishing an academic advising task force, and charging members of the campus community to expend more energy toward promoting quality academic advising. A team of people with expertise in institutional research, admissions, academics, computer programming, and student affairs can develop a coordinated academic advising system. The remainder of this chapter explores how this might be accomplished from the perspective of a chief administrative officer.

Academic Advising and the Educational Mission

How an institution's mission statement is written and used may well express the priorities of the academic community, including that of academic advising. On the one hand, mission statements may be used to guide the direction and planning activities of an institution; on the other, they may be rarely reviewed or considered at all. Thoughtful administrators and their advisory boards and staffs take responsibility for assuring that the institution's mission statement is used as an overarching rationale for the educational enterprise they are charged to lead. Just as an institution may state that its mission is undergraduate liberal arts education, it can also state that it endorses and emphasizes academic and personal development of students and that it strives to facilitate educational growth through advising and programming activities designed to be responsive to the needs of students. Mission statements are, after all, usually written by the institutional leaders responsible for their implementation.

While it is one thing to prepare a written mission statement to guide an institution's approach, it is another to put that statement into operation. Although mission statements should specify the values of the institution and serve as guides to the development of programs that are consistent with those values, it is sometimes quite difficult to bring such ideal consistency into reality through the operating policies of the organization. There are both formal (official) and informal (operative) approaches to using educational missions and goals. It is especially effective to assess the institutional mission from a goal analysis perspective, such as that of Perrow (1961). He differentiated between official goals and operative goals by noting that the former are reflected in general purpose/mission statements, charges, articles of incorporation, annual reports, and public statements, whereas the latter are reflected in operating policies, leadership decisions, promotion criteria, and the like. The process of goal analysis using such a model is highly recommended, for without careful evaluation one cannot be assured that the institution's goals are effective or viable. As Borland (1983, p. 42) points out, "Accepting superficial statements of goals without real analysis of the operational goals affecting one's own subsystem can be a behavior fatal to the potential success of an administrator." The use of goal classification systems, such as Perrow's, can be most helpful in identifying anticipated changes in students that can be attributed to experiences in the academic environment. The educational process stimulates continual change, and it is the responsibility of college and university leaders to assure current and prospective students that the institution's programs and policies will help them achieve their academic and personal potential. Putting the educational mission of the institution into operation can be aided immensely if members of the academic community are encouraged to know their institution's mission statement, to work to assure its fulfillment, and to suggest changes in it when appropriate. Connecting the academic advising program more directly to the goals and objectives implicit within the institution's mission can have a profound effect.

The relationship between the student and the institution is of utmost importance to the quality of the educational experience. When institutional leaders encourage faculty and staff to establish close, caring relationships with students through the academic advising system, mentoring relationships often result. Such relationships (McCaffrey and Miller, 1980) are generally viewed as a rather natural way for students and their advisors to interact within a supportive educational environment. The educational process is a very special experience that comes about when learners, both more and less knowledgeable, interact to expand their knowledge and understanding. The academic advising system can be made to become an integral part of this process, and it is the wise academic administrator who uses it judiciously to promote the institution's mission.

Academic Advising and the Institutional Image

In a very unique way, academic advising can be used as a vehicle for observing what students experience throughout their education. To some extent, academic advising is a kind of glue that can hold the higher-education experience together for many students. At the very least, it has a major influence on the image of the institution in the student's mind's eye, both during the college years and long afterward. A serious disservice is done to the reputation of the institution when students perceive that they are "put in a bind" because of poor advising or, worse, no advising at all. In effect, academic advising has great potential as a source of positive (or negative) public relations for the institution as a whole. Nothing does more damage to the image of an institution than disgruntled, frustrated, and unhappy students who view the institution as a cold, uncaring, and unconcerned place where one must "sink or swim" without the aid of an organized support system. There is little an institutional representative can say to undo the anger and disappointment that occur as the result of bad advice received and acted upon or a computer error that went undetected until the final graduation check was completed. The potential for positive institutional regard, active alumni contributions, and referrals of prospective students and donors to the alma mater is significantly diminished. Poor-quality academic advising will likely result in the institutional image being tarnished and public relations efforts being undermined. Much of the way the larger community views the institution is a direct result of the image portrayed by students and alumni. To the extent that student satisfaction with the college is dependent upon positive, healthy relationships with other members of the academic community, academic advising is critical.

When the academic advising process is experienced as being effective, personalized, accurate, and efficient, the public image of the institution is enhanced. Students who are pleased with their educational experiences and the support services provided them by their institution are especially effective as recruiters of prospective students and become unofficial public relations agents. To offer low-quality academic advising services or to reduce the quality of academic advising because of financial considerations is a shortsighted approach to budget management and reflects misplaced priorities.

Through the services they offer, higher-education institutions make visible the way they define their functions. The educational function should include not only academic programs but also extracurricular life activities that encourage student development through cognitive learning, affective development, and practical competence (Bowen, 1977). Such a definition requires attention to the total development of students rather than, as with narrower approaches, solely encouraging intellectual growth. A college's approach to educational and student support programs and the philosophy underlying that approach are important marketing considerations. One of the best formal vehicles for communicating such matters is the college catalogue, which provides students with information about the breadth and depth of the curricula, the sequencing and frequency of courses, special services and facilities available, academic regulations, academic advising programs, and other essentials. This document is an official institutional statement and is referred to in the event of contractual disputes between students and the institution. As a result, the catalogue often becomes the academic advising program's media vehicle, the primary publication that outlines everything one needs to know about navigating the educational milieu. The college catalogue, therefore, becomes a primary tool in the academic advising process. Whether used for educational planning purposes for full-time day students or for part-time evening or nontraditional students, the catalogue must be accurate and comprehensive. Not only do institutional leaders have a responsibility to ensure that adequate, accurate information is available in the catalogue, they need to be aware that, in many ways, the college catalogue reflects the institution to the public at large as well as to students in attendance.

Academic advising is, or certainly should be, a concern of the institution's board of governors, whose responsibility it is to ensure that the college has programs and policies that enhance planning, curricular quality, accessibility, and the delivery of essential student support services. In turn, the institution's leadership must ensure the development and implementation of systematic educational program planning and academic advising that are essential to a high-quality educational experience. Educational consumers and their patrons expect their dollar's worth of service and support; oftentimes they view academic advising as one of the more obvious manifestations of these commodities. It is evident that one of the most integrating factors on a college campus can be the academic advising program. From the board of governors to the faculty-staff advisors, the thread of continuity is provided through advising that exhibits the caring, supportive campus environment so important to all concerned. The institution's public image may be sustained largely by this thread also. While an institution's image is directly linked to the quality of its educational programs, the programs cannot stand alone; they require strong student support and enhancement services, including academic advising, to exist. If this principle of higher-education administration is overlooked, the success of the institution may be jeopardized.

Academic Advising and Organizational Structures

Academic advising calls for a special relationship between students and those who represent the institution. Too much is at stake in the establishment of these relationships to let them develop in unplanned ways. Therefore, administrators have responsibility for creating organizational structures that will enhance both the establishment and the maintenance of these important relationships. Such structures help identify who will do the advising, what it is intended to accomplish, and how the institution's resources will be brought to bear. Determining the goals and objectives of the program, selecting the personnel who can best accomplish those goals, and finding the funds to support the system are all essential elements that the institution's administration must address.

One important principle that should be applied as these plans are being formulated concerns *whom* to involve. Since developmental academic advising (see Chapter One) involves much more than course scheduling alone, the thoughtful administrator will seek to involve not only those responsible for the formal curricula—the faculty—but those responsible for the informal and cocurricular areas as well. The collaborative effort of both academic affairs and student affairs personnel is needed. In one sense, the academic advising program can become a focal point for promoting cooperation and collaboration between these organizational components. After all, these two areas complement each other in influencing educational outcomes for most students. It is suggested strongly that these sometimes highly diverse areas be intentionally brought together to create and carry out the academic advising function.

Goals. In order to establish meaningful goals, those responsible for the academic advising program need to ascertain what it is that students truly need in order to successfully pursue their educations. It is crucial, therefore, that students' needs be assessed initially, to guide the establishment of program goals and objectives, and regularly thereafter to evaluate programs and make adjustments. Careful assessments can identify the different needs of subpopulations. For example, some students may function quite well when required procedures, multiple options, and established processes for movement from admission to graduation are clearly communicated. Others, who are faced with multiple choices, who are academically underprepared, or who are faced with other mitigating personal, social, cultural, or physical exigencies, may need special or more frequent assistance (see Chapter Ten). An institution has an ethical and social responsibility to ensure that all students have access to the resources and support they need for successful achievement of their educational objectives. To admit students with special needs or limitations for which the institution is neither prepared to deal nor willing to give support clearly calls an institution's integrity into question.

Colleges vary in the degree of autonomy they grant students, and an institution's goals and program orientation will be influenced by how mature and independent it perceives its students to be. Some goals, however, are common to every quality academic advising program. One of these is teaching students how to make informed, intelligent decisions. Since educational, career, and life planning processes all call for decision-making skills, every student needs to learn to make judgments without undue dependency on others. It also makes sense for advising programs to help students learn assessment and goal-setting techniques in order to aid in the planning process. Developmental theory indicates that humans tend to move toward increasingly complex modes of behavior, skill, and activity throughout their lives. To facilitate healthy development, academic advising programs can do much to involve students in understanding their own needs and motivations, actively guiding their own life progress, and taking responsibility for their actions. Another goal common to quality advising programs is making campus and community resources accessible so that students can use them in achieving personal goals. The best plans can fail if essential human, physical, and financial resources are unrecognized or not available. Achieving success, whether in an academic environment or elsewhere, requires a number of coping skills. The academic advising system needs to take these factors into account as goals and objectives are being established.

Selecting and Motivating Staff. No approach to staffing the academic advising programs is "right" for all institutions; the situation will be different for each college or university. However, the administration should think the decision through very carefully, because whom it selects to implement the advising program will be a major factor in the program's ultimate success. Not only must advisors know the academic programs, processes, and procedures involved but they must also be able to relate well with students and faculty. Knowledge about one academic area is not enough; students need and have the right to accurate, timely, and complete information at all points throughout their educational experience. Academic knowledge, in and of itself, is not enough, for the student's personal development is also paramount to the developmental advising process. Although difficult to implement, academic advising needs to be viewed as an educational function for all seasons of a student's educational life. Consequently, the staff should include individuals with a variety of backgrounds and skills: faculty members who can bring in-depth knowledge about the academic dimensions to their work; student affairs staff members who understand the developmental processes through which students move and who are familiar with extracurricular learning opportunities; and students who can, with supervision, help meet the heavy demands placed on the advising program and who often have a special understanding of the problems and needs faced by other students. As mentioned earlier, the advising program offers a unique opportunity for the academic affairs and the student affairs programs to cooperate for the benefit of the institution and its student consumers.

Motivational systems that reward activities valued by the organization lead to innovation, improved effectiveness, and feelings of individual importance. Salary supplements, although desirable, are not the only means for motivating advisors. People are motivated when their individual needs are responded to appropriately and in a timely fashion. Some advisors view advising as a personal responsibility and derive much satisfaction from doing it well. Others consider extrinsic values or rewards of greater import; they may wish to undertake greater coordinating, leadership, or supervisory responsibilities within the advising program. Desirable incentives for them may be released time from teaching, committee work, and other responsibilities or, in some instances, receiving an organizational title or special project grant. Likewise, recognition for participation as an academic advisor can be included in promotion and tenure guidelines, with evaluation of advising effectiveness given significant weight. It is also a relatively simple matter to create a special recognition program for campus achievement to honor those who contribute significantly to the mission of the institution, such as honors day recognition of the top advisors, along with letters or certificates of commendation. A shortcoming on many campuses is the lack of official institutional recognition of those who daily toil to make the institution a better place in which to live and learn.

Motivational systems can sometimes be built into merit pay programs or released time arrangements for attending professional development activities or conferences. Opportunity to participate in a campus-wide or special subunit advising project that crosses organizational boundaries with faculty, staff, and students from other administrative areas may be both stimulating and enjoyable for advisors. For institutions that use a management-by-objectives approach, many such special projects and activities can be built into the system and recognized and rewarded accordingly.

One of the best learning experiences a student can obtain while in college is to work as a student helper who aids other students in their educational process. Not only is this an excellent learning opportunity, it is a most enjoyable and rewarding one as well. Staffing the advising program with student paraprofessionals who are trained and supervised by professional advisors has much to recommend it. For student paraprofessional advisors, academic credit or developmental transcript recognition can be included in the reward system. Many upperclass students welcome the opportunity to be of service to their peers, especially if they understand the implications such activity has for careers in the educational or helping professions.

An important theme in any motivational system, whether it is designed for students, faculty, staff, or a combination of these, is that expectations must be made clear and incentives should be tied directly to individual needs. A key to the successful motivation of academic advisors is directly in the control of their immediate supervisors. It is imperative that senior-level administrators work closely with those supervisors to ensure that effective management techniques are employed and that systematic advisor staff development continues to emphasize skill development. Issues of power, authority, and turf can constitute serious obstacles to the success of an advising program and may arise when noncollaborative, highly competitive situations are allowed to exist. If faculty members see academic advising as their territory alone, developmental academic advising may never become a reality. If professional advisors do not believe that students can be trusted to function as objective peer advisors, then students will never have an opportunity to become involved. Reiterated here is the importance of seeking to establish a collaborative advising effort designed to respond to the academic, intellectual, emotional, social, career, and other personal needs of students. Building a collaborative advising model with shared responsibilities reduces negative effects of power issues by actually empowering people through their active involvement in the advising system. Power then becomes a positive, productive force, and territory becomes a jointly owned property.

Academic Advising as Educational Process

It is not difficult to view academic advising as a microcosm of students' total educational experience. If the institution views the educational process as being developmental in nature, wherein students are aided in moving from their present levels of knowledge and skill to increasingly advanced, more complex levels, then the advising program will reflect this posture in its approach. Likewise, if the prevailing view of education is compensatory in approach, then the advising program will focus on a remedial approach to working with students. There is a growing belief that effective developmental and preventive approaches to providing student support reduce the need for remediation. The choice of focus is crucial to the orientation of those responsible for creating academic advising systems and should influence substantially the criteria for selection of advisors and the types of training and in-service education provided them.

It has been asserted that developmental change occurs when students are challenged to respond to new and previously unexperienced questions and life situations by making personal accommodations in their thinking or mastering new knowledge (Sanford, 1967). If human development is a direct result of experiencing differentiation and reintegration (Chickering, 1969) and if there are critical periods when college students exhibit a certain readiness to achieve new developmental tasks (Havighurst, 1952), then the advising process can benefit from advisors' abilities to identify the predictable points at which students are ready for, and in need of, new information, new challenges, and new opportunities. Students will progress through these critical points whether or not the institution seeks to be systematically responsive to their needs, but without organized support in the form of developmental academic advising, many students will drop by the wayside because they lack the ability to handle such matters without help.

There are several critical points during the student's progression through the educational process that can be readily identified and responded to by advisors. These include (a) the pre-enrollment period, (b) the initial entry period, (c) subsequent registration periods, and (d) the final enrollment period. These transitions may be experienced differently by different people, but the need to face the challenges posed by each juncture is similar for all students. A developmental academic advising program can, for many students, make a significant difference as to how effectively such critical points are transcended.

Pre-Enrollment Period. Pre-enrollment advising is often totally lacking, with prospective students left largely to their own devices as to how they arrived at the decision to select, apply to, and enter a particular institution. Too often the "admissions counselor" is little more than a salesperson out to recruit students. Obviously, no college can survive without an adequate number of students being enrolled, but what is done to ensure that the institution is the best choice for a particular individual, both academically and personally? It is at this point that the institution's advising system should first be utilized by focusing on the decision-making processes used and on helping the student assess his or her educational goals and plans. If the institution cannot meet the special educational needs of a given student, it has an obligation to inform the student accordingly. How the student plans to finance the costs of going to college should also be examined. Established policies and procedures, important as they are, are often designed for convenience in administering the institution. It is equally important that they ensure prospective students the information they need to make one of the most important decisions they will make in life.

This information can be of value in every institution, not only to those responsible for student advising but for other administrative and academic units as well. A telephone dictation system is extremely useful in meeting a number of needs. For example, if an admissions officer makes contact with a prospective student on a recruiting trip, the officer can develop a page of related variables that identify special concerns and interests of that person regarding particular academic and student services, campus policies and procedures, and other specific information. The officer can then phone this information into the dictation center where it can be used to create relevant, personalized correspondence with the prospective student and become the foundation for a data base. People responsible for the interest areas referred to can be alerted about the prospective student, and the advising office can use the information to initiate the pre-enrollment advising process through correspondence and personal contact. Such a well-orchestrated and integrated approach aids all campus units to do their jobs better and sets a positive tone for the prospective student because of its efficiency, promptness, and personalized approach.

Initial Entry Period. Once the application procedure is complete and the prospective student is admitted, new and more specific decisions are in order. It is important to make the transition from high school or another college to the institution as smooth and enjoyable as possible. Whereas general information is needed during the pre-enrollment period, specific information is necessary during the initial entry period. Specifics concerning financial aid packages, housing assignments, academic procedures, special support services, student organizations such as fraternities and sororities, new student orientation programs, and related areas are high priorities for the entering student. At this point, long-term goals may become secondary to the immediacy of getting started in this new educational enterprise. Developmental academic advisors may be of particular value during this transition process. The parent-student relationship may be strained because of the decision to go to college and leave home. Many students will exhibit great apprehension about entering into the higher-education process, and that needs attention. Some will have second thoughts and some will experience pre-entrance panic. The challenge being experienced at this time presents an excellent vehicle for stimulating personal change and development.

The initial entry period is also an excellent time to add to the data base begun during the pre-enrollment period. Earlier data, including academic records, test scores, references, and personal interests, can now be augmented with placement test scores, personal assessment data, family background information, high school activities data, personal problems checklist information, and other data that can be used not only to aid the student in making the transition to college but also for both short and long-range planning purposes. Again, the information gathered should reflect the needs of the many administrative units within the college that can use the data in responding to students' needs and in achieving institutional goals.

During the initial entry period, it is important for the advising program to obtain information that will be useful to the educational planning process and to facilitating students' development while they are in college. Predictor variables need to be selected that can be used to help students build strengths that will ensure a successful college experience. Some of these variables include information about academic problems, personal problems, personal goals and aspirations, health problems, special interests, previous leadership experiences, and family background. These data can be of great value to advisors working with entering students who are making the difficult adjustment to college. In many instances, this adjustment is initially more difficult in the personal-emotional area than it is on the academic-intellectual level.

Many of these major transitional issues become increasingly apparent during the initial term of college enrollment. Identification of the specific factors affecting success and satisfaction with college is important. At this point, developmental academic advising depends on the availability to students of a well-organized, easily accessible, and truly supportive advising program. As the challenge of the initial transition to college increases during the first term of study, the need to establish a meaningful advising relationship increases. One of the first tasks an individual faces in a new environment is to establish human contact that provides an initial support base. The support base is important to building the security necessary for taking the risks involved in undertaking new endeavors. The advising system can provide this kind of support intentionally. During the initial entry period, advisors and student paraprofessionals can be assigned to small groups of students for the purpose of building support bases and an identity group, as the model program described in Chapter One. As noted earlier, a mentoring relationship is particularly important to students' ability to navigate the higher-education process successfully. The more academic advising can be integrated into the educational processes, the greater the chances that students will achieve academic success.

Subsequent Registration Periods. In most instances, the tensions and challenges of the college experience lessen over time. Nevertheless, every new term offers another potentially critical point of challenge for the student. Is personal and academic development progressing as expected? Has the student learned to work within the system? Are campus and community resources being utilized to help meet the student's personal and educational goals? Are career decisions being made and has the student taken action to gain necessary information about career options? These and related questions tend to come to the fore with every passing academic term, and it is the advisor's responsibility to raise them with students accordingly. If a solid, trusting relationship is established initially, the challenge of these advisor questions will be viewed as important, albeit uncomfortable, by the students, and they will understand that the advisor's intention is to stimulate their development.

One excellent vehicle for stimulating intentional developmental activity throughout the college years is the student development transcript (Brown and DeCoster, 1982). Advisors can use this special record, which identifies and records information about activities and experiences not noted on the academic transcript, to challenge students to become involved more fully in the learning and growth opportunities available. When students' personal, noncurricular goals are identified, this transcript can aid in accomplishing them. It can keep the student's attention on important areas of concern and give the student a graphic portrayal of how well personal objectives are being achieved. In the long run, such a record might be of great value to a prospective employer as well. Too often the personal activities that account for most of what students learn are neither recorded nor recognized. The student-development transcript approach can readily be brought into being on any campus with the capacity for a computerized information system.

Final Enrollment Period. Not all students attend college to complete a degree program. Some have other goals, such as transferring to another institution, whether for graduation or other reasons. Nevertheless, when a student is ready to exit, the advising system should be organized to help ensure a smooth transition out of the institution. It might be of value to have an end-of-the-year forum for each class, to evaluate students' experiences during the year. Some type of exit interview is desirable, whether for graduating seniors or for those leaving earlier. Like the transition from high school to college, the transition out of college into the "real world" is a critical time for most students. The many significant questions and concerns faced by students at this time need attention. If an ongoing developmental academic advising system has been implemented, students will be likely to take full advantage of it in examining possible preparations for the changes that must be made. At the very least, the advising program should provide an evaluation of the student's educational experiences at the institution. After all, a college's responsibility for facilitating the growth and development of students does not end when the student decides to leave or completes all course requirements.

Influencing Change in Academic Advising

If the student assessment and academic advising evaluation are carried out as proposed earlier, their results may well point to the need for certain alterations to the advising system. If the data suggest that revisions to the advising system are needed, a small group of individuals with appropriate expertise can be assigned to work together on an academic advising review and planning task force to guide that change. At this time, the chief administrative officer can ensure that both academic and student affairs staff members are involved and that the charge to the task force is to incorporate a collaborative approach. In many ways, selecting the membership of the review and planning group may be one of the most important decisions made throughout the entire process.

Personal involvement in any activity builds vested interest in its success, and academic advising is no exception. It is therefore wise to establish a support network that includes important members of the academic community, even chronic nay sayers, who can and will influence others (see Chapter Fifteen). Building such a base requires that people become involved in defining and solving the problem. To do this effectively calls for considerable one-on-one contact between members of the task force and significant others on campus. Although this process is often subtle and time-consuming, it is worth the investment of time and effort. While people brought into the process in this way may not always work actively to support the project, they will tend to work less or not at all to defeat it. With this kind of groundwork, a foundation is established on which to build support from others on campus, such as faculty members, administrative councils, and student government bodies. Others outside the institution, such as parent groups, can be brought into this activity as well, although there is greater hazard involved since they do not possess the same degree of commitment to or understanding about the college as do faculty, staff, and students. Figure 1 graphically depicts how the various components involved in the process of change can fit and flow together.

An *initial step* in effecting change is compiling data that inform and test observations and assumptions about the perceived problems and their solutions. For advising systems, helpful information includes student and faculty expectations of the advising process, visibility, availability, and accuracy of advising information, where and when advising occurs, who advises and what motivates their work, and other available advising evaluation data.

Analysis of the collected data and other information is the *second step* in the process. Comparisons between student and faculty expectations and the present program are necessary. Interpreting the available data and objectively testing them against what is known about past performance and outcomes are essential if intelligent planning is to follow. In some instances, it may be necessary to identify other areas that need evaluation before continuing.

The *third step* in the change process calls for the engineering of a better system. Required is an evaluation of the skills and competencies needed by potential advisors to implement an effective advising process. One approach that may be useful here is reflected in the Reality Analysis, Skills Assessment approach proposed by Miller, Carpenter, McCaffrey, and Thompson (1980) in their Action-Planning Model. This approach calls for rating the importance of a particular skill to the accomplishment of a given task and the assessment of level of skill achievement on the part of present staff members. Such a procedure often results in the discovery that present and prospective advisors may not possess high levels of skills in some essential areas. Should this be the case, there will ultimately be need for implementation of special advisor training activities. Initially, some individuals may feel threatened by the newly identified expectations and skills required to carry out the advising function. However, as individuals help shape the new system, have information about it, and have training and educa-

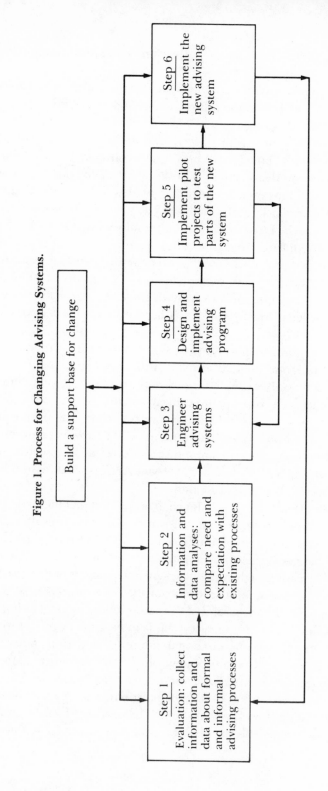

Figure 1. Process for Changing Advising Systems.

tional programs made available to provide them with opportunities for skill development, the fear of change and of potential failure is minimized.

When planning for in-service education, it helps to involve advisors already skilled in the areas under consideration in teaching those skills to other advisors. This approach helps create an active partnership in the process rather than a "we-they" attitude. Feelings of helplessness or lack of power work against an effective collaborative approach. Effective in-service techniques include role plays, videotaped practice interviews, opportunity to practice new approaches in a protected laboratory-type setting, and ample opportunity to discuss and digest the basic philosophy, concepts, principles, and approaches involved. Important areas for training have been identified by Gordon (Chapter Sixteen) and Ender and Winston (1982).

The *fourth step* in the process for change concerns designing the new program, including its organizational structure, its basic goals and objectives, its staffing patterns, its training, staff maintenance, and rewards procedures, its systematic integration into the academic processes, and its budgeting structure. The initial plan should be reasonably elaborate for it will be reviewed by many throughout the campus community and must be interpreted so as to exhibit practical, functional characteristics that easily lend themselves to the particular campus.

As new systems are designed, it is essential that the leadership examine closely the potential consequences that may result. It may prove helpful to begin by implementing pilot projects to test some of the changes before finalizing the new system. This *fifth step* is useful particularly when the new systems represent major changes and investments of efforts. Results of the pilot projects need to be factored back into the design of the system before implementing the new model. If the entire new system is to be implemented initially within one of the organizational subunits on a pilot basis, the choice of site needs careful attention. Consideration needs to be given to the level of vested interest in the particular unit for making the project successful as well as the potential influence a given unit has on others within the institution. The purpose of a pilot project is to both test the effectiveness of a particular approach and to use the pilot program to convince others on campus as to its feasibility and desirability for their use. Successful pilot implementation builds positive attitudes and influences others to be supportive. Clearly steps three, four, and five are closely interrelated for it is here that new ideas are planned, developed, and tested. Once proven viable, they can then be better and more efficiently implemented within the institution, which is reflected in *step six*. Establishing a systematic planning process to guide the task force's work is extremely useful and adds credibility to the new advising systems that result.

Even when the new advising system is in place, however, the full job is not complete. Continued communication with others throughout the campus community about the advising program is necessary to gain support and momentum. Success is sometimes less apparent to others than to those most directly involved. Therefore, success needs to be communicated and shared in order for it to be understood and accepted. Too often, meritorious work and projects go unrecognized because individuals believe merit should be obvious to others and clearly recognizable to supervisors and other authorities on campus. It is the wise program leader who makes sure that others are kept posted on what is being done.

Summary

This chapter emphasized three primary themes important to the establishment of a developmental academic advising system from the perspective of an institution's chief administrative officer. First, the academic advising process is an excellent vehicle for viewing in microcosm what college students experience as they progress through their undergraduate education. In many ways, academic advising is the single area that all students are most likely to be exposed to while in college. Higher-education administrators can take advantage of this fact and see that the advising system is used as a resource for institutional research and evaluation to obtain better profiles of students' needs, experiences, and activities.

Second, the development, implementation, maintenance, and management of academic advising programs can become an excellent focal point for promoting collaboration and cooperation among the many campus divisions, especially those of academic affairs and student affairs. Too often these areas function with complete and total disregard for the other's existence. This can promote undesirable levels of territoriality and lines of organizational demarcation that limit the effective integration of a total educational process that pervades the campus community. When staff and faculty members view certain roles, functions, and responsibilities as being the exclusive domain of one group or organizational entity, pecking orders and adversary relationships often occur. These factors tend to limit rather than expand the capacity of the institution to create truly educational and developmental environments for students. A developmental academic advising approach calls for an integration of the intellectual-educational with the affective-social-career areas of personal development. Both the formal and the informal curricula are essential to the total development of students. The promotion of a collaborative relationship between academic and student affairs programs within the academic advising system can better bring about the desired integration.

The third theme concerns the need for systematic planning to create more effective and efficient academic advising systems. The process of change can be predicted and this knowledge can be helpful to those responsible for the advising program. If change is needed, and it certainly is in most institutions' advising programs, then administrators should plan that change in thoughtful, systematic ways. The process for changing advising systems outlined in this chapter may be of help to this end.

Developmental academic advising is probably the wave of the future. Institutional leaders need to become aware of its potential for creating educational environments that will aid them to more effectively achieve their educational mandates. The fact that such approaches are likely to increase student retention is a plus that cannot be overlooked.

References

Astin, A. W. *Four Critical Years: Effects of College on Beliefs, Attitudes, and Knowledge.* San Francisco: Jossey-Bass, 1977.

Astin, H. S., and Kent, L. "Gender Roles in Transition." *Journal of Higher Education*, 1983, *54* (3), 309–324.

Blocher, D. H., Dustin, E. P., and Dugan, W. E. *Guidance Systems*. New York: Ronald Press, 1971.

Borland, D. T. "Organizational Foundations of Administration." In T. K. Miller, R. B. Winston, Jr., and W. R. Mendenhall (Eds.), *Administration and Leadership in Student Affairs: Actualizing Student Development in Higher Education*. Muncie, Ind.: Accelerated Development, 1983.

Bowen, H. R. *Investment in Learning: The Individual and Social Value of American Higher Education*. San Francisco: Jossey-Bass, 1977.

Brown, R. D., and DeCoster, D. A. (Eds.). *New Directions for Student Services: Mentoring-Transcript Systems for Promoting Student Growth*, no. 19. San Francisco: Jossey-Bass, 1982.

Chickering, A. W. *Education and Identity*. San Francisco: Jossey-Bass, 1969.

Ender, S. C., and Winston, R. B., Jr. "Training Allied Professional Academic Advisors." In R. B. Winston, Jr., S. C. Ender, and T. K. Miller (Eds.), *New Directions for Student Services: Developmental Approaches to Academic Advising*, no. 17. San Francisco: Jossey-Bass, 1982.

Havighurst, R. J. *Developmental Tasks and Education*. New York: Longmans, Green, 1952.

McCaffrey, S. S., and Miller, T. K. "Mentoring: An Approach to Academic Advising." In F. B. Newton and K. L. Ender (Eds.), *Student Development Practices: Strategies for Making a Difference*. Springfield, Ill.: Thomas, 1980.

Miller, T. K., Carpenter, D. S., McCaffrey, S. S., and Thompson, M. J. "Developmental Programming: An Action-Planning Model." In F. B. Newton and K. L. Ender (Eds.), *Student Development Practices: Strategies for Making a Difference*. Springfield, Ill.: Thomas, 1980.

Perrow, C. "The Analysis of Goals in Complex Organizations." *American Sociological Review*, 1961, *26*, 854–863.

Sanford, N. *Where Colleges Fail*. San Francisco: Jossey-Bass, 1967.

Terenzini, P. T., Pascarella, E. T., and Lorgan, W. G. "An Assessment of the Academic and Social Influences on Freshman

Year Educational Outcomes." *Review of Higher Education,* 1982, *5* (2), 86–109.

Walsh, E. M. "Revitalizing Academic Achievement." *Personnel and Guidance Journal,* 1979, *56* (8), 446–449.

Weissberg, M., and others. "An Assessment of the Personal, Career, and Academic Needs of Undergraduate Students." *Journal of College Student Personnel,* 1982, *23,* 115–122.

4

Foundations
for Academic Advising

Russell E. Thomas, Arthur W. Chickering

Most U.S. colleges and universities pay lip service through expressions in bulletins and catalogues to concern for students' "personal" development. Such concern is manifested in academic and student support programs ostensibly designed to facilitate "total" development for each student. In fact, such programs typically reflect a conceptualization of the student population as white, male, Protestant, and in the traditional age range. In other words, they seem to assume that all students are alike and give little attention to the varied stages of their development. Academic advising is a support service that is rarely undertaken with careful consideration for the various levels of development that both students and advisors go through.

Shipton and Steltenpohl (1981) assert that "if colleges are to truly enhance individual development and prepare students to cope with succeeding stages of development, faculty and staff advisers and counselors need to be prepared to assist students of all ages in clarifying their life, career, and academic purposes" (p. 691). It must be assumed that colleges sincerely intend to facilitate the total development of each student if a case is to be made for helping staff members prepare themselves for such an undertaking. Given such an assumption, developmental theory becomes extremely useful in that it provides advisor and student a solid conceptual base for their joint work.

Rationale for the Use of Developmental Theory in Advising

Personal development is assumed by faculty, academic administrators, and student affairs staff to be the major, if not exclusive, domain of the student affairs branch of higher education. This assumption rests on the conceptualization of the student as a being whose life is clearly divided into two separate worlds: the academic, or curricular, and the nonclassroom, or extracurricular. Obviously, such a division of any student's life makes as much sense as the artificial delineations among interrelated academic disciplines. How a student functions in academic arenas is closely related to how that student has felt, what that student has experienced, and how the student has developed in nonacademic arenas. One student who is working part time, newly married, and active in student government and another who is a feminist with years of active involvement in civil rights groups will both function academically in ways that reflect their out-of-class experiences. Contrariwise, the academic experiences of students often serve as catalysts to out-of-class interests, activities, and behavior. Thus, a freshman English literature class may trigger or facilitate a student's assertion of independence from parents. A student taking an exciting laboratory science course may come to realize that even in the "hard" sciences there are many unknowns. Such realizations can be unsettling to students and result in reconsideration of their majors. Thus, given the intricate interplay of academic and personal development, separating the two is administratively convenient but obviously absurd and ignores the wholeness of each student. Academic advising based on developmental theory legitimately recognizes this wholeness and serves to encourage effectively wholesome development of each student's life in and out of the classroom.

What about academic advising not based on developmental theory? It would be like *most* advising as currently carried out. For example, a student receiving academic advising from a full-time academic advisor will likely receive a cordial greeting, a short presentation on general requirements, a copy of courses needed for the desired specific program or major, and a schedule of classes. The emphasis will be on giving the student advice or information he or she "needs," in the opinion of the advisor. The information flow is mainly from the advisor to the student. Little relevant knowledge about the student is acquired or even seen as necessary. In addition, the advising process is influenced by the departmentalized, disciplinary structure of the curriculum at most colleges and universities, the large numbers of students to be served by relatively few persons at most institutions, the popularity and convenience of computerized registration, administrative concern for cost-effective practices, student desire for ease and comfort, faculty preoccupation with research and publication, and faculty preference for light teaching and advising loads. In these circumstances, students and staff may both be inclined to approach advising in a rather egocentric, perfunctory manner and see it as a necessary evil to be endured and negotiated as quickly and painlessly as possible.

Advisors who give no thought to students' developmental needs are most likely to practice the same kind of advising they received as undergraduates. In contrast, advisors who approach their task armed with developmental theory literally "see" students differently, fully and realistically recognizing each student as a complete individual. Advisors without knowledge of developmental theory tend to view students stereotypically, according to sex, age, race, ethnic origin, socioeconomic class, major, year in college, the American College Test (ACT) or the Scholastic Aptitude Test (SAT) scores, geographic origin, and/or body build. Although the brevity of meetings between students and advisors does not allow for recognition of much more than superficial characteristics, advising based on developmental theory readily acknowledges that "what you see" is not all there is and may not even begin to convey the real person the student is. This knowledge operates to counter judgments based on incomplete first impressions.

The next section contains several brief vignettes of students and advisors. These examples illustrate the complexity of the personalities involved in academic advising and provide a real-world context in which to consider developmental theories.

Student Profiles

Kathy, nineteen years old, is a freshman athlete who comes from a middle-class home and whose parents are highly supportive and proud of her prowess in swimming; she is presently considering majoring in history, physical education and recreation, or sociology.

Donald, twenty-two years old, is a junior majoring in hotel management and was a developmental student during his freshman and sophomore years. He has had to work throughout his high school and college years to supplement the income that his disabled parents receive. His parents have mixed views about the value of a college education.

Adahm, twenty-seven years old, an international student, is a sophomore pursuing a B.S. in engineering, although he has an avid interest in archeology. His family is oil-rich and his father is highly supportive of his attendance at a U.S. college. Although he has made an effective academic adjustment, socially he is very uncomfortable, as there are only two other males at the college from his native country.

Marshall, forty-six years old, an Afro-American, is now a senior in accounting and recently returned to school after an absence of twenty-one years. He is married with three teenagers and his wife strongly encourages him to complete his baccalaureate degree. He has been a bookkeeper for fifteen years and hopes for career advancement after he obtains his degree.

Martha, thirty-four years old, is a transfer student from a local community college now working on a major in nutrition. A single parent with eight- and eleven-year-old boys, she has completed an A.A. program in nursing. She works full-time in nursing with some familial support in caring for her children while she attends classes.

Ricardo, eighteen years old, is a Chicano student who has achieved advanced placement in mathematics and chemistry. Through an individualized honors program, he will complete his undergraduate studies in two and a half years. He works as a research assistant to a noted chemist on the faculty. His parents are generally supportive and quite proud of his accomplishments although they sense his growing dissatisfaction with certain ethnic values and customs.

Advisor Profiles

Yolanda, thirty-eight years old, an assistant professor of ceramic art, has major responsibility for advising all art majors in her department. She is a native Australian, has worked in her craft for eighteen years, and now teaches and advises in a small, private liberal arts college. Once married, now divorced, she is presently living with one of her colleagues in a college-owned residence. She tends to be a solitary person who enjoys her privacy.

Vern, a forty-five-year-old associate professor in electrical engineering, is an Afro-American who has taught for six years after working as an engineer for several years and completing his doctoral studies. He is married to an accomplished concert pianist and has two children, both presently in senior high school. He has aging parents with many physical ailments. Experientially, he is the most qualified faculty member in his department.

Charlotte, twenty-nine years old, is a full-time advisor in a centralized advising center and an adjunct assistant professor in child psychology. She has worked as a graduate assistant, an instructor in elementary psychology, and a care giver in a daycare center. She was an excellent student throughout her educational career. She is married to a computer analyst and has a two-year-old boy.

Harold, forty-nine years old, is director of University College, which houses an undergraduate centralized advising center, and a professor of theater. He has over twenty years of teaching and advising experience following a brief acting career and a period of radio-television directing. He has been awarded favorite teacher honors for several years, enjoys student contact, and often holds classes in his home. Presently married, having been married and divorced twice before, he is an extremely active person with intense interest in gourmet cooking and enjoys entertaining.

Elizabeth, sixty-four years old, counseling and personnel services professor and student personnel director of the College of Education, has major responsibility for the undergraduate academic advising of all education majors. She has authored a textbook on family counseling and serves in the university senate and on many college-wide committees. Actively involved in many charity organizations, she has an invalid husband who suffered a stroke four years ago. She has no children.

These vignettes suggest varied backgrounds and situations that advisors and students bring to the advising relationship. When advisors understand the varied backgrounds of their students, they can respond more effectively. Also, students need to realize that advisors are themselves people, with an assortment of strengths and weaknesses, struggling with their own developmental tasks, the substance of which may be identical to tasks the students are considering. Academic advisors employing a developmental perspective will more readily recognize the interplay of their own and their students' personal strivings. Two theorists whose ideas flow naturally from such acknowledgment of developmental tasks are Erikson and Neugarten.

In reflecting on the work of Erikson and Neugarten, Chickering (1975) notes that their studies of the life cycle "suggest some fundamental concerns and developmental tasks which lie behind the desire for a degree, the pursuit of a better or different job, the wish to read more widely and experience more deeply, to meet new persons and new ideas, to explore dimly seen horizons" (p. 207).

Life Cycle Theory and the Advising Relationship

By becoming familiar with the work of Erikson (1950), Gould (1972), Levinson and others (1978), Neugarten (1963 and 1970), Sheehy (1976) (summarized in Figure 1), and other life cycle theorists, advisors will be able to identify their own status and that of their students' age groupings. These theorists generally point out normative features, tasks, concerns or issues, and processes of the adult life cycle. For example, Marshall, our forty-six-year-old returning adult student, will be able to better accept the curious and perhaps surprised reaction from both teachers and students regarding his present enrollment in school when he recognizes that most forty-six-year-old men have become somewhat locked into their occupations whereas he has full intentions to change his job status (Task from Figure 2: Revising career plans). He might also be interested to discover that his return to school to attain a degree may be one more manifestation of his attempt to enhance his competence and boost his self-confidence.

Gould (1972) found in his studies that adults grouped according to age identify certain salient themes. Thus, the nineteen- to twenty-two-year-old age group verbalized the major theme of getting away from or leaving their parents (Figure 1). Ricardo, our Chicano honors student, may be engaged in such thinking, and his leaving may involve physical, social, and cultural elements. Indeed, many advisors encounter students who lack clear academic objectives since their presence on a college campus represents, primarily, their attempt to escape from parents and, secondarily, a concern for establishing a basis for some future occupational pursuit.

Levinson and others (1978) focused on adult male development and viewed development as shaped by both internal and external factors, the latter being one's own inner timetable and the social forces present in a person's environment. Thus, individual development proceeds through the interactions of each person and environment. The various ages from late adolescence through late adulthood are characterized by age-related personal concerns, general orientations, problems, dilemmas, developmental tasks, roles, and responsibilities (Figure 2) (Chickering, 1981). Martha, our thirty-four-year-old single parent, may very likely have left her family of birth to start her own family and delayed "getting into the adult world." Rather, she "settled down" and is now concurrently getting into the adult world and becoming her own person. She illustrates normative differences between men's and women's life cycles in our present-day culture. Yet there are many students today,

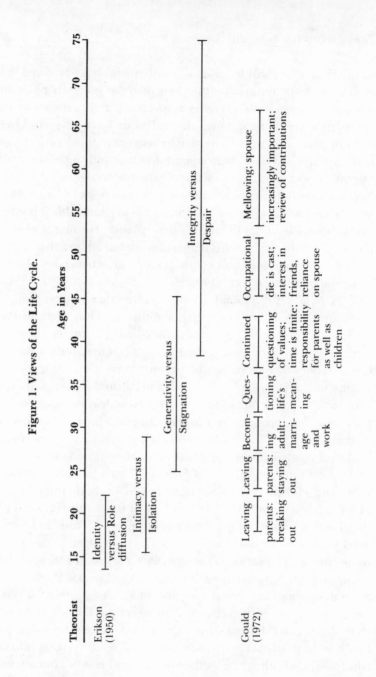

Figure 1. Views of the Life Cycle.

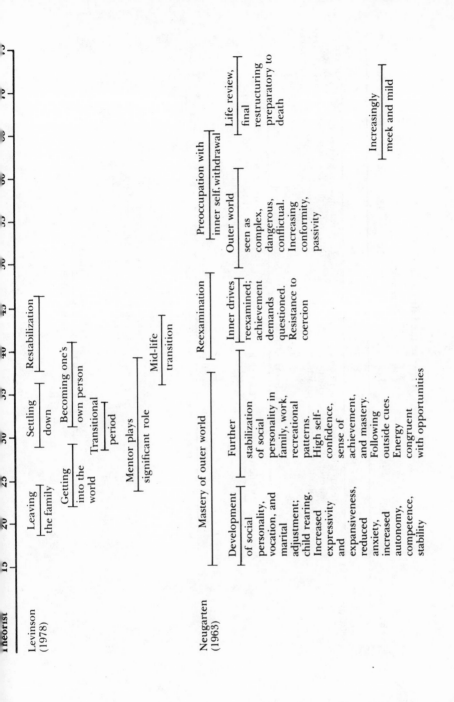

Figure 1. Views of the Life Cycle, Cont'd.

Age in Years

Theorist	15	20	25	30	35	40	45	50	55	60	65	70	75

Neugarten (1970)

Time since birth

Future stretches forth; time to do and see everything; achievement orientation; death is an abstraction

Time left to live

Time is finite, time enough only to finish a few important things; sponsoring others; personalization of death

Death is no crisis; how and where are important

Sense of self-determination

Sense of life cycle and inevitability

Average age women marry

Children First Last

Last child to school

Last child leaves home; not a significant crisis; increased freedom and home satisfaction

Many women work

Few women work

40 percent women work

50 percent women work

Introspection, stock-taking, conscious self-utilization; menopause is not a significant crisis; normal events are not crises if timing is appropriate

Sheehy (1976)

Pulling up roots

Provisional adulthood

Age 30 transition

Putting down roots

Mid-life transition

Restabilization and flowering

Becoming One's Own Man (BOOM)

16–23 Late Adolescence and Youth	23–35 Early Adulthood	33–45 Midlife Transition	43–57 Middle Adulthood	51–63 Late Adult Transition	63+ Late Adulthood
Achieving emotional independence					
Preparing for marriage and family life					
Choosing and preparing for a career					
Developing an ethical system					
	Deciding on a partner				
	Starting a family				
	Managing a home				
	Starting an occupation				
	Assuming civic responsibilities				
		Adapting to a changing time perspective			
		Revising career plans			
		Redefining family relationships			
			Maintaining a career or developing a new one		
			Restabilizing family relationships		
			Making mature civic contributions		
			Adjusting to biological change		
				Preparing for retirement	
					Adjusting to retirement
					Adjusting to declining health and strength
					Becoming affiliated with late adult age groups
					Establishing satisfactory living arrangements
					Adjusting to the death of a spouse
					Maintaining integrity

Source: Chickering, 1981.

both male and female, whose lives are aptly characterized by the sequential patterns articulated by Gould, Levinson, and Sheehy. The parallels and differences in the work of Gould and Levinson seem to result in more congruent views of adult development and a complementary, coherent picture of the various phases of adulthood.

The work of Erikson (1950) and Neugarten (1963, 1970) enriches the view of human development from a life cycle perspective (Figure 1). "Neugarten, more than any other theorist, elaborates the role of age and timing in adult development. The shift from 'time since birth' to 'time left to live' sets boundaries for other major changes; from sense of self-determination to sense of inevitability of the life cycle, from mastery of the outer world, through re-examination, to withdrawal and preoccupation with inner self and sponsoring others; from achievement to self-satisfaction. She found that when normal events were 'on time'—children leaving home, menopause, death of a spouse, even one's own death—they were not experienced as crises. Departure and death of loved ones causes grief and sadness, as does the prospect of one's own leaving, but when it occurs at times and in ways consistent with the normal expected life cycle, most persons manage the event or the prospect without major upset" (Chickering, 1975, p. 207). These thoughts highlight several points regarding the life cycle that advisors and students confront in their relationships. Depending on the life cycle phases of student and advisor, they may or may not be able to relate effectively to each other. Life cycle differences may render the advisor helpless, ineffective, or hazardous to the student. For instance, Charlotte, our full-time advisor, may yet be preoccupied with concern for achievement, mastery, and expansiveness, as are many, if not most, of her students. She will probably be able to identify with them; however, in some cases, she may not be helpful in their struggles because of her own unfinished business. Neugarten's point about events being "on time" is another key concept. An advisor would expect that Kathy, nineteen years old, might view her father's death at age forty-one as almost unmanageable, whereas Marshall, our forty-six-year-old, will probably be able to carry on reasonably well if his sickly, seventy-three-year-old father dies.

72416

Although not a life cycle theorist, Super's discussion of career development from a life span, life space perspective points out that most people generally will play nine major roles in four physical theaters over the course of their lifetimes (1980, p. 283). Those roles here are listed chronologically:

- child (including son and daughter)
- student
- "leisurite" (no standard term is available to describe the position and role of one engaged in the pursuit of leisure-time activities, including idling)
- citizen
- worker (including unemployed worker and nonworker as ways of playing the role)
- spouse
- homemaker
- parent
- pensioner

Super further notes that these roles are sometimes played in combinations (two or more simultaneously) or singly, initiated and abandoned at various times, and are not necessarily sex-linked. "The constellation of interacting, varying roles constitutes the career" (Super, 1980, p. 284). In the order in which they are typically entered, the principal theaters in which these roles are played are (1) the home, (2) the community, (3) the school (including college and university), and (4) the workplace. Acknowledging the presence of other theaters such as the church, the club, the retirement home, and so on, Super points out that all persons do not enter these theaters. Student affairs staff, faculty, and administrators, as persons functioning in careers in the school as a major theater, are in positions to be affected by this theater as well as to affect the lives of others, namely, students entering on a temporary basis.

Super (1980) further notes that "the simultaneous combination of life roles constitutes the *life-style*; their sequential combination structures the *life space* and constitutes the *life cycle*. The total structure is the career pattern. Roles wax and wane in importance and in the quality of performance; theaters are entered and deserted. How this is done is a result of the interaction of personal and situational variables" (p. 288). Donald, our twenty-two-year-old hotel management major, plays several roles simultaneously, including child, student, worker, and homemaker, in at least three of the major theaters—the home, the school, and the workplace. Donald has a distinctive life-style, to a great degree determined from without. In the near future he will cease to operate as a student and will be expected to move on to other roles in new theaters, while continuing to play some present ones in current theaters.

For students in the traditional age group, the advisor can observe and may be a vital part of the school theater facilitating their "playing" several roles, defining their personal life space, and establishing their initial career pattern. Referring to Donald again, the advisor may help him resolve inevitable conflicts between his student and worker roles. At other times, such conflicts may arise over his student and homemaker roles, given his parents' physical disabilities. At times, advisors themselves will experience such problems. Thus, neither student nor advisor ceases to experience expectations of others and personally held notions about the roles he or she plays.

Developmental Theories

In an insightful discussion of general developmental principles associated with varied vocational developmental theories, Beilin (1955, pp. 55-57) identified several key common elements of diverse developmental theories, including those that focus on intellectual and moral development. The following list points out some of these principles:

1. Development is a continuous process.
2. The developmental process is irreversible. (While not fully accepted today, the key point here is the notion that, once a person has arrived at a particular stage of development, that person is changed forever. While that person may return to a previously achieved stage, such a return carries with it new capacities. Achievement of each new stage subsumes previously achieved stages of development.)

3. Developmental processes can be differentiated into patterns, thus making process and products more predictable and, hence, more manipulable.
4. Where development is proceeding normally, maturity is a natural outcome.
5. Normal, healthy development is characterized by increasing differentiation and then integration of new elements.
6. The pace of development is rapid at the outset and slower as time passes.
7. Normal, healthy development proceeds from dependence to increasing independence.
8. Normal, healthy development proceeds from the egocentric to social behavior.
9. Normal, healthy development results from the interaction of several variables operating simultaneously or in succession.

Thus, behavior is seen to proceed from the simple to the complex, from the concrete to the abstract, from egocentric to social.

Perry's Scheme and the Advising Process and Relationship. Perry and his associates (1970, 1981) set forth a scheme of intellectual and ethical development worthy of consideration by advisors for its useful insights into the thought processes of their students. Perry's scheme consists of four categories that incorporate nine positions. The first category is dualism; in position 1 students perceive their world in such polar terms as we versus they, good versus bad, and right versus wrong. "Right answers for everything exist in the absolute, and are known to authority whose role is to mediate (teach) them" (Perry, 1970, p. 9). In position 2, also in the dualism category, students see diversity as unnecessary confusion in ill-qualified authorities or as simply exercises created by authorities to force or encourage them to find the answer for themselves. Position 3 is in the second category, *multiplicity:* the students accept diversity and uncertainty as legitimate but still temporary in areas where the authority (the advisor) simply has not determined the answer yet. In position 4, still in multiplicity, students see legitimate uncertainty (and therefore diversity of opinion) as extensive and elevate it to the status of an unstructured epistemological realm of its own in which each person is entitled to his or her own opinion, a realm that is posed against authority's realm where right-wrong still prevails. However, in position 4 students may discover qualitative contextual relativistic reasoning as a special case of "what they want" within authority's realm (Perry, 1970, p. 9).

In position 5, in the category of *relativism*, students think of all knowledge and values, including authority's, as contextual and relativistic and subordinate dualistic right-wrong functions to the status of a special case in context (Perry, 1970, pp. 9–10). In position 6, still in the relativism category, students start to think or consider the necessity of orienting themselves in a relativistic world through some form of personal commitment (as distinct from unquestioning commitment to some simple belief in certainty) (Perry, 1970).

The last category, *commitment in relativism*, contains the last three positions. In position 7, students make an initial commitment in some area, perhaps a major. In position 8, students begin to experience the full implications of commitment and explore the subjective and stylistic aspects of responsibility. Finally, in position 9, students experience the affirmation of identity among multiple responsibilities and realize commitment as an unfolding, ongoing activity through which they express their life-styles (Perry, 1970).

How might the above ideas be useful to an advisor? First, a caution: There are no implicit values attached to the various levels of intellectual and ethical functioning. In other words, there are no "better" or "worse" levels. Students and advisors functioning at dualistic levels are as valuable and worthy as those students and advisors who are functioning at relativistic levels. While the temptation exists to link "higher" levels with "better" and "lower" levels with "poorer," such thinking should be resisted. Next, let's make a few assumptions about our representative students and advisors profiled earlier. One safe assumption we might make is that the students will be operating at varied positions, as will the advisors. Ethnicity, sex, age, and life circumstances will not accurately predict those positions. Rather, how one perceives momentary circumstances, one's ethnicity, sex, and age will be influenced by one's functioning position. Perry (1981, p. 97) notes "the development we have traced in college students reveals itself now as 'age-free.' " To elaborate on how this theory will be helpful, consider a few of our students.

Kathy, our nineteen-year-old freshman, undecided on a major, may be operating at an intellectual level represented by dualism. While striving to find the "right" major, she may think that what she really needs is for her advisor to tell her what she should do. Certainly, her advisor will know what is right for her, she thinks. "After all, if he has asked me what I think, he is probably just trying to make small talk and to help me relax. I'm sure he'll eventually get around to telling me what direction I should take. My parents have even told me not to worry. The university officials assured us during orientation that whatever help we might need in choosing a major, I could count on my advisor. Right now, I need him to tell me what to major in for the next four years." But what if her advisor does not tell her what to major in? How will she react? What should her advisor be careful to do or not to do? What about the timing of his responses to her? What of the advisor's developmental stage? If the advisor is also at the dualistic stage, he may very gladly tell her what to do. Or if her advisor is encountering some major personal crises, wherein choices must be made, and is functioning at the multiplistic stage, he may not be emotionally prepared to help her consider alternatives in a dispassionate, objective manner, although he may be able to identify with her in her dilemma. If her advisor has satisfactorily resolved in his past such critical decisions and has moved to commitment in relativism, he may be emotionally and intellectually prepared to help her choose an acceptable major while helping her own the choice. Thus, the developmental level of her advisor will interact with her developmental level to her benefit or detriment. Certainly, her advisor should avoid talking down to her or being patronizing because of her dualism.

Ricardo, our freshman honors student, may be well along the way toward multiplicity; much of his excitement as a research assistant may derive from the revelation that many "authorities" do not know the answer and perhaps are not even sure of all the questions. Indeed, he may be learning to view his ideas and hunches as equally valid or promising as some authorities' ideas. If so, Ricardo certainly will view his advisor differently from Kathy.

Ricardo, while respecting his advisor's opinions and knowledge, will be more likely to see his advisor as one who can provide information about varied courses from an official point of view. But Ricardo will also want to check out what his fellow students think about these courses. What kinds of behavior will Ricardo's advisor need to exhibit to be most helpful? Ricardo will need to begin to examine the quality of varied opinions, to analyze why certain persons express or hold certain opinions or positions, and to think critically about his own ideas and opinions. He certainly should be encouraged to articulate coherent reasons for his choices of certain courses and to carefully weigh the pros and cons of his and others' arguments for particular choices.

(For additional insights, see Miller and McCaffrey's (1982) detailed, comprehensive treatment of Perry's scheme.)

Advising and Moral Reasoning Development. Most advising will involve, directly or indirectly, decision making that relates to future careers, and such careers entail related life-styles. Therefore, Kohlberg's thoughts regarding value or moral development have particular import for advising. Kohlberg describes moral development as involving three levels, each divided into two stages, with shifting orientations toward two key concepts, justice and role taking. Kohlberg (1971) defines justice as "the primary regard for the value and equality of all human beings, and for reciprocity in human relations" (p. 14). The concept of role taking involves taking "the point of view of another person by imagining oneself as the other person, in order to anticipate his actual behavior" (Theodorson and Theodorson, 1969, p. 356).

Rest (1982) notes that "the six stages can be thought of as concepts of how people cooperate with each other" (p. 31). At each stage, an individual will hold "a different conception of the possibilities and conditions for cooperation" (p. 31). A student at stage 1 (the punishment and obedience orientation) would define as right whatever the advisor demands. The student would not be inclined to question authority (the advisor) but rather to value "unquestioning deference to power" (Kohlberg, 1971, p. 164). A student at stage 2 (the instrumental relativist orientation) would approach the relationship as a loose "contract." "Cooperation is viewed as single one-shot exchanges—you do me a favor and I'll do a favor for you" (Rest, 1982, p. 31). Thus, a student at this stage will go along with the advisor and use the relationship to extract a needed letter of reference or recommendation. The student's commitment is to self rather than to the relationship.

The student at stage 3 (the interpersonal concordance or "good boy-nice girl" orientation) reasons in a manner "based on the notion of friendship and affectionate relationships—people establish an ongoing cooperative relationship because they like and care for each other" (Rest, 1982, p. 31). A student at stage 3 then will perhaps seek to obtain approval of the advisor and to be liked by the advisor by being "nice." The student at stage 4 (the "law and order" orientation) reasons on the basis of "a conception of a formally organized social system, where people occupy various roles in the social structure and cooperate with each other by doing their respective jobs and following formal law" (Rest, 1982, p. 31). Certainly, survival in many institutions of higher learning demands such reasoning by both students and advisors.

At the postconventional, autonomous, or principled level, a student at stage 5 (the social-contract, legalistic orientation) may presuppose "a society-wide network of cooperative relationships, but goes beyond stage 4 in requiring that social arrangements reflect the general will of the participants as decided through some consensus-producing procedure such as voting" (Rest, 1982, p. 31). The student at stage 6 (the universal ethical principle orientation) "goes beyond due process and consensus government and appeals to ideals" (Rest, 1982, p. 31). Indeed, "at this level, there is a clear effort to define moral values and principles that have validity and application apart from the authority of the groups or persons holding these principles, and apart from the individual's own identification with these groups" (Kohlberg, 1971, p. 164).

Within the advising relationship, the advisor who desires to foster the moral development of a student will usually display genuine respect for the student and create an open, trusting relationship wherein challenges to currently held values will be fully heard or perceived. Thus, the support for the individual will be firmly established to enable challenges to be interpreted and responded to without alarm or defensiveness. Also, the advisor will be actively engaged in encouraging the student to consider the value considerations underlying various choices made. The responsive advisor may consider where the student stands on various issues regarding choice of a major, course selections, extracurricular activities, politics, religion, and social mores. So informed, the advisor can urge a student to explore through various concrete experiences the reordering of priorities associated with various roles and related responsibilities. For instance, involvement with student government entails many exciting opportunities. Yet, this public service activity also carries with it a host of generally negative aspects—namely, open scrutiny of all decisions by a campus press, media review of all controversial decisions, and so on. Yet, to the aspiring public servant student, such an experience goes a long way toward bridging the gap between vague comments about the joys and sorrows of public service found in the *Occupational Outlook Handbook* and the tough realities.

In moral development, the advisor's developmental level heavily determines the advisor's efforts to foster the development of a student. In particular, the developmental level of the advisor can be critical in dealing with someone of a different age, race, or sex. For instance, an eighteen-year-old engineering student who encounters a sixty-year-old advisor may experience great tension, attributable to the considerable age gap and possible moral development gulf. Or the woman or black student may encounter great difficulty with the biased white, male advisor who may very well unconsciously hold many stereotypes regarding women and minorities. Thus, even if the advisor, in this case, is relatively mature in moral development, such built-in biases will interfere with his efforts to foster the moral development of such students. Given some awareness of such attitudes and attendant behaviors, this advisor may be ready to deal with his problems in this area. Following awareness of strongly held prejudices, the advisor needs to accept or own such thoughts and strive to heighten his or her awareness of the myriad, subtle behavioral manifestations of such feelings and thoughts. Nondefensive solicitation of honest feedback from women and minority advising colleagues and students may elicit insightful observations. Deliberate behavioral modification efforts can be undertaken concurrent with various forms of self- or other-administered cognitive and insight therapy. All of the preceding suggestions assume that the advisor wants to be rid of his prejudice. If not, the idea of this advisor influencing in a positive light the moral development of his women and minority students will remain just an idea.

Developmental Change. As a hopeful indication of the potential impact of a developmentally oriented advising approach, Sanford (1966), in referring to change-promoting institutions, noted, "If an institution is a system of subsystems, and if a change in any one of them can change the whole, then it should be possible to make certain modifications in a college program, which would reduce overall rates of mental illness among students, or increase the overall level of their development" (p. 49). In light of this comment, there are several critical aspects of universities and colleges that are highly related to positive human development. Perhaps the following comments begin to answer the question "What would the ethos of a developmentally oriented college or university be?"

In considering the thoughts of Chickering (1969), Heath (1981), and Miller and McCaffrey (1982), several critical conditions emerge. For instance, while Chickering pointed to a college's clarity and consistency of objectives, Heath cited internal coherence, and Miller and McCaffrey noted a college's sense of shared purpose. All seem to be saying that for a college to have a developmental climate, its inhabitants should possess a modicum of agreement as to its central focus and destiny. Heath (1981) seems to be saying that prior to such agreement, the faculty, student affairs staff, administrators, and students should be accurately and reflectively aware of their college's character, strengths, weaknesses, values, and outcomes. From such would naturally flow a clear sense of shared purpose.

Faculty, administrators, and student affairs staff should be known by students and have enough close contact with them to be seen as realistic and accessible role models. These persons should be mature and competent as well as willing and able to make appropriate demands of students while offering requisite encouragement. In displaying their competence, faculty should evidence genuine respect for each student's competence.

Heath (1981) says the institution should be empathically responsive: "A school that is empathically responsive has faculty and students who value being open to and responsive not just to their own privatistic concerns but also to the needs of others; it has the empathic skill to transcend its immediate preoccupations to be concerned about its contribution to societal needs. Its faculty genuinely care about the growth of its students and seek to educate in ways that enhance the historic liberally educating goal of deepening a youth's humaneness and identification with others" (pp. 97–98). Consistent with these ideas, Miller and McCaffrey (1982) note a college should strive for congruency between individual needs and its environmental characteristics. The student culture of a developmentally oriented institution should be one characterized by positive, intimate, meaningful relationships versus negative, superficial, aimless interactions (Chickering, 1969; Miller and McCaffrey, 1982).

The climate of a change-promoting institution will be characterized by reasonable freedom of choice in most areas of faculty and student life. Thus, the developmentally oriented institution will provide ample opportunities for students, and other members of the academic community, to make meaningful decisions in all areas of their lives and to control their destiny. Realistically, advisors find themselves functioning in institutions whose bureaucratic structures and political climates actually work against the development of students and staff alike. In such cases, the individual advisor must work doubly hard in a developmental way with staff, administrators, and students. As an individual change agent, such advisors can and must, if they are to remain true to their convictions of the validity of developmental academic advising, create supportive islands of change promotion with their students. They must thoughtfully set in motion positive, developmental waves within their units or departments, college or university. Within every college or university, kindred souls can be found. One key to fostering the idea of developmental academic advising in a neutral or antidevelopmental institution is the building of coalitions of developmentally minded individuals, across disciplinary and organizational lines. Thus interdisciplinary teams of faculty, counselors, and administrators can be marshaled to engage in head-to-head and heart-to-heart conduct and dialogue to foster needed institutional change.

Ultimately, all institutions should become thoughtful and humane in their organizational configurations, policies and practices and be designed in such a manner that their structures fit their constituents and not vice versa.

Practical Implications of Developmental Theory

Given the provision of a developmental environment or climate, growth in intellectual and moral development and successful coping with life cycle concerns will more easily occur. Sanford (1966) noted, "The institution which would lead an individual toward greater development must, then, present him with strong challenges, appraise accurately his ability to cope with these challenges, and offer him support when they become overwhelming" (p. 46). Further, Sanford (1966) suggested that an advisor might seek to ascertain the student's potential, present skills, attitudes, beliefs, knowledge, emotional needs, feelings of self-esteem, and coping mechanisms. The advisor should also determine how the student is functioning in the higher-education environment. Then the advisor can weigh such varied data, draw upon relevant developmental theory, and structure or guide the relationship in ways that respect the rights of each student and support the responsibility for individual decision making of each student.

Awareness: An Enabling Quality. If advisors expect to employ any of the theories previously discussed, they need to be keenly aware of how they perceive and are perceived by others, namely their students. We assert that advisors, concerned with facilitating the optimal personal development of each student, will be "accurately and reflectively self-aware" of their strengths, weaknesses, values, and interpersonal relationships and thereby capable of "adapting to the demands of various adult roles" (Heath, 1981, p. 94). Thus, Charlotte, the relatively young general advisor, may be quite capable of relating more easily to young undergraduate females than Elizabeth, our sixty-four-year-old professor. Or Vern, our forty-five-year-old Afro-American engineering professor, may relate more comfortably to Adahm, our male international student, whose cultural values are rooted in a male-ruled and female-subjugated culture, than would Charlotte. Advisors will find it quite beneficial or even necessary to be cognizant of what they have in common with and how they differ from each student. Given such awareness, they will be capable of predicting how these personal commonalities and differences will interact. Let's explore a few of these possible critical variables on which advisors and students may be alike or different.

Possible Variables for Matching Advisor and Student. Assume that each advisor possesses the requisite information and adequate training for advising and that the advising relationships are characterized by mutual caring, respect, and commitment. What impact will differences of sex, race, values orientations, interests, life-styles, socioeconomic backgrounds, or introversion-extroversion leaning make? For a white, female engineering student, with no previous contact with a minority faculty or staff person, being assigned to Vern, a black engineering professor, may require a major, or even insurmountable, adjustment in currently held thoughts and feeling about blacks. Or assuming that Charlotte, our twenty-nine-year-old, full-time advisor, is a sensitive, attentive person, one can readily imagine occasions where her sensitivity, attentiveness, and caring will be misinterpreted by a young male student, such as Adahm, who is lacking, but desiring, close interaction with members of the opposite sex.

Regarding impact of interests and personality, how might Yolanda, our art professor, relate to the male student who is very people-oriented and desires to teach others all facets of art versus the female student who views Yolanda as a role model? Will not "natural affinity" or mutual attraction be operative in these relationships?

Harold, our extrovert university advising center director, will very likely tend to attract many students by virtue of his outgoing personality. It is also probable that many of these students will share his values orientation, some of his interests, and various aspects of his apparent life-style.

Thus, a critical set of personal variables with many practical implications for the quality of the advisor-student relationship need consideration. Good "fits" in many cases will be readily apparent. In other instances, obvious differences may be worked through.

Variations in Stage and Age. To facilitate individual movement from one developmental stage to another, it is desirable to have some difference between the advisor and student in level of development. Given the assumption that most undergraduates are at Perry's dualistic and multiplistic levels, most advisors should be at Perry's relativistic level or above and Kohlberg's stages 3 and 4, which constitute his conventional level, or above. These differences in levels of development are sufficient to create some tension or dissonance in the student that will serve to motivate and facilitate student growth. Implicit in this discrepancy between advisor and student in levels of development is the assumption that the advisor is capable of differing responses, depending upon the formal or informal assessment of the developmental stage of the student.

Regarding age and stage interactions, ideally, for the traditional-age undergraduates, advisors should be older than their students, in addition to the desired stages just noted. While peer advising has often been found to be as effective as traditional advising, such peers are as likely as not to have been effective by virtue of the close identification between advisor and student. However, when desiring developmental growth, more than identification will be necessary. An older advisor sincerely needs, as Heath (1981) notes, to be capable of being empathically responsive. Sensitive advisors need not to have lived all the experiences of their students in order to empathize with these individuals. Thus, being older and at a higher developmental level will contribute to the creation of a setting wherein the roles the advisor will play will be perceived and accepted more readily by the student. Such roles as evaluator, teacher, role model, and mentor are more consistent with the general conceptualization of an advisor who happens to be older than with one who is younger. Thus, our twenty-nine-, thirty-eight-, forty-five-, forty-nine-, and sixty-four-year-old advisors will all be acceptable on at least the age dimensions and fully acceptable if they meet the ideal criteria for developmental stages for working with most traditional-age students.

Variations in Life Cycle Status. In most advising cases, the student and advisor will be dealing with different life cycle issues. Generally, most advisors are older and at a different place in the adult life cycle than their typically young adult students. Such differences should usually work to the benefit of both advisor and student. Ideally, the advisor has already successfully negotiated such

life cycle tasks as achieving emotional autonomy, initiating preparation for a career, and building a clear set of personally relevant
values. Advisor-student conflict may arise when both are struggling
to resolve the same life cycle concerns. Emotionally, the advisor may
very well be incapable of serving in a developmental advising
capacity. For instance, advisors caught up in the throes of a mid-
life career change may have little cognitive and emotional energy
available to relate objectively to young students preoccupied with
choosing majors that will prepare them for careers. In such instances, advisors must retain a clear sense of their competencies and
deficiencies and be careful to refer students when they are unable
cognitively or emotionally to be of help. Developmental academic
advising entails giving students the best advisors have to offer.

Staffing Concerns. The brief discussions of theory and applications lead naturally to several suggestions regarding present
staffing arrangements of advisors.

In the advising program now in operation on the campus,
all advisors should first examine current advising approaches,
noting the implicit or explicit theoretical bases for the approaches.
Through well-structured inventories, specific skill assessment can
be accomplished that will help advisors to ascertain their present
level of listening and responding skills. In addition, the collective
competencies of the total advising staff will be appraised. Concurrently, the present level of development of each advisor should be
assessed. The college or university concerned about effective developmental academic advising needs to review its training or preparation, formal or informal, of academic advisors. An honest appraisal, establishing solid baseline data, would include efforts to
assess the advisors' knowledge of developmental theory and their
ability to apply such knowledge. This will likely prove to be a more
sensitive and difficult, although necessary, task.

The collection of all these data will yield a comprehensive
picture of the relative homogeneity and heterogeneity of the entire
advising corps of an institution. The accomplishment of this
appraisal phase will clarify the nature of the needs for a professional
development program aimed at encouraging developmental academic advising. With many institutions having standing college- or
university-wide committees charged with oversight or continuous

review of the quality of academic advising and with many student
government bodies concerned about the quality of academic advising, the vehicles and impetus for undertaking such staffing concerns seem built-in or ready-made.

Professional Development Concerns. A discussion of staffing
concerns leads comfortably to an exploration or enunciation of
professional development guidelines.

Mixed by age, sex, ethnic origins, and level of developmental
stage functioning, how should or can an institution best structure
a professional development program on developmental academic
advising that itself is developmental in structure? As a given, many
advisors are engaged in competing roles and functions that tax their
available time and energy. Advisors must be able to realize substantial intrinsic and extrinsic rewards by virtue of their participation
in any professional development program on developmental academic advising. Also, advisors must experience administrative support for following through on such knowledge and skill gained
through professional development efforts.

Inherent in developmental theory is recognition of individual differences and the uniqueness of each person. Thus, careful
attention should be given to the very structure of any educational
and training effort. Referring to the life cycle theory, advisors'
maturity should be openly acknowledged. In acknowledgment of
developmental stage theory, the leaders of any professional development effort need to be capable of flexibly responding to varied levels
of functioning of advisors. Indeed, the program directors of any
such efforts need to be prepared to provide the requisite amounts
of support and challenge needed to facilitate the acquisition of
knowledge, attitudes, and skills necessary to carry out developmental academic advising. (For explicit ideas and suggestions on
implementing developmental instruction, please refer to Knefelkamp and Cornfield, 1979.) Support could possibly be manifest by
providing specific instructions, a clear structure, and a warm,
respectful, caring atmosphere in the initial phases of a program.
Having established such a climate, the program leaders may then
provide a variety of approaches to learning and skill development.
Such approaches should be designed to accommodate the varied
levels of development of the advisors and their preferred learning

styles. (See Chapters Fifteen and Sixteen for a more in-depth examination of advisor development approaches.)

While these comments assume a somewhat ideal situation, in most institutions there are existing incentives for and constraints against developmental academic advising. Any reasonable professional development effort must honestly acknowledge and deal with these forces. In other words, it is likely that incentives will need to be strengthened and constraints weakened and eliminated.

With the continued concern about sufficient college student enrollment, developmental academic advising can be seen as one powerful dimension of facilitating student retention. Administrators may well need to be persuaded that such efforts are worth the advisor's time and energies. Indeed, such efforts may need to be shown to be cost-effective. However, such costs will likely include more than dollars and cents. In the process of selling developmental academic advising to administrators, the program leaders must realize that the level of developmental functioning of administrators does influence their verbal and nonverbal behavioral responses. Thus, attention must be given to the mode of presenting the notion of developmental theory and academic advising with a developmental slant. These and other issues or concerns must be satisfactorily handled if a responsive, vibrant developmental advising effort is to be a reality on college and university campuses across the nation.

Summary

This chapter set forth several theoretical foundations for the dynamic developmental processes involved in academic advising. It shared vignettes of students and advisors whose lives exemplify the various ages and stages of development. Contributions from life cycle, psychosocial, career, and cognitive development theorists were described. In addition, the conditions for and dynamics of developmental change were explored. The chapter ended with implications of the theories, noting such issues as matching students and advisors (on the bases of ethnicity, sex, race, and so on), staffing, and professional development. Readers (advisors) should now have some useful lenses through which to view what they are confronting developmentally in themselves, how a particular advising procedure or activity might affect the development of a student, and what specific development issues a student might present. Such understandings can generate a greater sense of control over what occurs in the advising relationship. Also, both advisors and students may experience less anxiety, given the greater predictability and understanding of the developmental goals of advising.

References

Beilin, H. "The Application of General Developmental Principles to the Vocational Area." *Journal of Counseling Psychology*, 1955, *2*, 53–57.

Chickering, A. W. *Education and Identity*. San Francisco: Jossey-Bass, 1969.

Chickering, A. W. "Adult Development—Implications for Higher Education." In C. E. Cavert (Compiler), *Designing Diversity '75, Conference Proceedings, Second National Conference on Open Learning and Nontraditional Study*. Lincoln, Neb.: University of Mid-America, 1975.

Chickering, A. W. "Life Cycle." In J. Lindquist and T. Clark (Eds.), *Institute for Academic Improvement Sourcebook*. Memphis, Tenn.: Memphis State University, Center for the Study of Higher Education, 1978.

Chickering, A. W., and Associates. *The Modern American College: Responding to the New Realities of Diverse Students and a Changing Society*. San Francisco: Jossey-Bass, 1981.

Erikson, E. *Childhood and Society*. New York: Norton, 1950.

Gould, R. L. "The Phases of Adult Life: A Study of Developmental Psychology." *American Journal of Psychiatry*, 1972, *129*, 521–531.

Heath, D. H. "A College's Ethos: A Neglected Key to Effectiveness and Survival." *Liberal Education*, 1981, *67*, 89–111.

Knefelkamp, L. L., and Cornfield, J. L. "Combining Student Stages and Style in the Design of Learning Environmentalists: Using Holland Typologies and Perry Stages." Paper presented to the American College Personnel Association, Los Angeles, March 1979.

Kohlberg, L. "From Is to Ought: How to Commit the Naturalistic Fallacy and Get Away with It in the Study of Moral Development." In T. Mischel (Ed.), *Cognitive Development and Episto-mology*. New York: Academic Press, 1971.

Levinson, D. J., and others. *The Seasons of a Man's Life*. New York: Knopf, 1978.

Miller, T. K., and McCaffrey, S. S. "Student Development Theory: Foundations for Academic Advising." In R. B. Winston, Jr., S. C. Ender, and T. K. Miller (Eds.), *New Directions for Student Services: Developmental Approaches to Academic Advising*, no. 17. San Francisco: Jossey-Bass, 1982.

Neugarten, B. L. "A Developmental View of Adult Personality." In J. Birren (Ed.), *Relations of Development and Aging*. Spring-field, Ill.: Thomas, 1963.

Neugarten, B. L. "Adaptation and the Life Cycle." *Journal of Geriatric Psychology*, 1970, *4* (1), 71–87.

Perry, W. G., Jr. *Forms of Intellectual and Ethical Development in the College Years: A Scheme*. New York: Holt, Rinehart and Winston, 1970.

Perry, W. G., Jr. "Cognitive and Ethical Growth: The Making of Meaning." In A. W. Chickering and Associates, *The Modern American College: Responding to the New Realities of Diverse Students and a Changing Society*. San Francisco: Jossey-Bass, 1981.

Rest, J. R. "A Psychologist Looks at the Teaching of Ethics." *Hastings Center Report*, 1982, *12* (1), 29–36.

Sanford, N. *Self and Society: Social Change and Individual Development*. New York: Lieber-Atherton, 1966.

Sheehy, G. *Passages: Predictable Crises in Adult Life*. New York: Dutton, 1976.

Shipton, J., and Steltenpohl, E. H. "Educational Advising and Career Planning: A Life-Cycle Perspective." In A. W. Chickering and Associates, The Modern American College: *Responding to the New Realities of Diverse Students and a Changing Society*. San Francisco: Jossey-Bass, 1981.

Super, D. E. "A Life-Span, Life-Space Approach to Career Development." *Journal of Vocational Behavior*, 1980, *16*, 282–298.

Theodorson, G. A., and Theodorson, A. G. *A Modern Dictionary of Sociology*. New York: Crowell, 1969.

Part Two

The Advising Process: Strategies and Clientele

The first five chapters in Part Two identify effective advising strategies and techniques and explain their impact on the developmental processes experienced by students. The remaining chapters focus on ways in which the advising process can address the special needs of several important undergraduate subpopulations and the unique needs of graduate students.

In Chapter Five, "Educational Planning: Helping Students Make Decisions," Virginia N. Gordon details the nature of the decision-making process and its impact on college students' academic and career concerns. The chapter begins by describing a five-stage decision-making model that can be applied to educational planning and career choice. Academic choices often confronted by students that require timely and thoughtful decisions are outlined and strategies are presented for providing assistance. Lastly, groups who often require special attention (such as undecided majors, students who decide to change majors late in their academic careers, and academically talented students) are discussed.

Wesley R. Habley ("Integrating Academic Advising and Career Planning," Chapter Six) advocates the integration of academic advising with a variety of student affairs and support services on campus, if delivery of effective career- and life-planning services is to be a reality. He presents an eleven-step intervention model that focuses on career planning and decision making within the context of an academic advising structure and relationship. The chapter concludes by suggesting programmatic implications and strategies for integrating career planning within a developmental approach to academic advising.

In Chapter Seven, "Enhancing Students' Intellectual and Personal Development," James C. Hurst and Gene A. Pratt discuss academic advising and its relationship to students' intellectual and personal development. They present an intervention model for conceptualizing from a broad institutional/system perspective an academic advising program that has as its goal the total development of students. They then describe several examples of programs that have integrated personal and intellectual development with academic advising.

Tools and techniques that individual academic advisors can use in their daily work with students are described by Thomas J. Grites in Chapter Eight. He describes a wide variety of information sources and instruments, such as ACT/SAT profiles, formal assessment instruments, academic transcripts, developmental transcripts, questionnaires, and anecdotal records. Several methods of delivering advising services are explored as well.

In Chapter Nine, "Using Computers in Academic Advising," Gary L. Kramer, Erlend D. Petersen, and Robert W. Spencer investigate the rapidly emerging widespread use of computer systems in academic advising programs. They outline several different approaches to the development of systems that provide timely, accurate information for use in academic advising and cite both advantages and disadvantages of each. Curriculum management systems currently in use in several institutions are also described.

Chapters Ten and Eleven focus attention on specific subpopulations of students who require special attention from academic advisors. Sue A. Saunders and Leroy Ervin (Chapter Ten) discuss the advising needs of, and suggest interventions for assisting, academic high-risk students, learning disabled and handicapped students, students who have extensive demands on their time—such as part-time students, scholarship athletes, and students in performing arts—and minority and international students. Roger B. Winston, Jr., and Mark C. Polkosnik (Chapter Eleven) address the specific, unique concerns of graduate and professional school students. They identify roles and functional responsibilities of graduate student advisors and suggest strategies for helping students during such critical phases of their study as entry into the department, program planning, comprehensive examinations, and thesis/dissertation research.

5

Educational Planning:
Helping Students
Make Decisions

Virginia N. Gordon

Educational planning is a process in which each college student is involved in self-assessment, exploring and integrating academic and career alternatives, and making decisions that are personally relevant for the present and the future. It is a continuous effort that reflects the maturity and ability of individual students as they approach each decision situation. Educational planning is not something that happens during registration nor is it a clerical function. Educational and career planning skills and knowledge are used throughout a lifetime. In the college years, these techniques and skills may be emphasized, learned, and practiced in a nonthreatening, supportive environment. The academic advising relationship can become the vehicle for a great deal of this learning, experimenting, reality testing, goal setting, and implementation.

Academic advising and decision making are two processes so inextricably joined that they are often used as vehicles for one another. College students not only need assistance in making academic choices but often need help in learning the critical skills associated with the decision-making process itself. In the college years students develop interpersonal relationships, develop autonomy and independence, build a vocational identity, and formulate a life-style for the future (Chickering, 1969). Educational and vocational decisions made during this period will have great impact on the future lives of students. The academic advising relationship can become a powerful influence in helping students formulate realistic educational plans that will aid in ensuring satisfying futures.

Analysis of Decision-Making

Many approaches for understanding and negotiating the decision-making process have been offered. Some are mathematical in nature, based on concepts of probability or a quantitative approach to alternatives and outcomes (Dilley, 1967; Gelatt and Clarke, 1967; Thoresen and Mehrens, 1967; Herr, 1970). Other approaches are concerned with the influences of information, risk taking, rewards, and social and economic factors on decision making (Lipsett, 1962; Clarke, Gelatt, and Levine, 1969; Herr, 1970; Holland, 1973).

Every advisor has experienced the fascinating differences in approaches individual students bring to the educational choice process. While many students view the choice of academic major or the selection of courses as discrete actions, they are in reality only extensions of previously made decisions. Students come to the advising situation with varying degrees of skill and confidence in decision making. Some have had limited experience and practice in this area because others, such as parents, have always made decisions for them. The advisor must approach these students very differently from those who have independently developed effective styles and strategies for making decisions and have confidently practiced these in a variety of settings. Understanding (a) the different approaches or theories of decision making, (b) the important variables involved, and (c) the levels of skills students possess are vital tools for academic advisors in helping students with educational and career planning.

Janis. Janis and Mann (1977) describe decision making in terms of a five-stage process that can be applied to educational planning and choice:

1. *Appraising the challenge.* The student will not acknowledge a decision situation exists until challenged by some disturbing information or event that forces him or her to change course; for example, the institution may force a major choice after so many credit hours or parental pressures may become too strong to ignore. At this point, the search for alternatives proceeds.

2. *Surveying alternatives.* The student now seeks information and advice in an effort to find some viable alternative majors, courses, or curricula. Some of these options may come from prior ideas, or new ones may be generated from the advisor's suggestions.

3. *Weighing alternatives.* Now each alternative that has been identified is evaluated. The pros and cons of each choice are studied. When one alternative has too many negative consequences, it is eliminated. Finally, just one alternative is left.

4. *Deliberating about a commitment.* After a decision has been made, a full commitment to accept it may be delayed until reactions of others to the decision and other consequences are considered.

5. *Adhering despite negative feedback.* If most feedback is positive and the choice seems to be the best one, action to implement it is taken. If too much negative feedback is encountered, the decision may be viewed as not right, and the process may start all over again with the student returning to the first stage.

Tiedeman and O'Hara. Tiedeman and O'Hara (1963) also view decision making as a process that becomes increasingly differentiated and comprehensive as an individual develops and matures. When a person faces a discontinuity in life, purposeful action is often initiated in the form of decision-making behavior. Some of life's critical decision points are when a student is ready to select a college, choose an academic direction, decide on a career field, or take a first job. Tiedeman and O'Hara describe the process a college student might experience as a decision is identified, dealt with, and made. The planning phase includes a period of exploration when the student considers many alternatives, none of which may be realistic. The student lacks important information necessary for a decision. During the next stage the student begins to crystallize some alternatives, based on more relevant information, and begins to weigh the advantages and disadvantages of each option. During the choice stage a decision is actually made, even though some doubts may still exist. Finally, the decision is clarified and former doubts disappear. Once the decision has been made, action plans are formulated and the planning phase is completed.

Tiedeman and O'Hara also describe action stages of induction, reformation, and integration where the decision is acted upon and individuals successfully integrate the decision into their self-concept.

Harren. Harren (1979) has designed a decision-making model based on Tiedeman and O'Hara's concepts that can provide a framework for advising interventions. Harren's model not only includes the stages in the process of deciding but also includes the characteristics of the decision maker and the environmental factors that influence decision making. Decision-making styles are the decision maker's personal approach to perceiving and responding to decision-making tasks. The rational and intuitive styles are characterized by an internal responsibility for decision, while the third style, dependent, implies an external control.

To summarize the process component of Harren's model, the following stages and processes are described (Harren, 1979, p. 121):

- *awareness:* appraisal of self-in-situation
- *planning:* exploration-crystallization
- *commitment:* integration with self-concept system; bolstering; action planning
- *implementation:* success and satisfaction outcomes; conformity-autonomy-interdependence

Harren postulates that many college freshmen are in an *awareness* stage. They find themselves in a new environment and begin to take honest stock of where they are and where they are going. This self-appraisal may cause them some anxiety if they realize that they need to make an academic and career decision. Only when this is internalized will they move on to the next stage, which Harren calls *planning*. While many undecided students are obviously in the awareness stage, many other ostensibly decided freshmen are as well.

During the planning phase of the process, students' self-concepts play an important role. This stage is characterized by "an alternating, expanding, and narrowing process of exploration and crystallization" (Harren, 1979, p. 122). Students begin to search for information and interpret it in a very personal way. This may be the most important task of the choice process and one that advisors particularly need to understand. Students bring to the information-gathering stage of decision making a unique mixture of past experiences, different levels of skills, motivation to perform the task, and different degrees of cognitive complexity.

While students are gathering data about certain majors, for example, they are reacting to each in terms of internal criteria that vary in degree of clarity and concreteness. The student with a rational decision-making style will approach the situation with objective deliberation. Information is gathered and decisions are made in a logical, orderly way. The intuitive style, on the other hand, involves a feeling approach where an emotional self-awareness forms the basis for decision making. The intuitive decision maker gathers information but reacts to it at an emotional rather than a thinking level. The dependent decision maker denies responsibility for a decision and projects the responsibility on others. For example, this student will expect the advisor, teacher, or other authorities to select the best major.

After data are gathered, the narrowing process of crystallization begins. Some students may have enough information to make a decision and move on to the commitment stage. Others may need to gather more data or may need to reassess their knowledge about their own personal characteristics (for example, values, abilities) before a decision can be reached. Many advisors have witnessed this expanding-narrowing process taking place in students.

Once a specific alternative is chosen, the student moves into the *commitment* stage. Students often do not publicly commit themselves to a decision once it is made until they discuss it in general terms with others to get reactions from them. If the feedback continues to be positive in nature, the students' confidence in commitment increases. Harren postulates that this is where individual students integrate the commitment with their self-concept. There is now a future orientation where the student actually begins the *implementation* stage with specific action steps and plans.

Once the decision is implemented, the student finds closure in several ways: integration into the self-concept system, reduction of any dissonance that was once felt, and reduction of any anxiety that was once present due to lack of information and planning. Harren states that decision-making styles are especially important during the implementation stage. Each style (dependent, rational, or intuitive) will influence the degree of satisfaction and stability that prevails over time. The dependent decision maker, for example, may conform to the decision at first but later may revoke it and recycle through the process again.

Harren offers not only a framework for identifying the needs of individual students in this area but provides insights into how the student-advisor relationship is affected by the complexity of the process. Advisors working with students in the awareness stage can help them expand their time perspectives, which includes assessing past experiences and projecting future goals so decisions made in the present incorporate these personal dimensions. Advisors need to determine how self-confident the student is in making decisions; some may need help in understanding the process. Feelings of anxiety may help students realize the importance of exploring alternatives, thus moving them into the planning stage.

Advisors may work with students in the planning stage by helping them expand and then narrow their academic options. This is the information-gathering aspect of the process. Students need to react to academic and career information in terms of their own personal realities. For example, do they have the ability to perform well in this or that major? Asking probing questions and helping the student clarify personal issues are important advisor roles.

Herein is reflected the "art" of understanding how a student makes decisions. This understanding is essential to effective advising.

Students in commitment need help with action planning: How do they implement their major decision? Whom do they need to see to finalize the decision? What procedures or forms need to be processed? Once the decision is implemented, the student should feel a sense of satisfaction and closure. The advisor's role at this point becomes one of support. The *Assessment of Career Decision Making* (Harren, 1980) instrument was developed by Harren to help identify where individual students are developmentally in this decision-making process.

Influences on Decision-Making Skills. Another important consideration in decision making is the way that personal, social, and economic variables interact and affect the decisions made by students at given times. The complex interdependence between these factors, while not fully understood at this time by theorists, may have important consequences for the individual student. Academic advisors, while not self-proclaimed experts in this field, may be able to raise questions and provide insights not otherwise identified by the student. Helping students gather all relevant information and facilitating an examination of data from many perspectives may be viewed as an important advisor contribution to the choice process. This may be considered a teaching role that is acknowledged by many as an integral part of the advising responsibility.

Learning effective decision-making techniques will not only influence academic success and satisfaction but will become an important part of the knowledge and skills acquired by the college student for life. Decision making may be taught by modeling. Advisors may engage students in specific tasks that are integral to the process; for example, they may help students identify the problem(s), identify and clarify values, and gather information. Effective decision making is a key to retention. Students who are experienced and confident in making educational and vocational decisions are more likely to complete a college degree (Cope and Hannah, 1975; Beal and Noel, 1980). Decision making can be one of the most critical skills learned during the college years. Practicing these skills in a relatively safe environment will prepare students and give them confidence in their ability to negotiate any challenge they encounter later in life in family affairs, community relationships, and work-related decisions.

Critical Academic Decisions

Tiedeman and O'Hara (1963) propose critical decision points that individuals face during their lives. It is not surprising that some of the most important ones occur during the college years. After the initial decision to select and attend a specific institution is made, one of the most immediate decisions is to select a college major. Choosing the specific courses geared to this major is another important task. The creation of an overall education plan as outlined later in this chapter encompasses these critical choices. Many students equate these decisions, however, with a career decision as well. While some openly admit confusion about academic and occupational relationships, many students assume their choice of major and career to be a simultaneous one.

Selecting a Major. It has been well documented that many freshmen enter college feeling very pressured to declare a major. That these initial choices are sometimes not realistic or suitable is evidenced by the tremendous number of changes of major before graduation (Titley, Titley, and Wolff, 1976; Foote, 1980; Titley and Titley, 1980).

Since the selection of a college major is the first important academic decision to be made, many students feel a choice, however tentative, is better than no choice at all. Rather than forcing closure on this issue prematurely, many campuses have instituted colleges, departments, or centers for students who honestly admit their need to explore.

Students are at many levels of certainty about a choice of major (Titley and Titley, 1980; Goodson, 1981; Gordon, 1982). Very few students know exactly what they want, have undertaken a thorough information search, and have the ability to succeed in the area they have chosen. A larger number of students have made tentative decisions and need to confirm or reject them during their first years in college. Another large group considers two or three alternatives but needs time to gather information and reality test their ideas before making a choice. Another smaller group of students enters college every year totally undecided about a major. These students need a great deal of academic and career advising as they progress through the process of exploration.

Advisors will work very differently with students in various levels of commitment to a major. Undecided students may need a great deal of self-assessment and information about many majors as well as learning how to pull it all together. They may also be laboring under self-inflicted or external pressures to choose. These students, who need to explore a variety of alternatives, may require a different approach than students needing to confirm a tentative decision. Decided students may also need information but may have a greater need to reality test their choice by taking courses or contacting workers in a variety of related career fields. Each level of commitment implies a different level of information needed. Assessment of these levels of decidedness through questionnaires or surveys administered during orientation or through advising services is of particular value to advising program leaders.

Occupational Relationships. Some students select a major on the basis of its immediate identification with an occupation. Other students choose majors assuming that life after graduation will take care of itself. Although advisors have heard the "what can I do with a major in . . .?" question for many years, it becomes increasingly prevalent when economic times dictate a more closed job market. This is of particular interest to liberal arts students who have traditionally found employment in diverse areas and who feel the pressure as freshmen to find occupational relevance within their major.

An important advisor role is to help students understand the value of a college degree in terms of becoming an educated person with a broad range of knowledge and skills, regardless of major. Although some may argue that higher education must respond to changes in society and the world, others propose that "vocationalism" is threatening the very heart of a liberal education. Rather than separating these two, students seeking "relevance" need help in bringing liberal learning and career planning together. Students who are vocationally oriented can become aware of the joy and value of becoming educated. Advisors can be an important catalyst in this critical understanding by giving students ample opportunity to explore such possibilities in some detail.

One aspect of helping students resolve the dichotomy between liberal learning and occupational training is to teach them how occupations are organized and what work tasks are involved so that they become more aware and broadened about many possibilities. Many students are looking for the "right" major that can lead them to the "right" occupation. They need to understand that many combinations of majors and occupations exist and that even the most obvious major-occupation connections do not always ensure a job after graduation. The need for a marriage of academic and career advising services is obvious here.

Although the decision about an occupational field may seem to many students to be the most critical decision made in college, it is in reality only one of many. Being a college graduate implies knowledge, abilities, skills, and a much broader capability to contribute in many career areas.

Selection of Courses. One of the ongoing decisions needing to be made throughout college is the choice of courses to schedule each term. Many students see these as relating only to the major they have selected. Advisors may hear from a student that certain courses need to be "gotten out of the way" their freshmen year, for example. Students need to be taught the scheduling process, the value of course exploration, and the important use of electives. An integral part of creating an educational plan includes a projection of all courses to be taken. Advisors should encourage students to provide a rationale for why they are taking certain courses and make sure they understand how the integrated whole works together.

When helping students select courses, advisors have certain tools available to help them determine levels of past achievements, including high school grades and American College Test (ACT)/ Scholastic Aptitude Test (SAT) scores. These tools are dealt with in detail in Chapter Eight. While these are only indicators, they are especially useful for first-year students. Scheduling courses in keeping with the students' level of competence is especially important during their initial period of adjustment to college in general. Many students need to learn the art of building a schedule. They need to learn how to select courses that provide balance and diversity. Even very bright students may not find academic success their first term in college if scheduled inappropriately. This area of educational planning is particularly within advisors' realm of expertise. Creating appropriate and realistic schedules can have a great effect on students' success or failure, especially during their first year in college.

Developing an Educational Plan

Educational planning involves many important tasks that eventually incorporate a set of short- and long-term goals. Certain conditions must be present before an educational plan can be of optimal value:

1. Students need a personal commitment and involvement in formulating a plan. If the plan is initiated by them and has relevance for them, it will provide a blueprint for an important period in their lives and have profound influence on their future. They will also take responsibility for its outcomes.
2. Students must be aware of the need for flexibility in carrying out any plan. Nothing remains static, and plans may need to be altered as new information or events indicate a change is desirable or necessary.
3. Students should be able to articulate their reasons for being in college and how the degree fits into their career and life goals.

Goal Setting. Goal setting involves imagining a desirable future while formulating present plans. Setting goals is a very difficult task for some students, and they may perceive planning without goals to be easier and just as effective. Academic advisors often work with students who cannot express goals or who do so in very vague and general terms.

Goals are sometimes identified by students as they make and act out certain decisions. These students move in comfortable and interesting directions that in time may thrust them toward a specific goal. Planning for the future does not necessarily mean systematic, elaborate goals must be set. Simply selecting an alternative and following it through its course may lead to a satisfying conclusion.

Whether a student is able to set concrete, far-reaching goals or whether a vague, ill-defined direction is taken, progress is being made.

One important advisor role is to help students question their values and describe what is implicitly important to them in making certain decisions. Students tend to make decisions based on previous knowledge, experiences, and prior choices. Only after making an implicit choice does one confirm it on the basis of hard fact. Students may alter or distort the facts in favor of the alternative chosen. Justifying a decision is one way of making sense out of a confusing jumble of intuition, emotions, and information. Choosing a mate, for example, may be a goal for many young people, but it is seldom accomplished by rational, logical means alone.

In formulating educational and career plans, students must be acutely aware of the role that environmental factors play in determining the outcomes of a decision. A "good" decision may have a "bad" outcome because of external factors beyond the control of the decision maker. Although goal-directed planning is viewed as desirable by most, a need for flexibility and adaptability is critical as the goal is being pursued. Some characteristics of a good educational plan might be that it is personally relevant and realistically based on one's interests and strengths, attainable within a reasonable time frame, and structured so that changes or modifications may be made when needed or desired without disrupting the entire plan. A good plan will present an academic challenge to the student while providing a practical perspective for the career-related concerns that many students have.

Advisor Responsibilities in the Planning Process. Advisors can play a key role in helping students initiate and monitor an educational plan. The responsibilities of advisors and students in this venture need to be negotiated very early in the relationship. Advisors often see themselves primarily as information givers. Much more is expected and needed by the student, however. Advisors can provide a mature, experienced opinion in many aspects of planning. Advisors can also act as sounding boards for ideas as the student progresses through each step of the process. Advisors can create an open, friendly climate so that students feel free to share ideas and dreams. They need to feel that someone has a personal interest in their present struggles and their future. It is the students' responsibility to actually make decisions so that they feel personal ownership of the plan once it is formulated. Students sometimes need to be reminded that they will live with the plan and will need to take responsibility for modifying or changing it when needed. They will know, however, that there are always supportive people around to listen, question, suggest, and congratulate them on a job well done.

Students Who Require Special Advising

There are certain groups of students who need special advising approaches to educational planning and decision making. Some of these include exploratory students who are not decided upon an academic or occupational choice, students whose initial choices of a major or career field are not attainable or desirable, preprofessional students (such as premedicine or prelaw) who have been denied entrance to a professional college or who have changed their minds about applying, and honors or gifted students. Chapter Ten explores the special needs of some of these students but the more general needs are discussed here.

Undecided Students. Students who enter college initially without any clearly defined educational or vocational goals comprise a large proportion of most freshman classes. Years of research on this special group have yielded no particular characteristics that describe them in general. Appel, Haak, and Witzke (1970) have factor analyzed some of the dimensions identified through research as relevant to decision-making behaviors. When applied to undecided students, six factors emerge:

1. *Data-seeking orientation.* Most undecided students freely admit they need information in order to make a decision about a major or an occupational field. This information can fall into several categories including self-information (What are my interests?), academic information (What is required for a chemistry major?), and career information (What can I *do* with a degree in chemistry?). The decision-making process incorpo-

rates several steps including gathering information, analyzing it, and synthesizing it. Few satisfying education and career decisions can be made without a great deal of up-to-date, comprehensive, realistic information.

2. *Situation-specific anxiety.* Many students, whether undecided or not, are anxious about making educational decisions that they often view are for a "lifetime." A certain amount of anxiety can be a healthy motivator and encourages students to seek the information and help they need in order to make informed choices.

3. *Generalized indecision.* Some students, however, are anxious about every decision they make, whether it is important or significant. If students cannot decide what to wear in the morning, they will assuredly have difficulty making the selection of an academic major. Goodstein (1965) refers to these students as "indecisive," which means they need a very different advising approach than undecided students. They need a referral for more in-depth counseling.

4. *Multiplicity of interests.* Many undecided students have so many ideas about a major or career field that they do not know how to narrow down their alternatives. This is particularly true of bright students.

5. *Concern with self-identity.* Knowing one's self in terms of values, abilities, interests, and aspirations is an integral part of career decision making. Developing and identifying self-concepts are important steps in this process. Undecided students need to gather information about the personal characteristics that make them unique. All students need time to develop a vocational identity during their college years. Some undecided students may require a longer exploration period than others.

6. *Humanitarian orientation.* Although undecided students as a group have interests that span every academic discipline and occupational field, many of them indicate an interest in the social sciences and helping professions. An interest and aptitude in math and science narrow academic options quickly, whereas social science and humanities interests span many areas. It is easier for students to see direct relationships between

science majors and occupations (for example, agriculture, engineering, and health areas) than for the social sciences.

Appel, Haak, and Witzke (1970) conclude that there are multiple causes of indecision, and undecided students constitute a heterogeneous group.

Other researchers have approached the causes of indecision from another perspective. Osipow, Carney, and Barak (1976) and Holland and Holland (1977) have identified various antecedents of indecision and have developed instruments to help diagnose an individual student's reasons for indecision. Their scales group these causes into self-identity factors, occupational information deficits, and external barriers.

As students select specific items that describe their personal reasons for being undecided, appropriate action steps may be initiated to eliminate that particular problem or concern. For example, students who select items indicating a personal conflict may need to be referred for counseling, while students indicating a need for occupational information may be referred to a career library or to workers involved in specific career fields.

Many academic and career advising programs assume that all undecided students need to start with self-assessment activities. While this is often the case, undecided students are so very different from one another that an individual approach is necessary. Self-assessment tools can help to pinpoint the direct reasons for a specific student's uncertainty.

When helping undecided students approach educational planning and decision making, it is imperative to ascertain the level of commitment to an academic choice (and indeed to the student's reasons for being in college). A student who has absolutely no ideas for a major needs to be approached from a different perspective than one who has several possibilities in mind. There are several advising techniques that will help all students begin the process of exploration in an organized way. The role of the advisor in this process is critical. The following steps may be considered a general approach to all undecided students:

1. Help students identify where they are in education planning and major selection. Help students verbalize all their ideas about majors and their degree of certainty about these choices. If students cannot verbalize a single idea for a major, the advisor may question them about courses preferred or disliked in high school, extracurricular activities in which they participated in high school, leisure-time activities, and work experiences. As the students talk about themselves, advisors can often relate academic majors and occupations to the interests they express.

2. Advisors can then provide information about these alternatives or suggest resources for them to contact for information. Some students may need to spend a great deal of time at this task if they need self-information in addition to academic and career information.

3. Once students have gathered this data, advisors can help them react to it in a rational, logical way. The emotional content of this analysis should not be ignored, however. Some students may use a more intuitive, feeling approach to decision making than others.

4. While students must be responsible for making the decisions, advisors can provide a great deal of support during this period and act as a sounding board for any decisions the students make.

5. After a choice is identified, the advisor can assist the students in formulating an action plan for carrying out the decisions.

6. Advisors can also help students evaluate decisions once they are made and implemented. Monitoring the educational plan can be performed by the student and advisor together. Each will bring a different perspective to this important step.

A particularly effective vehicle for helping undecided students with the information-gathering step that is so critical to educational planning is the freshman orientation or seminar course. A course format has many advantages: (a) Undecided students receive immediate attention. (b) A group (the class) provides the critical support that students need during their first few weeks in college. (c) Instructors are assigned as the student's academic advisor in some systems, which helps to build a familiarity and identity that an undecided student needs while exploring. (d) Immediate adjustment concerns may be identified and resolved. (e) Self-assessment activities may be accomplished in class and processed immediately. (f) Academic major information may be provided in an organized and comprehensive way. (g) Educational and occupational relationships may be explored. (h) The decision process may be learned during the activities in class. (i) By giving academic credit for the class, the institution shows support and emphasizes the importance of educational planning and decision making.

Most students who enter college with no firm commitment to an educational direction usually appreciate the opportunity that the freshman orientation course provides for exploring in an orderly way. A few may not be developmentally ready to undertake such a task, however. Any approach, whether it is individually, in groups, or in a class setting, should take into account the differences in maturity among students.

Major Changers. Another large and often neglected group is made up of the students whose initial educational decisions change. Titley and Titley (1980) estimate that over three fourths of all students change their major at least once during their college years. This has been substantiated in other research studies (Foote, 1980; Slaney, 1980).

There are many valid reasons for changing majors or occupational goals. Some students decide very quickly that their original academic choices are not what they want. The program they had chosen may have course requirements they were unaware of, such as intensive math and science. After taking a certain number of courses in a given major, some students find it is no longer of interest to them. Others may find their high school backgrounds and abilities in certain subjects are not sufficient for them to succeed in their initial choices. Many students who select academic programs that lead to specific occupations find new information about that particular career field that causes them to initiate a change, or they learn about occupations or fields of which they were unaware before entering college.

Students who realize they have made an unrealistic or uninteresting choice are in a critical transition period and need special advising help. They not only need to identify alternative majors, but they need to know the resources on campus that can aid them during this transition. Some students have made decisions that pleased significant others in their life and may be unsure of how to inform them of a change. Others may need to convince themselves that this change is a positive and productive one.

An academic advisor can help a student understand how course work already taken can fit into new curricula. Referrals may be made for career counseling if the advisor and student agree this is appropriate. Some students may need to spend some time exploring by experiencing a work environment before another decision is made. Throughout this process, an academic advisor's attitude and availability are keys to students' needs for support and guidance. Some major changers drop out when they feel they are floundering and have no direction. Professional counselors and advisors as well as faculty need to be aware that the major changers on campus need special attention during this sometimes difficult transitional period.

Upperclass Major Changers. Students who admit or confront their need for a new academic decision early enough are usually able to change majors with few or no penalties in loss of course credit or time. A few students, however, see a change as a sign of weakness and continue on in an academic area even though they know it is not the best one for them. Other students drift until they discover that they have upperclass hours, and at this point they are uncertain as to where to turn for help.

Academic advisors usually find this a difficult and challenging group with which to work. On one hand, a great deal of time, energy, and money have been spent. On the other hand, a student unhappy with a major or occupational field may regret this decision for a lifetime. Sometimes a compromise is the best solution. If a student is a high achiever, a graduate degree in an alternative field may be a solution and may even strengthen a student's marketability (for example, an engineering undergraduate may continue on for a master's degree in business administration or a home economics major may apply for a graduate program in psychology). A student who does not want a graduate program, who cannot afford the expenditure of either time or money required for graduate school, or who does not have the credentials for graduate school may need to weigh the advantages and disadvantages of lost time and money versus a change of major to a different field.

Advisors can often help students articulate new goals in a specific form and help them see alternative routes to these goals. Advisors can also help students systematically look at possible changes from all perspectives so that when the student makes the decision, the most probable outcomes have been considered.

Professional College Changers. Another important group needing help with educational and vocational planning is the preprofessional student who is rejected from professional colleges or the upperclass student who decided not to apply to professional colleges even though that was an initial goal.

The fear of rejection is always in the back of most preprofessional students' minds, and they often select an undergraduate major as something "to fall back on, just in case." Some preprofessional students select themselves out of a professional program because they realize their grades or scores on standardized admissions tests are too low. Others simply change their minds about wanting to be a physician or a lawyer. Still others find the financial drain would be too great.

Whatever the reasons for not continuing on to a professional education, a special kind of academic advising is needed. As upperclass students, they need to understand how their current course work can be applied to other undergraduate programs. Others will simply need to work with a placement officer to determine other occupational alternatives with their current major. Some of these students may also look at other graduate programs. The advisor's role is to help them identify realistic alternatives and help them work with the appropriate resources on campus. An advisor can provide the personal support these students need as they explore alternative programs and goals.

Honors/Gifted Students. Students with high academic potential are another challenging group needing special help with educational planning. Electing the honors program option generally signifies that students have a strong desire to learn and have a need for intellectual recognition. Many, however, do not have the maturity or experiences necessary to make long-range vocational plans.

Perrone, Male, and Karshner (1977) have identified some career development concerns unique to gifted and talented students: (1) They are told at an early age that they are capable of succeeding in any career and may avoid testing their true competencies because of fear of failure or avoidance of success. (2) Since they receive so much reinforcement, they may find it more difficult to measure up to such expectations. (3) They tend to foreclose too early on a career choice, based solely on recognition and success in a particular academic field. (4) Their career interests and values need to be based on a wide range of experiences that are not usually part of the school curriculum. (5) Talented individuals often experience conflict between achieving excellence and being normal. (6) Talented people may become lifelong students because the role is comfortable. (7) Talented students may view a career as their principal means of self-expression and worth.

Multipotentiality presents a dilemma for gifted students since it carries beyond intellectual ability. Bright students often engage in a wide variety of social, athletic, and community activities. Since multipotentiality is a characteristic of most gifted students, selection of careers cannot be based on interests and abilities alone. Honors females, in particular, need to clarify their values and understand their motivation so that sex-role stereotypes are recognized as possibly limiting the alternatives they consider.

Overall, the research on exceptionally bright college students has identified some personal characteristics that are important to consider when advising or counseling them. Intellective measures such as test scores and grade point average (GPA), for example, have not proved the best predictors of college persistence or satisfaction for this group. There is a growing awareness that these students have unique characteristics beyond their ability to achieve that affect the ways they make educational decisions, plan careers, and later adjust to work environments.

Academic and career counselors helping honors students with educational planning and decision making might consider the following tenets in advising them:

1. Some entering honors freshmen need help with adjustment concerns during the first weeks in college. Even bright students, for example, may fall back on ineffective high school study habits and not realize the differences in college courses, curricular requirements, and testing procedures.

2. Many honors students must adjust to the personal and social changes in a new environment and the increased personal responsibility and independence it requires. Although it is often wrongly assumed these students are more capable of this adjustment than others, they too need a great deal of personal contact and support. A few bright students are bewildered and discouraged during their first term in college with their poor academic showing.

3. Some honors students may have made an educational decision so early in their life that they may not have explored any other alternatives. They need time to confirm their choice in a nonpressured atmosphere. Since even the most "decided" students may have doubts, they need the opportunity to compare this choice with other similar and realistic options. Students who have many academic interests also need the opportunity to explore in an open, supportive climate. The danger of a bright student locking in too soon is an example of what Erikson (1968) describes as "identity foreclosure." According to Chickering (1969), many students are not capable of establishing a personal identity until they are juniors or seniors. Developing self-concepts is a critical component of the educational and vocational decision-making process.

4. Some bright students need to be encouraged to stretch themselves and take risks. Advisors can play an important role in encouraging students to stretch their intellectual potential in new and challenging directions.

Students with Special Needs. There are many other special types of students who approach educational planning from different perspectives (see Chapters Ten and Eleven). Adult students often attend college for short-term goals, such as improving their skills for work or wanting something better than their present situation. Other adults simply want to learn for learning's sake and want an educational plan that offers them the opportunity to take a variety of courses and assimilate a broad spectrum of knowledge.

Disabled students and those with learning disabilities also need a very individualized approach to educational planning. Advisors need to work with the appropriate resources on their campus to assure that these students are recognized and counseled in ways that make the college experience a positive and successful one. International students need special attention in scheduling courses initially and in formulating education and career plans that are realistic for their culture.

On many campuses, advisors may be working with very diverse student populations. Advisors need to be sensitive to the needs of each individual student since there may be special needs associated with that student that may not be apparent on first contact.

Summary

Academic advising can become a critical link in helping students with educational decisions and career and life planning. Advisors with knowledge of academic programs, occupational alternatives, and theoretical approaches to the decision-making process can become critical partners in helping individual students successfully plan for the future.

Effective academic advisors recognize that all students confront certain decision-making situations but each student will approach and solve the decision from a very unique developmental perspective. There are certain types of students who need special approaches to educational planning, such as the undecided, major changers, or honors students.

Higher education is training the leaders of tomorrow. Future citizens of society need to be adroit at problem solving and to be comfortable with goal-oriented behavior. Advisors can become role models and provide the support and structure on which tomorrow's citizens will learn, practice, and succeed in developing the effective decision-making skills that will be used over a lifetime.

References

Appel, V., Haak, R., and Witzke, D. "Factors Associated with Indecision about Collegiate Major and Career Choices." *Proceedings of the 78th Annual Convention of the American Psychological Association,* 1970, *5,* 667–668.

Beal, P. E., and Noel, L. *What Works in Student Retention.* Iowa City, Iowa: American College Testing Program and National Center for Higher Education Management Systems, 1980.

Chickering, A. W. *Education and Identity.* San Francisco: Jossey-Bass, 1969.

Clarke, R., Gelatt, H. B., and Levine, L. "A Decision-Making Paradigm for Local Guidance Research." *Personnel and Guidance Journal,* 1969, *44,* 40–51.

Cope, R. G., and Hannah, W. *Revolving College Doors.* New York: Wiley, 1975.

Dilley, J. S. "Decision-Making: A Dilemma and a Purpose for Counseling." *Personnel and Guidance Journal,* 1967, *45,* 547–551.

Erikson, E. *Identity and Crises.* New York: Norton, 1968.

Foote, B. "Determined- and Undertermined-Major Students: How Different Are They?" *Journal of College Student Personnel,* 1980, *21,* 29–34.

Gelatt, H. B., and Clarke, R. B. "Role of Subjective Probabilities in the Decision Process." *Journal of Counseling Psychology,* 1967, *14,* 332–341.

Goodson, W. "Do Career Development Needs Exist for All Students Entering College or Just the Undecided Major Students?" *Journal of College Student Personnel,* 1981, *22,* 413–417.

Goodstein, L. "Behavior Theoretical Views of Counseling." In B. Steffre (Ed.), *Theories of Counseling.* New York: McGraw-Hill, 1965.

Gordon, V. N. "Are Undecided Students Changing?" *Vocational Guidance Quarterly,* 1982, *30,* 265–271.

Harren, V. A. "A Model of Career Decision Making for College Students." *Journal of Vocational Behavior,* 1979, *14,* 119–133.

Harren, V. A. *Assessment for Career Decision Making: Preliminary*

Manual. Carbondale, Ill.: Department of Psychology, Southern Illinois University, 1980.

Herr, E. L. *Decision Making and Vocational Development.* Boston: Houghton Mifflin, 1970.

Holland, J. L. *Making Vocational Choices: A Theory of Careers.* Englewood Cliffs, N.J.: Prentice-Hall, 1973.

Holland, J. L., and Holland, J. E. "Vocational Indecision: More Evidence and Speculation." *Journal of Counseling Psychology,* 1977, *24,* 404-414.

Janis, I. L., and Mann, L. *Decision Making: A Psychological Analysis of Conflict, Choice and Commitment.* New York: Collier Macmillan, 1977.

Lipsett, L. "Social Factors in Vocational Development." *Personnel and Guidance Journal,* 1962, *40,* 432-437.

Osipow, S., Carney, C., and Barak, A. "A Scale of Educational-Vocational Undecidedness: A Typological Approach." *Journal of Vocational Behavior,* 1976, *9,* 233-243.

Perrone, P., Male, R., and Karshner, W. "Career Development Needs of Talented Students: A Perspective for Counselors." *School Counselor,* 1977, *27,* 16-23.

Slaney, R. "Expressed Vocational Choice and Vocational Indecision." *Journal of Counseling Psychology,* 1980, *27,* 122-129.

Thoresen, C. E., and Mehrens, W. A. "Decision Theory and Vocational Counseling: Important Concepts and Questions." *Personnel and Guidance Journal,* 1967, *46,* 165-172.

Tiedeman, D. V., and O'Hara, R. *Career Development: Choice and Adjustment.* New York: College Entrance Examination Board, 1963.

Titley, R. W., and Titley, B. S. "Initial Choice of College Major: Are Only the 'Undecided' Undecided?" *Journal of College Student Personnel,* 1980, *21,* 293-298.

Titley, R. W., Titley, B. S., and Wolff, W. "The Major Changers: Continuity or Discontinuity in the Career Decision Process?" *Journal of Vocational Behavior,* 1976, *8,* 105-111.

6

Integrating
Academic Advising
and Career Planning

᭜ᬺᬻ. ᭜ᬺᬻ. ᭜ᬺᬻ. ᭜ᬺᬻ. ᭜ᬺᬻ. ᭜ᬺᬻ. ᭜ᬺᬻ. ᭜ᬺᬻ.

Wesley R. Habley

As higher education entered the decade of the eighties, it became increasingly apparent that many changes had taken place on college campuses during the previous ten years. These changes signaled the need for increased attention to the area of career and life planning for students.

Background to the Present Dilemma

The National Center for Education Statistics reported a 42 percent increase in the number of college students, from nearly 8 million in 1969 to over 11.5 million in 1979. It is significant to note that there were substantial increases in the number of part-time students and in the number of students who were employed while attending college. The socioeconomic backgrounds of those going to college had also changed substantially. Although brighter students from economically advantaged families with better-educated parents continued to be most likely to attend college, the enrollment of traditionally underrepresented groups, such as blacks, women, and adults, increased significantly during that ten-year period (National Center for Education Statistics, 1969, 1979).

Finally, as might have been predicted, the nature of student concerns and issues noticeably shifted as a result of the increasing diversity of the student body. Although the changing concerns of students were reflected in all aspects of campus life, the issue of career orientation was the most obvious change in student attitudes. This shift in student concern has been reported in the Carnegie surveys of 1978 (Johnson, 1979). In those surveys, student affairs administrators at 586 colleges and universities were asked to describe how students had changed since the 1969–70 academic year. They responded by saying that students in 1977–78 were more career-oriented, more concerned with material success, more concerned with self, and more practical. These opinions underscore the notion that students perceive a college education as the entrée to a career.

Surveys of student attitudes also lead to the same conclusion. In summarizing the findings of the Carnegie studies of 1969 and 1976 and the American Council on Education/University of California at Los Angeles (ACE/UCLA) survey of 1979, Levine (1980) used the term *vocomania* to describe college students' orientation to careers. In 1969, when students were asked to identify the most essential outcomes of a college education, they ranked learning to get along with people first and formulating values and goals for their lives second (Trow, 1975). By 1976, those two expected outcomes were replaced respectively by (a) detailed grasp of a special field and (b) training and skills for an occupation (Roizen, Fulton, and Trow, 1978). During the seven-year period between the studies, the changes in the percentages of students reporting the essential outcomes were training and skills for an occupation (+ 8 percent); detailed grasp of a special field (+ 6 percent); formulating life goals and values (– 9 percent); and learning to get along with people (– 10 percent) (Roizen, Fulton, and Trow, 1978).

A final indicator of increasing student concern for career preparation has been the shift of student choice of major toward vocationally oriented fields. Among the fields that have gained in student popularity are business, agriculture, biology, the health professions, and technical areas. On the other end of the spectrum, education, the humanities, and several social science fields have decreased in popularity (Astin and others, 1980; Creager and others, 1969).

Against this backdrop of increasing student concern for career preparation, higher education and American culture have been faced with a major dilemma. This dilemma has been created by the rapid rate of technological growth coupled with the responsiveness of higher education to that growth.

Alvin Toffler (1970) has observed that the discovery and transmission of new knowledge have increased and continue to increase, at a geometric rate. His example of progress in the field of transportation provides a vivid illustration of that growth. Between 6000 B.C., when the chariot traveled at the rate of 8 miles per hour, and 1825, when the steam locomotive reached the speed of nearly 14 miles per hour, there was little gain in the application of new knowledge to the field of transportation. However, during the last 160 years, the speed of travel has increased over 1,000-fold, to the point where astronauts now orbit the earth at a rate of 18,000 miles per hour. An additional indication of the technological explosion is the dramatic increase in scientific and technological literature. The number of scientific journals and articles is doubling every fifteen years to the point that today, on a worldwide basis, scientific and technical literature increases at the rate of 200,000 pages per day or nearly 70,000,000 pages per year (Toffler, 1970).

Faced with accelerating technological growth, higher education has been unable to develop new programs, particularly in career-related areas, that keep pace with that growth. An important factor in the inability to respond is simply that new knowledge is being discovered faster than it can be transmitted through traditional means. By the time knowledge has been discovered, applied, reported, sorted, transmitted, and learned, it may have already become obsolete. Coupled with the overwhelming growth in the knowledge industry is higher education's inability to quickly redirect its energies and resources. Suffice it to say that higher education, as are most public institutions, is slow to change.

The dilemma then, is that students are becoming much more concerned with career-related curricula at the same time that higher education is less able to provide the learning experiences necessary for such specialized training. And the dilemma is not likely to diminish in the near future.

Responding to the Dilemma

Because it is neither possible to slow the rate of technological growth nor to develop totally effective and responsive change strategies within higher education, it becomes critical for institutions to develop programs for assisting students in coping with a life and a career in which change and technological growth are the only inevitabilities. It is in this context that many institutions are adopting a holistic student development approach to the career- and life-planning needs of students. Such an approach broadens the scope of educational planning from a narrow focus on training for job skills to the broader goal of education-for-life skills. Although there are those who would argue that the mission of higher education has been, and continues to be, the development of life skills, students tend to want to focus on preparation for the narrower, more pragmatic, more materialistic world of work.

Super's Life-Career Theory. One response to the need for a broader approach to the career- and life-planning needs of students is portrayed in the theories of Super (1976) whose concept of the life-career rainbow represents a scheme based on the total development of the individual, rather than focused only on a job or occupation. His theory expands the term *career* to mean the combination and sequence of the roles that one plays in a lifetime and the pattern in which those roles fit together at a given point in time. In describing the life-career rainbow, Super identifies nine life-career roles that may be played by an individual within five life-career theaters (see p. 151).

Super includes several other basic tenets that are critical to the understanding of his theory. First, the roles and theaters are interrelating continuously. It is conceivable that an individual will

Life-Career Roles	*Life-Career Theaters*

Life-Career Roles	*Life-Career Theaters*
1. son/daughter	1. home
2. student	2. community
3. worker	3. school
4. spouse	4. workplace
5. homemaker	5. retirement community or home
6. parent	
7. leisurite	
8. citizen	
9. pensioner	

play several roles simultaneously in different theaters. Second, the various roles may be dominant or subordinate at different stages in life. At one stage work may predominate, with parenting occupying a less prominent position. Conversely, there may come a time when the needs of the family are most important, moving job concerns into a less prominent position. Finally, Super differentiates between the terms *occupation* and *career* by defining occupation as a series of work tasks and career as a sequence of jobs in one particular role, that of worker.

Definition of Academic Advising. Super's theory provides the stimulus for a more encompassing definition of the academic advising process. If one is to assume that the higher-education experience does more than prepare students to get a job, then it also follows that the academic advising students receive as they seek a college degree should lead them to examine the various roles and theaters of life. This approach to the advising function requires that the academic advisor be an active participant in the career- and life-planning process. Not only should advisors be aware of the complexities of human development and the various roles and theaters in which the student must function, but also the advisor must assist the student in utilizing the variety of institutional options that can meet the challenges provided by those roles.

Advising literature is replete with definitions and descriptions of the advising process that focus on the interaction between the student and the advising program. Crockett (1978, p. 10) states that "academic advising assists students to realize the maximum educational benefits available to them by helping them to better understand themselves and to learn to use the resources of an educational institution to meet their special educational needs." Grites (1979, p. 1) focuses on the interaction dimension of the advising relationship by stating that academic advising is "a decision-making process during which students reach their maximum educational potential through communication and information exchanges with an advisor." Both of these definitions focus on securing the most productive outcomes from the advising relationship and have student development as the underlying theme. Crookston underscores the importance of the advising process by defining academic advising as teaching. He states, "Advising is concerned not only with a specific personal or vocational decision, but also with facilitating the student's rational processes, environmental and interpersonal interactions, behavioral awareness, and problem-solving, decision-making, and evaluation skills" (1972, p. 12).

It is clear that each of these definitions of academic advising is student-centered. Furthermore, each definition supports the contention that the advising relationship should be characterized by learning, growth, sharing, decision-making, and maximizing the higher-education experience. None of the definitions describes academic advising as a function that focuses solely on the world of work.

O'Banion's Model. O'Banion (1972) has developed a model for the academic advising process that provides a conceptual framework for sequencing the activities suggested by the Crockett, Grites, and Crookston definitions of academic advising. He describes academic advising as a five-stage process in which each stage in the process builds upon learning and decision-making that takes place in the earlier stages. More importantly, however, O'Banion's model clarifies the significant interrelationship among life planning, career planning, and academic advising. The five stages in the O'Banion model are (1) exploration of life goals, (2) exploration of career/educational goals, (3) selection of an educational program, (4) selection of courses, and (5) scheduling of courses.

Critics of advising programs are quick to point out that most advising focuses on the last two stages of the model. This is due, in part, to the fact that these two stages are information-based. They require minimal understanding of the student development and decision-making processes and focus almost entirely on the exchange of factual information between the advisor and student. That is, once a student has selected an educational program, student and advisor adhere to a predetermined pattern for the selection and sequencing of courses and follow published institutional guidelines for course scheduling.

Although the O'Banion model clearly describes five important stages in the advising process, problems arise that have made it difficult to move his theory into practice. These difficulties stem from the traditional delivery of academic advising by faculty, which remains the most prevalent delivery system for advising. Yet many faculty are not able to provide the full range of services suggested by the O'Banion model. There are at least two major reasons for this. First, some faculty assume that because a student has chosen a particular major, it also follows that the student has an understanding of and commitment to that major and that student commitment to a major is indicative of previous exploration and reasoned decision making. Of course, this assumption is generally faulty. Changing majors is, indeed, a common occurrence. But the assumption does permit faculty advisors to focus primarily on the course selection and scheduling stages of the O'Banion model.

The second, and more pervasive, problem with the implementation of the O'Banion model is the capacity of the faculty advisor to provide the support necessary for accomplishing the first three stages in the process. Faculty advisors are discipline-oriented and, therefore, may not have the skills necessary to assist students in the exploration of life, career, and educational goals that leads to the selection of an educational program. Even more significant is that even if faculty advisors have the desire and the skills necessary to assist students in the first three stages of the O'Banion model, lack of time and the sheer number of students make it difficult to complete those tasks. These problems make it virtually impossible for the O'Banion model to reach the implementation stage in an advising system that relies *solely* on faculty members for the delivery of services.

An Advising Process/Intervention Model

In spite of the seemingly insurmountable barriers created by the intersection of student careerism, increasing technological growth, and higher education's incapacity for rapid change, the ability of an institution to provide career- and life-planning services remains a critical element in meeting the needs of today's students. And although the academic advising process continues to offer the possibility of providing the most meaningful medium to deliver those services to students on an individual basis, the inability to convert existing theory into practice, exacerbated by the low skill levels of advising personnel, has fostered an unfortunate impasse in the delivery of career- and life-planning services.

Perhaps the major assumption that has led to these circumstances is flawed. That assumption is that if academic advising, career planning, and life planning are inextricably related in theory, then it should follow in practice that the academic advisors can deliver the full range of career- and life-planning services. This is, in reality, a spurious assumption. The scope and depth of skills needed to assist students in these areas are of such magnitude that it is not possible for an academic advisor to provide all of those services to each student.

Realistically, a fully functioning model for delivering career- and life-planning services requires the careful integration of all student support services on the campus. These functions include, but are not limited to, advising, orientation, counseling, placement, learning assistance, testing, and educational opportunity programs. The exemplary program of career and life planning does not require the academic advisor to become a specialist in all areas. As Lindquist (1982) suggests, the advising program should serve as the hub of a support services model, and the academic advisor should become the key contact in the implementation of a comprehensive career- and life-planning program. The academic advisor is in a position to identify planning concerns, to make tentative assessments on the scope of those concerns, and, if the advisor's skill level is appropriate for dealing with the concerns, to provide direct assistance to the student. It is very probable, however, that individual advisors cannot meet all those needs. Consequently, student affairs units and other support agencies must play a major role in the delivery of career- and life-planning programs. That role is to (1) assist the advisor in understanding and identifying areas of student need, (2) provide the advisor with an understanding of the basic services offered, and (3) serve as a referral and feedback resource for advisors.

Clearly then, the success of career- and life-planning services is highly dependent on the extent to which well-organized and integrated student affairs and other support services interface with the function of academic advising. Without this integration, the ability to deliver effective career- and life-planning services will be minimized.

Once the importance of the integration of academic advising with other career- and life-planning services is understood, it becomes possible to define an advising process that delineates the roles played by both the academic advisor and the other support services that are involved in the career- and life-planning process. In addition, it becomes possible to define advising as a sequential pattern that identifies critical intervention points for the academic advisor. The advising process/intervention model (Figure 1) depicts the relationship between advising and other support services and also provides a sequential pattern for structuring the advising relationship.

In the model, eleven tasks in the career- and life-planning process are presented. An important aspect of this model is that there is no presumption regarding the skill levels of individual academic advisors. Rather, advisors must exhibit attitudes and understandings conducive to the effective functioning of the model. These attitudes and understandings include (1) concern for student development, (2) willingness to participate in both the advising program and the training necessary to implement it, (3) awareness of institutional policies and procedures, and (4) a thorough understanding of the roles played by student affairs and other support services.

At each step in the model, an academic advisor may work with the student to accomplish the particular task or, if necessary,

Figure 1. Advising Process/Intervention Model.

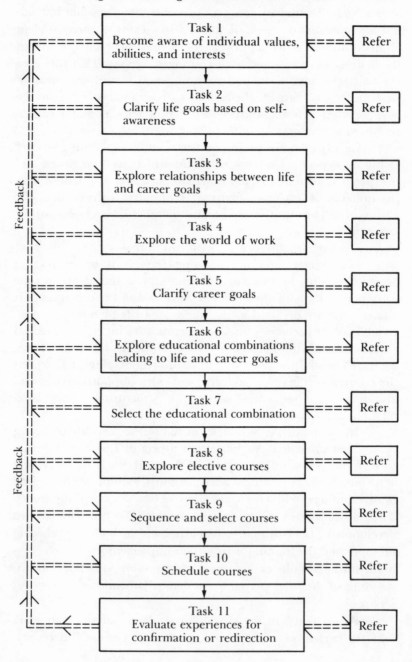

refer that student to available support services that can provide the student with more specialized assistance. In that sense then, the model is applicable to the variety of advising structures that exist in colleges and universities. In those institutions where faculty advising is the primary delivery system, it could be expected that there would be a heavy reliance on support services, particularly in tasks 1 through 5. Institutions with specialized or centralized advising programs would probably be in a position to deliver some or all of the services necessary to assist students in the accomplishment of the first five tasks.

Since the model stresses the relationship between the advising process and a variety of services that support that process, coordination of effort is a paramount concern. It is essential that the units involved in the model participate in collaborative planning efforts that minimize duplication of services and maximize cooperative programming. Even more essential, however, is the development of an advising support network in which services are efficiently organized and clearly communicated not only to advisors but also to students.

Another feature of the advising process/intervention model is that it provides a feedback mechanism so that advisors and students may return to earlier tasks if decisions and actions taken in accomplishing a later task are not supported by the student's actual experiences. This aspect of the model underscores the importance of continual evaluation in the career- and life-planning process.

Finally, the model may be used as a tool to assist students in gaining greater insights into both the complexity and the importance of sound planning and decision making in relation to career and life planning. The model also provides the student with a series of exploratory goals that direct the planning process. Each task, if successfully accomplished, increases the probability of success in completing ensuing tasks. And the progressive realization of goals stipulated in each task leads to the more encompassing activation of career and life plans.

Task 1: Become aware of individual values, abilities, and interests. This exploratory activity is often difficult to accomplish, but it is an absolutely essential task in the career- and life-planning process. Although most students provide evidence of their values in conversation with their advisors, few have taken the time to articulate and prioritize those values. And far fewer students are aware of either the role that values should play in the career- and life-planning process or the problems that can be created when values are in conflict with each other. Students who need assistance with this task are identified by the inability to identify and/or verbalize value statements.

In the value awareness portion of task 1, it is sometimes helpful for an advisor to focus on selected values of the individual students, and it is most critical for the advisor to be nonjudgmental, adhering to the premise that values are personal determinations and are unique from one individual to another. It is possible to begin the discussion of values by asking the question "What is important to you?" Unfortunately, very few students will be comfortable responding to such a general inquiry. Therefore, it is suggested that advisors raise value issues with students by presenting several values and asking for students to respond to them. Possible value issues that could be raised are independence, security, helping others, education, variety, prestige, leadership, and/or leisure time. This is a limited list of possibilities, but these values have significance in the career- and life-planning process.

In assisting students to a better understanding of abilities, the advisor should have a number of tools available to stimulate discussion. Among these are the high school transcript, standardized and placement test results, and college academic record. Although these sources of information provide a general picture of academic ability, it is important to note that the discussion of abilities should also include a look into the future. Students should not only be encouraged to focus on their existing abilities as evidenced by such information but also on the abilities they would like to develop and those which they would like to improve.

Finally, the advisor should encourage the exploration of students' interests. This has been a somewhat neglected facet of awareness, but it is crucial in the establishment of the relationship between career and life goals that takes place in task 3. In many cases, the discussion of interests will lead to areas outside the domain of academe. This discussion could be stimulated by asking students how they spend their leisure time or what hobbies they have. The insights that are gained from this discussion play an important role in educational decisions.

Task 2: Clarify life goals based on self-awareness. Drawing on the understandings gained in task 1, task 2 involves asking students to make broad statements about some of their goals in life. Students begin formulating statements of their expectations for themselves that are centered on home, community, school, and workplace activities. One way for the advisor to assess the completion of this task is to ask the student to write brief statements on each of Super's life-career theaters and life-career roles. These statements should be general in nature; that is, the statements should not be so specific as to preclude options that may surface in later tasks. It is important for advisors to address the consistency, or lack thereof, between these broad statements and the values, abilities, and interests that were investigated in the first task.

Task 3: Explore relationship between life and career goals. It is at this juncture that the student and the advisor work together to reach a deeper understanding of the interplay among life and career goals. Preoccupation with jobs is common among students. One indicator of the need for attention to this task comes from the student who consistently refers to career and life goals as if they were bipolar dimensions.

Super's (1976) life-career rainbow is an excellent resource for this task. Of major significance is Super's description of the life-career roles and his broader definition of career as the combination and sequence of the roles that one plays in a lifetime and the pattern in which those roles fit together at a given point in a person's life. It is critical that students understand that the workplace is only one of five life-career theaters and that the role of worker is only one of nine roles in the life-career rainbow.

Finally, it is extremely important for the advisor to begin a discussion of the significance of the collegiate experience in developing skills that can be used in each of life's theaters and roles. This discussion should help to counteract the vocationalism that is characteristic of many of today's students. By exposing the student to the need for a multidimensional approach to the selection of appropriate educational goals, it is possible to expand student receptivity to a wide variety of educational options that the student had not previously considered.

Task 4: Explore the world of work. Although many students gain employment experience through part-time or summer jobs, few of them understand the relationship between the world of work and conscientious life and career planning. Although the first three tasks provide the advisor with indications of the need for assistance, this task is one that should be addressed with all students. This assertion is based on the notion that all students can benefit from an in-depth exploration of the relationship between individual personality and the world of work.

In order for an occupation to meet individual needs, there should be a match between the individual's values and abilities and the environmental characteristics of that occupation. Holland's (1973) theory of careers proposes that personality and work environments are closely related. Four working assumptions summarize Holland's theory.

1. Most persons can be characterized as one of six personality types: realistic, investigative, artistic, social, enterprising, or conventional.
2. There are six basic working environments: realistic, investigative, artistic, social, enterprising, and conventional.
3. People search for environments that will let them exercise their skills and abilities, express their attitudes and values, and take on agreeable problems and roles.
4. A person's behavior is determined by an interaction between his personality and the characteristics of his environment [1973, p. 2-4].

Holland's theory is the basis for the *Self-Directed Search*, a self-scoring instrument that measures the six dimensions of personality listed above. The popularity of both Holland's theory and the *Self-Directed Search* are testimony to the need for students to give serious consideration to the working environments associated with particular occupations. More importantly, however, the work of

Holland serves as the focal point for understanding the interrelationship between life and career planning and the world of work.

Task 4 may be the most difficult task with which an advisor and a student must wrestle. This assertion is based on two factors. First, academic advisors have only limited knowledge of the variety of working environments. This knowledge may have been gained through firsthand work experience or through observation of a variety of occupations. The second factor that makes task 4 difficult to accomplish is the changing nature of the world of work. It is not realistic to expect an academic advisor to keep abreast of the continuously changing world of work. As a result, the advisor must rely heavily on support services for developing programs that assist students in completing this task. (Several program ideas that aid students in the exploration of the world of work are described in the final section of this chapter.)

Task 5: Clarify career goals. Task 5 is a benchmark in the career- and life-planning process. Tasks 1 through 4 focus on self-awareness and information gathering, but task 5 is the first task that requires action-oriented decision making from the student. At this point the student has worked with the advisor, and possibly support programs, to obtain an assessment of self, an awareness of the relationship between life and career goals, and a general understanding of the world of work. Synthesis is the key to clarifying career goals. The academic advisor can assist the student in synthesizing the information gathered in the first four tasks to the point where career options can be identified. Although many students have decided on a specific direction by this time, it is critical to note that the outcome of this task is not necessarily the identification of a major. Rather, the outcome of task 5 should be the identification of career areas that appear to be consistent with the individual student's needs. Students who are unable to define those career areas may need to return to earlier tasks for re-examination. In other instances, decision-making deficits may require an advisor to refer the student to supporting programs.

Task 5 is critical in another sense, for it is the point at which traditional academic advising systems begin to offer assistance to students. It should be obvious that the definition of advising that undergirds the advising process/intervention model includes dimensions that have not commonly been identified with the advising function. To attempt to meet the career- and life-planning needs of students without careful attention to the first four tasks of the model is analogous to departing for an unknown destination without the aid of a map and in a vehicle that you do not know how to operate.

Task 6: Explore educational combinations leading to life and career goals. In task 6, the curriculum of the college or university enters the career- and life-planning process for the first time. In this task the advisor and the students explore institutional alternatives for implementing the career goals that were derived in task 5. It is important for the advisor and the students to examine combinations of majors, minors, sequences, and course clusters. There may be more than one way for the students to achieve their life and career goals through the creative design of an educational program, and it is incumbent upon the students and the advisor to explore each of the available alternatives. The institution may provide a major that is tailored to a particular student's career and life goals. In other cases, the only route to achieving a goal may be through a double major or a major-minor combination. However configured, the identification of alternatives and combinations within the institution that lead to the students' career and life goals is the desired outcome of task 6.

It is probably necessary for the advisor and the students to consider the selection and scheduling of introductory courses at this stage. This is particularly useful if students have multiple alternatives available to them or if their career goals are still broadly defined. Although this interim stage will require the investment of an academic term, it should enable the students to confirm or narrow the choice of educational combination.

Task 7: Select the educational combination. A segment of Crockett's definition is descriptive of task 7: "Use the resources of an educational institution to meet their special educational needs" (1978, p. 1.0). The resources of the institution are not only the majors, minors, and sequences offered but also the variety of combinations that can be orchestrated to meet the individual goals of the students.

Although this task requires the making of a critical decision, it is far from being a point of no return. Through activities accomplished in the previous six tasks, the students and the advisor should be in a position to identify which of the alternatives will most likely lead to the accomplishment of the students' goals. Certainly, previous courses taken and information gained through other sources either have enabled the students to confirm initial career direction or have reduced the number of alternatives to the point where those alternatives are manageable.

It is also possible, however, that a student may have discovered that the institution does not offer an educational combination that is consistent with her or his goals. If this is the case, the advisor and the student should explore the possibility of transfer to another institution that offers a program more consistent with those goals. Since few advisors are equipped to respond to this concern, a referral to another support agency should probably result.

Task 8: Explore elective courses. The utility of elective courses is sometimes overlooked in the academic advising process. This is due, in part, to students' concern with completing required courses in their academic programs. While there are academic programs in which the student has little latitude in course selection, most degree programs permit students to explore elective courses. These elective courses can be used to provide students with the opportunity to explore new subject areas, investigate subjects that may not be directly related to the chosen educational program, or pursue other areas of interest. It is important for the advisor and the student to take advantage of electives as a mechanism for rounding out the academic program.

Task 9: Sequence and select courses. At this point in the academic advising process, attention is focused on the selection and sequencing of courses. The advisor and the student must take into account such things as prerequisites, required courses in the major and minor fields, general education requirements, and elective courses in arriving at a class schedule that is reflective of the student's goals and abilities. Care should be taken to uncover "hidden prerequisites" in the sequencing of courses. A hidden prerequisite is a course that precedes a specific requirement but is not listed as a required course. In many cases, the decisions and understandings that have been reached in the accomplishment of previous tasks make this activity rather routine.

Task 10: Schedule courses. Depending on the registration system and the availability of courses, this task is also rather routine. Registration procedures are usually well defined. The only real advising concern that surfaces during course scheduling is the inability of students, for whatever reason, to enroll for the courses that have been selected. Since this situation arises fairly often, it is important that the advisor and the student discuss alternative course selections. If alternative strategies for closed classes are developed prior to the registration process, then the frustration of students can be minimized. More importantly, the availability of alternative strategies will reduce the possibility of students' making ill-considered judgments and selecting courses that are not consistent with their individual goals.

Task 11: Evaluate experiences for confirmation or redirection. As with any planning or decision-making model, evaluation must be an ongoing activity. In this task, the advisor and the student must evaluate the outcomes of the learning experiences that take place in the classroom. In many cases, this evaluation will lead to the confirmation that the student has indeed developed an educational plan that is consistent with his or her career and life goals. If this occurs, the advising process returns to task 8 in a recurrent pattern each term.

In other cases, the learning experiences that take place may lead the student to question the educational plan. If this situation occurs, the advisor and the student should investigate the possible sources of the problem. The feedback mechanism in the advising process/intervention model suggests that it is possible to return to any earlier task to examine the concern. In some cases, student dissatisfaction with choice of educational plan may stem from the inability to perform the academic work necessary for a given program. In other situations, courses in the major subject may cause the student to re-evaluate career goals or the balance between life and career goals. The student and the advisor may return to any of the tasks in the advising process/intervention model for clarification. If that is done, it is most appropriate to repeat the sequence of tasks that follow.

Programmatic Implications for Career and Life Planning

As discussed earlier, adhering to such an encompassing definition of academic advising requires a substantial institutional commitment to the integration of advising with other units on the campus. Although there are a wide variety of support services on most campuses, each campus organizes those functions somewhat differently. In addition, the organizational structures employed to deliver academic advising services vary widely from campus to campus. As a result of these two factors, it is difficult to define the career- and life-planning services that may be delivered in terms of the offices that provide them. It is much more useful to provide programmatic suggestions and allow the reader to determine both the efficacy of those suggestions and the service agencies within the institution that might be called upon to implement them. The final section of this chapter deals with program ideas that may be employed to enhance the career- and life-planning process.

Curricular Options. Perhaps the most visible method for delivering career- and life-planning services to students is through incorporation into the curriculum. Wherever possible, curricular possibilities should be explored not only because such activities lend academic credibility to the task of career and life planning but also credit-bearing experiences are most attractive to students. There are at least three levels in which career and life planning can be incorporated into the curriculum: exploration, introduction to a discipline, and internship or cooperative programs.

At the exploration level, many institutions offer credit-generating courses that assist the student in understanding the basic concepts necessary for examining the career- and life-planning process. In these exploratory courses, students make assessments of their values, abilities, and interests and equate those assessments with working environments. In addition, many of these exploratory courses assist students in the development of decision-making skills. Because the focus of these courses is on exploration, less emphasis is placed on the selection of an educational combination. Rather, students learn a process that can be applied to the selection of a major or, for that matter, to the redirection of a career later in life. The availability of exploratory courses can be of great assistance to students and academic advisors, particularly in dealing with tasks 1 through 5 of the advising process/intervention model.

A second exploratory option is the orientation course or freshman seminar. Although orientation courses generally faded from existence during the 1960s, there is an indication of resurgence of this activity. The orientation course is aimed at assisting the freshman student in adjusting to the postsecondary environment. These courses may include traditional topics, such as academic requirements, student affairs program, and student rights and responsibilities. Many courses now include career- and life-planning modules in them. These modules may not be as thorough as complete exploratory courses, but they do provide the student with basic understandings of the relationship between academic planning and career and life goals. As such, orientation courses can provide students and advisors with additional support. (See Chapters One and Seventeen for more details about courses.)

The second level of incorporating career- and life-planning concepts into the curriculum is through the development of courses that provide an introduction to a specific discipline. Such courses should not be confused with survey courses. These introductory courses include topics such as history of the field, degree requirements, options within the discipline, and career opportunities. Where possible, observation of and participation in activities related to the discipline are structured into the course outline. Introductory courses in specific disciplines are extremely beneficial in the advising process, providing the resources to which advisors may refer students who have narrowed their goals to two or three academic programs or allowing the student who has tentatively decided on a major to obtain the information necessary to finalize that decision. Finally, if the course is required of students who have already selected the major, it can either be a confirming experience or may provide the stimulus to search for a more appropriate discipline.

Internship or cooperative programming is the third level at which career and life planning may be infused into the curriculum. If experience is the best teacher, then internship activities can provide the capstone learning experience for clarifying career and life goals. Such activities are designed to give students the benefit of intensive involvement with a particular occupation. Generally, these experiences are only available to senior students, although occupational experiences in some curricula may take place earlier. In addition, at some institutions the lack of available sites to place interns makes the experience unavailable to all but the best students. Nevertheless, the offering of such experiences is an important component of the career- and life-planning process.

Extracurricular Options. Advisors and students should be aware of the role of extracurricular activities in the development of an educational plan that is consistent with career and life goals. The full range of extracurricular activities provides students with the opportunity to gain self-awareness and to develop skills that can be utilized throughout life. Extracurricular involvement includes four major areas: structured programming, student employment, student organizations and activities, and volunteerism.

In the first extracurricular area, the term *structured programming* is used to define any set of formalized learning experiences that take place outside the classroom. For the most part, such programs offer similar experiences to those that have been structured into the curriculum but differ from curricular options in that they are not offered for credit and, generally, are shorter in length and more limited in scope.

Examples of such programs are life-planning workshops, career development seminars, career exploration groups, or vocational counseling workshops. Generally, activities of this type are sponsored by counseling services, the advising office, or the office of career planning and placement and require the commitment of students to participate actively. Because these programs require an investment of student energy over time and because they offer no academic credit, it is sometimes difficult to stimulate and maintain that participation.

Another example of structured programming is the single-session information program. This program can be used in a variety of ways. Among these are degree requirements, major requirements, career options in a particular discipline, or registration procedures. Although such sessions have a limited focus, they often provide students with specific information that may be useful in accomplishing tasks in the advising process/intervention model.

Student employment is the second area in which advisors and students may capitalize on activities outside the classroom. Because an increasing number of college students are involved in part-time work experiences, it may be possible to relate those experiences to the career- and life-planning process. Although it is true that students may be required to take whatever position is available to them, it is often possible to find part-time and summer employment that is related to the educational plan. Even jobs that are peripherally related to the academic discipline should be encouraged. Employment options can stimulate the exploration process and should not be overlooked as a source for clarifying career and life goals.

The third area of extracurricular involvement is participation in student organizations and activities. Departmental clubs and special interest organizations provide students with the opportunity to develop skills in leadership and group interaction. In addition, many of the departmental clubs provide programs that present information useful in the career- and life-planning process. A fully developed program of student organizations and activities is an enhancement to career- and life-planning services on the campus.

Finally, volunteerism is an extracurricular program that can introduce students to a wide variety of career options. Volunteerism is particularly useful for students who hope to enter helping professions, such as education, health services, social work, or other areas of public service. In addition, volunteer activities provide students with the opportunity to develop human relations skills that are necessary in almost any life situation. Although most students would prefer an employment opportunity, often volunteerism is the only way that they may gain exposure to a particular career area, and, as a resource for advisors and students, volunteer work should not be overlooked.

Use of Human Resources. Although the career- and life-planning process is an activity that requires a great deal of interaction between the student and the advisor, there are, in addition to support agencies, other human resources that can assist in the process. Among these are peers, alumni, retired adults, and community employers. In most cases, these human resources remain virtually untapped.

Students comprise what is perhaps the most underutilized human resource on the campus. Students who are well trained and closely supervised can deliver many of the services that have traditionally been provided by academic advisors. Although it may not be possible to provide peer counselors with the depth and breadth of training necessary for many tasks in the advising process/intervention model, it is possible they can be called upon to assist in the delivery of programs that support the career- and life-planning process. In addition, peers can be of great assistance in the exploration of elective courses, the selection and sequencing of courses, and the scheduling of courses. The design of an effective peer program may free the academic advisor for the more complex tasks found in the advising process/intervention model.

Unfortunately, the institution's only contact with alumni may come in the annual fund-raising appeal. In many cases, alumni would like to support the institution but find themselves unable to make a financial contribution. Soliciting alumni participation in career- and life-planning programs is one way to promote continuing alumni-institution contact while assisting undergraduate students in the career- and life-planning process. Alumni may be invited to participate in on-campus discussions with students about majors, careers, and life experiences. Such programs can be both informative for students and stimulating for the alumni.

Another concept in which the alumni may be involved is shadowing. The shadowing concept puts an individual student in contact with an alumnus who is willing to share career and educational experiences. In addition, the shadowing concept offers two distinct advantages. First, because the student will most likely visit with the alumnus at her or his place of work, the student can gain additional insights into the world of work. Second, the alumnus is not required to travel to campus to participate in the program. As a result, alumni can participate in campus programming without a substantial commitment of time and travel.

Both the campus-based and shadowing programs may also be implemented using retired adults in the community. This constituency usually has the time and, in many cases, a great deal of interest in making contact with traditional-age college students. Many institutions offer reduced tuition or other benefits for senior citizens to attract them to the collegial environment. The possibilities for learning and sharing between retired adults and college students can form the basis for an excellent career exploration program.

Finally, although the community setting varies greatly from campus to campus, the resources of the community should not be overlooked. Area business and industry can provide more than placement for internships and cooperative programs. Many business leaders are willing to participate in group or individual programs that assist students in the career- and life-planning process. And involving those individuals can produce the peripheral benefit of improving "town-gown" relationships.

Computer-Assisted Career Exploration. During the last ten years, there has been a concerted attempt to incorporate computer technology into the career- and life-planning process. Among the more prominent efforts in this area are the DISCOVER system marketed by the American College Testing Program and the System of Interactive Guidance and Information (SIGI) that has been developed by the Educational Testing Service. In addition, several statewide vocational networks offer computerized career exploration programs. Although the cost of these systems may appear to be prohibitive, when calculated on a per-user basis, the cost factors become more reasonable.

Computer-assisted career exploration activities offer three significant advantages. First, computers can provide a systematic examination of career and life values. And, as a result, computer systems are capable of providing students with an efficient and comprehensive understanding of the first three tasks in the advising process/intervention model. Since these are usually the most complex and time-consuming tasks in the model, the use of computer-assisted activities can prove to be an excellent resource. Second, most computer-assisted career exploration systems provide in-depth data on the world of work including occupational outlook, minimum educational requirements, and job descriptions. This information is extremely valuable in accomplishing task 4 in the model. Finally, because most of these systems are user interactive, they provide students with an introduction to the computer. Although this skill is not directly related to career exploration, it is certainly a valuable skill in this increasingly technological age.

Assessment Instruments. The availability and utility of assessment instruments that may be used to support the career- and life-planning process are of such magnitude that an entire chapter, indeed a volume, could be used to describe them (see Chapter Eleven for some examples). Because of the wide variety in both content and application of assessment instruments, it is important that several principles regarding their use be presented. First, the selection of an instrument should be made carefully so that the instrument measures what is needed to support the career and life process. Second, those who administer and/or interpret the assessments should be thoroughly trained in measurement. Finally, assessment instruments should be considered as only one piece in the career- and life-planning puzzle. There is no instrument that conclusively measures the most appropriate career and life goals for an individual.

Summary

The career- and life-planning process is inextricably woven into the function of academic advising. Because the academic advising process is one in which all students participate, it is essential that academic advisors equate that process with the broader mission of career and life planning. In this chapter, an advising process/intervention model that depicts and describes eleven sequential career- and life-planning tasks has been presented. The model underscores the need for integration of academic advising with other support services on the campus and provides the framework for structuring the relationship between advisor and student.

References

Astin, A. W., and others. *The American Freshman: National Norms for Fall 1979.* Los Angeles: Cooperative Institutional Research Program, Laboratory for Research in Higher Education, Graduate School of Education, University of California, 1980.

Creager, J. A., and others. *National Norms for Entering College*

Freshmen—Fall 1969. Washington, D.C.: American Council on Education, 1969.

Crockett, D. S. (Ed.). *Academic Advising: A Resource Document*. Iowa City, Iowa: American College Testing Program, 1978.

Crookston, B. B. "A Developmental View of Academic Advising as Teaching." *Journal of College Student Personnel*, 1972, *13*, 12-17.

Grites, T. J. *Academic Advising: Getting Us Through the Eighties*. Washington, D.C.: American Association for Higher Education–Educational Resource Information Center (AAHE-ERIC)/ Higher Education Research Report No. 7, 1979.

Holland, J. L. *Making Vocational Choices: A Theory of Careers*. Englewood Cliffs, N.J.: Prentice-Hall, 1973.

Holland, J. L. *The Self-Directed Search*. Palo Alto, Calif.: Consulting Psychologists Press, 1977.

Johnson, S. *Survey of Institutional Adaptations*. Berkeley, Calif.: Carnegie Council for Policy Studies in Higher Education, 1979.

Levine, A. *When Dreams and Heroes Died: A Portrait of Today's College Student*. San Francisco: Jossey-Bass, 1980.

Lindquist, J. "When Advising Is the Hub." Paper presented at the Sixth National Conference on Academic Advising, San Jose, Calif., October 1982.

National Center for Education Statistics. *Opening Fall Enrollment, 1969*. Washington, D.C.: U.S. Government Printing Office, 1969.

National Center for Education Statistics. *Opening Fall Enrollment, 1979*. Washington, D.C.: U.S. Government Printing Office, 1979.

O'Banion, T. "An Academic Advising Model." *Junior College Journal*, 1972, *44*, 62-69.

Roizen, J., Fulton, T., and Trow, M. *Technical Report: 1975 Carnegie Council National Surveys of Higher Education*. Berkeley: Center for Studies in Higher Education, University of California, 1978.

Super, D. E. *Career Education and the Meanings of Work: Monographs on Career Education*. Washington, D.C.: U.S. Government Printing Office, 1976.

Toffler, A. *Future Shock*. New York: Random House, 1970.

Trow, M. (Ed.). *Teachers and Students: Aspects of American Higher Education*. New York: McGraw-Hill, 1975.

7

Enhancing Students' Intellectual and Personal Development

᪥᪥᪥ ᪥᪥᪥ ᪥᪥᪥ ᪥᪥᪥ ᪥᪥᪥ ᪥᪥᪥ ᪥᪥᪥ ᪥᪥᪥

James C. Hurst, Gene A. Pratt

Historically, "student development" appears to have been an enigma to academic affairs and student affairs alike. The difficulty inherent in understanding, defining, and measuring the phenomena of change in student intellect, affect, and behavior is a major challenge to all educational enterprises.

The temptation to label complex constructs with a simple descriptor has led to the myth and the tyranny of the "credit hour" in higher education. The credit hour is a myth; although it is a unit of time spent in a designated activity, most administrative and academic personnel treat it as an actual unit of student growth or development. It comprises a tyranny—readiness for graduation is determined by counting them, verification of a major is determined through the discipline in which they occur, faculty work load is defined by the number taught each semester, departments and colleges are funded according to the number generated each term, credit hours produced by institutions justify allocations received from legislatures, and in many cases advisors recommend class schedules as a reflection of "hours" needed in specified disciplines and activities. The credit hour seems to have become an entity in itself and is endowed with the validity of a unit of measurement that in turn dictates.

The real tragedy of this circumstance is that students, quick to model and adapt, begin to think in terms of goals related to credit hour accumulation rather than experiential increments of human development. It is certainly easier to determine class standing, from freshman to senior, by numbers of credit hours earned rather than by predetermined and measurable levels of maturity. A danger lies in the acquired belief that the college experience is constructed around the credit hour rather than systematically planned experiences leading to greater maturity within a developmental framework.

Nowhere is this danger more prevalent than in the advisor/advisee interaction. The enlightened advisor looks beyond the credit hours to be arranged into a term-by-term class load, diligently helping students identify opportunities and experiences designed to induce in them the characteristics of the educated person. The enlightened advisor works to build advisory systems designed to have an impact on not just one student at a time as the student comes to the office but on whole populations of students as active agents in the educational enterprise.

Student affairs professionals have, in recent years, acquired significant sophistication in the area of student development and are therefore in a position to provide leadership for professionals in academic affairs, especially in the realm of academic advising. This chapter describes a blueprint for understanding student development in general and intellectual and personal development in particular, introduces a model for the process of advising, and describes a variety of advising activities as actual examples of the blueprint and the model. With student development theory as a blueprint, a process model as the tool, and practical applications to provide a perception of finished products, the advisor is prepared to avoid the entrapment of myths and tyrannies and to guide students through experiences designed to create in them the essence of the educated person.

Student Development Theory

Widick, Knefelkamp, and Parker (1980) reviewed the theories and models of student development and categorized them into five general approaches. *Psychosocial theories* emphasize development through a series of life stages that converge to define the life cycle (Erikson, 1963; Chickering, 1969; and Keniston, 1971). *Cognitive development theories* describe development as a series of irreversible stages and processes by which the individual perceives and reasons about the world (Piaget, 1964; Perry, 1970; Kohlberg, 1971; and Loevinger, 1976). *Maturity models* define "whole" individuals composed of self-systems of intellect, values, self-concept, and interpersonal relationships and relate these systems to growth dimensions (Heath, 1977). *Typology models* deal with characteristic and stable ways in which individuals perceive and respond to situations through a sequence of development (Heath, 1964; Cross, 1976). *Person-environment interaction models* emphasize the interdependence of individuals and their environments in each shaping the other (Stern, 1964; Pervin and Smith, 1968; Holland, 1973; and Moos, 1976). All these theories or models are in essence blueprints of student development, each drawn from a different perspective. Each is in its own way valuable to academic advisors as they assist students along developmental paths.

A Student Development Model. Drum (1980) described a model for student development that seems particularly adaptable for use by the academic advisor. He identified five assumptions to describe both the finished product and the process of student development. The areas within which development occurs in students include cognitive structures, esthetics, identity formation, physical self, moral reasoning, interpersonal relatedness, and social perspective.

Drum's first assumption is that development in students is characterized by greater richness and complexity within the seven areas, greater internal consistency and integration across areas, and the ability to process ever finer discriminations with regard to good and poor quality, good and poor judgment, functional and non-functional moral reasoning, and the consistent communication or projection of an integrated person.

The second assumption that Drum identified in this effort to describe a blueprint of student development is that, as development occurs, the beliefs, values, and judgments of the student move from an external locus, based on what the student perceives as presses from external sources, to a more internalized and integrated set of personalized beliefs, values, and judgments.

The third assumption deals with process rather than product and identifies development as continuous. It is characterized by a gradual and consistent blending from a less mature stage into one that is more mature.

Assumption four modifies the third assumption slightly with the notation that, although developmental change may be continuous, it is certainly not systematically one dimensional. Developmental advancement includes regressions, periods of stabilization, and periods during which great leaps of change appear to take place.

Finally, the fifth assumption notes that such quantitative changes as shifts from an existing value, the acquisition of new skills, the better acquisition/utilization of data in decision making, and the development of slightly different tastes or preferences are building blocks upon which future change may occur with greater intensity and breadth.

Table 1 summarizes Drum's blueprint for student development. As can be seen in that table, he has identifed seven areas of development and has broken each of those areas down into three levels. Those seven areas can be outlined as follows:

1. *Cognitive structures.* Students progress from a simplistic point of view, wherein everything is perceived as an absolute (black or white, right or wrong), through a relativistic view, in which a wide variety of perspectives can be identified as relevant to any belief, to a reflective stance, wherein students are capable of using multiple perspectives to come to a conclusion with which they feel comfortable.

Table 1. Drum's Analysis of Student Development.

Areas of Development	Levels of Development		
	Basic	Expansive	Refined
Cognitive structures	Simplistic	Relativistic	Reflective
Esthetic development	Instilled preferences	Broadened appreciation	Enhanced sensitivity
Identity formation	Conforming	Experimental	Intentional
Physical self	Unintentional practices	Selective management	Personal responsibility
Moral reasoning	Externalized locus	Internalized locus	Integrated
Interpersonal relatedness	Self-centered	Role-dominated	Intimate
Social perspective	Ethnocentric	Culturally relativistic	Anthropocentric systems

Source: Drum, 1980, p. 25.

2. *Esthetic development.* Students move beyond instilled preferences, which are often the unexamined inheritances from one's
family, through a broadened appreciation of esthetic richness,
to an enhanced sensitivity wherein the students pursue personalized images of beauty in art, drama, music, architecture, and
other elements in the environment.

3. *Identity formation.* This is one of the most crucial areas of
development for the college student. Students move away from
an identity formation based on blind conformity, through a
process of careful experimentation with a variety of introspective experiences associated with identity formation, to a final
stage wherein the student is clearly able to discuss the questions
"Who am I?" and "In what direction am I presently moving?"

4. *Physical self.* This development appears to be inseparable from
cognitive and affective development. The college experience
has long been perceived as a time and place to address continuing physical development. Drum uses the "unintentional
practices" concept to describe the unexamined incorporation of
family-taught ideas about physical health development. Advanced levels of development move through a phase of selective
management of good health practices to a level of personal
responsibility wherein the individual demonstrates an under-

standing of a comprehensive program of good health practices and incorporates the understanding in daily life.

5. *Moral reasoning.* This dimension of student development parallels the importance of identity formation. Earlier stages of moral development are characterized as having an external-ized locus that guides a student's conclusions with regard to morality and immorality. Conformity to parental standards sets societal trends; the conclusions of peers and expectations of authorities rob the student of individuality. On the other hand, a totally internalized locus for moral reasoning implies greater reflection along the lines of "I am the judge of what's best" but fails to incorporate the balance between external and internal contributions to moral reasoning. The integrated locus identified by Drum describes an individual able to integrate personal reflection with external factors in order to formulate an integrated moral stance that shapes beliefs and guides behaviors.

6. *Interpersonal relatedness.* Students progress through earlier levels of development characterized as self-centered, through middle developmental levels that are role-dominated, to the highest form of interpersonal development characterized as one wherein intimacy is attained through relationships of commit-ment, autonomy, freedom, trust, openness, and self-awareness.

7. *Social perspective.* Students progress through an ethnocentric, cultural relativistic, and anthropocentric path of increasing maturity. Less mature persons perceive their own culture as the only standard of the human condition, while more mature persons are capable of a more objective assessment of various cultures as a rich variety of expression of the human condition.

Developmental Advising. The advisor enlightened by Drum's student development blueprint is one who goes far beyond simply filling free time with college courses and credit hours toward a thoughtful, reflective, and studied process whereby the student's *cognitive structures* are enriched through experiences designed to challenge simplistic and relativistic ways of thinking and to incor-porate more reflective cognitive processes. The enlightened advisor will direct and encourage the student to expand *esthetic* horizons beyond instilled preferences through a broadened appreciation and to enhance the student's sensitivity toward a personalized image of beauty. The *identity formation* of the student is a central concern of the enlightened advisor, who will assist a student in moving beyond that identity that conforms blindly to childhood experiences, through experimental activities, toward an intentional identity that is the result of careful thought and reflection. Students whose *moral reasoning* is based primarily upon the influence of external presses will be assisted by the enlightened advisor in identifying and exploring internalized moral conclusions so that an integrated set of moral standards will emerge and guide the thoughts and actions of the student. The advising of the dedicated advisor will finally assist the student to acquire the capacity to develop his or her *physical self*, a mature *social perspective*, and *interpersonal relatedness* that is satisfying in its reciprocity along the dimensions of commitment, autonomy, freedom, trust, openness, and self-awareness.

The unenlightened advisor fills time with credit hours and courses; the enlightened advisor helps the student identify those challenges and experiences designed to elicit greater approximation to a blueprint of the fully functioning person.

Advising Intervention Model

Advising typically occurs with an advisor sitting at a desk or table with a student poring over class schedules for the purpose of identifying a schedule of classroom and laboratory activities for the student to undertake during a given term. Indeed, this one-on-one circumstance can be a very powerful and effective method of advising. It is not, however, the only format that may be used. Indeed, although potentially effective in a one-on-one situation, it has severe limits when larger-scale impacts are called for.

Morrill, Oetting, and Hurst (1974) developed a three-dimensional conceptual model of intervention strategies for student development that is particularly relevant to the advising process.

The three dimensions of the model as depicted in Figure 1 follow:

1.   The target of the intervention stated most simply may be either (a) the individual or (b) the environments that influence the

Figure 1. Dimensions of Intervention for Student Development.

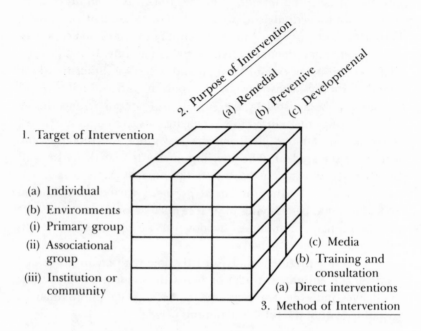

Source: Morrill, Oetting, and Hurst, 1974. Copyright © 1974 by Morrill, Oetting, and Hurst. Used by permission.

individual. The environments that affect the individual include (i) primary groups, (ii) associational groups, and (iii) institutions or communities.

2. The purpose of the intervention may be (a) remedial, (b) preventive, or (c) developmental.

3. The method of reaching the target population may be (a) direct intervention with the target by professionals or administrators, (b) consultation and training of other helping professionals or paraprofessionals, or (c) the use of media as the vehicle for the intervention.

Any intervention of an advising nature may be classified along all three of the dimensions described in Figure 1. That is, every advising intervention is characterized by who or what the intervention is directed toward, why the intervention is attempted, and how the intervention is implemented.

Targets of Advising Interventions. Traditionally, the *individual* has been perceived as the exclusive target of intervention; that is, the interaction between an advisor and a student has been the procedure by which advising took place. The didactic interaction between advisor and advisee is, of course, a powerful and effective process if both have prepared in advance and perceive their task as identifying experiences and activities designed to shape human development rather than simply creating a schedule of classes for enrollment. The key to enhancing dyadic advising lies in the training and orientation of both the advisor and the student. Unfortunately, programs designed to train students to be good advisees are all but nonexistent. There appears to be a prevalent assumption among higher-education professionals that advisors and advisees should instinctively know and be able to implement the process of good advising. In fact, however, there are many more poor than good processes and role models in existence so that inadequate and ineffective procedures are often transmitted from one faculty/student generation to the next.

Ivey (1971) proposed microcounseling as a procedure for interview training. The adaption of Ivey's microcounseling procedure appears to have great potential for training advisors and advisees for a more effective dyadic advising interaction. Essentially, Ivey describes a videotape-assisted procedure wherein trainees, in this case both advisors and advisees, view vignettes of effective and ineffective interactions between an advisor and an advisee. This provides the trainee with the ability to discriminate between good and poor advising. Ivey's model proceeds by interspersing brief didactic explanations of good and poor advising with opportunities for advisors and advisees to observe themselves in a dyadic interaction on videotape. Critiquing of the tape through immediate feedback assists the trainees in acquiring the skills, abilities, and attitudes prerequisite to good advising. Ivey's training paradigm described here or, for that matter, any training paradigm must be an expression of a theoretical formulation if it is to be effective. The conceptualization of student development proposed by Drum earlier in this chapter provides an excellent theoretical base on which such training could take place. For example, a training module using Ivey's model could be developed to train the advisor in how to challenge the student to acquire experiences in each of the seven areas of development. (See Chapters Fifteen and Sixteen for additional discussion about training.)

The dyadic interaction between advisor and student, then, continues to be one of the potentially most powerful procedures by which advising takes place. The individual student is, of course, the target of the intervention in this instance. The process can be greatly enhanced through intentional training and preparation of both advisor and advisee. The systematic training of faculty advisors and of new students entering the educational system through an intentional training paradigm such as that proposed by Ivey (1971) appears to hold great promise for enhancing and improving this traditional approach.

The *environment* within which an individual lives and interacts has a profound effect upon the individual. Lewin (1935), Holland (1973), and Barker (1978) have all written extensively about the impact of the environment upon the individual's behavior and thinking. The three-dimensional model outlined earlier in this section identifies three possible environments of an individual that can be the target for intervention: primary group, associational group, and institution or community.

Within an environmental context, the *primary group* continues to be one of the most powerful influences on individuals. Primary groups are defined as the intimate, continuing personal associations that occur frequently on a face-to-face basis; they are characterized by interpersonal intimacy as opposed to simply physical or geographical proximity. Examples of primary groups on a college or university campus are married student families, sororities and fraternities, religious groups, professional and scholarly societies, roommates or hall mates, and undergraduate or graduate students in the same departmental major. The most common examples of primary groups are families and small groups of friends that are maintained through an extended period of years.

Typically, the conjugal family is the most powerful shaper of behavior and attitudes through the first seventeen years of life. The family then has great potential as a target of intervention designed to assist with the academic advising of a student. Inevitably, advising will occur in a home, either implicitly or explicitly. Advising by the family or primary group can be enhanced by efforts on the part of an elementary or a secondary school system or, for that matter, a postsecondary institution to provide families with accurate information concerning academic options within the institution, the job market, and the world of work in general, prerequisite academic preparation for college majors and various careers, and so on. Back-to-school nights, written materials, career exploration days to which parents and family are invited, and television or newspaper spots are all examples of procedures that can be used in preparing a primary group to better advise a student. In a later section of this chapter, an actual state-wide intervention with the primary group as the target is described.

Associational groups can be advising targets. Bierstedt (1970) described associational groups as collections of individuals who share a consciousness of similar interests, goals, or needs and who join together in some organized way to pursue those interests. Associational groups usually meet relatively frequently to pursue similar interests, goals, and needs. Examples of associational groups are fraternities and sororities, student clubs or guilds, student government groups, and classes. The influence of peer groups on individual behavior during early and late adolescence is well documented (Newcomb and Wilson, 1966; Feldman and Newcomb, 1969). Experienced faculty advisors are usually able to recount stories of individuals who have selected a course of study for an eventual career not through a systematic procedure wherein their interests, skills, abilities, and career characteristics are assessed but rather as a result of what a peer associational group approves or disapproves. Interventions with associational groups in the higher-education system have the potential for informing, training, and shaping constructive attitudes among the associational groups so that the associational group will have a positive influence upon its members. Seminars, workshops, and group efforts can easily be designed to provide advisee training, assess individual skills and interests, explore traits and characteristics associated with various careers, and enlighten the associational group in procedures through which support can be extended to its members.

Finally, the *institution or community* can be the target of advising intervention. Intervention at the institutional level is considerably more complicated than with associational groups. These levels of intervention differ in that members of the institutional group may have only infrequent contact and probably do not know everyone in the organization, as they would in an associational group. They all, however, identify with the institution in some fashion. (If asked, any member could identify him- or herself as a student, a faculty member, or a staff member in the college.)

An example of an advising intervention at an institutional level would be the creation of a new advising center for a college of arts and letters. If the goals and principles of developmental academic advising were adopted, if advisors were trained and evaluated on the basis of those goals and principles, and if publicity was directed toward students to inform them of both the change in philosophy and the availability of new services, then an intervention directed at an institutional level, a college of arts and letters, can be said to have occurred.

A specific instance of one such institutional intervention was at the University of Utah. This institution designed a two-quarter hour course to address the potential problems encountered by high-risk students upon entrance. Students enrolled in this course showed higher grade point averages and retention rates than those in control groups (Landward, 1979).

Purposes of Intervention. The three-dimensional model by Morrill, Oetting, and Hurst gives three purposes for advising interventions: for remediation, for prevention, and for personal development of the students.

Every experienced advisor has had the experience of advising a student who has just been placed on academic suspension as a result of poor academic performance that, in turn, has been the result of poor advising that mismatched student skills and abilities and the demands of a particular college major. Sometimes the influence of the primary group or an associational group has influenced the student in a mismatched direction. Advising interventions to remediate problems that have already occurred are often the most difficult and frequently unrewarding activities for an advisor. Enlightened advisors and institutions make every effort to identify potential problems before they occur so that interventions for *remediation* will be minimized.

Prevention is the result of accurate prediction and a systematic effort to avoid problems before they arise. Early warning programs wherein advisors are notified during the term of advisees who appear to be in academic trouble are an example of preventative advising efforts. Careful assessments of student skills, abilities, and interests prior to initial enrollment in an institution or course of study are also an example of an effort to create a proper match between a student and an academic program and to avoid a mismatch that could eventually lead to a problem and the necessity for remediation. The prevention of problems can also take place through an alert advisor noting that a student is deficient in specific skill areas, such as numerical, verbal, or study habits. Referrals to programs designed to teach generic numerical, writing, or study habit skills are all examples of advising interventions for *prevention*. Reflection on Drum's (1980) model for student development also has utility for advising intervention planning.

Ideally, advisors would not have to struggle to repair damage to advisees but instead could assist students in developing potentials. Advisees with no academic deficiencies and with apparent major career choices that seem appropriate have as much right to the attention of advisors as those who have deficiencies and problems. The effort of the advisor in providing intervention for *personal development* is to identify the horizon of the student's interests and potential in all of the areas identified by Drum (1980) and then assist the student in identifying those activities that will help develop that potential. Banning (1980) describes a "management template" system for campus ecology that is a model for matching campus resources to student interest and potential.

Methods of Advising Interventions. The typical one-on-one dyadic advising relationship, although effective, has a very narrow range of influence. The range, of course, is restricted to the individual receiving the advising. Other methods of intervention may increase the range of influences and in a sense provide greater efficiency in affecting greater numbers of students, primary groups, associational groups, and the institution.

Most advising is simply a *direct* intervention wherein advisors are directly involved in intervening with any of the four target groups previously mentioned (individual, primary group, associational group, institution). It is the method typically accepted. There are, however, other methods by which advising can occur.

Training and consultation programs can be methods of advising students. Training paraprofessionals (as discussed in detail in Chapter Sixteen) to provide advising is a relatively common procedure at many institutions. If done appropriately, a faculty member or student affairs professional will select, train, and supervise upperclass students or part-time individuals in the advising process. The success of these "indirect" methods is a direct reflection of the care taken in the selection, training, supervision, and evaluation process. Consultation on the role and function of advising within a family, associational group, or institution may also be an effective way to have an impact on an advising program. Consultation leading to the increase of rewards for good academic advising or elevating the status of advising through including it as a variable to be considered in promotion and tenure considerations may enhance the advising process.

Media may be used for advising intervention. Interventions with individuals, primary groups, associational groups, or institutions may occur through fact sheets, bulletins, programmed training manuals, slide presentations, videotape presentations, and radio and television spots. Most of these media interventions can be adapted to reach any of the four target groups identified by Morrill, Oetting, and Hurst (1974). The introduction of computer-assisted learning opens wide horizons for potential advising interventions and is developed in detail in Chapter Nine.

Examples of Advising Intervention Strategies

The three-dimensional cube model developed by Morrill, Oetting, and Hurst may be used to plot the types of interventions that presently exist in an institution and can further be used to plan for the types of interventions that should be adopted. When used correctly, it is capable of expanding the horizons of any individual advisor and can certainly be used as a tool to assist a center for academic advising that has as its mission the enhancement of advising at an institutional or community level. The following examples will illustrate the application of the three-dimensional cube model.

Target: Primary Group, Purpose: Preventive, Method: Media. A perennial problem at the University of Wyoming that appeared to be worsening in the early 1980s was that freshman students entering the institution were underprepared in basic math and English skills. In addition, incoming students appeared to be making selections for academic majors and career plans that were unrealistic with regard to academic skill level and generic academic ability. The result of these circumstances was enormous pressure on the advising system of the university to assist students. Frequently, students would enroll for classes beyond their skill levels and, through poor academic performance, would jeopardize their future in higher education. A method to prevent these problems much earlier in the student's life was needed. The greatest potential for addressing the problem appeared to be more adequate academic advising in the home, so that parents and siblings would be better prepared to advise students as early as the middle and secondary schools on the appropriate preparation necessary for success in college.

During the winter and early spring, the Center for Academic Advising designed an "open letter" from the president of the university to all students in grades seven through twelve and their parents. The letter was written in a very forthright manner, indicating to students and parents the general kinds of precollege academic preparations that were necessary if students were to experience a full measure of academic success at the university. A copy of the letter was then sent to the state superintendent of public instruction and to all district superintendents and middle and high school principals in the state in order to elicit cooperation and reduce defensiveness that might arise through the project. The letter was released to all newspapers in the state in April 1982 and was published as a quarter-page advertisement purchased by the university (see Figure 2).

The response to the president's open letter across the state was vigorous and positive. Some minor instances of defensiveness

Figure 2. President's Open Letter to Students in Grades 7 through 12 and Their Parents.

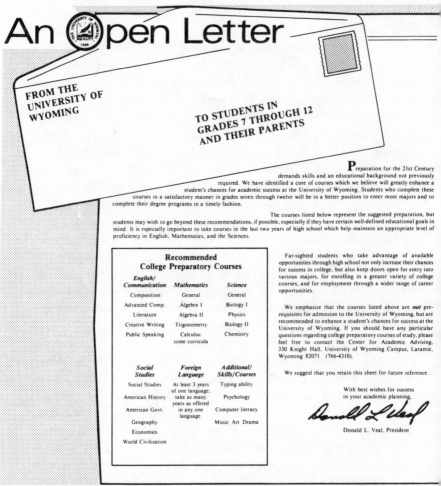

An Open Letter

FROM THE UNIVERSITY OF WYOMING

TO STUDENTS IN GRADES 7 THROUGH 12 AND THEIR PARENTS

Preparation for the 21st Century demands skills and an educational background not previously required. We have identified a core of courses which we believe will greatly enhance a student's chances for academic success at the University of Wyoming. Students who complete these courses in a satisfactory manner in grades seven through twelve will be in a better position to enter most majors and to complete their degree programs in a timely fashion.

The courses listed below represent the suggested preparation, but students may wish to go beyond these recommendations, if possible, especially if they have certain well-defined educational goals in mind. It is especially important to take courses in the last two years of high school which help maintain an appropriate level of proficiency in English, Mathematics, and the Sciences.

Recommended College Preparatory Courses

English/ Communication	Mathematics	Science
Composition	General	General
Advanced Comp.	Algebra I	Biology I
Literature	Algebra II	Physics
Creative Writing	Trigonometry	Biology II
Public Speaking	Calculus: some curricula	Chemistry

Social Studies	Foreign Language	Additional/ Skills/Courses
Social Studies	At least 3 years of one language; take as many years as offered in any one language.	Typing ability
American History		Psychology
American Govt.		Computer literacy
Geography		Music Art Drama
Economics		
World Civilization		

Far-sighted students who take advantage of available opportunities through high school not only increase their chances for success in college, but also keep doors open for entry into various majors, for enrolling in a greater variety of college courses, and for employment through a wider range of career opportunities.

We emphasize that the courses listed above are *not* prerequisites for admission to the University of Wyoming, but are recommended to enhance a student's chances for success at the University of Wyoming. If you should have any particular questions regarding college preparatory courses of study, please feel free to contact the Center for Academic Advising, 330 Knight Hall, University of Wyoming Campus, Laramie, Wyoming 82071 (766-4310).

We suggest that you retain this sheet for future reference.

With best wishes for success in your academic planning,

Donald L. Veal, President

were noted among some of the smaller schools where the preparation suggested by the president was not yet available in their curriculum. In each such case, however, intent was expressed to insert the appropriate preparatory course material in the middle or high school curriculum. Numerous calls were received by the Center for Academic Advising and the president's office, expressing appreciation for the apparent interest of the university in the preparation of students for the college experience.

The concept developed in the open letter was further referred from the general nature of the information in the open letter to more specific information at the departmental level. The Center for Academic Advising considered carefully the feasibility of a project designed to provide each home of middle and secondary school students in the state with a brochure providing such specific information concerning the appropriate precollege preparation for every college major offered at the university. The director of the Center for Academic Advising contacted every department head and academic dean in the institution and secured from them information concerning what middle school and high school preparation would be considered essential, recommended, or at least a good background. This project was initiated during the fall of 1982, with the intent of distributing a brochure to every household of middle and secondary school students in the state during the spring of 1983. The initial draft of the brochure was ready for review at the beginning of spring semester, 1983.

Again, the state superintendent of public instruction was informed of the project and wrote a letter of support for the project and the brochure urging cooperation from all district superintendents and high school and middle school principals in the state in the distribution process. The president of the university also sent a letter of explanation to superintendents and principals that identified the brochure as follow-up to his open letter. The brochures were sent to all middle and secondary schools in the state with instructions for their distribution to parents of the children enrolled.

The printing and distribution process was completed during April and early May, 1983. Again, the project was perceived in a very positive light by the great majority of individuals who provided a response. It was becoming clear by this time that a number of middle or secondary schools across the state were vigorously pursuing revision or enhancements of their curricula in order to provide students with the academic preparation specified in both the president's open letter and in the follow-up brochure provided.

Although it would be extremely difficult to measure quantitatively the impact of the intervention described in this example, families appear to be much better informed and better able to advise students concerning the academic course work in which they should be enrolling in order to pursue college majors and eventual careers. It is hoped that in the ensuing years, entering students at the University of Wyoming will be better prepared for their selected majors and will thus experience greater academic success. This example indicates that the use of media can be an effective method in providing a preventive intervention by better preparing primary groups (in this case the student's family) to provide more accurate advising.

In conclusion, although this intervention was originally designed with the primary group as a target, the efforts of the middle and secondary schools across the state to modify their curricula may be classified as an institutional intervention. Thus, a secondary target of intervention was the middle and secondary schools in the state.

Target: Individual, Purpose: Preventive, Method: Training. Unfortunately, freshmen entering a college or university usually have a limited or inaccurate view of the advising process. The typical expectation of the entering freshmen appears to be limited to what they have experienced in their middle or secondary school wherein a schedule is filled out and a counselor or an advisor signs a card that validates the schedule. The majority of entering freshmen have never received any training to prepare them for the advising process nor have they ever witnessed a demonstration or modeling of a competent advising interaction.

The University of Wyoming developed a training procedure, not unlike that developed at other institutions, wherein, through the use of a series of videotape vignettes, trainees are shown models of various advising interactions between advisors and their students, ranging from those that are obviously inadequate to challenging and competent demonstrations. Each vignette lasts three to five minutes and can be used in a variety of ways. Simply showing the vignettes with a follow-up discussion and critiquing of strengths and weaknesses results in trainees reporting significant improvement in their perception of the advising process. The vignette may also be used to precede actual practice sessions wherein trainees assume roles of advisor or student and deal with the problem presented on the vignette (for example, the use of the American

College Testing (ACT) profile or of the transfer student's transcript in advising) in the trainee's own preferred way. Observers to the role-play interaction serve as consultants to the process and enrich the training activity. The fact that the vignettes are on videotape makes them easily modified and updated on a periodic basis. The trainees involved may be either faculty members who are serving as advisors or students who may wish to improve their general advising skills or their ability to advise students of special subpopulations, such as student athletes, minority students, foreign students, or nontraditional students. There is no limit to the advising topics that may be addressed in the vignettes.

One university that implemented a procedure similar to that described here reported a dramatic turnaround in the willingness of faculty members to attend advisor training workshops. Previous efforts that emphasized lecture about the content of advising were very poorly received, but when the lecture method was replaced with the active vignette videotape role-play process, rave notices were received.

Target: Individual, Purpose: Developmental, Method: Media. New student orientation programs, commonly occurring during the summer, provide an ideal place for advisee training to occur. The training may emphasize the adequacy of information and content associated with the institution, curricular and cocurricular offerings, or the process wherein the advisee systematically assesses the advisor. One institution developed a series of slides with accompanying narration and music designed to introduce students to every college and major in the institution. Although the information was printed in the annual bulletin, the packaging of the slide presentation brought possible majors and eventual careers to life for students. The advantage of the slide show was the ease with which each college and department could update and modify the various portions of the program. Potential criticism of the slide show by academic departments was eliminated by involving every department and college in the actual creation of the various sections of the slide show.

Several universities have instituted ongoing new student orientation programs including one- or two-credit orientation courses wherein students are made aware of university policies, procedures, jargon, student affairs programs, and college majors offered (and job and salary expectations). They also engage in self-assessment in terms of study skills, interest inventories, value systems, learning alternatives, and career planning (Dooley, 1982; Standing, 1982; and Beatty, Davis, and White, 1983).

Target: Institution, Purpose: Developmental, Method: Consultation. A number of years ago, Colorado State University recognized the importance of implicit and explicit reward systems in shaping the status and values associated with academic advising. Most institutions of higher education have awards and recognition for good teaching or research. Fewer systematically recognize creativity, innovation, and dedication in the advising of students. With the assistance of the development office in the identification of funds, an annual award was established for faculty advising. Initial recipients of the award were faculty members who not only demonstrated adequate advising on an individual basis but developed advising programs that had an impact on entire departments. Not only are the awards powerful reinforcers for the direct recipient, but the description of the advising intervention that is publicized in campus media appears to have encouraged departments to explore innovative and effective methods of advising.

Target: Associational Group, Purpose: Remedial, Method: Training. The use of paraprofessionals as either advisors or preadvisors (dealing primarily with routine, clerical matters of advising such as developing a preliminary class schedule) is relatively common practice in higher education. Those programs that are conscientious in defining the specific job intended for the paraprofessionals and carefully select, train, supervise, and evaluate paraprofessionals report significant success. One implicit advantage of using students as paraprofessionals is that the students may be drawn from specified associational groups on campus and given a specific assignment to impact the associational groups from which they are drawn. One example would be the selection of a paraprofessional from each house in a Greek system. After thorough training and with continuing supervision, these individuals could serve as the contact within the house for preadvising to occur. The same circumstance could be true of floors in a residence hall or with other student special interest groups. With vigorous activity on the part of assigned professionals, the attention given to the advising process among the other members of the associational group could be enhanced and reinforced. The role of the paraprofessional could also be greatly enhanced with the development and use of videotapes and slide shows such as those mentioned in previous examples.

Conclusion

The movement from unenlightened to enlightened advising is one of the significant challenges of higher education at this time. Inefficiency and loss of human potential will result from a process in which time blocks are simply filled with courses. The enlightenment of advisors through a commitment to student development, both in theory and practice, appears to be a key ingredient in answering the challenge. The adoption of a theoretical model to describe student development and of a conceptual scheme for the intervention process has been suggested here as prerequisite to enlightened advising. If typical faculty advisors are to acquire a knowledge of student development theory and an attitude of guiding students through a series of experiences designed to elicit development, a vigorous and sustained training program is essential. The creation of an institutional center for academic advising or the equivalent is suggested as the focus for such a vigorous and sustained effort.

The training task of such a center is not limited to student development theory. A process model such as that described here (Morrill, Oetting, and Hurst, 1974) is also an essential part of the content. Advisors whose perceptions are limited to the dyadic interaction model of advising will have their own creativity encumbered with ignorance. Advising interventions with primary groups and associational groups are especially relevant to academic departments and even colleges. It is within these entities that students form themselves into primary and associational groups along lines of common academic interests.

Advising as a strategy for intellectual and personal development must be based upon an understanding of the developmental process in the students who will present themselves as advisees.

Faculty advisors traditionally advise for intellectual development, identifying opportunities for students. Personal development, however, usually relies on extracurricular opportunities in the campus environment and, therefore, more informed advisors. The presence of a centralized office or location with a charge to provide leadership in this training and informational task for advisors seems prerequisite to accomplishing all that needs to be done. With advising identified as a critical factor in student retention, there is no choice but to allocate the resources necessary for the training and support tasks noted in this chapter.

References

Banning, J. H. "The Campus Ecology Manager Role." In U. Delworth, G. R. Hanson, and Associates, *Student Services: A Handbook for the Profession.* San Francisco: Jossey-Bass, 1980.

Barker, R. G., and Associates. *Habitats, Environments, and Human Behavior: Studies in Ecological Psychology and Eco-Behavioral Science.* San Francisco, Jossey-Bass, 1978.

Beatty, J. D., Davis, B. B., and White, B. J. "Open Option Advising at Iowa State University: An Integrated Advising and Career Planning Model." *National Academic Advising Journal*, 1983, *3* (1), 39–48.

Bierstedt, R. *The Social Order.* (3rd Ed.) New York: McGraw-Hill, 1970.

Chickering, A. W. *Education and Identity.* San Francisco: Jossey-Bass, 1969.

Cross, K. P. *Accent on Learning: Improving Instruction and Reshaping the Curriculum.* San Francisco: Jossey-Bass, 1976.

Dooley, L. R. "Great Expectations and Harsh Reality in the Advising and Orientation Course." In *Proceedings of the Sixth National Conference on Academic Advising*, 1982, pp. 61–62.

Drum, D. "Understanding Student Development." In W. H. Morrill and J. C. Hurst (Eds.), *Dimensions of Intervention for Student Development.* New York: Wiley, 1980.

Erikson, E. *Childhood and Society.* (2nd Ed.) New York: Norton, 1963.

Feldman, K. A., and Newcomb, T. M. *The Impact of College on Students.* 2 Vols. San Francisco: Jossey-Bass, 1969.

Heath, D. *Maturity and Competence: A Transcultural View.* New York: Gardner Press, 1977.

Heath, R. *The Reasonable Adventurer.* Pittsburgh, Penn.: University of Pittsburgh Press, 1964.

Holland, J. L. *Making Vocational Choices: A Theory of Careers.* Englewood Cliffs, N.J.: Prentice-Hall, 1973.

Ivey, A. E. *Microcounseling: Innovations in Interview Training.* Springfield, Ill.: Thomas, 1971.

Keniston, K. *Youth and Dissent.* New York: Harcourt Brace Jovanovich, 1971.

Kohlberg, L. "Stages of Moral Development." In C. M. Beck, B. S. Crittenden, and E. V. Sullivan (Eds.), *Moral Education.* Toronto: University of Toronto Press, 1971.

Landward, S. "Increasing the Academic Survival Rate of High-Risk Students." In *Proceedings of the Third National Conference on Academic Advising,* 1979, pp. 58–59.

Lewin, K. *Dynamic Theory of Personality.* New York: McGraw-Hill, 1935.

Loevinger, J. *Ego Development: Conceptions and Theories.* San Francisco: Jossey-Bass, 1976.

Moos, R. H. *The Human Context: Environmental Determinants of Behavior.* New York: Wiley-Interscience, 1976.

Morrill, W. H., Oetting, E. R., and Hurst, J. C. "Dimensions of Counselor Functioning." *Personnel and Guidance Journal,* 1974, *52* (6), 354–359.

Newcomb, T. M., and Wilson, E. E. *College Peer Groups.* Hawthorne, N.Y.: Aldine, 1966.

Perry, W., Jr. *Forms of Intellectual and Ethical Development in the College Years: A Scheme.* New York: Holt, Rinehart & Winston, 1970.

Pervin, A., and Smith, S. H. "Further Test of the Relationship Between Satisfaction and Perceived Self-Environment Similarity." *Perceptual and Motor Skills,* 1968, *26,* 835–838.

Piaget, J. "Cognitive Development in Children." In R. Ribble and

V. Rockcastle (Eds.), *Piaget Rediscovered: A Report on Cognitive Studies in Curriculum Development.* Ithaca, N.Y.: School of Education, Cornell University, 1964.

Standing, R. "New Approaches to Orientation." In *Proceedings of the Sixth National Conference on Academic Advising,* 1982, pp. 38–39.

Stern, G. G. "B = F (P, E)." *Journal of Personality Assessment,* 1964, *28* (2), 161–168.

Widick, C., Knefelkamp, L., and Parker, C. A. "Student Development." In U. Delworth, G. R., Hanson, and Associates, *Student Services: A Handbook for the Profession.* San Francisco: Jossey-Bass, 1980.

8

Techniques and Tools
for Improving Advising

Thomas J. Grites

Even if a solid theoretical foundation for developmental academic advising has been introduced throughout the institution and if the best educational plans and strategies have been presented, the overall success of the advising program ultimately rests with individual advisors. To assist the advisor *and* the student in achieving maximum educational success through the academic advising process, a variety of resources and materials are available. These advising "tools" can be used by the advisor to facilitate, monitor, and review the educational and developmental progress for each student.

This chapter examines a wide sampling of publications, assessment instruments, institutional resource documents, campus agencies, and human resources that can be useful to academic advisors. Applications of these materials and several techniques for using them most effectively are also suggested.

Publications

Much of the success of any advising program can be attributed to the quality of information available to both students and advisors. Clarity, conciseness, relevance, accuracy, and availability are essential characteristics of publications designed to enhance the advising process. Some institutional publications that should be reviewed for their effectiveness include admissions materials, the college catalogue, student handbooks, advisor handbooks, and the schedule of classes. Each of these is described here in some detail.

Appropriate use of these publications results in more accurate, active, and productive advising; therefore, advisors should become involved in their development. Students can thus be encouraged to become more active and responsible in the advising process and for their education.

Admissions Materials. How can admissions literature help academic advisors? First, this information must represent an accurate picture of what the campus actually provides. This material helps shape the expectations for students, parents, and counselors. If these expectations are not met, the advising process suffers—often because the advisor becomes the primary individual to whom the dissatisfaction is expressed. As Chickering (1973, p. 75) stated, "When the institution does not have the necessary capacity, when it lacks competence on the faculty, when it lacks critical facilities or other resources and has no access to them, then it must be candid about its limitations." The "truth-in-advertising" recruitment effort helps avoid a potentially negative initial advising session.

Second, the student's application can serve as a vehicle for communication. Many demographic characteristics are identifiable through applications; personal statements provide further information about the student's goals, abilities, interests, and expectations. One specific part of the application has a special relationship to advising, and that is the "choice of major." Students are often assigned to their advisors by this single criterion, no matter how inappropriate or uninformed that choice might be. Furthermore, some applications allow no option to be "undecided," which *forces* the student to make an uninformed choice. Either situation increases the potential for an uncomfortable initial advising session. Advisors' access to applications can assist them in helping students adjust to academic life.

Systematic reviews of admissions publications, including the application, need to be made with a special consideration for their potential impact on the advising process.

College Catalogue. The single most important publication affecting the advising process is the college catalogue, which is often considered "the bible." Students and advisors are expected to read and understand the degree requirements and all other academic and institutional policies. Most catalogues indicate the student's responsibility in meeting the requirements and policies of the institution, yet the advisor is often the interpreter and monitor of them.

The college catalogue, then, is one of the bonds of the advising relationship; it is a tool that both student and advisor should study and reference frequently. This document will also likely serve as primary evidence in any litigation concerning academic policies (see Chapter Fourteen). With such importance placed on this official publication, the need for clarity and accuracy is obvious. Institutions should review their catalogues frequently to ensure that they articulate the intentions of the institution.

Student Handbook. The student handbook is another publication that can enhance the advising process. Many such handbooks reiterate and detail the most important academic policies included in the catalogue, and this reinforcement is always helpful. Beyond this repetition, however, is usually a description of many student services and resources for assistance with all kinds of matters, ranging from career indecision and poor study skills to resolving roommate, alcohol, and financial problems. All student clubs and organizations are usually described in this publication as well.

To advise students developmentally, the advisor can use the student handbook to identify other campus resources that will assist students to improve their decision-making, studying, leadership, coping, and valuing abilities and skills.

Advisor Handbook. The advisor handbook is a publication designed explicitly for use by the advisor, rather than by the student directly. Unlike many of the other publications described, which are fairly uniform in their content, advisor handbooks vary greatly. At one extreme are the voluminous documents that virtually repeat much of the college catalogue and also include curriculum worksheets, referral sources, and advising definitions, procedures, and methods; these are often distributed in loose-leaf binders so that additions and deletions can be made easily. In contrast, some handbooks are designed to include only information specific to the advising role and not found elsewhere. Some happy medium should be achieved so that the unique information is not buried in the duplicate material.

Whatever the format and content, the advisor needs a well-conceived handbook and must become familiar with it in order to use it effectively. Efficient use of this publication results in fewer phone calls, fewer unnecessary referrals, more resourceful advisors, and more satisfied students.

Schedule of Classes. Another institutional publication necessary for good advising is the schedule of classes for the upcoming term and academic year. Not only does this schedule list courses, times, rooms, and instructors, but it also often includes recent policy or procedure changes, deadline dates, and other announcements that might not have been available when the catalogue or the handbooks were printed. The advisor and the student should carefully review *all* material included in the class schedule rather than only the specific course offerings. When used properly, this tool prevents such unpleasant circumstances as erroneous registrations (wrong section, time conflicts, and the like), inappropriate courses (to meet requirements or level of difficulty), and loss of the money required to pay fees for late registration or extra terms.

External Publications. Beyond the publications produced by the institution, advisors may wish to review a variety of external publication sources that can provide ideas for individual advising and for overall programmatic efforts. Some of these include: Crockett's (1978, 1979) resource documents, which contain numerous practical suggestions and examples of adaptive material; Grites' (1979) monograph, which synthesizes the available literature on academic advising and provides recommendations for the future; Winston, Ender, and Miller's (1982) sourcebook, which establishes the concept of developmental academic advising; the *NACADA Journal,* newsletter, and conference proceedings published by the National Academic Advising Association, which provide ongoing reports of concepts, programs, and research in the field of academic advising; and books like this one.

Assessment Instruments

Advisors have available a variety of assessment instruments to aid them in advising for personal and academic development.

SAT/ACT Profiles. Most institutions require scores from the College Entrance Examination Board Scholastic Aptitude Test (SAT) or the American College Testing Program (ACT) as part of the admissions process. These scores are used to predict college success and, therefore, determine whether a student should be admitted, and they are sometimes used as well to determine levels of placement in mathematics and English courses. In addition to the simple test score reports and analyses, however, each testing company provides a profile for each student who took the test. This profile includes a wealth of self-reported information about the student that is invaluable in the advising process, especially for the first meeting of the student and the advisor.

The SAT student report (Exhibit 1) includes responses from the Student Descriptive Questionnaire. These responses provide the advisor with information about the student's specific college choices, potential majors and careers, activities, interests, and special assistance needs. A complete description of the Student Descriptive Questionnaire and its use was published by the College Entrance Examination Board (1982).

Similar to the SAT College Report, the ACT Assessment College Report (Exhibit 2) provides the advisor with information about extracurricular activities in high school and those anticipated in college, educational and vocational plans, and areas of special interest or needs. In addition, the ACT report provides information from an interest inventory that students complete at the time of their registration for assessment. The interest inventory yields three profile scores: a percentile ranking in each of six basic interest areas;

Exhibit 1. The SAT Student Report.

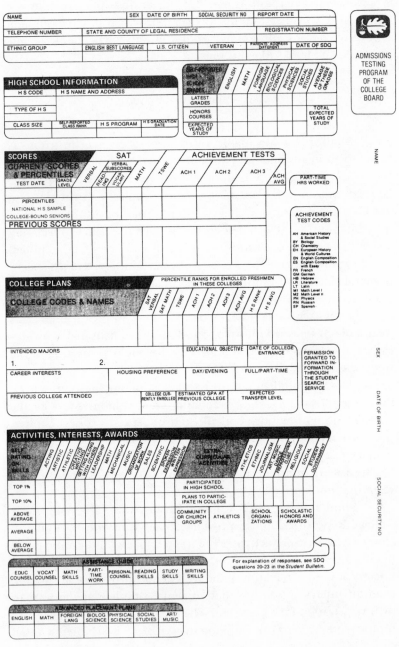

Reprinted by permission of Educational Testing Service, the copyright owner.

coordinates for the Map of College Majors, which plot a location that encompasses a group of potential college majors for that student; and a region designation for the World-of-Work Map, which identifies a number of "job families" and occupations that seem suited to the student's interests. These additional scores are especially useful to the advisor when discussing both immediate and long-range educational and career plans. A thorough description of the use of the Student Profile Report, including its use in group advising, is found in Crockett (1978).

Whether the institution uses SAT or ACT scores for admission, the advisor should, first of all, be provided a copy of the appropriate report. It is surprising to find how many institutions retain these reports in the admissions or registrar's office and do not distribute them to advisors. *These reports provide one of the best developmental advising tools available.*

Once they are distributed, the advisor should attempt to look for two primary situations—compatibilities and inconsistencies—as the basis for initial advising. Are the intended majors, career interests, and requisite abilities (as measured by the actual scores) similar? For example, does the intended engineering major have a relatively high math score for your institution? Or does the aspiring lawyer have relatively high verbal/English scores, irrespective of intended major? If these indications are compatible, then the student's initial educational plan is probably appropriate; if they are not, however, the advisor should call inconsistencies to the attention of the student so that they are either clarified or so that some alternatives can begin to be explored.

Along another dimension, the advisor should make the same comparisons in the areas of self-rating of skills and assistance (SAT) and of special educational needs and interests and accomplishments (ACT). Are the student's self-ratings consistent with the educational plan and/or test scores? For example, does the business student's self-rating of writing, leadership, and speaking skills rank "above average" on SAT or "HI" on ACT? Or does the student (any major) indicate a need for special assistance in academic skills development or counseling services? When these self-ratings are consistent with the educational plan, the advisor is able to activate the developmental process. When they are not, the advisor must first

Exhibit 2. ACT Assessment College Report.

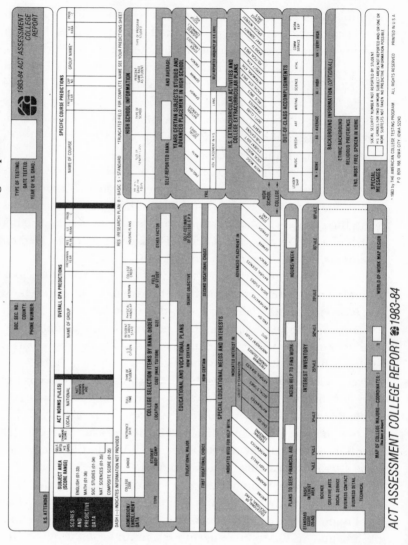

CAREER PLANNING AIDS (For Student Use)

The Map of College Majors and the World-of-Work Map use your **interest** scores to help you identify college majors and occupations ("jobs") you may want to consider. As you use the maps, keep in mind that they are based on INTEREST SCORES ONLY. Because interests and abilities may differ, BOTH need to be considered in career planning.

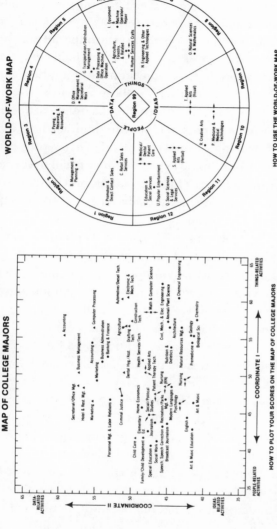

WORLD-OF-WORK MAP

HOW TO USE THE WORLD-OF-WORK MAP

1. Copy your World-of-Work Map Region number (_____) from the Interest Inventory section on the reverse side.

2. Use your region number to locate your region on the World-of-Work Map. Look at the career families in your region **and** the adjacent regions. The jobs in these families generally involve activities corresponding to your interest scores. Although your region on the map does not indicate which job you identify (and programs of study) you may want to **explore**.

3. Ask your counselor or advisor for a copy of ACT's Career Family List*, which contains examples of jobs in each of the career families. You may wish to consider some of these jobs (and related programs of study) as you make career plans.

*The Career Family List appears in *Using the ACT Assessment on Campus* (sent to colleges) and in the *ACT Assessment Counselor's Handbook* (sent to high schools).

MAP OF COLLEGE MAJORS

HOW TO PLOT YOUR SCORES ON THE MAP OF COLLEGE MAJORS

1. Copy your map coordinates I (_____) and II (_____) from the Interest Inventory section on the reverse side.

2. Locate your score for coordinate I on the map, and draw a vertical line from that point to the corresponding point at the top edge of the map. Then locate your score on coordinate II and draw a horizontal line from that point to the corresponding point at the right edge of the map.

3. Make an "X" where the two lines cross. This point shows the location of your **interests** as compared to those of students in a wide variety of 4-year college majors/programs (indicated by ●) and 2-year college majors/programs (indicated by ▲). The closer you are to a major, the more similar your interests are to the interests of college students in that major. Although your location does not indicate which major you should **enter**, it should help you identify majors you may want to explore.

explore the inconsistencies, clarify them, and initiate the student's development from a different perspective.

The third major dimension along which the advisor should compare student responses is that of high school and college extracurricular activities. Does the student indicate a variety of high school activities and few plans for college activities? Does the student indicate too many college activities that might detract from academic endeavors? Or does the student indicate little or no involvement either in high school or college? Whatever the pattern of responses, the advisor should explore in more detail the extracurricular plans of the student. This exploration provides a basis for general discussion and provides the advisor with more complete information about the student.

As advising tools, the SAT and ACT profiles include a wealth of information that students have already provided. These provide a solid basis for discussion upon which to build the total developmental advising process. Appropriate distribution, training, and use of them will certainly result in more effective advisors and students more aware of their own development.

Other Assessment Instruments. Although SAT or ACT scores are used primarily for admission, they are sometimes used for math and English course level placements. Many institutions have supplemented these with other standardized tests in specific curricular areas, and some have developed their own. Placement tests have been designed for English, math, foreign languages, and certain science courses. Since the advent of open admissions policies and additional educational opportunity programs, a variety of basic skills assessment tests have been developed. In New Jersey, for example, all freshmen entering public institutions (and some private) must take the New Jersey College Basic Skills Placement Test *after* admission but before their initial registration.

In addition to the assessment of specific academic skills, many institutions assess other skills and characteristics of their students. Various instruments are available to assess goal setting, career exploration, and individual learning-style behaviors. When appropriately trained in the use of these instruments, advisors are better able to recognize student behaviors, plan an active, intrusive advising approach, and determine student growth as a result. Descriptions of some of these instruments follow.

Setting one's educational goals is not as easy a task for college students as one might assume. Students often have unrealistic, ill-conceived, distorted, or confusing goals for their college experiences. The College Student Goals Inventory (CSGI) (Gill and Freuhling, 1979) and the Student Developmental Task Inventory, Second Edition (SDTI–2) (Winston, Miller, and Prince, 1979) are two instruments that advisors can use to assist students in developing their educational goals and objectives.

The CSGI assesses the importance of eight goal areas for students and their perceptions of how the institution is helping them achieve those goals. From the 100 items, the degree of *student need* is determined by the difference between the importance and the achievement of the goals. From these data, various remedial, developmental, and preventive efforts can be established and facilitated by the advisor.

As a more direct individual student approach, the SDTI–2 uses 140 items to yield scores in three developmental task and nine subtask areas. The instrument is self-scored, and the advisor assists students in identifying generalized areas that may need development, in creating a developmental plan, and by reviewing their progress periodically. Winston, Miller, and Prince (1979) have also developed an accompanying self-assessment instrument, the Student Developmental Profile and Planning Record, which requires much less interpretation and provides space to log one's developmental progress. The SDTI–2 can also be used to assess institutional programs for student development and for research, but its primary purpose is for individual student assessment.

Both the SDTI–2 and the CSGI contain subscales on educational and career planning, but another instrument often used to assess the student's occupational plans more specifically is the *Self-Directed Search: A Guide to Educational and Vocational Planning* (Holland, 1970). This programmed booklet of several activities helps students assess their interests and abilities in six general occupational classifications. Although it is completely self-scoring and self-interpretive, the author provides recommendations for later student action, including assistance from such persons as advisors.

A new area of educational research that has implications for the advising process is that of learning styles. The conditions under which students seem to learn best have been described according to the interactions involved, the concreteness versus abstractness of the activity, and the external influences surrounding the activity. Knowledge of a student's learning style enables the advisor to assist that student in course selection and in encouraging other activities from which the student can best learn. The reader is referred to Claxton, Adams, and Williams (1982) for a concise review of several learning-styles instruments and the description of two programs where they have been used by both students and faculty to make adjustments in the learning process.

The use of both tests and inventories as tools in the advising process is obvious. Results of these instruments provide data about the student that might not otherwise be readily available. Having these results in advance provides the advisor with a springboard from which to begin the developmental aspects of academic advising. For example, knowing that a student is deficient in reading skills and/or good study habits has serious implications for the simple advising task of course selection. Without the knowledge of these deficiencies and the intervention by the advisor, the student could easily be "programmed for disaster" by registering for several courses that primarily require taking lecture notes and reading the text as preparation for examinations, as is often the case in survey courses taught in lecture halls. Alternative types of courses, such as art and music performance, speech, foreign language, and perhaps writing and math, must be considered so that this student is not overburdened with the (reading) tasks for which assistance is necessary. Another prime, but often unrealized, example exists where the student's academic abilities appear to be strong, as indicated by SAT/ACT scores and high school grades, but the study habits and skills are weak. Similarly, the student might have been exposed to limited modes of instruction in high school, and the nature of the academic environment in college becomes a real shock. Furthermore, unrealistic educational and career goals might emanate from the high school setting. These incompatibilities could be the major reasons for the attrition of college freshmen (Gordon, 1984).

The use of these additional tests and inventories makes the advisor more aware of potential difficulties. When the student is also made aware of them, the advisor can assist in remedying the deficiencies and preventing attrition. This additional information also assists the advisor in determining what other campus agencies and resources are available for the student to correct the deficiencies and in making an appropriate referral. A more complete description of these resources is presented later in this chapter.

Institutional Resource Documents

Within the institution itself are several types of documents that can assist advisors.

Transcripts. Probably the most frequently used advising tool is the transcript of previous academic work, whether it is from the student's high school, previous college(s), or the present institution. Transcripts reflect the student's past academic performance and serve as an additional predictor of future academic success.

Many smaller institutions provide advisors with the high school transcripts of their new freshmen. Beyond their academic predictive value, these transcripts often include useful comments from counselors about the student's interests, abilities, potentials, and possible difficulties. These comments, along with the student's self-reports, provide the advisor with information that facilitates a more personalized advising relationship. New freshmen are often anxious and tend to be both relieved and impressed when someone in their new and strange environment shows a personal interest in them as individuals. The appropriate use of this information establishes a comfortable, working advising relationship for the future.

Advisors of transfer students must rely on the transcripts from previous institutions in order to determine course equivalencies and to assess future course planning. In many institutions, the transfer course equivalencies are determined prior to the advisor's receipt of the transcripts; this insures consistency in the evaluation and allows for more productive advising in the time available, especially at the beginning of the advising relationship.

Too often, however, the use of previous transcripts terminates with the course-equivalency determinations. Their full use as advising tools requires the advisor to read beyond the list of courses and become more intrusive to determine reasons for certain academic situations and past decisions. For example, is there a major discrepancy in the student's performance from one term to the next? If so, this could be due to academic ability, change of academic or career plans, personal circumstances, living arrangements, or "freshman-itis." Or is there a pattern of course withdrawals? Such a pattern could reflect study skills deficiencies, overcommitments of time, or even poor advising. Without examining transcripts for such indicators and attempting to determine their source, the advisor is completing only part of the advising task. A more thorough use of transcripts as advising tools results in better developmental advising.

Finally, advisors normally receive institutional transcripts for their students at the end of each term (or the beginning of the next). These often also include the student's current registration as well as certain demographic information. The advisor should use these transcripts much the same as those from other institutions.

One additional feature of some institutional transcripts (or version of the official transcript) is the graduation audit of graduation requirements, which is displayed in detail on each. This feature is associated with the use of a computer in advising and is described more fully in Chapter Nine. Suffice it to say here that such computer assistance should be sought wherever possible. The time saved (by both students and advisors) in determining course requirements is much better utilized in making advising the true developmental process that it should be.

Beyond these simple records of data about the student, Brown and Citrin (1977) have described a more comprehensive student record—the student development transcript. This document is able to portray student progress along such developmental dimensions as "intellectual, academic, personal, moral, social, cultural, and physical" (p. 163) and can serve to stimulate institutional goal setting, to motivate student developmental progression, to diagnose student strengths and weaknesses, and to prescribe activities for both current and lifelong development. They offer experiential or competency-based checklists and a portfolio as possible formats to record student data, activities, and experiences. This approach to student transcripts is clearly reflective of the student development concept emphasized throughout this book.

Transcripts, then, serve as advising tools beyond the simple reflection of courses completed. The capable advisor will use them to analyze the student's potential, to determine possible difficulties, and to monitor the student's progress toward established educational goals.

Questionnaires. Although a wealth of information is made available through transcripts, other specific details are often desirable, either for the institution or for the advisor. These additional details are usually solicited through questionnaires designed by directors, committees, or individual advisors.

Some of the informational items might include the student's hobbies, musical interests, favorite books and movies, and special talents that indicate how leisure time might be spent; the expectations of college (that is, responsibilities, values, academic work load, social adaptations, and confidence in meeting these) that could indicate inconsistencies with what the campus provides; or the (continuing) student's assessment of progress toward established goals, such as choosing a major, avoiding dismissal, or remedying deficiencies.

Each institution, or indeed each individual advisor, will determine the need for this supplemental information. It is assumed that whatever additional information is solicited is valuable to the overall success of the advising program as delivered by individual advisors. Such questionnaires should not be used precipitately.

Anecdotal Records. As the advising relationship progresses, the advisor will not be able to review all the materials mentioned previously in this chapter for each advising session, especially when the number of advisees is large. It becomes important, then, for the advisor to review quickly what has already been achieved and what has been planned. The best way to be able to make this review is by keeping notes from each previous session and sharing them with the student. These notes might include specific course selections and/or recommendations, suggested explanations of new or alternative options to be considered, or specific tasks designated for the student to accomplish by the current advising session. Crockett (1978) provided a suitable format for keeping such notes (see Exhibit 3).

This advising tool is, perhaps, the only one that is created solely by the advisor. The advisor's own shorthand, organization, and emphases are recorded. There is no imposition or interpretation implied; the advisor's individuality prevails.

Calendars, Checklists, and Worksheets. Since the advising process often becomes overshadowed by many other ongoing campus activities, it is helpful to be reminded when certain advising activities should occur. An easy way to achieve this is by distributing lists of dates and activities that are relevant to the advising process. These are usually done for each term and distributed to all advisors.

Advising calendars usually include those dates that are most important to the advising process. These dates often appear in some of the other publications mentioned earlier but are now provided in a different format. These calendars are usually single sheets that can be attached to the advisor's desk, door, wall, or bulletin board. Creative artwork often makes them visually attractive so that students, as well as advisors, become aware of them. Such dates as apply to registration, schedule adjustment, applications for graduation, financial aid, honors programs, preregistration for the next term, and course withdrawals to avoid academic and/or financial penalties are included. Brief advising tasks or strategies are often suggested throughout the calendar as a means of preparing advisors for the upcoming critical dates. An example of such a calendar is shown in Exhibit 4.

Advising checklists serve as reminders about the content of advising sessions rather than emphasizing the specific dates as in the calendar. These, too, reinforce what is already printed but help to ensure that the advisor doesn't overlook some important aspect that could jeopardize the student's future academic plans. When advisors see many students, particularly during the peak advising periods, they cannot possibly remember if they provided the same information to each student. The checklist reduces the possibility of oversight. Some have also been designed to serve as a check on the advisor's personal approach or style of advising.

Exhibit 3. Sample Anecdotal Records.

Advisee Conferences

Advisee: _____

Instructions: For each conference with the above named student, please
record the date, general subject of the conference, approximate length of the conference, and any comments. Group
subjects of conferences under the headings of *academic*,
career, *personal*, or *other*. This form should be kept in the
student's folder in your office.

Date	Subject of Conference	Conference Length	Comments

Exhibit 4. Sample Advisor Calendar.

Sept. 1 - 3:   Orientation, Advising and Registration

Hold group or individual appointments with new advisees to discuss the advising relationship, course requirements, registration efforts, co-curricular activities, campus services, and career options.

Sept. 8 - 14:   Drop/Add period

Make an extra effort to be available.

Oct. 1 - 12:   Early Academic Monitoring

Verify final schedules of advisees, their addresses, phone numbers, etc.

Discuss any academic difficulties to determine possible need for assistance from Skills Center or course withdrawal to save 50% tuition.

Oct. 8:   Last day to withdraw for class(es) with 50% refund

Oct. 20:   Distribution of graduation certifications for December graduates.

Nov. 8 - 12:   Preregistration for Spring Term.

Consider use of "veteran" advisees to assist you.

Midterm check for academic difficulties; make appropriate referrals; advise that Nov. 19 is the last date to withdraw with a "W" grade, if appropriate.

Nov. 12:   Graduation certifications due.

Nov. 19:   Last date to withdraw from class(es) with a "W" grade.

Dec. 1 - 15:   End of Term "crisis counseling" (as needed)

Consider "I" grades, "F" grades in favor of concentrating on others, or even an official withdrawal from the College if appropriate.

Assist the students with study tips on preparation for final exams and papers.

Jan. 1:   Last date to apply for financial aid for Spring Term.

Some of the advising content that might be suggested on these checklists includes an overview of the advising process, specific course/graduation requirements, academic honesty, grading and retention policies, and an assessment of the completeness of information about the student. Advisor behaviors that should be "checked" include one's availability, knowledge of the academic policies and procedures (which change frequently in some institutions), knowledge of referral sources, and completeness of advising (that is, the total developmental approach). An example of such a

Exhibit 5. Sample Advisor Checklist.

Preparation

_____ I have posted my office hours and other times that I am available for advising.

_____ I have reviewed the catalogue, schedules of classes and advisor handbook for academic policy changes.

_____ I have reviewed the names of my advisees, and I have updated their files.

Practice (with the student as an active participant)

_____ We have reviewed the student's academic plan.

_____ We have reviewed the progress toward realizing that plan.

_____ We have discussed any potential academic difficulties and their possible remedies.

_____ We have reviewed specific graduation requirements.

_____ We have discussed future course selections.

_____ We have discussed the student's involvement in other campus activities.

_____ We have discussed any additional concerns the student may have.

_____ We have established a future meeting time and have outlined what tasks need to be accomplished by that time.

Follow-up

_____ I made specific notes about my advisee's situation.

_____ I felt I maintained an individualized, caring relationship with my advisee.

_____ I clarified certain misunderstandings.

_____ I suggested possible alternatives to the student's choices, opinions, or directions.

_____ I encouraged the student to assume more responsibility in the advising process.

checklist is shown in Exhibit 5, and others are included in Crockett (1978).

Advisor calendars and checklists can be combined into one document or distributed separately. In either case, they are very inexpensive tools that assist advisors throughout the term. They also serve as subtle reminders that advising is an ongoing process, that it does not start and stop on specific dates. The appropriate use of these simple reminders can improve the overall advising *program* significantly because they serve to improve the process *individually*.

Advising worksheets, or curriculum guides, are used by most academic departments. These sheets show the summary versions of the major, minor, general education, and elective course requirements, and they are often made available throughout the campus.

Though they do simplify the course advising process, they may have also *inadvertently served as the major obstacle to developmental advising*. Having the student's curriculum very clearly outlined on paper, with spaces available to indicate that courses have been completed, has given the misleading impression that academic advising is merely a "check-off" process. When advisors and students share this perception, developmental advising is lost. The worksheets are useful tools that expedite the course-scheduling function of advising. It is incumbent upon the advisor, however, to maximize the advising time made available by this expediency to create and maintain the developmental nature of advising as described throughout this book.

Campus Services, Agencies, and Personnel

Rather than advising tools that are used by the individual advisor, the following are resources that advisors might use to supplement their own advising. The knowledge of these resources and the appropriate use of them, either through referral or consultation, will result in better-informed students and advisors.

Every institution has various offices, programs, and personnel that provide specialized services to students. These resources often have a direct influence on the developmental advising program. In some cases, the advisor must become more keenly aware of their assistance. A number of these resource units are described here.

Learning Resource Center. This is one of the most important referral units for the advisor. These centers usually provide remedial or tutorial assistance in all areas of study, but they are most frequently used for writing, math, reading, and study skills improvement. Since students often feel embarrassed or stigmatized by receiving such assistance, the influence of the advisor in making such a recommendation is important. When viewed in a positive, constructive way (by the advisor and student), the results are usually positive and constructive. For students on academic probation, the service is critical; for those who experience only periodic difficulties, it is recommended; and for those who seem to have no learning skill problems, it is nonetheless reassuring.

Career Development Center. This is a significant referral unit, especially for "undecided" freshmen and graduating seniors. These two developmental periods are often the most anxious for college students, at least as they relate to jobs and careers. The freshman feels pressure to decide but does not have enough information to do so wisely; the senior suddenly realizes the meaning of entering the professional world to apply what was learned but not knowing the competitive criteria upon which to be judged. Professionals in the career center are able to assist students all along this continuum of anxiety. The center is usually well equipped with print, nonprint, and computer-assisted media that facilitate career decision making. The advisor should become fully knowledgeable of this important advising resource and should use it appropriately throughout the advising relationship.

The function of job placement for graduates is often attached to the career development center. The most common placement efforts are to maintain job listings; to arrange for on-campus interviews by major industries, agencies, graduate schools, and business firms; to provide a credentials service; and to teach resumé writing and interview skills. In addition, many centers attempt to collect job placement data on the graduates. Whereas the advisor would probably refer students to the center for most services, the job placement data can be used in the advising office. It is important to know how many graduates of a specific program are employed in entry-level positions, how many have advanced, and in what areas of the country and at what salaries they are employed. Of course, not all the data will be favorable, and such information should be provided as well. In any case, the advisor should have access to such information and should be able to use it effectively with students.

Counseling and Testing Center. This is another important referral unit on campus. In most institutions, this office provides educational-vocational counseling that is more sophisticated than most advisors can provide, as well as individual or group psychological services. The latter should be provided only by the appropriately trained staff of the center; however, some advising situations could warrant the advisor's direct assistance and can be achieved through (telephone) intervention by the counseling staff. Though advisors can be trained to use certain minimal psychological recognition and referral skills, their limitations must be recognized. Academic advisors should not attempt to become (or be made into) therapists.

Many different kinds of services have been administratively placed under the counseling center. The functions of learning assistance and career development are sometimes located here. Many community colleges provide their primary academic advising services through this center. Some institutions have attempted to integrate these services into a unit called the CAP center, that is the center for counseling, advising, and placement.

Whatever the administrative arrangement, the advisor must be familiar with the functions and services of the center. Referrals to this resource unit and/or consultation with its personnel can both prevent future advising problems and remediate those that have already occurred.

Registrar's Office. This is another resource unit frequently used by advisors. Though the information provided here is rather specific (deadline dates, forms and signatures required, issuing of grades and transcripts, and sometimes the determination of graduation requirements), it is nonetheless important to the advising process. Such routine information does not lend itself directly to developmental advising, but the advisor can attempt to make it so. When a student has failed to meet a deadline, complete a form, obtain a signature, request a transcript, or fulfill a requirement, the advisor has the opportunity to reinforce the student's responsibility in the total learning process. When such circumstances are related to life or work situations, these apparently meaningless events are transformed into developmental learning activities. The advisor might also use this resource to obtain the most complete, accurate, and current information on students, since all permanent academic transactions are stored here.

Other Resource Offices. Various other resource offices may be available to students and advisors on each campus. Most of these have very specific functions or are designed to serve a specific clientele of students, but the advisor should be aware of them and use them if necessary. Such offices include financial aid, admissions, and centers for women, international, minority, (older) adult, commuter, handicapped, veteran, and undecided students. Often, an office of institutional studies will be useful not only to determine certain academic behavior patterns (changing majors, dropping courses, and the like) but to obtain information on attrition as well. It is helpful for advisors to know these patterns so that appropriate preventive measures can be attempted.

Other Advisors. A readily available, yet often overlooked, resource for improved advising is one's own colleagues. One advisor may have a particular strategy, technique, or format that works especially well with certain kinds of students, and such effective means should be shared. This sharing should occur across the campus, that is, *across* academic disciplines, administrative reporting lines, and specific service areas. At least once each academic term, some planned sharing activity should be scheduled. Once this activity has become regularized, the meetings are used both for sharing and for assessment of use by the others. The goal is to have each advisor provide a specific idea; the result is improved advising by all.

One effective means of sharing advisor techniques is through videotaping. This is not always practical, but when accomplished, it is very illustrative. Though some commercial advising videotapes are available (from the American College Testing Program), those produced on campus with one's own advisors, students, and situations are usually quite effective. Furthermore, those that are candid, rather than staged, are also often more effective. Those responsible for advising programs should investigate the possibility of videotaping as a resource for all advisors.

The Student. The best resource for the advisor to assess how to proceed developmentally is the individual student. As the student provides various information, the advisor decides which tools and/

or other resources need to be used. The specific advising tool used throughout this process is the interview skill of questioning.

Hyman (1982) described the application of this skill in the college classroom as being essential to the thinking process. Many of his tactics and strategies are also applicable to the advising session. For example, rather than simply acknowledging that a student's course selections fulfill certain academic requirements, the advisor should ask *why* the student made those choices or why the student did *not* choose other options that would meet the same requirements. Similarly, the advisor might ask the student to provide a rationale for the choice of a major. Very often the reasons are inappropriate or incompatible for this student, or they have been made in haste and under pressure. The effort here is to challenge students to think about their choices so that the advisor can then proceed to advise developmentally.

One obvious implication from this procedure is that some "file" is established for each student. An advising file would typically contain such items as the SAT/ACT profile, transcripts, test results, questionnaire data, anecdotal records, and curriculum worksheets. Additional items might include academic notices, specific correspondence to/about the student, the student's resumé, or various forms used in the advising process. This file is reviewed periodically and should be forwarded to the new advisor if a change is made.

All the advising tools and resources described here are not used by each advisor with each student. The widest range is presented so that advisors have an idea of what is available to them. The specific selection of the best ones must be made by the advisor, appropriate for the individual student. The next section of this chapter describes some of the techniques through which the tools and resources can be used.

Techniques and Strategies

Academic advising has traditionally been viewed as a one-to-one, faculty-student relationship. In reviewing the developmental nature of advising and the possible tools available to accomplish this task, the obvious question is "How can I find the time to do this?" The techniques described here are provided to assist the advisor in creating more advising time, in making the best use of the time available, and in maintaining the developmental nature of advising.

Group Advising. Advising several (five to eight) students at a time obviously results in an economization of advising time. More students can be advised in shorter periods of time *and* without sacrificing the quality of advising. Group advising helps to illustrate the commonalities of student concerns; to identify and clarify advising facts, myths, rumors, and misinterpretations; and to encourage the exploration of various courses, majors, and careers. One-to-one advising, on the other hand, breeds boredom for the advisor through the repetition of common information, prevents the sharing of common concerns among students, and can inhibit student development. The group advisor, similar to the classroom teacher, facilitates discussion, suggests alternatives, and answers specific questions; this is developmental advising at its peak. The advisor may be even *more* effective by meeting with eight students for a total of forty-five minutes than by meeting individually with each one for fifteen minutes.

A variation of group advising is the team approach where two or three advisors conduct sessions together. Student participation might range from twenty-five to seventy-five students per session. This approach has the same advantages as the group session with one advisor but also provides for a broader-based expertise regarding policies, requirements, and other information. It exemplifies the use of other advisors as resources that was described in the previous section. Furthermore, Grahn, Kahn, and Kroll (1983) found that the team approach not only reduced the amount of advising time but did so with no significant overall loss in student knowledge of academic policies and procedures or in student satisfaction with advising.

All of this evidence is not to say that individual advising should be discarded; it should not. Advisors should, however, consider the group approach as an alternative, especially during the peak advising periods of preregistration, registration, and schedule adjustment.

Peer Advising. Students have always assisted other students with all kinds of matters throughout higher education. Many institutions have taken advantage of these strong peer relationships to formalize tutorial, orientation, residence hall, counseling, and academic advising programs in which students provide specific assistance to other students. (Several successful peer-advising programs are described in Chapter Seventeen.)

Where no formal peer-advising program exists, however, the individual advisor can create one. The advisor can simply suggest that a highly motivated and interested, usually upperclass, student assist lower-division students in the advising process. This student can assist in scheduling appointments, reviewing graduation requirements, ensuring that all necessary information is available to the advisor, and completing forms. Between advising sessions, the peer advisor can help verify student schedules, addresses, and participation in suggested activities. The amount of assistance that an advisor can expect depends upon the student's availability and the compensation provided. Some students are paid; some earn independent study credit; and some volunteer.

Whether formalized or not, the concept of peer advising should be reviewed as a technique for improving the advising program. Peer relationships are strong and should be utilized as a developmental advising effort.

Advising Contracts. Kramer and Gardner (1983, p. 26) described the advising contract as "a shared definition of what is to be accomplished, the principal duties of each party, and the procedures to be used to monitor, evaluate, or change that relationship." This description can be considered analogous to homework assignments for a course, and it can be applied to a variety of advising situations.

For example, the initial advising session might be used to establish the respective student and advisor responsibilities in the relationship. These responsibilities can be written in the form of a contract that will prevent confusion and faulty assumptions in the future. This is similar to reviewing a syllabus and the grading mechanisms for a course. More specifically, the advisor might "contract" the student to visit the learning resource center at least three times prior to the next advising session in order to improve certain academic skills needed in a current course. Or the advisor might require the student to obtain written approvals for some requested course of action.

The use of advising contracts is advantageous for monitoring the progress toward certain educational objectives, for determining alternatives when contract conditions are not being met, and for an ongoing review of student growth and development. It can be especially useful with students who need considerable structure in their learning environment. This must not be overdone, however, or the developmental process will be negated. The advisor must decide when such a technique is appropriate for a specific student.

Self-Advising. One measure of the effectiveness of a developmental advising program is how well students are able to advise themselves. Advisors should encourage self-advising whenever possible. They might, for example, refuse to meet with students until a tentative course plan has already been outlined; they might encourage students to discover the answers to questions about career opportunities, graduate school admissions, or job interview techniques.

At a minimum, students should know how to fulfill the graduation requirements. They should also learn how to determine alternatives for themselves, how to make decisions about those alternatives, and how to accept the responsibility and consequences of those decisions. Such outcomes exemplify academic advising as a developmental process that enhances the quality of higher education.

Summary and Implications

This chapter has provided a comprehensive set of advising materials and techniques that advisors might use in the developmental advising process. The advisor is the facilitator in this process and, therefore, must select from this set those elements that are most appropriate for the individual student and circumstance, in accordance with the overall student development process model.

To set goals, for example, two published instruments have been described; several instruments and strategies for self-assessment have also been included. The various resource offices identified here provide continuous opportunities for the instruction and consultation phases of the process, and institutional publications, personnel, and perhaps a version of the student development transcript provide mechanisms for evaluation of both the environment and the student.

In order to be able to select and use these materials most effectively, an advisor training program, such as those described in Chapter Sixteen, is necessary. The training program enables the advisor to achieve the maximum potential use of the available advising tools and resources, and it must include strategies for introducing them, especially for those advisors who are not familiar with student development literature. Participation in such a program is itself a developmental activity for the advisor. This awareness serves to ensure the same kinds of results with the students who are seeking to attain specific educational and personal goals.

References

Brown, R. D., and Citrin, R. S. "A Student Development Transcript: Assumptions, Uses, and Formats." *Journal of College Personnel*, 1977, *18* (3), 163–168.

Chickering, A. W. "College Advising for the 1970s." In J. Katz (Ed.), *New Directions for Higher Education: Services for Students*, no. 3. San Francisco: Jossey-Bass, 1973.

Claxton, C., Adams, D., and Williams, D. "Using Student Learning Styles in Teaching." *American Association of Higher Education Bulletin*, 1982, *34* (9), 1, 7–10.

College Entrance Examination Board. *College Guide to the Admissions Testing Program (ATP) Summary Reports*. New York: College Entrance Examination Board, 1982.

Crockett, D. S. (Ed.). *Academic Advising: A Resource Document*. Iowa City, Iowa: American College Testing Program, 1978.

Crockett, D. S. (Ed.). *Academic Advising: A Resource Document (1979 Supplement)*. Iowa City, Iowa: American College Testing Program, 1979.

Gill, J. S., and Freuhling, J. A. "Needs Assessment and the Design of Service Delivery Systems." *Journal of College Student Personnel*, 1979, *20* (4), 322–328.

Gordon, V. N. *The Undecided College Student: An Academic and Career Advising Challenge.* Springfield, Ill.: Thomas, 1984.

Grahn, J., Kahn, P., and Kroll, P. "Faculty Team Approach to Group Advising." *Journal of College Student Personnel,* 1983, *24* (3), 214-218.

Grites, T. J. *Academic Advising: Getting Us Through the Eighties.* Washington, D.C.: American Association for Higher Education–Educational Resource Information Center (AAHE-ERIC)/ Higher Education Research Report No. 7, 1979.

Holland, J. L. *The Self-Directed Search: A Guide to Educational and Vocational Planning.* Palo Alto, Calif.: Consulting Psychologists Press, 1970.

Hyman, R. T. *Questioning in the College Classroom.* Idea Paper No. 7. Manhattan, Kans.: Center for Faculty Evaluation and Development, Kansas State University, 1982.

Kramer, H. C., and Gardner, R. E. *Advising by Faculty.* (2nd ed.) Washington, D.C.: National Education Association, 1983.

Winston, R. B., Jr., Ender, S. C., and Miller, T. K. (Eds.). *New Directions for Student Services: Developmental Approaches to Academic Advising,* no. 17. San Francisco: Jossey-Bass, 1982.

Winston, R. B., Jr., Miller, T. K., and Prince, J. S. *Assessing Student Development: A Preliminary Manual for the Student Developmental Task Inventory (Second Edition) and the Student Developmental Profile and Planning Record.* Athens, Ga.: Student Development Associates, 1979.

9

Using Computers
in Academic Advising

Gary L. Kramer, Erlend D. Peterson,
Robert W. Spencer

Increased computing power and reductions in size, cost, and operational complexity in computers have dramatically increased their use in higher education and will undoubtedly expand computer applications in the future (Sampson, 1982). Computer-based systems are prevalent in most facets of student life programs in both two-year and four-year colleges and universities. In addition to academic advising, forms of computer assistance are used to aid the processes of student development, career counseling, admissions, financial aid, counseling-test administration, instruction, job placement, housing, and study skills (Blandford, Bridle, and Darling, 1980; Davidson and Gulak, 1980; Erwin and Tollefson, 1982; Mayberry, 1978; Sampson, 1981; Shatkin, 1980; Wedemeyer, 1978).

The use of computer technology can enhance the quality and accuracy of academic information for practically any advising delivery system.

Institutional Challenges and Academic Advising

Especially today, universities and colleges face challenges in offering a sound advising program. They are asked to provide advisors who are knowledgeable about academic degree requirements, to organize and disseminate complex student information accurately, and to personalize the advising process.

The 1980s represent an era not only of educational accountability but also of increased pressures on the institution to provide better services to students, and to do so with fewer resources. On the one hand, students want and need academic advisors who are accessible and able to provide specific, accurate information. On the other hand, because of insufficient budgetary support, advising students is often assigned a secondary role, and many advisors are neither knowledgeable about academic requirements nor available for or interested in advising (Spencer, Peterson, and Kramer, 1982b). Hence, an unfortunate dichotomy within the institution results in an unresolved dilemma for the student seeking specific academic information.

The complexity of student information as well as monitoring the fulfillment of academic requirements makes it more difficult for institutions to provide up-to-date information. Keeping up with current graduation requirements alone is an arduous task, as is the need for institutions to maintain contractual responsibilities for preserving student degree requirements by date of program entry. In place of the single department, common core degree program, many departments now offer multiple majors within multiple subspecializations. Degree requirements tend to change annually, as do general education and university requirements. The multiplicity, complexity, and frequency of changes in degree requirements create a great challenge for academic advisors (Spencer, Peterson, and Kramer, 1982a).

If the repetitive and clerical burden of tracking and monitoring academic requirements were removed from advisors, perhaps then the "personal touch" that most advisors want to offer students could be enhanced. Indeed, individualized academic and career planning could then receive primary emphasis.

Computers and the Advising Process

Because institutions are becoming increasingly complex and because information to students is often repetitive, the use of computer-assisted programs to facilitate, manage, and monitor student academic progress becomes especially important. Several aspects of the helping process are generally repetitive and do not appeal to most advisors (Sampson and Pyle, 1983). Computers can usually handle these aspects more easily and more cost-efficiently than can personnel.

Computers cannot replace people as advisors; there is no such thing as "computer advising." But, accompanied by personal advising, the use of computers has demonstrated efficiency and program improvement. Advising by computer can be an effective tool in assisting students and advisors to know and monitor academic requirements. It can relieve much of the clerical burden of the academic advisor.

This chapter describes, first, the cost effectiveness and definition of computer-assisted advising. Then the chapter introduces several institutional models of computer-assisted advising. Finally, it presents guidelines for analysis and design of computer-assisted advising and concludes with a computer-assisted advising paradigm.

Cost-Effectiveness of Computer Use. Over the past several years, the unit cost of computing has steadily decreased (Dertuzos and Moses, 1979). And just as significant, computing power and capabilities have greatly increased. Computers have become less expensive while becoming more powerful and, in the long run, have become cheaper than human labor (Bonham, 1983; Sampson and Pyle, 1983).

However, there is one caution. If an advisor is willing and able to take advantage of timely, accurate, and useful information provided by the computer, then the potential for dollar saving in the institution does exist. But if the advisor fails to take advantage of the information, then the institution has a very expensive automated system that is not being utilized and is simply wasting money (Duffy, 1982).

Use of computer technology in advising can mean cost benefits. In recent years, machine costs have decreased by 87 percent, whereas people costs have increased by 100 percent (U.S. Department of Labor, Bureau of Labor Statistics, 1980). (Computer costs are derived by comparing the IBM 370 series with the IBM 4300 series.) Computer costs are one of the few things in American society that are becoming less expensive (Spencer, Peterson, and Kramer, 1982a).

Computer-Assisted Advising. Computer-assisted advising in its simplest form is a computer program that stores and matches the degree requirements and the student's academic record. The computer produces an evaluation report that shows the graduation requirements and the student's progress in completing those requirements. The progress report may be printed in any variation or format the university or college desires. In most cases, the report includes:

1.   all requirements for graduation (institution, general education, major and specialization)
2.   specific courses that will satisfy the requirements
3.   all courses the student has completed
4.   individual requirements, waivers, or substitutions
5.   additional credit (advanced placement [AP], College Level Examination Program [CLEP], military credit, and so on)
6.   a statement of proficiency in completing the requirements
7.   whom to see and where to go for additional assistance (Spencer, Peterson, and Kramer, 1983)

In summary, the academic advisor should know about graduation requirements that are in effect for the student being advised, course requirements that satisfy the student's major degree requirements, courses completed by the student, and exceptions, waivers, substitutions, or special approvals given the student.

Computer-assisted advising can provide the academic advisor with information in each of these areas. Use of computer technology not only increases accuracy but also reduces advising costs in time and money by freeing the advisors to spend time advising students more effectively rather than clerically maintaining a tracking program.

Landmark Developments in Computer-Assisted Advising

The use of the computer to assist in academic advising and degree audits began at the University of California (UC), Berkeley, and Georgia State University (Peterson and Kramer, 1981). Additional computer advising programs emerged very slowly. By 1980 approximately 12 colleges and universities in the United States had implemented computer-advising programs. But between 1980 and 1983, interest grew and university personnel increased their efforts to use computer technology to support academic advising and degree audit. In a 1983 American Association of Collegiate Registrars and Admissions Officers (AACRAO) survey, 132 colleges and universities reported they had computer degree audit programs.

Although the basic concept of computer-assisted advising was similar among the 132 colleges, the individual approaches to computerization of academic information were as different as the names used to describe them. For example, Georgia State University called its system PACE (Programmed Academic Curriculum Evaluation); Purdue University entitled its system Academic Progress Report, and the University of North Carolina named its report Automated Degree Audit.

University of California, Berkeley. The College of Letters and Science at the University of California, Berkeley, developed the first operational computer-assisted advising program in 1968. It provided a two-page graduation summary of the college and general education requirements. The computer listed the summary information on a preprinted first page. The second page was an unofficial transcript of all courses completed. At the end of each semester, the College of Letters and Science Advising Center obtained from the registrar's office a computer tape of students' grades. It was merged with the college's student course history tape, which was a cumulative computerized academic record for each student. The computer then matched the individual student record with the requirements and printed the progress report. The progress report was distributed to students by the college advising center personnel each term.

Berkeley's College of Letters and Science depended on its own student computer record system. Since it was not integrated with the official university student record system, errors crept into the college system, causing credibility problems and eventually termination of the computer system in 1977. Even though the Berkeley system was discontinued, it influenced other institutions to attempt a computerized advising system. It also provided an example of what developers of computer-assisted advising programs should not do. Those who observed Berkeley's experiences learned the importance of integrating the computer advising system with the official student academic records of the registrar's office. The lack of accuracy of the advisement report brought about the system's demise. Each semester increased the number of errors in the College of Letters and Science's student record tape, until the college was forced either to make major modifications to the system or discontinue it. Frequency of errors caused a loss of credibility in using a computer system among faculty, students, and administrators.

Georgia State University. Georgia State University developed its degree audit system (PACE) at about the same time as UC Berkeley did. In 1976 programming changes were made to make the program more efficient, and it has since become a very effective tool for advisors at Georgia State. The terms *degree audit* and *advising evaluation* refer interchangeably to the PACE system. It provides a self-advising report that is distributed to the students each quarter through the colleges. The degree audit system is designed with a common computer base that allows different degree program "masks" to define the requirements within each college. A requirement for a mask can be specified in a number of ways, such as:

1. a specific course or courses
   - English 111 (or)
   - English 111 and English 112 (or)
   - English 111 or English 112 (or)
   - English 111 and English 112 or
     English 113 and English 114
2. a selection of one or more courses from a given list

- any three classes from
  History 106
  History 111
  History 112
  History 113
  History 114
  (or)
- any two from the following options
  Physics 101 and Physics 102
  Geology 101 and Geology 102
  Anthropology 101 and Anthropology 102

3. a specified number of hours from a given department and at a specific level (that is, freshman, senior, and so on)
   - ten hours from department of English (course level 100 or 200)
   - fifteen hours from departments English (course level 300 or 400)
   - twenty hours from any department except Physical Education (course level 400)

4. a specified sequence of courses (a given set) or a choice of a set from a given number of sets (Singletory and Greene, 1983)
   - select ten hours from courses
     English 111, English 112, English 113
     Journalism 101, Drama 102 or
     from departments of Foreign Languages and History

The system is carefully designed to follow the same format as the degree statements printed in the institution's catalogue.

Purdue University. In 1969 Purdue University developed the first complete degree-tracking program, entitled the Academic Progress Report. The program began in the college of business and because of its success, it was later expanded throughout the entire university. The curriculum degree requirements and student records were stored on computer tapes. Initially, the degree audit reports were generated once a semester. In recent years the records have been transferred to computer disks that give immediate computer access for requesting the progress reports, although hard-copy reports are actually processed on an overnight basis.

The progress report is affectionately known as the "bingo sheet" because of its matrix format. Originally it was restricted to the student's actual major, but now the program can match the student's record against any valid major/minor combination in any school. Academic Progress Reports are produced automatically each term and distributed to the schools for use by academic advisors and students in preparing the course request form for the next term's registration.

Brigham Young University. In 1976 Brigham Young University implemented the first comprehensive on-line computer-assisted academic advising program with integrated and interactive computer data files. The system provides the user with immediate and direct access through computer terminals to the curriculum degree requirements and student academic records. The user can generate an individual progress report upon request. By entering the student name or student-body number, the computer program locates the student academic record, matches it with the degree requirements for the semester the student officially entered the degree program, and displays the results on the terminal screen within two to three seconds. If a hard-copy record is desired, the request is entered in the computer and the report is printed immediately. The Advisement by Computer (ABC) progress reports are mailed to students each term of their enrollment.

Miami-Dade Community College. Miami-Dade Community College has developed a system that not only deserves recognition for a community college system but also incorporates a broad perspective of the type of academic and career counseling that all colleges and universities can use as a model. The system, entitled Advisement and Graduation Information System (AGIS), provides a concept of helping students in an open admissions environment. It assists students in class selection, and more importantly, it assists advisors and instructors to monitor individually each student's progress and needs. AGIS includes nine computer programs to assist a person in individualized instruction or advising. It maintains three files for each course/program—course file, student file, and student index file. The system identifies specific courses that are suggested or required for sixty-eight associate of arts programs, and it maintains accurate and up-to-date information on the graduation status of each student.

Computer-Assisted Advising Models. Computer-assisted advising systems vary according to the philosophy and resources of the institution. Most advising programs operate somewhere between a batch process (that is, a group of jobs to be run on a computer at one time) and a comprehensive, interactive on-line (that is, immediate and direct computer access, either by group or individual) system. And the method to manage curriculum or advising data may vary according to the organization of the institution. Centralized institutions (interdependent academic colleges) and decentralized institutions (autonomous academic colleges) will likely insert data differently. Some excellent models represent each of these variables. Reviewing the advantages and limitations of the models following and the suggestions in the section on "Analysis and Design of Computer-Assisted Advising" should provide insight for the institution considering development of a computer-assisted advising program.

All computer-assisted advising programs operate on the principle of matching degree requirements with student academic records to produce a degree progress report. However, here is a list of unique approaches and the institutions that designed them.

1.   The University of Denver developed a simple, efficient, and cost-effective system by batch processing the data once a semester and storing the data on computer tapes. The system was developed inexpensively and costs approximately two cents per progress report printed.

2.   Purdue University developed a unique progress report design. On one page it includes thirty-five segments of information including a matrix format that plots the degree requirements for the eight semesters of the baccalaureate program. In each box it shows the department name and course number of the required course. If the student has completed the course, it also prints the earned grade, semester and year taken, and number of credit hours.

3.   North Carolina State University designed their automated degree audit system as a centralized system with decentralized

decision making and data loading. There are nine schools and eighty departments. Each department and school is responsible for coding and entering the information. The system is a table-driven mask with embedded codes for the requirement options.

4. Georgia State University's advisement and degree-auditing system is not only one of the oldest systems but it is the only transportable system that is sold to other universities. Most degree audit systems are designed to the institution's environment. The Georgia State PACE system has been successfully implemented at several other colleges and universities.

5. Brigham Young University's system is unique for its total on-line computer capabilities as one segment of a larger student information system. It uses a "data base" approach; that is, degree and student academic records files are interactive. Every access gives the most accurate and up-to-the-minute evaluation. Two other unique characteristics, discussed later in this chapter, are the use of a curriculum identification (ID) number and a group structure of stated requirements and options.

6. Miami-Dade Community College has an expanded and comprehensive approach to advising. Academic advising is supported through three systems. Their Advisement and Graduation Information System (AGIS) goes beyond degree tracking to include on-line computer access to recommended courses for transfer by degree program for Florida's colleges and universities. The Academic Alert System is used early in the semester to identify both students who have academic difficulty and those who are outstanding students. The system generates either early warning letters or letters of encouragement. The third support system, the Standards of Academic Progress, is used at the end of the semester to identify students who have weak academic records.

Analysis and Design of Computer-Assisted Advising

The success and efficiency of a computer-assisted advising system depend on careful system planning and properly developed computer files. A curriculum management system and an integrated student record system must be in place before computer-assisted advising can succeed. Other systems that should be in place are the classroom scheduling and timetable system, registration, and graduation.

A good curriculum management system can be divided into three logical files: (1) information necessary for currently approved courses, (2) historical courses, and (3) catalogue information relating to courses.

The curriculum computer files must contain all catalogue information plus other monitoring information necessary for curriculum management. Generally, the curriculum computer files include the following information:

1. *Currently approved courses:* department name, catalogue number, record sequence, credit hours, lecture hours, lab hours, college and department assignment, effective years and terms, optimum minimum and maximum size, course title, semesters or terms offered, effective grade rule, curriculum identification number, class fee, special enrollment approvals, lab or quiz section approval, class type, and last action date
2. *Historical course information:* curriculum identification number, title code, department name, catalogue number, course titles, effective years and terms, credit hours, grade rule, number of students, last change date (The curriculum descriptions include department names/catalogue number, curriculum ID, from term/year, title, prerequisites, description, date when last revised.)
3. *Catalogue information:* college department major, specialization, degree requirements, prerequisites, narrative statements, effective catalogue year

The most important element in a degree audit system is the concept of a curriculum unit. Catalogue numbers and course descriptions change over time, though the course remains essentially unchanged in content; that is, the course represents the same curriculum unit. The most prominent example is freshman English. During a few decades, the course number for freshman English may have evolved from English 1 to English 10, English 15, English 100, English 101, English 105, English 110, English 111, and finally

English 115, while credit hours and content have remained basically the same. It still constitutes a single curriculum unit. A unique curriculum identification number embedded in the class record— for example, freshman English curriculum identification number 1144—eliminates the requirement of maintaining a table to identify the course history with equivalency.

The curriculum identification number can also facilitate the integration of transfer work. The visual information in the system, such as department abbreviations, course numbers, and course titles, can remain exactly as it appears on the transfer transcript. But a curriculum identification number, embedded in the transfer class record, can be immediately integrated and recognized in the degree audit and computer-advising programs.

Another design consideration that makes a computer degree audit system more effective is the use of groups in the statement of degree requirements. The statement specifies whether all the classes of that group must be completed or only a certain number of them, whether a certain number of credit hours in the group need to be completed, or if there is a combination of classes and credit hours. These groups can be combined with "and's" and "or's."

Either the system should automatically enter into the degree requirements area any change to a course in the curriculum file, or it should identify the need to change the degree requirement area when the curriculum file changes. For example, if Statistics 221 has a number change to Statistics 223, the system should automatically search the degree requirements and replace each entry of Statistics 221 with the new entry, Statistics 223. If Statistics 221 is deleted, the system should notify each department who uses the course in its degree requirements that the course has been deleted.

The curriculum management file, along with the degree requirements in the student-assisted advisory programs, can also be useful to departments in their curriculum planning. For example, if the system has a file containing the number of students who have officially declared a major in accounting, the courses they have completed, their current enrollment, and their class standing, the curriculum planners in the accounting department can compare their file to the degree requirement file to determine how many sections of each class they must offer and how many student spaces they must provide in the coming term, semester, or year.

The on-line curriculum management system can provide decentralized updating and maintenance throughout the colleges or departments. The system should include the proper edits and checks, according to institutional or college policy.

Most institutions are aware of the need to review their present system, identify their needs, determine their goals, know their limitations, and methodically design, implement, and evaluate a new system. Unfortunately, some institutions do not know and must learn later at great cost the following tips for designers of computer-based advising systems.

Integrating Academic Information Files. The systems that are effective today in computer-assisted advising are those that first integrated their academic information files (that is, registration, curriculum, records, and basic or student master). Both the student and the advisor want to know all factors that compose the academic record. Knowing which completed courses apply toward academic requirements is important, but knowing how current enrollment applies is also vital. Thus the key to programming is to interface all files that compose an academic record and thereby achieve a comprehensive student progress report.

Updating Academic Requirements. A well-trained and knowledgeable terminal operator responsible for inserting academic requirements is central to the success of the advising report. There are basically two ways to organize curriculum data insertion. One way is to centralize all data inputs, that is, to assign a clerical person the responsibility to insert all approved academic requirements for the institution. Another way is to decentralize the responsibility of maintaining and updating curriculum files. Each academic college is then responsible for its own curriculum and its own advising report. Before deciding which major system to use the institution should consider these issues: (1) the resources to hire and train one person or several, (2) the philosophy and management of curriculum approval, (3) the coordination and distribution of the advising report, and (4) the procedures to resolve discrepancies in any one of the data files. There are merits and limitations in each of the two methods. The philosophy or organization of the institution and the type of advising system will determine which method is better.

Tracking Academic Requirements. Sensitivity to the institution's current methods of tracking academic requirements, to current report formats, and to ideas from faculty, administrators, advisors, and computer personnel can make the designers' jobs much easier and more successful. Can the designers convert current tracking methods to a computer program? Can the computer produce reports in the current formats? The challenge is to produce a computer-tracking document that is familiar to its users. For example, the organization of degree requirements in the catalogue could be the first clue to what the college community finds comfortable and likes to use to describe its requirements. Furthermore, the involvement of faculty, college administrators, advisors, and computer personnel gives these users a feeling of ownership of the report. The committee that develops a computer-assisted advising program should realize that the greater the efforts to understand and work within the present format of academic requirements and to involve the program's users, the greater the possibility to win acceptance of the computer-generated report. Frequently, a user rejects a new report because it is in a format not readily understood. And in designing computer-assisted advising programs, many institutions changed a cold faculty reception to a warm one simply by redesigning the output to appear similar to previous degree audit forms.

Resolving Advising Problems. Computer-assisted advising provides a solution to the most fundamental advising problems. Institutions that have developed computer-assisted advising programs have found them to be an effective tool to improve the advising process. But whatever degree of success computer technology attains, college advising personnel are strongly encouraged to be available, knowledgeable, and interested. Advising students must still be personable. One might think that students who have received a computer-generated advising report have been advised. Such is not the case. Most academic advisors know that monitoring academic requirements is no more than half the responsibility of advising students. The personable, caring approach to academic advising is essential. Albert Einstein said it best:

The concern for man and his destiny must always be
the chief interest of all technical effort; never forget it
among your diagrams and equations.

In summary, an institution contemplating the development
of a computer-assisted advising program should first:

1. create and foster an ongoing dialogue among faculty, advisors,
    students, and administrative and computer personnel concern-
    ing advising information needs (In particular, the computer
    progammer plays a critical role in meeting user needs. The
    more specific and detailed the request for computerized advis-
    ing information, the better.)
2. carefully and comprehensively define the role of academic
    advising in the institution
3. determine essential academic information needs
4. provide flexibility in program development to allow for
    changes in academic requirements
5. isolate the most difficult academic program track (A "worst
    case" approach stretches program development to include the
    most extreme and awkward variables.)
6. clearly delineate program objectives
7. implement the program in phases, methodically (Haste can
    make waste.)
8. seek continually to evaluate and improve the computer-assisted
    advising program by soliciting feedback from all users of the
    system (Spencer, Peterson, and Kramer, 1983)

A Computer-Assisted Advising Paradigm

Brigham Young University developed a computer-assisted
advising program that monitors and tracks a student's progress
from entry into the institution through graduation. The computer
program provides a detailed individual evaluation of all graduation
requirements for each student according to date of entry into the
institution for tracking general education and institutional requirements and according to year/term of entry into the major for

tracking major requirements. Students, faculty, and administrators have immediate access to this information via on-line computer terminals or hard-copy printout. Each term a student is enrolled, a computer-printed summary of the student's progress toward graduation is mailed to the student's local address. The report includes the following features illustrated in Exhibits 1 to 3.

- page 1—general education and university requirements (see Exhibit 1)
  1. date of report
  2. academic field—college, major, degree type
  3. name, address, and social security number of student
  4. a summary of completed general education requirements and a listing of deficiencies
     Note:
     a. subject area
     b. classes required
     c. course or evaluation used to complete the requirement
     d. classes deficient
     e. application of current enrollment
  5. a summary of university requirements, courses completed, courses deficient, and application of current enrollment
- page 2—major requirements (see Exhibit 2)
  1. date of report
  2. student name and social security number
  3. departmental information
  4. date of entry into major
  5. major grade point average (GPA)
  6. tracking by classes
  7. tracking by credit hours
  8. tracking by group combinations
  9. application of current enrollment
  10. application of substitution course
  11. application of waived course
  12. application of transfer course
  13. unique narrative information
  14. statement of academic requirement completion
  15. statement of academic requirement deficiency

16. office and phone number where student can obtain additional assistance
- page 3—current enrollment and unofficial transcript (see Exhibit 3)
  1. date of report
  2. student name and social security number
  3. listing of classes student is currently enrolled in
  4. unofficial transcript—listing of classes completed in chronological order
  5. a summary of transfer classes completed, including name of institution and dates of attendance
  6. summary of advanced placement
  7. summary of CLEP
  8. summary of college credits
  9. semester GPA summary

Students receive the computer-assisted advising report before the drop/add deadline of the current semester and the registration deadline of the subsequent semester or term. Thus the report serves the students in three distinct ways. *First, it allows students to verify current enrollment,* especially in light of any class adjustments they might have made since the initial registration. This aspect of the report has substantially reduced students' complaints of not knowing their complete and official registration until the end of the semester when grade reports come out. *Second, the report can be used as a planning document for registration.* The completion/deficiency aspects of the report help students know what courses they must yet fulfill. *Third, the analysis of courses completed and the application of other means to fulfill requirements at the university provide the students a sense of control and monitoring of their academic program.*

The computer-assisted advising program also identifies classes repeated and states GPA requirements. It can be used to project curriculum demands, plan course offerings, check the accuracy of the transcript, and identify the number of semesters required for a given major or change of major. This information is readily available via an on-line system. For example, to assess the advantages and disadvantages of changing majors, a student may sit

Exhibit 1. General Education and University Requirements.

```
                    BRIGHAM YOUNG UNIVERSITY              OCTOBER 19, 1983
                    ADVISEMENT BY COMPUTER/                         ①
                    GRADUATION PROGRESS REPORT

                    COMMENCEMENT:  AUG 1984          DEGREE:  BS
COLLEGE:  ENGR. SCI.+TECH.  MAJOR:  MANUFACTRNG TECH   MINOR:
②
③         ┌Mary Student                  555555555
          ┤867 S. Stubbs Ave. #1
          └Provo, Utah  84601
```

	REQUIRED	COMPLETED	DEFICIENT	CURRENT ENROLLMENT (NOT INCLUDED IN CALCULATION OF DEFICIENCIES)
UNIVERSITY GRADUATION REQUIREMENTS		CLASS/CREDIT HOURS OR EVALUATIONS		
BASIC ACADEMIC SKILLS				
④a BASIC READING	1	READING	0	
BASIC WRITING	1	WRITING	0	
④b BASIC MATH	1	BASIC MATH	0	
ARTS & SCIENCES				
ARTS & LETTERS ELECTIVES	3	ART & LETT 1	0	
④c		ART & LETT 2		
		ART & LETT 3		
NATURAL SCIENCE				
BIO. SCI. REQUIRED	1	BIOLOGY BRD	0	
PHYS. SCI. REQUIRED	1	PHY SC BROAD	0	④d
NAT. SCI. ELECTIVE	1		1	CHEM 103 ④e
SOCIAL SCIENCE				
AMERICAN HERITAGE	1	AM HERITAGE	0	
SOC. SCI. ELECTIVES	2	SOC SCI 1	0	
		SOC SCI 2		
ADVANCED ACADEMIC SKILLS				
ADVANCED WRITING	1	ENGL 316	0	
FOREIGN LANGUAGE OR MATH	1	MATH 223	0	
PHYSICAL EDUCATION	1.0	FILLED BY ASSOC DEG		
PHYSICAL FITNESS	0.5	FILLED BY ASSOC DEG		
BOOK OF MORMON	4.0	REL A 421 (2.0)	0.0	
		REL A 422 (2.0)		
RELIGION ELECTIVES	10.0	REL 138 (2.0)	0.0	
		REL A 327 (2.0)		
⑤		REL C 351 (2.0)		
		REL C 333 (2.0)		
		REL A 301 (2.0)		
UPPER DIVISION	40.0	43.5	0.0	
RESIDENCE HOURS	30.0	90.5	0.0	
TOTAL HOURS *	128.0	164.5	0.0	
* D CREDIT ALLOWED	18.0	EARNED 6.0		

Exhibit 2. Composite of Requirements for the Major.

```
①——JUL 26, 1983        M A J O R   R E Q U I R E M E N T S              PAGE 2
②—STUDENT MARY              555555555     YEAR TERM ENTERED ..... 81 FALL————④
    ┌COLLEGE .... ENGR. SCI.+TECH.         RESIDENCE HRS REQUIRED  10.0
③───┤DEPARTMENT . MANUFACTRNG TECH        MAJOR HOURS COMPLETED . 73.5
    │MAJOR ...... MANUFACTRNG TECH         MAJOR GPA ............. 2.79————⑤
    └MAJOR CODE . 395320                   DEGREE ................ B.S.

⑥—COMPLETE THESE 15 CLASSES         *     C S   131 ................  3.0 B+
                                    *     ECON  110  TRANS ECON 220   3.0 B—②
    MFG T 124  CURRENTLY ENROLL  0.0 *    ENGL  316 ................  3.0 C+
    MFG T 131  ................  3.0 B— * PHSCS 105 ................  3.0 C
    MFG T 132  ................  3.0 A— * PHSCS 106 ................  3.0 D+
    MFG T 225  ................  3.0 C+ *
    MFG T 229  ................  3.0 B  * 1 CLASS DEFICIENT
    MFG T 230  ................  3.0 C+ *
    MFG T 331  ................  3.0 A— *****************************************
    MFG T 332  ................  3.0 B— *
    MFG T 335  ................  4.0 C+ *       IF NO PREVIOUS DRAFTING, DES T
    MFG T 336  ................  3.0 B— * 111 REQUIRED.
    MFG T 338  ................  3.0 B— *
    MFG T 345                          * COMPLETE THESE  8 CLASSES
    MFG T 360  ................  3.0 B+ *
    MFG T 430  ................  3.0 A— *  MFG T 291R ................  0.0 P
    MFG T 431  ................  3.0 B— *  MFG T 291R ................  0.0 P
                                    *     MFG T 291R ................  0.0 P
    2 CLASSES DEFICIENT             *     MFG T 291R ................  0.0 P
                                    *     MFG T 291R
    *********************************     MFG T 291R
                                    *     MFG T 291R
    COMPLETE  1 OF THESE CLASSES    *     MFG T 491R ................  0.5 P
                                    *
    MFG T 399R                      * 3 CLASSES DEFICIENT————————⑫
⑩——MFG T 498R SUBST MFG T 533  3.0 B+ *
                                    *********************************
    THIS REQUIREMENT IS COMPLETE    *
    *********************************  * COMPLETE  7.0 HOURS ————————⑦
                                    * FROM THESE CLASSES
    ┌EITHER COMPLETE THESE 3 CLASSES *
    │                               *     C S   420
    │   MATH  121 ................  3.0 C+ * C S   440
⑧──┤   MATH  122 ................  3.0 B— * EL EN 444
    │   MATH  223 ................  3.0 B— * EL EN 350
    │                               *     MATH  322
    └OR COMPLETE THIS CLASS         *
                                    * 7.0 HOURS DEFICIENT
        MATH  112                   *
                                    *     MFG T 291R EACH SEMESTER EXCEPT┐
⑭—THIS REQUIREMENT IS COMPLETE      * WHEN REGISTERED FOR MFG T 491R.    ├⑬
                                    *     8 HOURS TECHNICAL ELECTIVES:   ┘
    *********************************  * SEE ADVISOR
                                    *
    COMPLETE THESE  9 CLASSES       * IF YOU HAVE QUESTIONS, CONTACT YOUR┐
                                    * ADVISEMENT CENTER AT 264 CB         ├⑯
⑪———ELN T 100  WAIVED ........  0.0 WV * (EXT: 4325)                     ┘
    ELN T 242  ................  3.0 C+ *
    DES T 211  ................  3.0 B  *
⑨——DES T 316  CURRENTLY ENROLL  4.0 *
                                    *
    (CONTINUED ON THE NEXT COLUMN)  *
```

Exhibit 3. Current Enrollment and Unofficial Transcript.

①——JUL 26, 1983   PAGE 3

②— STUDENT MARY
    555555555

③——————⌐   C U R R E N T   E N R O L L M E N T
                     │   SUMMER TERM 1983
                     │CHEM   103   001   1.0   MFG T 224   001   3.0
                     ⌊DES T 316   001   4.0   MFG T 224 L 002   0.0

④————————————————U N O F F I C I A L   T R A N S C R I P T

TRANSFER CLASSES			FALL 1980			WINTER 1983		
⑤—DIABLO VALLEY CO			MFG T 131	3.0	B-	(CONT)		
ATTENDED 70-76			MFG T 132	3.0	A-	MFG T 336	3.0	B-
ASSOC 1972			MATH 100E	2.0	B+	MFG T 430	3.0	A-
ASTR 110	3.0	B	REL A 327	2.0	A-	MFG T 533	3.0	B+
BUS 169	3.0	B	REL C 351	2.0	C-	MFG T 401R	0.5	P
BUS 186	3.0	B				MATH 224	3.0	W
BUS 191	3.0	B	WINTER 1981			MFG T 291R	0.0	P
BUS 240	3.0	D	REL A 421	2.0	B+			
BUS 294	3.0	C				SPRING TERM 1983		
COMSC 101	1.0	A	SPRING TERM 1981			CHEM 100	3.0	C
COMSC 120	1.0	P	REL A 422	2.0	A	ENGL 316	3.0	C+
COMSC 150	3.0	B				MFG T 360	3.0	B+
ECON 220	3.0	B	FALL 1981					
ECON 221	3.0	C	DES T 111	3.0	C			
ENGL 122	3.0	A	MFG T 225	3.0	C+			
ENGL 123	3.0	A	MFG T 230	3.0	C+			
GEOL 120	3.0	C	MFG T 335	4.0	W			
H ED 124	3.0	C	MATH 121	3.0	C+			
HIST 120	3.0	C	MFG T 291R	0.0	P			
HIST 121	3.0	C						
HIST 124	3.0	B	WINTER 1982					
HUMAN 110	3.0	A	DES T 211	3.0	B			
HUMAN 112	3.0	B	MFG T 229	3.0	B			
MATH 120	4.0	C	MFG T 335	4.0	C+			
MATH 122	1.0	P	MATH 122	3.0	B-			
PE 102	0.5	B	REL C 333	2.0	B			
PE 122	0.5	A	MFG T 291R	0.0	P			
PE 150	0.5	A						
PE 150	0.5	A	SPRING TERM 1982					
PHYS 110	3.0	C	MATH 223	3.0	W			
PSYCH 122	3.0	B	PHSCS 105	3.0	C			
SOC 110	3.0	B	REL A 301	2.0	A-			

⑥—ADVANCED PLACEME			SUMMER TERM 1982		
ATTENDED 76-76			C S 131	3.0	B+
CHEM 111	3.0	P	PHSCS 106	3.0	D+

BYU CLASSES			FALL 1982		
FALL 1976			MFG T 331	3.0	A-
ACCT 203	3.0	W	MFG T 332	3.0	B-
C S 133A	2.0	W	MFG T 338	3.0	B-
C S 133B	1.0	W	MFG T 431	3.0	B-
REL A 421	2.0	W	MATH 223	3.0	B-
MATH 110	4.0	W	MFG T 291R	0.0	P

SUMMARY OF COLLEGE CREDITS————⑦

	EARNED	GRADED	POINTS	GPA
SPRING TERM 1977		WINTER 1983				TOTAL	164.5	162.0	450.70	2.78

SPRING TERM 1977			WINTER 1983							
ACCT 203	3.0	W	ELN T 242	3.0	C+	BYU	90.5	90.0	252.20	2.80

at a video terminal and match courses completed against any degree program.

Summary Remarks on Computer-Assisted Advising Programs

Generally, a computer-assisted advising program should provide a detailed individual evaluation of all graduation requirements for each student, including general, major, and university academic requirements. Students, faculty, and administrators should have immediate access to this information through terminals or through hard-copy printout. Perhaps the most significant feature of a computer-assisted advising program is its capability to provide students and academic advisors an immediate assessment of student progress toward graduation. A computer-assisted advising program should include other capabilities to:

1. state and track all requirements for graduation (institution-wide, general, and major)
2. categorize requirements within the major (college, department, major, and specialization)
3. individually tailor, insert, and track an approved degree program
4. track the number of classes, number of semester hours, and combinations of each
5. list prerequisites for required courses
6. show narrative information
7. include all credit, substitutions, and waivers (institutional credit, transfer credit, and miscellaneous credit such as AP, CLEP, and military)
8. provide instant update capability
9. allow students to "shop" for a major and review immediately change-of-major consequences
10. track requirements as frequently as every semester, but track each student by date of entry into the major
11. track two or more majors

Schools using a computer-assisted advising program have been able to provide advisors with informative reports on academic requirements that have the following characteristics:

1. accurate and up to date
2. less expensive than a photocopy
3. informative, allowing an advisor to focus on a student's education and career objectives
4. essential to graduation evaluation
5. adaptable to any type of advising (that is, faculty, advising centers, peer advising, or professional advising)
6. efficient in cutting clerical costs and in giving advisors time to work directly with students

Perhaps the question "Should a computer-assisted advising program be developed at my institution?" needs to be reworded to "When will my institution implement such a program?" Computer-assisted advising is indeed the best solution to the most fundamental advising problem—getting accurate academic information to advisors and students.

The Next Generation of Computer Systems

The present state of the art of computer usage in academic advising is still rather primitive. During the 1960s and 1970s, many institutions showed primary concern for systematizing academic records, especially the transcript, moving away from total dependence on hand-created, paper records. This chapter describes the results of this progress, which have greatly simplified and improved the accuracy of administrative records and have also provided accurate, pertinent information that is highly useful in the academic advising process. This advance has improved the quality of advising on many campuses by providing timely and accurate academic data recording students' progress toward graduation and identifying possible obstacles, such as prerequisite course sequences and other "hidden requirements."

The next generation of computer software needs to incorporate interactive features similar to the SIGI and DISCOVER programs for career exploration and guidance. An interactive computer-assisted advising system should allow students and their advisors to keep accessible critically important information about values, interests, academic background and performance, intellectual abilities and skills levels, and career aspirations. This program should not only provide information about academic status but also help students explore the full range of learning opportunities within the collegiate environment and relate their programs of study to other important areas of their lives, including their future careers.

References

Blandford, R., Bridle, H. D., and Darling, A. L. "More Time for Applicants with On-Line Admissions." *College and University,* 1980, *52,* 135–142.

Bonham, G. "High Tech and Meaningful Work." *Change,* 1983, *15,* 10–11.

Davidson, J., and Gulak, P. "Prospectus: Waiting List Subsystem." Unpublished manuscript, Department of Resident Life, University of Maryland, 1980.

Dertuzos, M. L., and Moses, J. (Eds.). *Future Impact of Computers: A Twenty-Year View.* Cambridge, Mass.: MIT Press, 1979.

Duffy, J. "Cost-Analysis." *Computer World,* 1982, *16,* 47–48.

Erwin, D. T., and Tollefson, A. L. "A Data Base Management Model for Student Development." *Journal of College Student Personnel,* 1982, *23,* 70–76.

Mayberry, M. E. "GRAD II—Placement's Answer to the Hidden Job Market." *Journal of College Placement,* 1978, *18,* 19–22.

Peterson, E. D., and Kramer, G. L. "Landmark Developments in Academic Advising." Paper presented at annual meeting of National Academic Advising Association (NACADA), Asheville, N.C., October 1981.

Sampson, J. P., Jr. "CASSI: A Computer-Assisted Approach to Helping Students Improve Their Academic Performance." *National Association of Student Personnel Administrators (NASPA) Journal,* 1981, *28,* 42–47.

Sampson, J. P., Jr. "Effective Computer Research Management: Keeping the Tail from Wagging the Dog." *National Association of Student Personnel Administrators (NASPA) Journal,* 1982, *19,* 38–44.

Sampson, J. P., Jr., and Pyle, K. R. "Ethical Issues Involved with the Use of Computer-Assisted Counseling, Testing, and Guidance Systems." *Personnel and Guidance Journal*, 1983, *61*, 283-287.

Shatkin, L. "Computer-Assisted Guidance: Description of Systems." Princeton, N.J.: Educational Testing Service, 1980.

Singletory, L. A., and Greene, J. E., Jr. "A Computerized Student Advisement and Degree Auditing System." Unpublished manuscript, Georgia State University, 1983.

Spencer, R. W., Peterson, E. D., and Kramer, G. L. "Advisement by Computer: A Tool for Improving Academic Advising." *College and University*, 1982a, *57*, 169-179.

Spencer, R. W., Peterson, E. D., and Kramer, G. L. "Utilizing College Advising Centers to Facilitate and Revitalize Academic Advising," *National Academic Advising Association (NACADA) Journal*, 1982b, *2*, 13-23.

Spencer, R. W., Peterson, E. D., and Kramer, G. L. "Designing and Implementing a Computer-Assisted Academic Advisement Program." *Journal of College Student Personnel*, 1983, *24*, 513-518.

U.S. Department of Labor, Bureau of Labor Statistics. *National Survey of Professional Administration: Technical and Clerical Pay*. Washington, D.C.: U.S. Government Printing Office, March 1980.

Wedemeyer, R. H. "Computerizing Student Financial Aid." *Journal of Student Financial Aid*, 1978, *8*, 23-28.

10

Meeting the Special Advising Needs of Students

❧❧❧ ❧❧❧ ❧❧❧ ❧❧❧ ❧❧❧ ❧❧❧ ❧❧❧ ❧❧❧

Sue A. Saunders, Leroy Ervin

The increasing diversity of undergraduate student populations in terms of age, ethnic background, career goals, and academic preparation is a concrete example of the changes taking place in higher education. Obviously, no one advising approach can possibly be comprehensive enough to meet the plethora of needs presented by such diverse student populations. If academic advisors are to serve as developmental educators rather than as mere "schedule makers," they need to have the background knowledge, skills, competencies, and personal characteristics to effectively promote development of successful behaviors—in the academic, vocational, and personal areas. Additionally, the institutional advising system must be flexible enough to meet diverse student educational needs rather than responding merely on the basis of a single advising model. This chapter will examine the (1) historical context that gave

rise to a more diverse undergraduate population, (2) needs manifested by a variety of student populations that require special
advising attention, and (3) advisor strategies that can be used to
address these student needs.

Trends Related to Student Diversity

If advisors are to work effectively with students who populate
postsecondary institutions in the 1980s, they are challenged to gain
a clear understanding of why the student body on a particular
campus is, in reality, likely to be a mosaic of student groups. A
knowledge of the changes in society and in higher education that
resulted in more students with special needs is a prerequisite to
understanding the pressures, conflicts, and opportunities faced by
both students and advisors.

When one views the historical development of American
higher education, the dramatically increasing rate of change is
readily apparent. Although the initial purpose was to train young
men for professions in the ministry or community service, higher
education has changed continually in order to be responsive to the
needs of society for trained members of newly developed professions, such as law, medicine, engineering, and business
administration.

Recently, much effort has been devoted to the demands of a
mass student market. The importance of the demands of student
consumers, coupled with the needs of institutions to maintain a
healthy fiscal condition, has led to a changing student body and
changing institutional missions. Specifically, these changes include
(1) enrollment of students who do not meet traditionally defined
entrance requirements, with the resulting creation of remedial
programs; (2) recruitment of older, part-time students along with a
concomitant need for appropriate student affairs programs; and (3)
the development of new technical fields that will be highly popular
with students (Carnegie Council on Policy Studies in Higher
Education, 1980).

The reduced number of young people in the traditional
cohort of college students has implications that will, by the year
2000, fundamentally change the composition of the student body.

For example, in 1960 student enrollments were composed primarily of young majority males, yet by 2000 more women than men will enroll in college and one fourth of all students will be minorities (Carnegie Council on Policy Studies in Higher Education, 1980). Minority students' increased access to traditionally white/Anglo institutions accounts, in part, for the projected increase of minority student attendance in college.

Research indicates that effective advising is related to positive outcomes for all college students. Systematic academic advising has been shown to be related to retention of students (Lenning, Beal, and Sauer, 1980), academic achievement (Wilson and others, 1975; Terenzini and Pascarella, 1980), satisfaction with college (Pantages and Creedon, 1978), and achievement of personal, social, and vocational developmental tasks (Hardee, 1962, 1970; Kramer and Gardner, 1977; Abel, 1978). Determining what constitutes effective academic advising, however, is a question that has not yet been answered conclusively (Brown and Sanstead, 1982). There are strong indications, though, that advising that significantly contributes to the totality of a student's higher-education experience purposefully emphasizes not only the immediate academic progress of students but also focuses on the student's developing sense of competence, future plans, and overall sense of identity (Miller and McCaffrey, 1982). Changing student populations, along with expectations that advisors function as developmental educators, require that the effective advisor must possess knowledge of needs of particular groups and strategies to use with students who evidence such needs.

The need areas emphasized in this chapter (academic under-preparation, academic and personal management, physical and/or learning disabilities, cultural differences, and academic standards and competition) are broadly defined and encompass large numbers of students on today's campuses. Some students can fit into several of the need areas. For example, the minority student who is academically talented and who has multiple family and job responsibilities fits into three of the need areas. Table 1 presents an overview of the needs, subpopulations, and advisor intervention implications covered in this chapter.

Academic Underpreparation

Underprepared students are not actually new to higher education. In fact, the first systematic program designed to assist students in reading and study skills was instituted at Wellesley College in 1894 (Cross, 1976). However, beginning in the 1960s, a significantly higher proportion of postsecondary students had deficits in reading, English composition, speaking, and mathematics of such magnitude that academic success was exceedingly difficult. The interest in academically underprepared students is not limited to open enrollment institutions, and even the most prestigious colleges and universities have established some types of developmental or remedial assistance. To maintain enrollment levels, colleges and universities have been accepting students with lower standardized test and IQ scores (Harris and Grede, 1977). However, advisors of underprepared students must face the realization that without appropriate intervention, these students are likely to drop out prior to graduation (Cope and Hannah, 1975).

Characteristics. In addition to the more obvious deficits in fundamental skills, underprepared students are likely to face a number of related concerns. The underprepared student may experience motivational problems, be more easily distracted from academic tasks (Mitchell and Piatowska, 1974), and, thus, is likely to have poor academic work habits. Also, low-achieving students are more likely than academically successful students to attribute poor academic success to luck rather than lack of ability (DeBoer, 1983). This pattern of attributions is likely to lead to a low level of confidence in academic abilities and an unwillingness to attempt challenging academic tasks.

Research indicates that underprepared students are also more likely to experience difficulties in educational planning. It indicates that they are less likely than their peers to have established appropriate and well-thought-out educational plans (Pollard, Benton, and Hinz, 1983). Therefore, underprepared students may have an unrealistic image of the purpose of school and study, and they may use a non-goal-directed approach to academic tasks. Motivational problems of the underprepared student also may stem from a lack of career focus (Grites, 1982). Underprepared students may not see the

Table 1. Special Advising Needs of Students.

Problem or Need	Predominant Subpopulations Associated with Problem or Need	Areas of Concern			
		Academic Competence	Personal and Social Development	Educational and Career Planning	Advisor Competencies
Academic underpreparation	1. Students with basic skill deficiencies 2. Nonnative English speakers 3. Older and returning students 4. Economically disadvantaged students 5. Learning and physically disabled students	1. Assessment of deficiencies 2. Management of time and study environment 3. Remediation of academic deficiencies	1. Improvement of academic self-concept 2. Overcoming social stigma of academic weaknesses 3. Development of personal motivation and persistence strategies	1. Creation of academic plans that maximize chances of success 2. Identification of realistic academic major and career goals	1. Understanding of learning and motivational styles 2. Ability to relate to underprepared students nonjudgmentally 3. Ability to use directive and encouraging advising approaches
Academic and personal management (students with multiple nonacademic responsibilities)	1. Student-athletes 2. Part-time and/or older students 3. Students pursuing performing arts careers	1. Management of time and study environment 2. Identification of academic strengths and weaknesses	1. Developing relationships outside of primary reference group 2. Overcoming feelings of alienation 3. Balancing importance of academic and nonacademic responsibilities	1. Assessment of feasibility of career choice in area of nonacademic skill (athletes, arts) 2. Development of alternative career plans 3. Creation of academic plans and schedules that are compatible with other responsibilities	1. Sensitivity to the pressures and demands of nonacademic interests 2. Ability to teach educational and career decision-making skills 3. Knowledge and appreciation of career options related to nonacademic interests
Physical and/or learning disabilities	1. Students with learning disabilities	1. Functional analysis of academic implica-	1. Adjustment to others' reaction to	1. Knowledge of functional requirements of	1. Knowledge of implications of learning or

2. Students with sensory disabilities 3. Students with movement and mobility handicaps	tions of disability 2. Development of strategies to compensate for or accommodate disability	disability 2. Development of coping strategies to deal with frustration and stress 3. Development of personal problem-solving and decision-making capabilities 4. Development of appropriate independence and autonomy	particular careers 2. Skill in career decision making 3. Assessment of academic major requirements affected by disability	physical disabilities 2. Knowledge of campus and community resources 3. Ability to relate to disabled students in a nonjudgmental manner 4. Ability to provide emotional support and encouragement
Cultural differences 1. Racial or ethnic minority students on predominantly white campuses 2. International students	1. For international students, assessment of written and spoken English and assistance for problem areas 2. Minority students may or may not have academic deficiencies	1. Ability to deal with alienation and subsequent stress 2. Development of social network and adult role models 3. Ability to cope with alien cultural values, social norms, and expectations	1. For international students, education received in U.S. should have relevance to home career structure 2. Development of role models for minority and international students	1. Ability to respond from a multicultural perspective 2. Knowledge of students' cultural values 3. Knowledge of and ability to use campus, community, and alumni resources
Academic standards and competition (students who face high levels of academic competition) 1. Academically talented students 2. Preprofessional students	1. Development of strategies to cope with high academic expectations and resulting anxiety 2. Development of appreciation for learning opportunities unrelated to grades	1. Identification of personal needs 2. Assessment of development and achievements in personal/social areas 3. Appreciate nonacademic aspect of college	1. Development of academic plans that encourage exploration of diverse career alternatives 2. Development of alternative career plans	1. Ability to understand stress and impact of possible failure 2. Knowledge of standards for competitive graduate and professional programs

relevance of esoteric college courses if they do not visualize the college degree as leading them to a meaningful vocation. Finally, underprepared students show significantly higher levels of anxiety, particularly in test situations, than do high achievers (Mitchell and Piatowska, 1974).

In addition, many academically underprepared students made late decisions to attend college and do not have college attendance reinforced by family members. Underprepared students are more likely to be first-generation college enrollees and may also come from economically disadvantaged backgrounds (Cross, 1976).

Many groups of college students exhibit underpreparedness in the collegiate environment. In fact, it can be argued that all entering freshmen are, to some degree, underprepared for the academic and personal rigors of postsecondary education. Nonnative English speakers and learning disabled students need specialized academic services in order to persist in postsecondary education. Older students who have not been involved in academic pursuits for a number of years are also likely to require assistance in developing academic skills. As mentioned, economically disadvantaged students may lack background knowledge and may have attended substandard elementary and secondary schools. However, a large number of underprepared students are distinguishable only by their common weaknesses in basic academic skills. It may be that these students were not at a point of receptivity to academic work during childhood and early adolescence.

Advisor Strategies and Competencies. Since underprepared students have deficits in basic skills, it is vitally important that the academic advisor encourage the student to receive an assessment of academic competencies and to participate in appropriate remediation activities. On most campuses there exist personnel with specialties in learning assistance who can assist the student and advisor. In most cases, the American College Test (ACT) or Scholastic Aptitude Test (SAT) scores and high school grades provide good initial screening information but do not provide necessary diagnostic information that can be used by learning assistance specialists. Standardized assessment instruments in reading comprehension, mathematics skills, English grammar, as well as more informal techniques (writing samples, classroom observation, and student self-report) can provide a wealth of diagnostic information. Once a diagnosis is completed, advisors can help the student seek out appropriate remediation services. Depending upon the types of learning assistance services available on a particular campus, the advisor's role and function differ. For example, on those campuses where underprepared students are required to participate in academic support services, the advisor's job is made easier because the program requirement eliminates the need to cajole or persuade students to avail themselves of needed services. The strategies discussed in this seciton will, however, focus on advisor interventions that can be used in conjunction with a variety of learning assistance services.

By necessity, the situation with underprepared students requires that advisors be proactive and possibly even intrusive (Glennen, 1976). Intensive advising, in contrast to more traditional advising, requires that the advisor take the initiative in contacting students. In discussing the counseling needs of underprepared students, Snow (1977) describes the need for proactive intervention by stating that most students do not seek professional counselors or advisors in their offices. Therefore, advisors must be activist initiators rather than passive respondents.

In interactions with underprepared students, advisors should assist students in assessing their needs and in determining both short- and long-range goals. The Student Developmental Profile and Planning Record (Winston, Miller, and Prince, 1979) is a good tool to use in helping students identify behaviors that need to be addressed in the goal-setting process. Common factors, in addition to academic skill deficiencies, that inhibit academic performance among underprepared students include test anxiety, difficulty in determining how much and where to study, reluctance to ask for assistance, difficulty in following academic tasks to completion, and stress associated with academic performance.

One way in which improvement objectives can be established and progress continually assessed is through a contract between student and advisor. At the New York City Technical College, students with academic difficulties are required to complete an academic agreement form and to participate in structured interview sessions with an advisor. On a regular basis, the advisor checks over each student's grades on tests, papers, and homework assignments. As students and their advisors select strategies for academic improvement, these are included as part of the official academic agreement. As a result of using this highly structured approach, Hudesman and others (1983) found that participants received higher grades than did students in the control groups.

One strategy that has been shown to meet a need of underprepared students is for the advisor to frequently monitor academic progress and to intervene quickly if progress deteriorates. At the University of Georgia, the Division of Developmental Studies has developed a computer-generated monitoring system that provides weekly reports to advisors (Dwinell, Saunders, and McFadden, 1984). A report is generated for each student in the division and includes information concerning (1) completion of course assignments, (2) class attendance, (3) tutorial session attendance, (4) an estimated course grade, and (5) an indication from each instructor as to whether the student is putting forth satisfactory effort in the course. This monitoring system allows advisors to quickly confront those student behaviors that are incompatible with academic success.

The stress experienced by academically underprepared students can and should be addressed by academic advisors. Williams, Decker, and Libassi (1983) completed a study in which two group treatments for improving academic performance were compared. The first treatment involved goal setting and time management while the second treatment also included identification of stressors and relaxation techniques. Results indicated that the second treatment group made significantly greater improvement in grade point averages. For the underprepared student, test anxiety coupled with basic skills deficits and general stress can be debilitating. On many campuses, counselors or psychologists offer relaxation workshops. Advisors of underprepared students should be alert to signs of anxiety and refer students to an appropriate resource.

Academically underprepared students can benefit from educational and career-planning experiences. The underprepared student's schedule for each term should contain courses that capitalize on academic strengths and challenge the student to improve weak areas. For example, the student with inadequate reading skills should be cautioned against taking three or four courses with heavy reading demands in the same term. Underprepared students should create a one- to two-year academic plan during their first term of enrollment. This plan should be structured to balance difficult and less-demanding courses and should demonstrate that a student is making reasonable progress toward meeting degree requirements. Additionally, the advisor can, by sensitive questioning and frequent contact, help a student clarify his or her purposes for pursuing postsecondary education. The advisor can also encourage underprepared students to begin choosing an area of academic specialization and ultimate career goals. Underprepared students should be encouraged to consult various campus personnel about the skills and abilities required for certain majors and related careers so that realistic and yet meaningful choices can be made.

The advisor who effectively serves underprepared students can help them overcome fears of failure and the stigma attached to academic underpreparedness. One who can communicate a belief that underprepared students are potentially successful is a powerful, encouraging force. The advisor's use of self-dislosure about his or her own areas of weakness can often motivate underprepared students (Grites, 1982). The use of successful student and faculty role models who overcame underpreparedness can also serve to encourage students and help them overcome the stigmatizing consequences of academic weakness.

Academic and Personal Management

The mythical image of the typical college student—that person whose primary responsibilities are to attend class, to participate in campus clubs, and to develop an active social network—obviously does not fit all students. Several subgroups of students, such as the intercollegiate athletes, full-time employees, or those in competitive performing arts training, face demanding and time-consuming responsibilities different from those of the typical "Joe College." Goals of these students are multiple—perhaps to achieve in athletics or the fine arts, or to gain financial stability and support a family while also being successful students.

Students Involved in Intercollegiate Athletics. Men, particularly scholarship athletes, provide a good example of the extensive demands placed on students with multiple nonacademic responsibilities. Edwards (1983) estimates that scholarship athletes devote thirty-five to forty hours per week to their sport on a year-round basis. This time estimate does not include travel time to sometimes distant arenas. Coupled with the emotional stress and physical fatigue associated with intense athletic competition, it is not surprising that the low graduation rates of athletes have been widely criticized (Underwood, 1980). The task of time management, although a simple one for many students, is a tremendous obstacle that is frequently not overcome by the scholarship athlete.

Coping with conflicting demands is not the only special advising need presented by athletes. The intensity of these demands is also associated with special needs in the career, personal, and social development areas. Athletes tend to develop social networks with others in their same sport (Lanning, 1982). Students outside the athletic milieu tend to view athletes as different or privileged, thus decreasing opportunities for creating diverse groups of friends.

The intensity of nonacademic demands is also likely to affect career decision-making issues. For example, athletes recruited to play "major" sports in college tend to aspire to play professional sports, yet fewer than 2 percent actually sign a professional contract (Underwood, 1980). The athletes' devotion to the goal of "going pro" tends to preclude development and planning for other career interests. Athletes are reinforced for their athletic ability by so many people that they do not emphasize the priority of choosing a career in the same fashion as nonathletes (Lanning, 1982).

Particularly for the scholarship athlete, the college or university environment also reinforces the relative lack of importance of meaningful educational and career planning. In recent years, much has been written about scholarship athletes who are advised to "major in eligibility" (Wittmer, Bostic, Phillips, and Waters, 1981). In other words, athletes are encouraged by athletic personnel to choose courses or majors based on whether the selected academic program will allow them to pass enough credit hours to remain eligible.

In addition to time management and career issues, the development of a healthy self-image is also a major concern to the scholarship athlete. The "blue-chip" athlete recruited to a major athletic power has been rewarded all of his or her life for athletic excellence. Therefore, that individual's sense of worth is based solely on athletic performance (Lanning, 1982). Oftentimes, however, for the beginning scholarship athlete, rewards for excellence fail to materialize. The quality of athletic competition at major universities approaches the professional level. Therefore, the star high school athlete is likely to "warm the bench" during the freshman year and thus may experience a grave and sometimes traumatic decrease in self-confidence. The likelihood of physical injury and resulting lack of ability to participate in athletics can have wide-ranging implications for self-esteem issues. Even an injury that temporarily removes an athlete from competition raises concerns about the transitory nature of athletic participation. The athlete's emotional reaction to injury may include debilitating confusion and severe resentment (Lanning, 1982).

Students in the Performing Arts. Students in the performing arts in many ways face conflicts similar to those of the student-athlete. Time management concerns are paramount. The time required to achieve excellence in music, drama, or dance is extensive. These students must spend many hours in daily practice, rehearsals, and, frequently, travel for concert tours or drama productions. Students who major in the performing arts also face limited job market opportunities upon graduation. The U.S. Department of Labor Statistics (1982) estimates that careers in music, dance, theater, and entertainment fields will have extremely restricted job openings for the forseeable future. Performing-arts students, because of the commitment required to pursue their art, are also likely to find that they are outside the mainstream of campus extracurricular life.

Students with Major Family and/or Job Responsibilities. Part-time students are also different from the "traditional student." Thus, these students, particularly if enrolled in a residential campus, may experience social isolation or loneliness similar to that of intercollegiate athletes and performing-arts students. Students with major nonacademic responsibilities may not view academic performance as their first priority and may, therefore, have difficulty in maintaining concentration. The part-time student may also be an adult learner and may be significantly older than the majority of undergraduates. Adult learners who have had a long hiatus from academic pursuits may experience a lack of self-confidence about their abilities.

In terms of career planning, older adult students, although they have extensive family or job responsibilities, are likely to have very specific educational goals and, at times, these goals may be unrealistic (Kuh and Sturgis, 1980). In addition, extensive nonacademic commitments may prevent spending the time necessary to explore a variety of career interests. It is important that the part-time student with multiple responsibilities have ample opportunity to broaden a number of alternative career choices. If students are not encouraged to question their pre-enrollment career choices and to investigate alternative careers, it is likely that many ultimately will be dissatisfied with their preconceived vocational goals.

Advisor Strategies and Competencies. How then is the academic advisor to assist students who are faced with multiple nonacademic responsibilities? One need common to all students with multiple responsibilities is that of effective study management. Therefore, students should be assisted in developing specific study plans, including study schedules, estimates of time required for various assignments, and reinforcements for completed study tasks.

Another important area of concern for students with multiple responsibilities is the need to examine and explore a variety of educational and career options. This need is particularly acute for the student-athlete or fine arts major. Students need to understand that an alternative career plan is needed—in case they are not successful in their first choice of a career. Advisors can and should take responsibility to ensure that students are informed about the number of athletes and arts majors who make a successful living in those fields. It has been suggested (Grites, 1982) that data about the success of an institution's former scholarship athletes should be made available. This type of data would also be helpful for any major or career goal with relatively limited opportunities for a successful long-term career.

The educational planning area is an important concern of students with multiple responsibilities and one with which advisors are charged to assist. It is important that the educational plans and academic schedules take into account a student's nonacademic responsibilities. Schedules must be balanced—that is, created to enhance a student's chance of academic success. A difficult task of the advisor in this area is to help students understand that attempting to complete full academic loads while trying to manage numerous outside obligations is flirting with discouragement and, ultimately, with academic failure. The creation of an academic plan (of at least two years' duration) that balances degree requirements, student interests, and obligations is a way in which the advisor can begin exploration of this issue.

Advisors must also be sensitive to the social and emotional development of this group of students. Advisors must possess the ability to appreciate the pressures and personal demands of nonacademic responsibilities. All too often, the academic community may be tempted to stereotype students in ways that do not enhance positive expectations. An example is the scholarship athlete who is often viewed as the "dumb jock." Advisors who succumb to these stereotypes likely will fail to provide the encouragement needed to ensure academic success.

Physical and/or Learning Disabilities

Recently, there has been an increased awareness among academic administrators, faculty, and student affairs professionals that accepting students with either physical or learning disabilities requires institutions and personnel to modify programs and services. The Rehabilitation Act of 1973, Section 504, was passed in an effort to assure equality of treatment of students with disabilities in educational environments. Thus, institutions have received additional incentives to make certain that all students receive benefit of the needed postsecondary services. In fact, Section 504 requires that institutions make modifications in their academic requirements to ensure that these requirements do not discriminate against students on the basis of handicap. Academic requirements that are essential to the program of instruction or to any licensing requirement, however, will not be regarded as discriminatory in the context of Section 504. For example, institutions must make certain that science and laboratory courses are adjusted to accommodate handicapped students and that auxiliary aids (such as recordings for the blind and braille typewriters) are available.

Students with physical and/or learning disabilities are a relatively new population in higher education. In the past, comparatively few students with physical or learning disabilities completed a postsecondary education. The majority of these persons were relegated to jobs with subsistence pay, elementary skill requirements, and few opportunities for advancement (Bowe, 1978). Due to improved facilities, federal legislation, and increased awareness that disability is not synonymous with incapacity, it is predicted that an increasing number of learning and physically disabled students will enter higher-education institutions (Schmidt and Sprandel, 1980).

Thus, increased numbers of learning or physically disabled students require that the academic advisor gather additional information about these student groups as well as cultivate a genuine sensitivity to the needs of these students. Both physical and learning disabilities have a diverse range of implications for daily living, for academic progress, for social development, and for career decision making. In addition, the identification, diagnosis, and even the definition of learning disabilities is a new area of professional inquiry, with a concomitant lack of consensus on these important issues. Implications of both physical and learning disabilities suggest that the academic advisor must possess enough knowledge about the nature of the disability to anticipate obstacles and roadblocks to successful progression in a college or university.

Learning Disabilities. The term *learning disabilities* encompasses a multitude of diverse learning problems. Brown (1980) describes many of these problem areas as follows:

- *dyscalculia:* inability to perform mathematical operations
- *dysgraphia:* inability to write letters and words in a satisfactory fashion
- *dyslexia:* inability to read and comprehend printed material
- *auditory perceptual problems:* inability to discriminate between similar sounds, to hear sounds in the order they were given, or to hear sounds if there is distracting background noise

- *cognitive problems:* difficulty in thinking, especially when it involves an orderly or logical approach, or in the ability to distinguish between two similar concepts
- *directional problems:* trouble distinguishing left and right, directions, geographical locations
- *perceptual problems:* trouble taking in and processing information through any of the senses

Not only do learning disabilities present difficulties in mastering academic tasks but they also affect social interaction and emotional development. Students with learning disabilities tend to have difficulties in concentration and impulse control (Lutwak and Fine, 1983). In addition, these students have been reported to have higher levels of anxiety (Schacht, Kass, and Schact, 1976), low motivation, low ego status, hypersensitivity, and difficulty in establishing social relationships (Kronick, 1978). Learning disabled students may experience a multitude of these manifestations or only one. The manifestations of learning disabilities, then, can make academic achievement difficult and progress in other personal developmental areas problematic.

There exist many misconceptions about learning disabilities. These misconceptions include the notion that these students are retarded, have emotional problems, will outgrow the condition, or that these students are simply low achievers (Makas, 1981). Additionally, a learning disability cannot be remediated in the same fashion as a deficit in academic skills. Instead, learning disabled students can learn to accommodate their disabilities and can be successful postsecondary students if the appropriate services are available. Because of these misconceptions and because of the complexity in identifying learning disabled students, it is difficult to ascertain how many of these students are enrolled in postsecondary institutions.

Learning disabled students have academic needs different from those of the traditional student. In the academic realm, a learning disabled student needs comprehensive analysis of the disability in order to know how that disability will affect academic performance and what services the student needs to accommodate the disability.

Numerous assessment strategies are needed to pinpoint the nature of a learning disability with enough precision to analyze its effect on academic skills. Students should take several standardized measures designed to ascertain (1) reading, spelling, and computation skills, (2) level of intellectual funtcioning, (3) ability to decode words, (4) knowledge of phonics, (5) perceptual abilities, and (6) auditory perception ability (Ryan, Davidshofer, and Miller, 1980). In addition to standardized measures, it is important that observational data from faculty and self-report information from the student be obtained. Finally, a comprehensive assessment should include the student's developmental history, including early school experiences and medical history. Because of the sophistication of these diagnostic strategies and the complexity of learning disabilities, a trained psychologist should administer and interpret the assessment data. The learning assistance centers on many large campuses have personnel on staff with expertise in learning disabilities. On a campus without appropriate personnel, community and public school resources can be sought. The Association for Children (and Adults) with Learning Disabilities (4156 Library Road, Pittsburgh, Pa. 15234) has numerous state and local chapters that can help individuals identify appropriate resources.

Often, learning disabled students also have basic skill deficiencies, although these students display a broad variability in the degree of deficits. Students with learning disabilities have typically struggled through elementary and secondary schools in an effort to compensate for the disability, and thus, in all likelihood, may not have internalized some of the fundamental skills in the same fashion as traditional students have.

Physical Disabilities. Physical disabilities are also diverse in nature and have wide-ranging implications for academic and social adjustment. If all activities, services, and programs available to the general student body are to be made available to the physically handicapped student, a number of special services must be created.

In the academic area, often physically handicapped students require specialized forms of learning assistance. Many congenitally disabled students, for example, have been educated in residential schools and thus may lack basic academic skills (Bryan and Becker, 1980). Therefore, physically handicapped students should receive a comprehensive analysis of their academic strengths and weaknesses. The University of North Dakota (Burrus, 1977) uses a functional analysis of academic skills adapted from Rusalem (1962) that isolates tasks required of students and identifies a list of needed adaptations. This type of analysis permits students to determine if they need, for example, readers, note takers, or special equipment such as tape recorders, braille writers, or special typewriters (Bryan and Becker, 1980). Completion of these analyses should be performed by those with expertise in working with the academic needs of handicapped students.

In order to cope with daily living and mobility, handicapped students are likely to need information and services unique to their particular situations. These students must be informed about buildings that are accessible and about the particulars of the handicapped transportation services. Oftentimes, handicapped students may need attendant care either for intermittent assistance or for the daily living tasks. Therefore, advisors of handicapped students may need to make referrals to resources that provide attendants.

Handicapped students' psychosocial developmental needs may require different types of interventions than those of the general student body. For example, the handicapped students who are attended by their parents may have unique concerns in attempting to develop autonomy and break away from intensive parental intervention upon enrolling in a residential college.

The issue of peer acceptance produces anxiety among most beginning college students. However, the handicapped student is likely to experience episodic depression, loneliness, and social isolation since the college student peer group typically emphasizes the importance of attractiveness, social conformity, and energetic physical activity. Also, nonhandicapped students often have mixed reactions to peers with physical handicaps, ranging from guilt to sympathy to curiosity to discomfort (Schmidt and Sprandel, 1980).

In the educational or career-planning areas, handicapped students must confront issues not germane to their nonhandicapped peers. It is likely that handicapped students have had less prior experience in making decisions about important life issues (Blosser, 1980). Therefore, these students may need to be taught how to clarify values, weigh alternatives, calculate risks, and assess consequences in relation to educational and career planning. Also, handicapped students may not have had sufficient opportunity to engage in work experiences. Thus, they may have very vague notions of their work values and occupational preferences. Finally, handicapped students may experience difficulty in obtaining pertinent information related to careers. Traditional sources of occupational information are written from the perspective of the able-bodied. Therefore, these sources often do not include information about the accommodations a handicapped person and employer must make to maximize chances of successful employment.

The diverse implications of both physical and learning disabilities are more extensive than can be addressed in this chapter. The typical academic advisor is not required to be an expert in various types of disabilities on most campuses. The office of handicapped student services provides direct assistance to students and can be helpful to advisors who wish to obtain needed information. The advisor has a responsibility to make referrals to the campus office of handicapped services and to suggest ways in which this office and other campus agencies might better serve students. Given the possibility that postsecondary institutions will enroll a higher proportion of disabled students, all advisors should develop strategies and attitudes appropriate for working with these students.

Advisor Competencies and Strategies. Probably the most crucial factor in determining the effectiveness of an advisor who works with disabled students is that advisor's acceptance of persons with disabilities. Academic advisors, as others in this culture, bring to their work attitudes that are on a continuum of acceptance (Walker, 1980). At the negative end of this continuum are the rejectors who, because of their fears and discomfort, judge disabled students as unsuitable for the postsecondary environment. Advisors who are highly verbal and scholarly may find it extremely difficult to avoid rejecting learning disabled students, assuming that these students are lazy, unmotivated, or stupid (Schmidt, 1982). Since many academic pursuits, such as field sciences, require physical mobility, the academic advisor may reject the notion that a physically handicapped student could successfully pursue a major in such an area.

A second type of attitude described by Walker (1980) is "mothering." The "mothering" advisor feels that the disabled student is incapable of personal responsibility and, thus, does virtually everything for the student. Often with learning disabled students, too much help translates into a lowering of standards and consequently the student does not acquire the essential academic skills. This "mothering" attitude is closer to the negative than positive end of the continuum. The "mothering" advisor does not promote students' increasing growth and self-sufficiency but instead encourages the student to forgo challenges for a comfortable complacency and continued dependency.

Often for many academic advisors, working with a disabled student is a completely novel experience. These advisors can be categorized using the Walker (1980) continuum as "novices." Although these advisors fall closer to the positive end of the continuum, they are tentative in their responses and need additional information to increase their confidence in working with disabled students. At the most positive end of Walker's continuum is the "wise one." These are people who treat a disability in an incidental, matter-of-fact fashion. They are forthright and honest with students and can provide realistic encouragement.

Can advisors' negative attitudes toward disabled students be changed? Walker indicates that exposure to accurate information and modeling from more experienced persons is extremely helpful. Advisor training should include information about disabling conditions and implications of these disabilities for academic progress, personal growth, and career development. More importantly, advisor training should include exposure to advisors who have been successful in working with disabled students. Schmidt (1982) suggests that well-respected scholars with disabilities who have been productive share their experiences with advisors. On campuses with well-organized centers for physically or learning disabled students, center personnel can share valuable expertise and often can provide experiential activities to show advisors what situations must be coped with. For example, advisors could experience reading material printed as a dyslexic student would perceive it, thus, for a brief period, experiencing some of the frustration these students encounter. Ideally, consciousness-raising activities should include faculty, students, and student affairs professionals as well as advisors. Since most educators and students fall into Walker's "novice" category, most members need additional information and are receptive to learning about disabilities.

The implications of a physical or learning disability in the postsecondary environment requires that campus or community resources be used to achieve optimal services for the student. The typical academic advisor cannot be expected to be an expert in all of these areas. The advisor will, however, need to become an effective manager of campus, community, governmental, and professional association resources. A wide range of resources are available to provide assessment and intervention assistance. A few of these include local departments of vocational rehabilitation, public school psychologists, campus offices for handicapped student services, and campus services for learning disabled students. In urban areas, there may exist chapters of the Association for Children (and Adults) with Learning Disabilities, the Cerebral Palsy Foundation, the Easter Seal Society, and Recording for the Blind. Higher Education and the Handicapped (HEALTH) Project of the American Council of Education is concerned with all disabilities, publishes worthwhile information, and will provide assistance to individual campuses.

Cultural Differences

While more minority group members are seeking higher education than ever before, they continue to be underrepresented in American postsecondary education. Although minorities account for 17 to 19 percent of the American population, they typically constitute only 10 to 17 percent of entering college freshmen (Smith, 1981). Even more significant are the data that indicate that minorities are less likely to receive degrees than majority students (Dearman and Plisko, 1979). Astin (1975) reported that black students dropped out from predominantly white colleges at a rate of 49.5 percent as compared to a dropout rate of 41.4 percent among white males and 30.9 percent among white females. Research on attrition indicates that academic factors such as inadequate basic skills and poor academic performance account for as much as half of the variance in attrition (Pantages and Creedon, 1978). However, the research of Astin (1975), Peterson and Rodriguez (1978), Cortina (1980), and Goodrich (1980) indicates that feelings of alienation, frustration, and helplessness may contribute significantly to the higher attrition rates of minority students on predominantly white campuses.

The enrollment of international students has, until recently, increased on campuses through the United States (Dillard and Chisolm, 1983). The adaptation process faced by international students is a difficult one and is receiving increased attention from researchers (Alexander, Workneh, Klein, and Miller, 1981). Many of the adaptation problems faced by international students result from the disparities in cultures that must be faced by internationals as they interact with fellow students, faculty members, and advisors (Dillard and Chisolm, 1983). Another major problem encountered by many international students is the difficulty in communicating since English is a second language. The nonnative speaker is likely to be unfamiliar with American slang and terminology unique to college students. Also, some nonnative speakers are likely to have learned effective English reading and writing skills but evidence pronounced difficulties in speaking and listening. Finally, the United States system of higher and secondary education is extremely different from systems in Asia, Western Europe, Africa, and South America. Therefore, internationals must cope with administrative procedures and faculty expectations that are unlike any in the home culture. For example, international students may be baffled by the expectation of American faculty members that students participate in class discussions. These differing expectations can lead to miscommunication and misinterpretation of actions between international students and faculty members or academic advisors. Therefore, in order to provide effective advising services, advisors need to be able to operate from a multicultural rather than ethnocentric position with international students.

Characteristics. In recent years a number of programs have been developed to meet the special academic needs of students who face cultural differences, particularly those from disadvantaged economic backgrounds. Federally funded Upward Bound and Special Services programs have been successful in increasing the basic skills of underprepared and disadvantaged minority students so that these students can compete adequately in postsecondary institutions (Young and Exum, 1982).

The social and psychological issues faced by minority students have obvious impact on ultimate success in the postsecondary environment and thus are important areas of intervention for the academic advisor. While generalizing about racial minorities as a group tends to obscure significant areas of uniqueness among minority cultures, general conclusions can be drawn about minorities immersed in a majority environment. Atkinson, Morton, and Sue (1979) argue that racial minorities tend to share world views quite different from those of whites or Anglo-Americans. Specifically, racial minorities and many international students tend to emphasize the role of the extended family; a shared rather than individual identity; and a unification of the body, mind, and spirit instead of the separation of these concepts subscribed to by those of European heritage (Smith, 1981). Minorities also share a sense of oppression and racial discrimination within the American society. Recent research indicates that minority group members, particularly black students, feel more estranged and alienated from the campus environment than their majority counterparts (Suen, 1983). Minority group members tend to face three common barriers to meaningful interaction: language differences, class-bound values, and culture-bound values (Atkinson, Morton, and Sue, 1979).

These social and psychological issues faced by minority students can become serious stressors for the minority student on a white campus (Gibbs, 1975; Maynard, 1980). When minority students perceive a lack of response to their special needs, increased alienation, stress, and poor academic performance result. The transition from a predominantly culturally homogeneous home environment with family and community support systems to the alien set of cultural values and social norms brings special anxieties to the freshman minority or international student (Henderson, 1979). The cultural context on American campuses frequently generates fear, frustration, and finally pessimism among international students (Dillard and Chisolm, 1983).

One developmental task of minorities, as other college students, is to clarify career goals and to determine areas of educational specialization. This task is made more difficult, however, by the fact that theories of career behavior have failed to consider the unique cultural values of minority group members as well as the restricted employment opportunities for minorities. Griffith (1980) has indicated that existing research on blacks fails to ascertain whether the career development patterns of blacks are caused by blacks or are the effects of restricted opportunities. Sue (1977) also maintains that the occupational and racial stereotyping of Asian Americans has precluded development of career development theories meaningful for this minority group. In terms of choosing academic majors, members of minority groups tend to select areas such as social science and education in which there are dwindling opportunities for career advancement (Smith, 1981). This phenomenon serves to continue the occupational stereotyping of minority group members and may well lead to pronounced underemployment of these persons.

International students face several concerns unique to their group. Typically, they recognize that their tenure in the United States will be brief and that they face another, sometimes difficult, transition, that of returning to their home culture. The learnings and values acquired in the United States may not "fit" in their homeland. Also, activities in their home countries have been changing and there is often difficulty in re-establishing friendship and social groups upon returning home. The concern about what is occurring at home and the difficulty in maintaining regular contact with friends and family are a continuing source of stress for international students (Bae, 1972).

Another issue confronting minority students is the small number of minority helping professionals available on most campuses. In a study of blacks on white campuses, Willie and McCord (1972) indicate that trust levels between blacks and whites are slow to develop. Minority students have been found to be unlikely to seek help from white professionals (Burrell and Trombley, 1983). When faced with personal or financial problems, these students sought help from family or friends. When confronting an academic concern, minority students were most likely to seek help from minority professionals. Although many studies indicate that an effective helping relationship can develop between a minority student and a majority professional (Jones and Jones, 1972; Peoples and Dell, 1975; Sue and Sue, 1977), the helping professional must be sensitive to the cultural background of minority students.

Advisor Strategies and Competencies. It appears that one primary concern of many minority students involves their feelings of alienation. Advisors can, to some degree, assist students in developing strategies to overcome alienation and resulting stress. Lee (1982) developed a black support group with the goal of addressing the personal and social needs of black students on a predominantly white campus. The group, led by black counselors, identified such discussion topics as (1) the stress of academic competition and negative expectations of majority professors and students, (2) lack of unity among blacks on campus, (3) pressure of maintaining one's black identity on a white campus, and (4) interpersonal stress between black men and women on campus. Group participants not only ventilated their frustrations but also shared effective coping strategies. Additionally, the use of blacks in leadership positions in this group provided participants with effective role models. Advisors can encourage the creation of similarly structured groups for both minority and international students. It is important that such groups focus on possible solutions to common concerns as well as providing a forum to ventilate feelings of frustration.

For many reasons, minority students tend to underutilize student affairs resources, particularly the counseling center. Reasons for this underutilization include lack of awareness, inaccurate perceptions of the service, and the belief that services are directed toward white students only (Benedict, Apsler, and Morrison, 1977). Advisors can be helpful to minority students in making certain that they are aware of opportunities available from student affairs programs. Miles and McDavis (1982) suggest that (1) information about student affairs programs should be disseminated in small groups, (2) individual sessions with personnel from the programs are useful in encouraging future utilization, and (3) peer counselors and helpers should be used to disseminate information about student affairs activities.

In the area of career planning, it is important that minority students have an opportunity to interact with minorities who have been successful in business or professional fields. These individuals can become significant, powerful role models to minority students.

Perhaps the most crucial competency to be acquired by advisors of minority and international students is the ability to operate in a multicultural context. The differences among cultures provide a fertile ground for miscommunication. Often the behavior of those from different cultures is misinterpreted when viewed from the perspective of one's own culture. Ho (1973) describes the Japanese female who presents herself as shy, hesitant, and self-deprecating, who may appear to be inhibited and exhibiting inappropriate behavior. However, when viewed from the perspective of Japanese culture, proper conduct demands nonassertive behavior in interactions with authorities. Advisors who work with students from differing cultural backgrounds can become more empathetic and sensitive by gaining increased knowledge about students' native cultures (Dillard and Chisolm, 1983). In addition to gaining knowledge, it is also important that advisors receive training in working with minority students. One multicultural training strategy involves videotaping sessions and receiving feedback from the minority student and trained personnel. Role playing has also been used effectively in developing a multicultural perspective. Advisors could be asked to assume the role of a minority or international student seeking help. This strategy allows the advisor to experience, albeit superficially, the kinds of miscommunications and feelings that can occur in this situation.

Academic Standards and Competition

Academically talented students who desire to excel in academic pursuits are often overlooked in the advising process because these students perform well academically and are apparently able to operate in a self-reliant fashion. These students seemingly pass through their college experience with minimal difficulties. Not only are academically talented students typically faced with high levels of academic competition, but students who desire to pursue professional degrees such as law or medicine are also likely to face intense academic competition. In addition, research about the needs of academically talented and preprofessional students is limited.

Characteristics. The most obvious characteristic of academically talented (honors) and preprofessional students is their academic capability. Yet there is growing awareness that these students may have unique concerns that can affect their social, personal, and career development. High levels of anxiety tend to accompany the pressure toward academic excellence. Research indicates that honors students are more anxious than nonhonors students (Gordon, 1983). Typically, talented students are expected by family, friends, teachers, and advisors to achieve at extraordinary levels. In addition, talented high school students face increasing competition at the undergraduate level and therefore may have to cope with the unfamiliar position of failure to be the most talented student in class. Also, increasing competition requires that these students work diligently and thoughtfully, which may not have been required at the secondary school level.

Because of the concern about maintaining high grades, academically talented students may choose not to pursue social and recreational interests. Therefore, these students may lack development of the social and relaxation strategies of less talented students.

In the career and educational planning areas, academically talented students approach this process somewhat differently from the general student population (Hoyt and Hebeler, 1974; Perrone, Male, and Karshner, 1977; Zaffrann and Colangelo, 1977). Specifically, honors students are noted for having many interests and high capability in several areas and thus may have difficulty narrowing alternatives (Gordon, 1983). Because of high ability, talented students may have been pressured by significant others to choose an academically rigorous or prestigious career even when these choices may be inconsistent with interests and abilities. Gordon (1983) indicates that honors students may need more assistance than less talented students in clarifying work values and life-style considerations relevant to career choices.

Advisor Strategies and Competencies. Most importantly, advisors should realize that honors or preprofessional students can benefit from the advising relationship and deserve attention equivalent to that of their underprepared peers. Advisors of talented students must be prepared to help them deal with failure to meet their expectations—a novel experience for most of these students.

Honors and preprofessional students may need an advisor's assistance in planning for alternate careers in the event that they fail to meet the level of competition required for certain professional schools. Some institutions have established special advising centers for students pursuing competitive professions. The Health Professions Office at the University of Texas and the Preveterinary Advising Center at Michigan are two examples. These centers help students understand clearly the academic requirements of competitive professions and provide useful career information. These alternatives provide a buffer for possible failure and can prevent a student from narrowing choices prematurely. Grites (1982) advocates that academically talented students be advised to take elective courses that have applicability in a variety of careers, thus promoting a broadly based undergraduate curriculum and exploration of several areas of interest. Some courses he suggests are writing, critical analysis, speaking, organization, leadership, and foreign languages. Courses such as statistics, computer sciences, and accounting may also encourage alternative career exploration.

Encouraging academically talented students to pursue nonacademic issues is sometimes a difficult task for advisors. One way in which this can be accomplished is through the use of a mentoring-transcript system. As described by Brown and DeCoster (1982), the mentoring-transcript system promotes a continuing, structured dialogue between a student and a mentor (faculty member, academic advisor, or student affairs professional). The dialogue emphasizes student achievement of such developmental tasks as personal identity, interpersonal relationships, intellectual competence, esthetic awareness, physical fitness, and multicultural awareness. Another part of this process involves students and mentors creating a transcript that documents achievement of developmental tasks. This transcript stimulates students to attend to developmental issues and can consist of experiential and competency checklists, portfolios, and narrative descriptions of progress. Elaborate mentoring-transcript systems have been established at Azusa Pacific, the College of Saint Theresa, and the University of North Dakota. Although not specifically designed for academically talented students, a mentoring-transcript system can foster developmental task achievement of these students.

Academically talented students can also benefit from peer assistance. Beginning honors students could be assigned an upperclass honors student as a peer advisor. The peer advisor can identify with the younger student's anxiety, frustration, and desire to excel. Additionally, older honors students can serve as positive role models for younger peers.

Summary and Conclusions

Postsecondary education is a changing landscape, with "new" students and "new" emphasis on the importance of academic advising. Students with special advising needs require that institutions establish meaningful and comprehensive programs. Typically, however, advisors may be unaware of the special needs of certain students. First, research about needs of special student populations is a relatively new phenomenon. Second, since special student populations are new to some higher-education institutions, advisors may lack experience in working with them. Therefore, advisors may be tentative in their responses and may miss opportunities for meaningful intervention with students.

Additional research needs to be completed about special student populations. Goals of such research should be to describe accurately the goals, perceptions, problems, and progress of students with special needs. There also exists a need to investigate, in a well-controlled fashion, the types of advising interventions that work most effectively with different types of student populations.

Since many advisors are "novices" in working with students who bring special needs, it is important that advisor training focus on helping advisors clarify their values about certain student groups and providing structured activities for advisors to practice their communication and referral skills. In order to provide all students with the most effective advising possible, advisors cannot become "rejectors" of certain student groups. An advisor who feels that a certain group of students "don't belong in college" can have devastating effects. Therefore, those who administer advising programs have the responsibility to confront directly advisor attitudes and values.

The relationship between individual students and their advisors is the crux of academic advising. Advisors can certainly not "be all things to all students" and thus should be aware of their strengths and limitations. Some advisors may not be effective with certain students and may need to refer or reassign them. Advisors should also interact with students independently, avoiding dependence on stereotypes of certain student groups. If the advisors are receptive to learning about special student populations and are able to approach advising from a comprehensive perspective, they can promote students' development in the social, personal, and vocational areas as well as the intellectual.

References

Abel, J. "Academic Advising Administration: Contributions to Student-Based Management Practices." *Journal of the National Association of Women Deans, Administrators, and Counselors,* 1978, *41,* 102–105.

Alexander, A. A., Workneh, F., Klein, M. H., and Miller, N. H. "Psychotherapy and the Foreign Student." In P. B. Pederson and others (Eds.), *Counseling Across Cultures.* (2nd ed.) Honolulu: University Press of Hawaii, 1981.

American College Testing Association. *Career Planning Program.* Iowa City, Iowa: American College Testing Association, 1983a.

American College Testing Association. *Vocational Interest Experience and Skill Assessment—VIESA.* Iowa City, Iowa: American College Testing Association, 1983b.

Astin, A. W. *Preventing Students from Dropping Out.* San Francisco: Jossey-Bass, 1975.

Atkinson, D., Morton, G., and Sue, D. *Counseling American Minorities: A Cross-Cultural Perspective.* Dubuque, Iowa: Brown, 1979.

Bae, C. K. "The Effect of Traditionalism on Social Adjustment and Brain Drain: A Study of Korean Students at the University of Wisconsin." Unpublished doctoral dissertation, University of Wisconsin, 1972.

Benedict, A., Apsler, R., and Morrison, S. "Student Views of Their Counseling Needs and Counseling Services." *Journal of College Student Personnel,* 1977, *18,* 110–114.

Blosser, R. E. "Career Development and Placement Services." In H.

Z. Sprandel and M. R. Schmidt (Eds.), *New Directions for Student Services: Serving Handicapped Students,* no. 10. San Francisco: Jossey-Bass, 1980.

Bowe, F. *Handicapping America: Barriers to Disabled People.* New York: Harper & Row, 1978.

Brown, D. *Steps to Independence for People with Learning Disabilities.* Washington, D.C.: Closed Look, 1980.

Brown, R. D., and DeCoster, D. A. (Eds.). *New Directions for Student Services: Mentoring-Transcript Systems for Promoting Student Growth,* no. 19. San Francisco: Jossey-Bass, 1982.

Brown, R. D., and Sanstead, M. J. "Using Evaluation to Make Decisions About Academic Advising Programs." In R. B. Winston, Jr., S. C. Ender, and T. K. Miller (Eds.), *New Directions for Student Services: Developmental Approaches to Academic Advising,* no. 17. San Francisco: Jossey-Bass, 1982.

Bryan, W. A., and Becker, K. M. "Student Services for the Handicapped Student." In H. Z. Sprandel and M. R. Schmidt (Eds.), *New Directions for Student Services: Serving Handicapped Students,* no. 10. San Francisco: Jossey-Bass, 1980.

Burrell, L. F., and Trombley, T. B. "Academic Advising with Minority Students on Predominantly White Campuses." *Journal of College Student Personnel,* 1983, *24* (2), 121–126.

Burrus, S. *University of North Dakota Functional Analysis of Handicapped Conditions.* Grand Forks: Student Opportunity Programs, Division of Student Affairs, University of North Dakota, 1977.

Carnegie Council on Policy Studies in Higher Education. *Three Thousand Futures: The Next Twenty Years in Higher Education.* San Francisco: Jossey-Bass, 1980.

Cope, R., and Hannah, W. *Revolving College Doors: The Causes and Consequences of Dropping Out, Stopping Out, and Transferring.* New York: Wiley, 1975.

Cortina, R. J. *From Educational Access to Academic Success: A Design for Improving Opportunities for Minority Persons in Wisconsin Higher Education in the 1980s.* Madison: University of Wisconsin System Committee, 1980.

Cross, K. P. *Accent on Learning: Improving Instruction and Reshaping the Curriculum.* San Francisco: Jossey-Bass, 1976.

Dearman, N. B., and Plisko, V. W. *The Condition of Education.* Washington, D.C.: U.S. Government Printing Office, 1979.

DeBoer, G. E. "The Importance of Freshman Students' Perceptions of the Factors Responsible for First-Term Academic Performance." *Journal of College Student Personnel,* 1983, *24* (4), 344–349.

Dillard, J. M., and Chisolm, G. B. "Counseling the International Student in a Multicultural Context." *Journal of College Student Personnel,* 1983, *24* (2), 101–105.

Dwinell, P., Saunders, S., and McFadden, M. "Monitoring the Progress of Developmental Students." Paper presented at Georgia Developmental Studies Conference, Athens, Ga., 1984.

Edwards, H. "Educating Black Athletes." *Atlantic Monthly,* 1983, *252* (2), 32–35.

Federal Programs Advisory Service. *Handicapped Requirements Handbook.* Washington, D.C.: Federal Programs Advisory Service, 1979.

Gibbs, J. T. "Use of Mental Health Services by Black Students at a Predominantly White University: A Three-Year Study." *American Journal of Anthro-Psychiatry,* 1975, *45,* 430–445.

Glennen, R. E. "Intrusive College Counseling," *School Counselor,* 1976, *24,* 48–50.

Goodrich, A. "A Data-Driven Retention Model for Improving Minority Student Persistence in Higher Education Institutions." Paper presented at the Spring Conference of the Wisconsin Association of Educational Opportunity Program Personnel, Lake Geneva, Wis., April 1980.

Gordon, V. N. "Meeting the Career Development Needs of Undecided Honors Students." *Journal of College Student Personnel,* 1983, *24* (1), 82–83.

Griffith, C. J. "Justification for a Black Career Development." *Counselor Education and Supervision,* 1980, *19* (4), 301–310.

Grites, T. J. "Advising for Special Populations." In R. B. Winston, Jr., S. C. Ender, and T. K. Miller (Eds.), *New Directions for Student Services: Developmental Approaches to Academic Advising,* no. 17. San Francisco: Jossey-Bass, 1982.

Hardee, M. D. "Faculty Advising in Contemporary Higher Education." *Educational Record,* 1962, *42,* 112–116.

Hardee, M. D. *Faculty Advising in Colleges and Universities.*
Washington, D.C.: American College Personnel Association,
1970.

Harrington, T. F., and O'Shea, A. J. *Career Decision-Making
System.* Circle Pines, Minn.: American Guidance Service, 1976.

Harris, N. C., and Grede, J. F. *Career Education in Colleges: A
Guide for Planning Two- and Four-Year Occupational Programs.* San Francisco: Jossey-Bass, 1977.

Henderson, G. (Ed.). *Understanding and Counseling Ethnic Minorities.* Springfield, Ill.: Thomas, 1979.

Ho, M. K. "Cross-Cultural Career Counseling." *Vocational Guidance Quarterly,* 1973, *21,* 190–196.

Hoyt, K. B., and Hebeler, J. R. *Career Education for Gifted and
Talented Students.* Salt Lake City, Utah: Olympus, 1974.

Hudesman, J., and others. "The Effects of Academic Contracting
and Semi-Structured Counseling Sessions on GPA for Students
in Academic Difficulty." *Journal of College Student Personnel,*
1983, *24* (3), 278–279.

Johnson, E., and McClelland, D. C. *Learning to Achieve Advanced
Level.* Glenview, Ill.: Scott-Foresman, 1984.

Jones, M. H., and Jones, M. C. "The Neglected Client." In R. Jones
(Ed.), *Black Psychology.* New York: Harper & Row, 1972.

Kramer, H. C., and Gardner, R. E. *Advising by Faculty.* Washington, D.C.: National Education Association, 1977.

Kronick, D. "An Examination of Psychosocial Aspects of Learning
Disabled Adolescents." *Learning Disabled Quarterly,* 1978, *1,*
86–93.

Kuh, G. D., and Sturgis, J. T. "Looking at the University Through
Different Sets of Lens: Adult Learners and Traditional-Age
Students' Perceptions of the University Environments." *Journal
of College Student Personnel,* 1980, *21,* 483–490.

Lanning, W. "The Privileged Few: Special Counseling Needs of
Athletes." *Journal of Sport Psychology,* 1982, *4,* 19–21.

Lee, C. C. "Black Support Group: Outreach to the Alienated Black
College Student." *Journal of College Student Personnel,* 1982, *23*
(3), 271–273.

Lenning, O. T., Beal, P. E., and Sauer, K. *Retention and Attrition: Evidence for Action and Research.* Boulder, Colo.: National Center for Higher Education Management Systems, 1980.

Lutwak, N., and Fine, E. "Countertherapeutic Styles When Counseling the Learning-Disabled Student." *Journal of College Student Personnel*, 1983, *24* (4), 320-324.

Makas, E. *Perspectives.* Washington, D.C.: Regional Rehabilitation Research Institute on Attitudinal, Legal, and Leisure Barriers, 1981.

Maynard, M. "Can Universities Adapt to Ethnic Minority Student Needs?" *Journal of College Student Personnel*, 1980, *21*, 398-401.

Miles, G. B., and McDavis, R. J. "Effects of Four Orientation Approaches on Disadvantaged Black Freshmen Students' Attitudes Toward the Counseling Center." *Journal of College Student Personnel*, 1982, *23* (5), 413-418.

Miller, T. K., and McCaffrey, S. S. "Student Development Theory: Foundations for Academic Advising." In R. B. Winston, Jr., S. C. Ender, and T. K. Miller (Eds.), *New Directions for Student Services: Developmental Approaches to Academic Advising,* no. 17. San Francisco: Jossey-Bass, 1982.

Mitchell, K. R., and Piatowska, O. E. "Effects of Group Treatment for College Underachievers and Bright Failing Underachievers." *Journal of Counseling Psychology*, 1974, *21*, 494-501.

Pantages, T. L., and Creedon, C. E. "Studies of College Attrition: 1950-1975." *Review of Educational Records*, 1978, *48*, 49-101.

Paul, W. *How to Study in College.* Boston: Houghton Mifflin, 1974.

Peoples, V. Y., and Dell, D. M. "Black and White Student Preferences for Counselor Roles." *Journal of Counseling Psychology*, 1975, *22*, 529-534.

Perrone, P., Male, R., and Karshner, W. "Career Development Needs of Talented Students: A Perspective for Counselors." *School Counselor*, 1977, *27*, 16-23.

Peterson, R., and Rodriguez, M. "Minority Student Perceptions of a University Environment." *Journal of College Student Personnel*, 1978, *19*, 259-263.

Pollard, K. D., Benton, S. E., and Hinz, K. "The Assessment of

Developmental Tasks of Students in Remedial and Regular Programs." *Journal of College Student Personnel,* 1983, *24* (1), 20–28.

Rusalem, H. *Guiding the Physically Handicapped College Student.* New York: Bureau of Publications, Teachers College, Columbia University, 1962.

Ryan, M. C., Davidshofer, C. O., and Miller, C. D. "Nature of Learning Disabilities: Identification and Programming for College Students." In P. Marx (Ed.), *The Handicapped Student on College Campuses—Advocacy, Responsibility, and Education.* Proceedings of Third National Conference of Association on Handicapped Student Services Programs in Postsecondary Education, Denver, Colo., May 1980.

Schacht, J. S., Kass, W., and Schact, M. "Personality Development and Learning Disabilities: Long-Term Follow-Up of Psychotherapeutic Remediation." Paper presented at Third International Scientific Conference of the International Federation of Learning Disabilities, Montreal, Canada, August 1976.

Schmidt, M. R. "Academic Adjustments and the Faculty Role in Working with Learning-Disabled Students." In M. R. Schmidt and H. Z. Sprandel (Eds.), *New Directions for Student Services: Helping the Learning-Disabled Student,* no. 18. San Francisco: Jossey-Bass, 1982.

Schmidt, M. R., and Sprandel, H. Z. "Concluding Remarks." In H. Z. Sprandel and M. R. Schmidt (Eds.), *New Directions for Student Services: Serving Handicapped Students,* no. 10. San Francisco: Jossey-Bass, 1980.

Smith, E. J. "Career Development Needs of Special Populations." In V. A. Harren, M. H. Daniels, and J. N. Buck (Eds.), *New Directions for Student Services: Facilitating Students' Career Development,* no. 14. San Francisco: Jossey-Bass, 1981.

Snow, J. J. "Counseling the High-Risk Student." In J. E. Roueche (Ed.), *New Directions for Higher Education: Increasing Basic Skills by Developmental Studies,* no. 30. San Francisco: Jossey-Bass, 1977.

Sue, D. W., and Sue, D. "Barriers to Effective Cross-Cultural Counseling." *Journal of Counseling Psychology,* 1977, *24,* 420–429.

Sue, S. "Psychological Issues, Theory, and Implications for Asian Americans." *Personnel and Guidance Journal,* 1977, *55,* 381–389.

Suen, H. K. "Alienation and Attrition of Black College Students on a Predominantly White Campus." *Journal of College Student Personnel,* 1983, *24* (2), 117–121.

Terenzini, P. T., and Pascarella, E. T. "Student Faculty Relationships and Freshman Year Educational Outcomes: A Freitter Investigation." *Journal of College Student Personnel,* 1980, *21* (6), 521–528.

Underwood, J. "The Writing Is on the Wall." *Sports Illustrated,* May 19, 1980, pp. 38–48, 53–72.

U. S. Department of Labor Statistics. "Outlook for Occupations: Writers, Artists, and Entertainers." In *Employment Analysis Trends: Occupational Outlook Handbook: 1982-83.* Washington, D.C.: U.S. Department of Labor Statistics, April 1982.

Wagner, C. S., and McKenzie, R. "Success Skills for Disadvantaged Undergraduates." *Journal of College Student Personnel,* 1980, *21* (6), 514–520.

Walker, C. "The Learning Assistance Center in a Selective Institution." In K. V. Lauridsen (Ed.), *New Directions for College Learning Assistance: Examining the Scope of Learning Centers,* no. 1. San Francisco: Jossey-Bass, 1980.

Walter, T., and Seibert, A. *Student Success.* New York: Holt, Rinehart & Winston, 1981.

Williams, J. M., Decker, T. W., and Libassi, A. "The Impact of Stress Management Training on the Academic Performance of Low-Achieving College Students." *Journal of College Student Personnel,* 1983, *24* (6), 491–494.

Willie, C. V., and McCord, A. S. *Black Students at White Colleges.* New York: Praeger, 1972.

Wilson, R. C., and others. *College Professors and Their Impact on Students.* New York: Wiley, 1975.

Winston, R. B., Jr., Miller, T. K., and Prince, J. S. *Assessing Student Development: A Preliminary Manual for the Student Developmental Task Inventory (Second Edition) and the Student Developmental Profile and Planning Record.* Athens, Ga.: Student Development Associates, 1979.

Wittmer, J., Bostic, D., Phillips, T. D., and Waters, W. "The

Personal, Academic and Career Problems of College Athletes: Some Possible Answers." *Personnel and Guidance Journal,* 1981, *60,* 52-58.

Young, E. D., and Exum, H. A. "Upward Bound and Academic Achievement: A Successful Intervention." *Journal of College Student Personnel,* 1982, *23,* 291-299.

Zaffrann, R., and Colangelo, N. "Counseling the Gifted and Talented Student." *Gifted Child Quarterly,* 1977, *21,* 305-325.

11

Advising Graduate and Professional School Students

≈≈≈≈≈≈≈≈

Roger B. Winston, Jr., Mark C. Polkosnik

> *Wanted.* A thoughtful *critic* who is also a
> constructive *counselor,* a stringent *taskmaster* who is
> also a supportive *colleague,* a model *scholar* who is
> also an effective *tutor,* a principled *bureaucrat* who
> also knows how to get around the system, a prodi-
> gious *researcher* who is also a charismatic *teacher,* and
> a respected *authority* in the field who is also available
> to students at any time. [Adapted from Heiss, 1970.]

This might well be a classified advertisement graduate or professional school students would use in seeking an advisor-sponsor-
major professor. These seemingly contrary or incompatible qualities and characteristics sought in an advisor reflect the complexity,
ambiguous roles, and contradictory demands placed upon advi-

287

sors by graduate students. Due to such ambiguity and to the wide differences among academic disciplines in terms of content, research methodologies, and desirable personality characteristics, very little has been written about the graduate education process and even less about what constitutes good academic advising.

In order to simplify the terminology in this chapter, *graduate student* refers to students who are in academic programs that focus primarily on research and scholarship and prepare them for careers as either college teachers or full-time researchers or who are in programs that focus on preparation of professional practitioners, such as counselors, psychologists, engineers, or secondary school teachers. This chapter, however, does not address traditional "independent professional schools," such as law and medicine. *Advisor* refers to faculty members who guide graduate students through their programs of study, serve as evaluators in written and oral examinations, and direct dissertations and theses. At some universities one person may perform all these functions with one student; at others, several faculty members serve the different functions.

In this chapter issues related to and roles fulfilled in the academic advising of graduate students are addressed. First, if advisors are to be effective, they must understand something about what graduate students experience (especially since many advisors may have forgotten or considered their own experiences unique and tend to exaggerate the superiority of their own graduate training). Second, the important roles and functions graduate student advisors fill are presented, followed by an explanation of appropriate interventions at different phases of graduate study. Finally, the unique needs of several student populations are addressed.

The Graduate School Experience

The graduate education process has been described as "infantilizing." Taylor (1975, p. 35) argues that "graduate students are adults who are 'hanging fire'. . . . They are . . . neither fully adults nor children. Many major life commitments are being held in abeyance; they are in a state of waiting." The graduate school experience is filled with uncertainty, stress, and ambiguity in relation to students' roles in the community, peer relationships, marital relationships, and student evaluation processes.

Roles in the Community. Adults in both biological and legal senses, graduate students are often treated as adolescents by the university, which places many of the same restrictions on them as on undergraduates. Most graduate students are middle class in their value orientations and family backgrounds but lack the income required for a middle-class life-style (Creager, 1971; Baird, 1976). Altbach (1970, p. 571) has commented that graduate students "are among the last persons in America observing the Protestant Ethic in that they forgo income and status now in the hope that they will obtain it later."

A return to graduate school often requires students to regress or to reassume roles that they have outgrown. For example, students who have completed their master's degree and have been teaching or providing professional services, often supervising several subordinates, are required to reassume the student role, which has little power or status associated with it. For many, this is a difficult psychological adjustment.

Socially, there are also difficult adjustments for returning students, especially those who are unmarried. Because of a lack of money (sometimes drastically less than a year before) and the isolation from eligible dating partners, many graduate students report feelings of loneliness, frustration, and hostility, which can spill over into their academic work. In fact, Rimmer, Lammert, and McClain (1982) found that the need for opportunities to meet other graduate students outside their department ranked high in importance among reported needs. That need ranked third, only behind the need for departmental orientation programs and assistance in job placement.

Another role confusion is often experienced by graduate students who also act as teaching assistants (TAs). TAs generally are viewed as faculty members by the undergraduates whom they teach, but the TAs must revert to a student role when dealing with the full-time faculty in the department. This confusion may be even more acute for those students who hold professional positions on the campus while also attending graduate school.

Peer Relationships. Students within a given department or program share a commonality of background and general intellectual interests and are subject to the same pressures as their peers; yet, they often are required to compete with fellow students for grades, assistantships, and attention from professors. This competition has been shown to be widespread and destructive. Baird (1969) found that competition increased stress among students but was unrelated to academic difficulty or high standards. It also tends to lead to game-playing and "system-beating" ploys (Sanford, 1976).

Peer relationships take on added significance in light of Polkosnik and Winston's (1983) findings that 47 percent of the doctoral students and 49 percent of the master's students reported that one half or more of the people they see socially are graduate students in their departments (over 30 percent reported all or most of their friends were fellow graduate students). The most common emotional problems reported by graduate students are feelings of isolation and loneliness (Halleck, 1976; Hoferek and Sarnowski, 1981). Many graduate students reported often feeling like "strangers in the crowd."

Marital Relationships. Almost all studies confirm that graduate school attendance places stress on student marriages (Hoferek and Sarnowski, 1981; Gilbert, 1982; McRoy and Fisher, 1982). Pressures are often caused by lack of recreation or shared time, lack of money, sexual dissatisfaction, and lack of communication. There is a differential effect on marriage depending on whether the husband, wife, or both are students. If only the husband is a student, there is a tendency for an intellectual gulf to develop between the husband and wife and/or for the wife to feel socially isolated. If the wife is the only student, she may develop feelings of isolation because traditionally husbands are expected to establish social relationships, but her husband cannot establish those relationships in the graduate environment. She also generally is expected to perform most of the household duties in addition to attending graduate school. There seem to be fewer problems and less dissatisfaction when both partners are students.

Student Evaluation Processes. Assessment of graduate student performance may be the single most ambiguous and stressful aspect of graduate study. Polkosnik and Winston (1983) found that over 75 percent of the surveyed graduate students reported that they at least occasionally did not know where they stood or how well they were doing; over 30 percent reported feeling this way often. Sanford (1976) maintains that this uncertainty, combined with perceptions of unfairness of evaluations, leads to destructive game playing that can disrupt the learning environment and adversely affect the quality of a student's graduate education. After studying intensively departments in three disciplines, Sanford concluded: (1) For many students, academic performance evaluations expressed through grades, assistantships, professional opportunities, and esteem of colleagues become more important than their own beliefs and satisfaction with their work. Grades replaced the substance of the discipline in importance. (2) Assessment creates and sustains considerable social distance between students and faculty members. "It is very hard to get close to a person if he [or she] exercises power over you as a result of his [or her] capacity to make fateful judgments of your character and competence" (p. 109). (3) Evaluation processes create a dependency relationship. "At a time when most young men and women are seeking some independence for themselves, graduate students find it necessary to please the powers that be, often without knowing precisely what it is that those powers want" (p. 110).

Advisor Roles and Functions

There are five essential roles and functions advisors must fulfill if they are to be judged successful. These include reliable information source, departmental socializer, advocate, role model, and occupational socializer. There are also two roles that are desirable for an advisor to fill but which may not be prescribed— friend and mentor.

Reliable Information Source. Graduate study often has a myriad of departmental and graduate school procedural rules and deadlines, not apparent to the uninitiated. Generally, for example, a student must apply for graduation months before completing the thesis or dissertation. The student, however, associates graduation with completion of requirements and, without a reminder from the advisor, may be required to miss the desired graduation date and/ or be required to register for unnecessary courses.

Most graduate departments have both formal and informal rules and policies that are haphazardly communicated to students, especially to those student generations that follow the initial policy decision. Many of the provisions of these policies are difficult to comprehend without an understanding and appreciation of the process, points of views, and theoretical orientations of influential faculty members and their decision-making approaches. Advisors must remember that students often do not have access to this history, and they therefore must, year after year, communicate these policies with all their options to students. Departmental graduate coordinators should annually compile accurate and clear statements of policy affecting graduate students and distribute them to each new student. Even if this is done, advisors must continue to seek to understand the informal structure and to guide students through the departmental policy and power maze. In a survey of graduate students at one university, it was found that almost 30 percent of the respondents reported that their advisors did not keep informed of policies and deadlines or did not pass the information along to them (Polkosnik and Winston, 1983).

Departmental Socializer. In addition to knowing what the formal rules and policies are, successful graduate students must understand the informal departmental structure. This may be referred to as learning to "psyche the system" or as departmental socialization (Heiss, 1970; Sanford, 1976). That students consider this important is reflected by the fact that over one fourth of those responding (in two separate surveys fourteen years apart) agree with the statement that "some of the best graduate students in my department drop out because they do not want to 'play the game' or 'beat the system' " (Creager, 1971; Polkosnik and Winston, 1983).

Strategies employed to beat the system include making a point to talk to particular professors at social gatherings, performing favors such as retrieving books from the library or doing secretarial tasks, or making a point to agree with or defend a professor's position or theoretical orientation. The greater the amount of competition and lack of shared purpose and theoretical orientation among faculty members, the more important it is for students to become expert at reading and reacting to the shifting departmental politics.

In order to appreciate the importance of the initial weeks of graduate study, one must understand some of what the student experiences. Research studies, though generally involving students in only one or two disciplines, present a consistent picture. Students enter graduate school with highly inflated or unrealistic expectations in terms of the amount of structure present, the academic or scholarly emphasis, the nature and quality of student-faculty relationships, and the breadth of interest outside the field of specialization (Winston, 1976). Entering students (especially master's level) have a high need for structure, low need for autonomy, and a high need for achievement with an external orientation. As students progress in their programs, they develop a more internal orientation, greater acceptance of responsibility for self and program of study, and increased integration of professional and personal roles (Barna, 1978). In studies by Valdez (1982), 81 percent of the first-year doctoral students experienced a moderate or major life crisis during the first semester, with 48 percent experiencing a major crisis. Butler (1972) and Goplerud (1980) also found high levels of stress among entering graduate students. Goplerud further found that the frequency of student-faculty contacts and development of a student support system mediated or lessened the stress. Substantial research has established that students who are members of supportive groups, compared to students without such groups, generally (1) performed better academically (Hall, 1969), (2) experienced less emotional and physical distress (Arnold, 1967), (3) suffered fewer severe physical and psychiatric illnesses (Bloom, 1975), and (4) were less likely to psychologically withdraw from the ambiguities of the graduate school environment and associated stress situations (Baird, 1969; Goplerud, 1980). Stress is also associated with competition, ambiguity about roles, departmental expectations and status, conflicting faculty demands, and interpersonal relationships (Baird, 1969).

What then are the advisor's responsibilities in the socializer's role? Advisors should ensure frequent contact outside the classroom during the first few weeks. Informal contact may be sharing a cup of coffee, going to lunch, or having short conversations in the hallway. It is the advisor's responsibility to initiate these contacts because many students, lacking knowledge of departmental norms and experiencing the uncertainty associated with entering a new environment, may be hesitant to take the risk. Advisors should take the initiative to introduce new students to established students and other departmental faculty in order to help novices begin to build their own emotional and academic support systems. Finally, advisors need to help students understand the realities of departmental politics, while helping students maintain enough of their idealism to fuel their own personal intellectual encounter with their discipline.

Advocate. It is important that students feel that there is a powerful person in the department who is knowledgeable about their skills, abilities, and background and who has their interests and well-being in mind. When assistantships and scholarships are awarded, students often feel that without an advocate they will be passed over. Soon after entering graduate school, students learn that their social position is determined in part by the influence and prestige of their advisor. They, therefore, reason that they are at a competitive disadvantage without an advisor who will champion their cause in the councils of the powerful.

The importance of having an advocate-advisor is often exaggerated by beginning graduate students who are overwhelmed by the authority of their field/profession and the institution (Bargar and Mayo-Chamberlain, 1983) and the scope of intellectual skills and material they believe must be mastered. The larger, more competitive and/or theoretically heterogeneous the department, however, the more important having an advocate becomes. That students feel the need for a "protector" is evident in the response students gave when asked whether their departments "favor the bright, imaginative student." Creager (1971) found 40 percent disagreed with the above statement; Polkosnik and Winston (1983) found over 47 percent disagreed with the statement. It seems clear that academic ability alone is not sufficient for success in graduate school. Since most students enter graduate school with the necessary academic skills and background, it is personality characteristics, inventiveness, endurance, and tenacity that often become the distinguishing features among students and, therefore, these are what bring rewards.

Advisors need to build relationships with students of sufficient closeness and depth that students can feel that their accomplishments and potential are appreciated. Advisors generally are knowledgeable about how "political" they must be within their department. It is essential that, no matter what the departmental climate, students feel that their advisor is a supporter—a person who is interested in their success. Without such support, students often come to feel isolated, even paranoid, and this can lead to destructive game playing, which can disturb the learning environment of an entire department and impede intellectual development.

Role Model. Academic advisors by definition are role models. A role model is a person who possesses skills and displays techniques that the student lacks and from whom, by observation and comparison with their performance, students can learn new behaviors or change existing behaviors (Kemper, 1968). Not only do students learn the terminology of the discipline or profession, but they also watch and learn how such professionals as historians, chemists, counselors, and accountants relate to each other, organize their lives, and approach their research, writing, and teaching. Research, however, suggests that students do not generally model their professional lives on one person but instead create a composite model, drawing from both negative and positive aspects of significant faculty and/or professional practitioners with whom they have contact (Bucher and Stelling, 1977). Results are mixed about the influence and impact on students of the model's sex. Some studies suggest that students prefer models of the same sex (Goldstein, 1979; Speizer, 1981). Other studies (Blackburn, Chapman, and Cameron, 1981) question this; in fact in a recent study, Erkut and Mokros (1984) found that female undergraduate students showed no marked preference for men or women role models, while men avoided female role models, preferring high-status, powerful male models. Female students who selected female role models generally were found to be seeking information about combining a rewarding professional and family life. Advisors are highly visible models of the practitioners of the profession or discipline. Whether or not they desire it, students will view advisors as exemplars who will shape their vision of what scholars, researchers, and professional practitioners should or should not be and do.

For students who plan to pursue careers in higher-education settings, it is from faculty, especially academic advisors, that students learn what Joseph Katz (1976) calls careermanship. It is in graduate school that would-be faculty and administrators learn to do the "politicking, committeeing, grant getting, pursuing of the fashionable and wooing of the powerful that are not an insubstantial part of the university's daily life" (Katz, 1976, p. 114).

There seem to be four conditions necessary for advisors to have a significant impact on students: accessibility, continuous contact for an extended period, casual relationships, and personally engaging relationships (Wilson and others, 1975; Hartnett, 1976). Advisor accessibility means both physical presence and approachability. Obviously, advisors must be on-campus and open to meeting with students if they are to interact; without meaningful interaction, little impact can be expected. Of equal importance are advisors' attitudes toward graduate students. If advisors communicate an attitude of helpfulness, support, interest in students' academic and personal lives, and respect for students' abilities and accomplishments, they will maximize their positive impact on developing researchers, teachers, and professional practitioners. Failure to provide this kind of interaction is most likely to produce a negative impact rather than *no* impact. The kinds of relationships that support student success cannot be established in a single interview or discussion once a term. Prolonged contact over a period of time is required in forming student-advisor relationships, as with other meaningful human relationships. Students must come to terms with issues of power and authority of faculty, personal competence as graduate students, and personal and intellectual compatibility with the advisor. Advisors, in turn, must deal with issues of the students' academic competence, personal and intellectual compatibility, and degree of commitment to the advising relationship. These issues can be addressed adequately only through repeated interaction, preferably both inside and outside the classroom. Research indicates that graduate student satisfaction with the educational process is heavily dependent on the quality and extent of faculty-student relationships (Heiss, 1970; Bowen and Kilmann, 1976; Hartnett, 1976; and Feild and Giles, 1980).

Studies in a variety of departments share a common finding—students seek relationships that include informal faculty interaction and contact, generally at a greater frequency than is reported in most departments (Sorenson and Kagan, 1967; Bowen and Kilmann, 1976; Hartnett, 1976; Winston, 1976; and Feild and Giles, 1980). Polkosnik and Winston (1983) found that 35 percent of the graduate students surveyed indicated that it was very important for them to have "a close personal relationship with [their] advisor"; 43 percent indicated that it was fairly important, while only 22 percent reported that it was unimportant. Over 20 percent of those surveyed also indicated they wished to have more contact with their professors outside the classroom and laboratory. Students seem to be seeking a sense of community that includes the faculty within their department. It seems improbable, if not impossible, to create the desired feeling of esprit de corps and collegiality unless there is frequent casual contact. Bowen and Kilmann (1976) reported that the greater the social distance between teachers and students, the less satisfaction students reported with their educational experiences. Sorenson and Kagan (1967) found that the quality of the interpersonal relationship between advisor and student was more important in determining whether the doctorate was received than was academic ability as measured by Graduate Record Examination (GRE) scores and undergraduate grade point averages (GPAs).

Occupational Socializer. Advisors play highly significant roles in the process through which students enter graduate school and emerge, three to five years later, as philosophers and philosophy teachers, mathematicians, historians and history teachers, and psychologists. The process has been labeled as professionalization (Katz, 1976), as acquiring an occupational identity (Becker and Carper, 1956), and as developing a professional self-concept (Pavalko and Holley, 1974).

There appear to be four essential steps in the process: development of interests and skills, acquisition of ideology, internalization of motives, and sponsorship (Becker and Carper, 1956). There are many varied reasons students *develop an interest* in a particular field or profession and decide to pursue a graduate or professional degree. Reasons for attending graduate school given by substantial majorities of graduate students across fields include (1) to continue intellectual development, (2) to increase earning power, (3) to study a subject for intrinsic interest, and (4) to satisfy job requirements or to enter a professional field requiring an advanced degree (Creager, 1971; Baird, 1976; Polkosnik and Winston, 1983). Once students are enrolled in graduate school, they are often overwhelmed and experience frequent feelings of insecurity when they confront perceived expectations that they must master unmanageable quantities of material and sophisticated research skills and techniques. Generally, during the first year, they read voluminously and gradually become comfortable with the field's terminology and approach to research. During the second year of study, students often report that they feel they are treated more as colleagues by faculty, and they may begin to question some of the basic assumptions of the field. Matters presented to undergraduates as facts come to be viewed as tentative conclusions that require additional research and/or conceptualization. They begin to lose some of the fantasy or idealized views of the field or profession; that is, they learn that lawyers are not like Perry Mason or that most chemists do not spend all their time on pure research. They learn that the field's basic assumptions were formulated by real human beings, some of whom may either be on the faculty or be acquaintances of departmental faculty. Students begin to appreciate the tentative, hypothetical nature of knowledge (Katz, 1976).

At about this time, the second step in the socialization process—*acquisition of ideology*—begins to take place. The emerging professional or scholar confronts questions about the worth of what he or she is doing, that is, "Why am I doing this rather than something else?" The answers to these questions are usually worked out through informal interaction with more advanced students and faculty; the neophyte tests the answers and then "buys" a set for himself or herself. Through this process, students come to view the field as worthwhile and adopt its ideals as their own. The more the field is viewed as a profession, the stronger the ideological identification (Becker and Carper, 1956).

During the third step in the socialization process—*internalization of motives*—students begin to focus their attention on postgraduation employment. Rumors about who got what position, salaries, and duties required by the position are shared in cliques and other student groups. Students begin to better understand the choices involved in work after graduation in their field through observing the actions of their graduating colleagues. It is not uncommon for students to begin to experience an anxiety similar to that experienced during the first year; they begin to question whether they have truly learned enough to function on their own as practitioners. Aspects of the field that were considered boring or unimportant take on a new significance. Students begin seriously to consider themselves as capable of becoming a full-fledged member of the field or profession.

Sponsorship is the final step in the socialization process. This process has been filled traditionally by students' advisors. Advisors write letters of reference that attest to students' knowledge, skills, and talents, and certify to the occupational world students' competence to function as practitioners in the academic discipline or profession. A dual obligation is involved: Sponsors place their professional integrity and reputation on the line by certifying that individuals will function competently; students are obligated to the sponsor to fulfill the ideals of the field and not to betray the trust placed in them. In so doing, students solidify their occupational identities.

As can be seen, advisors play a vital role, far beyond teaching facts, research techniques, and skills, in transforming students into physicists, writers, and agronomists. Consequently, advisors need to give students a chance to see them as practitioners of the field who publicly affirm the field's ideals, not just as teachers of the field's subject matter. In addition, they need to know students on an intimate enough level that upon completion of their programs of study, they can act as their good-faith sponsors. It is a sad state of affairs when, at the end of three or four years, an advisor must struggle to write a convincing letter of reference.

Other Desirable Advisor Roles. While reliable information source, departmental socializer, advocate, role model, and occupational socializer are essential roles expected of all advisors, it is desirable also that advisors be friends and mentors, but these roles cannot reasonably be "required." Most students, upon entering graduate school, hope to have advisors who are their friends. This is, however, difficult to actualize due to the position of authority advisors hold in students' academic lives. Friendship depends to a great degree upon compatibility of personalities and shared experiences. Advisors can increase the probability of becoming friends with their students by sharing informal activities and minimizing the inequality of the authority role, but unless there is a basic personal affinity, friendship will not result. By making the effort to become friends, whether ultimately successful or not, advisors lay the foundation for a successful advising relationship. Provided relationships of respect and trust are established with students, advisors can fulfill effectively their responsibilities without also being friends.

The mentor role, as defined by Levinson and others (1978), is not determined by formal roles but in terms of the character of the relationship and the function it fulfills. The mentor serves as a teacher, sponsor into the field, host and guide who welcomes the neophyte into the new occupational and social world and its values and customs, role model, and counsel and moral supporter in times of stress. All of these roles have been described previously as reasonable expectations from advisors. Mentors and protégés must, however, mutually select each other and be willing to invest emotionally in one another. These kinds of emotional involvements cannot be legislated. Like friendship, the promise of the relationship may be offered but may not be realized.

There are also problems associated with the mentor relationship once formed. First, mentor relationships by definition are transitory (usually lasting two to three years) and when they end, like termination of a love relationship, the endings are seldom civil and often bitter and filled with recrimination (Levinson and others, 1978). Mentor relationships require high levels of emotional commitment. Second, there is the danger of producing academic clones, stifling creativity, and producing intellectual conformity (Blackburn, Chapman, and Cameron, 1981). Third, because mentors tend to select protégés who are similar to them and because most graduate faculty members are white males, women and minority group members tend to be excluded (Combs and Tolbert, 1980; DeCoster and Brown, 1983). Fourth, it is very difficult for advisors in professional fields to be mentors because the advisors are teachers and are not generally professional practitioners or at best are part-time practitioners. Consequently, advisors lose much of their power to be mentors for professional practitioners once the student has graduated. Students who pursue careers in higher education, however, may retain their advisors as mentors after graduation.

Advisor Interventions at Critical Phases of Graduate Study

There are four critical moments or phases of graduate study when advisors can assist students in gaining the maximum benefit from the experience, while causing the least psychic distress: (1) entry into the department and building a program of study, (2) comprehensive examinations, (3) dissertation research and writing, and (4) separation and job placement (Bargar and Mayo-Chamberlain, 1983).

Building a Program of Study. Whether program curricula are highly structured or relatively unspecified, students and advisors need to devote attention to planning a program of study that takes into account student interests, past academic preparation and background, career goals, comprehensive examination requirements, and present level of personal development. As Bargar and Mayo-Chamberlain (1983) pointed out, program building must begin with the assumption that students have an intrinsic interest in the subject matter but perhaps a less than total commitment to the career area. In other words, many are still in the exploration stage of career development (McCaffrey, Miller, and Winston, 1984). Consequently, the early part of the program of study should be designed to assist the student to experiment with and explore various options within the field. It is essential that the advisor raise these issues with students in order "to help them resolve any uncertainties but also to legitimate the uncertainty and the process of its resolution" (Bargar and Mayo-Chamberlain, 1983, p. 411). To decide to change specialty areas within a field or even fields of study is no disgrace for either the student or the advisor.

Another consideration in program building is helping students overcome the passive stance often associated with the undergraduate student role. From such a stance, students see knowledge and authority as external and education as the accumulation of facts, theories, and skills. Even though a foundation in the history, background, and tested theories and research techniques in the discipline is essential, it is also vital that students develop independent problem-solving skills and synthesize their insights with currently accepted facts and theories (Bargar and Mayo-Chamberlain, 1983).

Other factors that require attention when planning a program of study are the student's career goals, present level of personal development, and expectations related to comprehensive examinations. Courses should be included in the program of study that give the student flexibility in postgraduate school career options—for example, certain courses may qualify a student to teach in several specialty areas while also helping the student gain expertise in at least one specialty. Advisors need to help students assess their level of intellectual and personal development and to identify activities that make them more effective scholars, researchers, or professionals. For example, if the student is shy or has difficulty speaking before groups, involvement in programs offered through various student affairs departments or in a graduate student or professional organization can prove helpful. It is also important that the program of study include courses that give students a solid foundation that will enable them to perform well on the comprehensive examinations. While a certain amount of independent study is a reasonable expectation, the advisor and student need to make sure that all major areas covered by the examinations are adequately addressed through course work.

Comprehensive Examinations. Preparation for written and oral examinations can be an essentially meaningless exercise in memorization and second-guessing or a time to review and sort out what has been learned and to organize it in personally meaningful ways that can serve as a coherent foundation for dissertation research and future practice. For most students, this is a period of high anxiety; advisors can (and should) intervene in ways that will assist the student in gaining the most from the experience and lessen the anxiety. Advisors should (1) share their view of the examination process and how it can be a positive learning experience, (2) help each student develop a study plan that will take into account work and learning styles and will assure adequate coverage of the areas to be tested, (3) make sure that the student understands the mechanics of the examination process, including evaluation and reporting results (this is an area in which most of the ambiguity can be removed), and (4) encourage the student to share his or her feelings of anxiety and apprehension with the advisor. While the last action will not eliminate the anxiety, being able to talk about it with someone "in authority" helps and allows the advisor to dispel some of the unfounded rumors that often seem creditable to the anxious student.

During the period of oral examinations, advisors can take several actions that will help each student through the experience and emerge with a feeling of accomplishment and closure. Before the examination, advisors should (1) openly discuss the student's feelings associated with the process, (2) tell the student what to expect from the advisor-chairperson and other members of the committee, (3) express confidence in the student's ability to perform well, and (4) explore with the student possible areas of questioning. It is important that the student feel she or he has an ally in the advisor but also understand that the advisor will not intervene in the examination process unless the questions are out-of-bounds or unreasonable. It is not the advisor's role to rescue students from difficult questions.

Once the orals begin, advisors should encourage appropriate questions from the committee and intercept inappropriate ones, encourage the student nonverbally, and ask well-thought-out questions that will allow the student to demonstrate her or his knowledge. After the orals, preferably the same day, advisors should give the student an honest evaluation of the performance, discussing substantive issues raised during the examination, and talking about the feelings associated with the experience. This gives closure to the examination phase and can help prepare the student to begin work on the dissertation.

The Dissertation. The dissertation should be the capstone of the doctoral program. It should make a contribution to the general state of knowledge in the field, enhance the student's skills as a researcher, and lay a foundation for a life as a researcher, scholar, or professional practitioner.

There are four phases in the dissertation research process: developing the topic, collecting the data, writing, and oral defense (Bargar and Mayo-Chamberlain, 1983).

Ideally, students will identify early in their study an area in the discipline that interests them as a research topic. If this is the case, then students will begin the topic development process with a good background in the research literature. Bargar and Duncan (1982) recommend that advisors (1) encourage students to discuss openly all cognitive and affective aspects of the endeavor, (2) listen to what the student says, rather than what the advisor thinks the student *should* say, (3) reflect back to the student what is heard in order to help the student understand how his or her ideas sound to another, and (4) ask the student to react to the advisor's understanding of the problem. During the formative stage, advisors should withhold their critique until they are sure that they really understand what and how the student proposes to research. Premature criticism can stifle creativity.

The advisor should guard against taking primary ownership of the student's research. In order for dissertations and theses to gain the approval of the student's committee, it is generally necessary that the research ownership be shared by the student and the advisor. Realistically, it cannot be totally independent research. Bargar and Duncan (1982) offer three tests advisors can use to determine whether they are taking over ownership or encroaching on the student's creative endeavor. First, has the advisor discovered a solution to a troublesome aspect of the research *and* does the advisor feel that it is the *correct* solution? Second, does the advisor sense the student has lost control in the creative effort? "If the advisor does not envision the student as the major actor in the creative research endeavor, perhaps he [or she] has begun to think that the student no longer controls the research endeavor" (Bargar and Duncan, 1982, pp. 22–23). Third, does the advisor feel increasing satisfaction with her or his ideas about solutions to research problems and less satisfaction with the student's solution? This is a good sign that the advisor is appropriating the student's research.

Once the problem is identified and a research methodology planned, the advisor should step back from the process and critically evaluate both its potential and its problems. Advisors should have a sense of how the doctoral committee will react and may avert later problems by alerting the student to possible concerns. An appropriate tactic is to request assistance from committee members in solving anticipated problems before the research begins.

Once data collection has begun, the advisor can perform several helpful services. Advisors can share their experience in the practical aspects of collecting and organizing the data or managing the experiment. They also can help students establish a reasonable timetable for completing each phase of the project and can check periodically with students in order to help them stay on schedule. Once the data collection is complete, the advisor can critically review with the students the findings and conclusions.

For many students, writing the dissertation is more difficult than actually performing the research. Some students have a tendency to avoid this final task and may, in some cases, never receive the degree because they could not find the energy to complete this last major task. It is important that both advisor and student develop a sense of disidentification in the review and critique of the manuscript. Students invest a great deal of their egos in their writing; advisors need to be careful that their criticism is helpful and not destructive. They must not take over ownership of the dissertation or impose their personal writing-style preferences, but must only provide objective editorial assistance.

The oral defense of the dissertation is in many ways similar to the oral examinations. It, however, has the unique quality of being a final rite of passage that signifies the student's entry into full membership of the community of scholars or the profession. Advisors should structure the oral so that the ritual aspect is not lost and that there is sufficient time for the student to receive congratulations from members of the committee and for the committee to share in the student's celebration. It is important that the student's accomplishment and hard work be acknowledged publicly. To hear "Congratulations, Dr. Jones" from those a student has admired and respected is often a cherished memory and an important punctuation point in one's life. It marks the end to the student status and emergence into the professional or academician role. Psychologically, this transition requires many adjustments and needs an easily identifiable starting point.

Separation and Job Placement. Many students experience postdissertation depression to varying degrees (Bargar and Mayo-Chamberlain, 1983). Some report feeling a sense of loss. It may be caused in part by the realization that they must move into a new job and make new friends, perhaps in a different part of the country. They will again face the same ambiguity and uncertainty experienced when entering graduate school but this time without an advisor to guide them. Advisors can help students through the process by first alerting students to the possibility of this happening before the oral defense, by being available to discuss openly the student's feelings, and by discussing the student's future plans. Advisors should be careful to make time for students after the defense so that students will not feel rejected now that they are no longer "students."

Most students will have begun the job search long before the oral defense. Those who have secured positions before completing the dissertation have incentives to complete their work promptly and are not required to deal with the anxiety of a job search while completing the dissertation.

Advisors can assist students in several ways in the placement process. As noted, students should plan their program of study to allow them flexibility to pursue several specialties. Especially for those students in depressed job market areas, such as the arts, humanities, and social sciences, advisors can suggest internships or summer employment in nontraditional areas in which job prospects are better. For example, anthropology students interested in ways different cultures deal with illness might do an internship in an inner-city hospital and take medical courses that could qualify them for a teaching position in a medical school (Gamson, 1979). Advisors can assist students in developing vitae that will attract potential employers, writing letters of reference, and making telephone calls to colleagues who have announced vacancies. Students have a right to expect assistance from their advisors in placement but should not expect the advisor to find them jobs.

Student Populations Requiring Special Attention

There are several groups of graduate students who possess unique needs and require special attention from advisors: women, foreign students, and terminal master's degree students.

Women Graduate Students. Research results about the differences between male and female graduate student experiences have been inconsistent. Holmstrom and Holmstrom (1974) found that there was a differential interaction rate with faculty that favored men and that women required higher qualifications than men in order to earn status in faculty eyes. Hartnett (1981), however, found that sex differences were related to the discipline and that no sweeping generalizations could be made in that regard. Since there is a shortage of women graduate faculty members who can act as women students' advisors and, given the current depression in higher-education funding that appears will remain the case for this decade, male advisors need to be aware of their women students' unique problems. First, married women students generally have more demands placed on their time than do their male counterparts. The wife is still generally expected to spend more time on domestic duties (including caring for any children) than is the husband, no matter whether the husband is a student or not. Second, women often experience a conflict between their personal and professional lives not experienced by men. Women often feel they are faced with a decision whether they will be a professional person or a wife and mother, a choice seldom considered by men. If women elect to seek a professional career, a marriage, and a family, they are faced with far more societal demands and conflicts than are their male counterparts (Adler, 1976). Advisors need to ensure that women students are not overtly or covertly discriminated against in terms of grades, assistantship opportunities, or amount of time given. They also need to guard against offhand remarks and sexist jokes that devalue women as persons, students, or future researchers, scholars, and professionals.

Foreign Students. While foreign students have all the needs of their domestic counterparts, they also have many additional needs of which the advisor must be aware. Many foreign students have language difficulties, especially in speaking, that can severely hamper their studies. If a student is admitted with inadequate language skills, the advisor must directly address the problem. Lee, Abd-Ella, and Burks (1981) also have found that many problems associated with interpersonal relationships, social adjustment, housing, and food are directly related to, or caused by, a lack of English-language proficiency. Spaulding and Flack (1976) concluded that students who had oral and written problems with English tended to have academic and social adjustment problems as well. Advisors are sometimes reluctant to raise the issue, fearing they will offend or embarrass the student. It is essential that the foreign student master English well enough to perform adequately; advisors should help them locate resources within the institution that can help them improve their proficiency. If these kinds of resources are unavailable, there is an ethical question of whether foreign students should be admitted.

Advisors must understand that foreign students often experience emotional difficulty caused by the cultural differences in addition to the anxiety normally associated with graduate study. These students, however, often experience difficulty finding help because many countries do not accept emotional disorders or problems as openly as in U.S. higher education (Halleck, 1976). Advisors need to be sensitive to foreign student experiences and often need to become directly involved in assisting them in receiving appropriate help. In order to accomplish this effectively, high levels of trust must be developed between advisor and student.

Students from developing countries often have a high fear of failure and thus overreact to criticism from faculty. Failure may be viewed as catastrophic, requiring them to return home in disgrace for themselves and their families. In some instances, they also, not irrationally, fear reprisals from their home governments. Consequently, advisors need to be aware of how their criticisms may be received and be prepared to deal with emotional fallout that may result. It is, however, important not to set up double standards with the rationale "they will never use this back home." One must ensure that all students gain the necessary skills and knowledge to function in the United States. To do less is to cheapen the foreign student's education and to cloud the academic credibility of the university and the integrity of the faculty member-advisor: No one is well served.

Master's Degree Students. Most of this chapter has been devoted to doctoral-level students, although much of what has been said generalizes to all graduate students. However, attention needs to be paid to the students whose goal is the master's degree. Some of these students will return for doctoral study after gaining professional work experience. Indeed, some doctoral programs require two to three years of professional work experience before beginning doctoral study.

It is important that these students not be viewed as second-class citizens or be made to feel that they are not as important as or less capable than doctoral students. Advisors need to keep in mind that master's degree students generally need more structure in their learning than do doctoral students and depend on authorities (faculty) to evaluate their performance more than do doctoral students (Barna, 1978). Even though in some cases specific courses and sequences of courses are less critical in advising master's degree students, this should not be translated into "take anything, it doesn't matter" or "these are the courses you must take to get the degree." Likewise, the same care should be exercised in directing master's theses or research projects as in directing dissertations.

Recommendations

Recommendations to advisors for effective advising of graduate and professional school students are based on the authors' thinking, along with that of Heiss (1970), Katz and Hartnett (1976), and Bargar and Mayo-Chamberlain (1983):

- Systematically strive to build relationships with students based on trust, openness, and shared commitment to the success of the student and advancement of the discipline or profession. It is very important that advisors share with students their confidence in each student's ability to be successful.
- Be available to students both for dealing with academic concerns and for informal social interaction.
- Hold ongoing seminars with students designed to promote interaction among students and engender interests and enthusiasm for the field. These seminars should be flexible in

structure and content. It may be wise to hold separate seminars for master's-level and doctoral-level students.

- Research, write, and publish with students as much as possible. This is effective role modeling.
- Make continuing efforts to stay informed about the rules, regulations, and policies that affect graduate students *and* regularly update and communicate this information to students.
- Through joint presentations with students at scholarly/professional meetings and social introductions, help students in the transition into the community of scholars/professions.
- Zealously remain vigilant to assure that students are not discriminated against, based on gender or minority background. "Innocent" jokes at the expense of women or minorities can be highly destructive to the personal and academic development of these students.
- When possible, lessen ambiguity about expectations, policies, procedures, evaluation, and grades. Give students as much *specific* feedback about their performances as possible. Frequent feedback, even when critical, is better than no information. Give praise and positive evaluations to students as often as one can honestly do so.
- Make certain that the department offers a well-organized orientation program to graduate study, the university, and the community, within the first week of classes each term students are admitted. If a departmental program is not offered, advisors with their more advanced students can offer such a program for the new students.
- Assist students as they near graduation in preparing for the job search and offer active assistance in securing positions.
- Treat students as adults who have a right to be involved in decisions that affect them.
- Confront directly students who lack the ability, attitude, or personality characteristics required to complete successfully the graduate program *and* function as a competent practitioner and help them explore alternative career options. It is wasteful and deceitful to begin erecting additional obstacles and withdrawing assistantships, hoping such actions will discourage marginal students and cause them to abandon their studies.

If academic advisors can implement many of these recommendations in their work with graduate students, there is the potential for greatly decreasing the unnecessary stress experienced by many graduate students and thereby improving the quality of their educational experience. Graduate study can be a journey of intellectual and personal discovery, not a demeaning and trivialized experience. Advisors, to a great extent, have the power to make the difference.

References

Adler, N. E. "Women Students." In J. Katz and R. T. Hartnett (Eds.), *Scholars in the Making: The Development of Graduate and Professional Students.* Cambridge, Mass.: Ballinger, 1976.

Altbach, P. G. "Commitment and Powerlessness on the American Campus: The Case of the Graduate Student." *Liberal Education,* 1970, *56,* 462-582.

Arnold, C. B. "Culture Shock and a Peace Corps Field Mental Health Program." *Community Mental Health Journal,* 1967, *3,* 53-60.

Baird, L. L. "A Study of the Role Relations of Graduate Students." *Journal of Educational Psychology,* 1969, *60,* 15-21.

Baird, L. L. "Who Goes to Graduate School and How They Get There." In J. Katz and R. T. Hartnett (Eds.), *Scholars in the Making: The Development of Graduate and Professional Students.* Cambridge, Mass.: Ballinger, 1976.

Bargar, R. R., and Duncan, J. K. "Cultivating Creative Endeavor in Doctoral Research." *Journal of Higher Education,* 1982, *53,* 1-31.

Bargar, R. R., and Mayo-Chamberlain, J. "Advisor and Advisee Issues in Doctoral Education." *Journal of Higher Education,* 1983, *54,* 407-432.

Barna, A. M. "The Graduate Experience in the Department of Counseling and Personnel Services." *Chrysalis,* 1978, *2* (1), 1-29.

Becker, H. S., and Carper, J. W. "The Development of Identification with an Occupation." *American Journal of Sociology,* 1956, *6,* 289-298.

Blackburn, R. T., Chapman, D. W., and Cameron, S. M. " 'Cloning' in Academe: Mentorship and Academic Careers." *Research in Higher Education,* 1981, *15,* 315-327.

Bloom, B. L. *Changing Patterns in Psychiatric Care.* New York: Behavioral Publications, 1975.

Bowen, D. D., and Kilmann, R. H. "Developing a Comparative Measure of the Learning Climate in Professional Schools." *Journal of Applied Psychology,* 1976, *60* (1), 71-79.

Bucher, R., and Stelling, J. G. *Becoming Professional.* Beverly Hills, Calif.: Sage, 1977.

Butler, H. F. "Student Role Stress." *American Journal of Occupational Therapy,* 1972, *26,* 399-405.

Combs, J. M., and Tolbert, E. L. "Vocational Role Models of College Women." *Journal of the National Association of Women Deans, Administrators, and Counselors,* 1980, *44* (1), 33-38.

Creager, J. A. *The American Graduate Student: A Normative Description.* American Council on Education Research Reports, Vol. 6, No. 5. Washington, D.C.: American Council on Education, 1971.

DeCoster, D. A., and Brown, S. S. "Staff Development: Personal and Professional Education." In T. K. Miller, R. B. Winston, Jr., and W. R. Mendenhall (Eds.), *Administration and Leadership in Student Affairs: Actualizing Student Development in Higher Education.* Muncie, Ind.: Accelerated Development, 1983.

Erkut, S., and Mokros, J. R. "Professors as Models and Mentors for College Students." *American Educational Research Journal,* 1984, *21,* 399-417.

Feild, H. S., and Giles, W. F. "Student Satisfaction with Graduate Education: Dimensionality and Assessment in a School of Business." *Educational Research Quarterly,* 1980, *5* (2), 66-73.

Gamson, Z. F. "Is a Career Part of Life?: Preparing Graduate Students for Today's Job Market." *Liberal Education,* 1979, *65,* 462-469.

Gilbert, M. G. "The Impact of Graduate School on the Family: A System View." *Journal of College Student Personnel,* 1982, *23,* 128-135.

Goldstein, E. "Effects of Same-Sex and Cross-Sex Role Models on the Subsequent Academic Productivity of Scholars." *American Psychologist,* 1979, *34,* 407-410.

Goplerud, E. N. "Social Support and Stress During the First Year of Graduate School." *Professional Psychology*, 1980, *11*, 283–290.

Hall, D. T. "The Impact of Peer Interaction During an Academic Role Transition." *Sociology of Education*, 1969, *42*, 118–140.

Halleck, S. L. "Emotional Problems of the Graduate Student." In J. Katz and R. T. Hartnett (Eds.), *Scholars in the Making: The Development of Graduate and Professional Students.* Cambridge, Mass.: Ballinger, 1976.

Hartnett, R. T. "Environments for Advanced Learning." In J. Katz and R. T. Hartnett (Eds.), *Scholars in the Making: The Development of Graduate and Professional Students.* Cambridge, Mass.: Ballinger, 1976.

Hartnett, R. T. "Sex Differences in the Environments of Graduate Students and Faculty." *Research in Higher Education*, 1981, *14*, 211–227.

Heiss, A. M. *Challenges to Graduate Schools.* San Francisco: Jossey-Bass, 1970.

Hoferek, M. J., and Sarnowski, A. A. "Feelings of Loneliness in Women Medical Students." *Journal of Medical Education*, 1981, *56*, 397–403.

Holmstrom, E. I., and Holmstrom, R. W. "The Plight of the Woman Doctoral Student." *American Educational Research Journal*, 1974, *11* (1), 1–17.

Katz, J. "Development of the Mind." In J. Katz and R. T. Hartnett (Eds.), *Scholars in the Making: The Development of Graduate and Professional Students.* Cambridge, Mass.: Ballinger, 1976.

Katz, J., and Hartnett, R. T. "Recommendations for Training Better Scholars." In J. Katz and R. T. Hartnett (Eds.), *Scholars in the Making: The Development of Graduate and Professional Students.* Cambridge, Mass.: Ballinger, 1976.

Kemper, A. B. "Reference Groups: Socialization and Achievement." *American Sociological Review*, 1968, *33*, 31–45.

Lee, M. Y., Abd-Ella, M., and Burks, L. A. *Needs of Foreign Students from Developing Nations at U.S. Colleges and Universities.* Washington, D.C.: National Association for Foreign Students Affairs, 1981.

Levinson, D. J., and others. *The Seasons of a Man's Life.* New York: Ballantine, 1978.

McCaffrey, S. S., Miller, T. K., and Winston, R. B., Jr. "Comparison of Career Maturity Among Graduate Students and Undergraduates." *Journal of College Student Personnel*, 1984, *25*, 127-132.

McRoy, S., and Fisher, V. L. "Marital Adjustment of Graduate Student Couples." *Family Relations*, 1982, *31*, 37-41.

Pavalko, R. M., and Holley, J. W. "Determinants of a Professional Self-Concept Among Graduate Students." *Social Science Quarterly*, 1974, *55*, 462-477.

Polkosnik, M. C., and Winston, R. B., Jr. "Graduate Student Views of Their Experience: 1969, 1983." Unpublished manuscript, University of Georgia, 1983.

Rimmer, S. M., Lammert, M., and McClain, P. "An Assessment of Graduate Student Needs." *College Student Journal*, 1982, *16*, 187-192.

Sanford, M. *Making It in Graduate School*. Berkeley, Calif.: Montaigne, 1976.

Sorenson, G., and Kagan, D. "Conflicts Between Doctoral Candidates and Their Sponsors: A Contrast in Expectations." *Journal of Higher Education*, 1967, *38*, 17-24.

Spaulding, S., and Flack, M. J. *The World's Students in the United States: A Review and Evaluation of Research on Foreign Students*. New York: Praeger, 1976.

Speizer, J. J. "Role Models, Mentors, and Sponsors: The Elusive Concepts." *Signs: Journal of Women in Culture and Society*, 1981, *6*, 692-712.

Taylor, A. R. "The Graduate School Experience." *Personnel and Guidance Journal*, 1975, *54*, 35-39.

Valdez, R. "First-Year Doctoral Students and Stress." *College Student Journal*, 1982, *16* (3), 30-37.

Wilson, R. C., and others. *College Professors and Their Impact on Students*. New York: Wiley, 1975.

Winston, R. B., Jr. "Graduate School Environments: Expectations and Perceptions." *Journal of College Student Personnel*, 1976, *17*, 43-49.

Part Three

Organizing
and Administering
Advising Programs

Part Three is composed of five chapters that address the administrative and organizational concerns associated with establishing and maintaining quality academic advising programs.

In Chapter Twelve, "Delivery Systems and the Institutional Context," Edward R. Hines analyzes the dynamics present in most institutions of higher education and how they influence the advising delivery system selected. He investigates the roles institutional characteristics (size, control, type, residential status, and program mix) have in determining appropriate organizational structures and ultimately the impact on the advising process. Consideration is given also to the overall organizational structure of the institution, budget and facilities management, and administrative leadership as they affect advising programs.

David W. King, Chapter Thirteen, surveys the important issues institutional leaders face as they administer advising programs. Particular attention is paid to institutional commitment as reflected in budget allocations, staffing, and availability of other resources. He examines the roles of an advising director or coordinator and discusses the competencies needed, such as political astuteness, diplomacy, and administrative/management skills.

In Chapter Fourteen, Donald D. Gehring points out some of the legal implications concerning advising practices and suggests ways to limit liability for both individual advisors and their institutions. He specifically addresses the issues of constitutional and contractual relationships and statutory mandates and gives examples to illustrate how advisors can meet the legal requirements.

As faculty members are currently in the majority of those providing advising services, Howard C. Kramer and Robert E. Gardner (Chapter Fifteen) focus on faculty development programs as a strategy for enhancing advising systems. The specific roles of the advising coordinator, as a catalyst for faculty development, are explored. Detailed examples of faculty development programs that can lead to the introduction of developmental academic advising concepts are presented. Pitfalls in the process are acknowledged, along with recommendations for a step-by-step process to achieve the goal of faculty appreciating advising as an opportunity for achievement, a channel for productivity, and an avenue of meaningful professional activities.

Chapter Sixteen concludes Part Three with a discussion of training programs to enhance the effectiveness of professional and paraprofessional advisors. Virginia N. Gordon reminds the reader that an advising program is as effective and responsive to student needs as the breadth and depth of knowledge of its advisors and the level of advising and interpersonal skills and techniques they use to communicate that knowledge to students. She presents a seven-step paradigm for setting up advisor training programs and illustrates key issues involved in implementing each step.

12

Delivery Systems
and the Institutional Context

Edward R. Hines

Academic advising, a time-honored area in higher education, now finds itself in the middle of a paradox. As a generic activity, the roots of academic advising go back to the American Colonial College (Rudolph, 1962). As an institutionalized function, academic advising is fairly new to higher education. Terms such as academic advisor, director of academic advising, and academic advising center are generally associated with the expansion of higher education since the middle of this century. In spite of the need for academic advising and its apparent success, negative elements detract from its legitimacy as an institutional function, thus causing a paradox. On the one hand, academic advising is dominated by institutional reward systems oriented to academic departments, as observed by Dressel: "Advising is caught up in a no-win situation in a culture predominantly devoted to content coverage, the departmental-disciplinary orientation, and a reward system that, at least in the universities, has little to do with the quality of either teaching or advising" (1981, p. 2). On the other hand, the reality of advising centers is that they do not directly generate enrollment. This occurs at a time when administrators and institutional leaders increasingly make enrollment-based decisions about the viability of programs and personnel. Virtually all higher-education activities and functions that are not direct generators of enrollment are subject to scrutiny.

This chapter will identify the organizational context of academic advising by discussing pertinent contemporary administrative and management concepts, examining major institutional characteristics and their relationship to academic advising, and reviewing major components in designing delivery systems for academic advising. These components include students, advisors, organizational structure, budget, and facilities.

Organizational Context of Advising

Academic advising takes place in an organizational context. This context is more than the organizational structure chosen for the delivery of an advising system. The predominance of the existing research pertaining to organizational structure deals with centralization. Should there be a centralized advising system, consisting of an advising center, a center with satellites, or a center with either formal or informal linkages to individual academic departments? Should there be a decentralized advising system relying primarily upon faculty in individual departments? In decentralized systems, there might be a central coordinator or a centralized office, but the emphasis of the advising system would be diffused, utilizing faculty as the prime delivery mechanism. These and other related questions are easier to answer, however, once the underlying characteristics of the college or university as an organization are identified and used as the basis for decision making about delivery systems.

This discussion of the organizational context of academic advising begins with two basic assumptions that grow from the literature on administration and management, and they pertain to open systems and to contingency management. It is assumed that colleges and universities are open systems with the characteristics of exchange with the environment, boundaries between the organization and the environment, uncertainty because of threats and constraints imposed by the environment, and the propensity to seek stability through adaptation, adjustment, and change (Thompson, 1967). Further, it is assumed that contingency management is appropriate (Kast and Rosenzweig, 1979) and is used either consciously or implicitly by virtually all higher-education administrators. The term *contingency* suggests that there is no "one best way" to manage. Instead, the approaches, strategies, and techniques chosen must fit the situation at hand. There are varied situations confronting higher-education administrators, and these situations call for multiple, varied management approaches and techniques. This flexible, adaptable orientation to management brings to light some of the contemporary thinking about colleges and universities as organizations. Four areas will be considered: colleges and universities as an organizational type, boundary spanning, differentiation and integration, and the growing importance of educational outcomes and productivity.

Academic or Professional Organization. A continuing frustration associated with colleges and universities viewed as organizations is that they do not fit the existing molds by which most types of organizations are classified. For instance, using a well-known organizational typology based upon identifying the prime beneficiary of the organization, it is observed that colleges and universities are service organizations, rather than business, commonweal, or mutual-benefit organizations (Blau and Scott, 1962). As service organizations, the clients are the prime beneficiary. If one conceptualizes a college as an organization oriented primarily to teaching, then the students as clients are the prime beneficiaries. However, colleges are also businesses having as prime beneficiaries the trustees or governing board as the "owners." Colleges also are commonweal organizations because in public service and research, the public-at-large is the prime beneficiary. Still further, colleges are mutual-benefit organizations because in many areas the membership is the prime beneficiary. This is true in graduate education, in research, and in most student associations and groups. Therefore, academic organizations exhibit characteristics representative of service, business, commonweal, and mutual-benefit organizations.

Another common view of academic organizations is along traditional lines, conceptualizing colleges and universities as collegial organizations. The *collegium* was a community of scholars, oriented to dispassionate inquiry, providing its members with a "sanctuary of scholarship" (Goodman, 1962). The primary functions of the university were to discover knowledge and offer social criticism. In a sense, academic advising was a core part of the institution, but as a direct service function, academic advising did not exist. The primary decision makers in the collegial organization were the faculty who made decisions collectively and democratically. Consensus was the byword, and there was an absence of conflict. In such an organization, students were viewed as protégés or junior scholars in residence. Great deference was paid to seniority and to academic rank. In such an organization, academic advising would be "prescriptive" or normative (Crookston, 1972).

Organizational Paradigms. In contemporary administration and management literature, there are four basic views or paradigms of organization and governance. As shown in Table 1, these paradigms are labeled economic rationality, bureaucratic or organizational, political, and academic or professional. In this discussion, each paradigm is applied briefly to the college or university, and the place of academic advising in each paradigm is identified.

One basic view of academic organizations is according to the *paradigm of economic rationality*. In economically rational organizations, there is maximum information about all decision alternatives, including their costs and benefits. With this information, the advantages and disadvantages of any decision alternative can be computed, frequently in cost-benefit terms. In economically rational organizations, efficiency often becomes a dominant organizational goal. Expressed as a ratio, efficiency is defined as means to ends, or input to output. The objective becomes one of achieving the smallest fraction possible in the ratio of input to ouput. The greatest amount of end product is generated by using the least amount of resources as input. In organizations where the paradigm of economic rationality is evident, decision making can proceed using computational techniques. Leadership may be largely a

Table 1. Models of Governance and Organization.

Area of Concern	Economic Rationality	Bureaucratic or Organizational	Political	Academic or Professional
Dominant mode of organizational behavior	Certainty	Regularity	Competitive	Ad hocracy (Organized anarchy[a])
Type of social structure	Unitary	Hierarchical, organized by subunits	Fragmented or syndical, dominated by power elites	Fragmented and loosely coupled,[b] dominated by academic elites
Organizational goals and mission	Clear, consistent, and dominant	Clear at higher levels, but may not be clear in subunits	Clear within subgroups, but outcomes dependent upon mutual adjustment	Symbolic, but often not operationalized
Leadership metaphors	Problem-solving technocrat	Titular or autocratic; figurehead or dictator	Mediator; statesperson	Problem-solving catalyst
Decision-making orientation	Computational	Coalitional within constraints of procedures, routines	Bargaining and compromise	Consensus with deference to academic elites
Information requirements	Extensive, systematic	Variable—dependent on procedural requirements	Little—intuitive or extensive justification	Variable—depends upon consensus

Sources: Adapted from Pfeffer, 1981; and Baldridge, Curtis, Ecker, and Riley, 1977.
[a]Cohen and March, 1974.
[b]Weick, 1976.

matter of problem solving. Of prime importance to such professional fields as econometrics and operations research, economic rationality can prevail in other parts of an organization, often in a small research unit or an office oriented to data generation. In an economically rational organization or in one following the tenets of economic rationality, academic advising would be a rather mechanistic function oriented largely to dispensing details pertinent to course selection, scheduling, and registration.

In another basic view of academic organizations called the *bureaucratic or organizational paradigm,* there is an orientation to organization and bureaucracy. This orientation assumes limitations in the information known about decision alternatives. As such, organizational leaders cannot maximize or optimize according to the dictates of quantitative analysis and computation. Instead, one must strive for the most satisfactory decision within given limitations and constraints. As coined by Simon (1957), the term *satisficing* is broadly applicable to most situations involving human behavior within organizations. In decision situations where satisficing is the rule of thumb, decisions become small adjustments on past organizational behavior. These adjustments provide the basis for the incrementalism used frequently in public agency budgeting. The two most predominant characteristics of this paradigm are that it seeks the most satisfactory resolution to immediate problems, and that, as a decision-making orientation, it is ubiquitous, as are organizations in everyday life. The organizational or bureaucratic paradigm, as the basis for an academic advising system, would have likely resulted in academic advising centers, especially in larger institutions, that grew rapidly in size as well as number in the 1960s. Comprehensive public colleges and community colleges would be included in this category. Along with advising centers, however, there would likely be the continuation of the traditional form of faculty advising. In any given institution, there could well be a hybrid form of both an advising center and faculty advising.

Still another view of academic organizations contained in this analysis is the institution as a political organization. Originating with political systems theory (Easton, 1965), the *political paradigm* gained rapid, widespread acceptance in the higher-education literature in the 1970s. Three characteristics of this paradigm are outstanding. First, the paradigm is oriented to process more than outcome; it deals with the ways in which decisions are made. The second characteristic of the political paradigm is its acceptance of conflict in a nonpejorative sense. Conflict between and among actors, groups, and organizations is a basic part of political life. Resolution of that conflict occurs during the political process by which decisions known as "policy" are made. The third outstanding feature of the political paradigm is the orientation to people and individuals who are known as the "players" in the game. Potential winners and losers in the game of politics emerge as a direct result of who is in the contest, what the stakes are, and what are the potential costs of losing as well as the gains from winning. The form and scope of academic advising in an organization dominated by politics are uncertain except that they might reflect the political strength of a particular actor or department on campus. Its continued sustenance may depend upon how that person or department negotiates and survives the political environment.

While each paradigm has applicability in an analysis of college and university organization, Table 1 suggests an *academic* or *profession paradigm* as a distinct type of organization. In academic organizations, the primary characteristic of organizational behavior is that it occurs on an ad hoc basis as the need arises. Cohen and March (1974) used the phrase "organized anarchy" to refer to academic organizations because goals were unclear, the technology was uncertain, and individual participation was variable. The social structure of academic organizations is not rigid, hierarchical, and "tight." Instead, it is loosely joined internally or coupled (Weick, 1976). While goals are important, they may not be clearly operationalized. Leaders are oriented to solving problems, and decisions are made according to the preferences of groups of influential professors and researchers who could be called "academic elites." In academic organizations, academic advising has evolved using two primary organizational mechanisms, the centralized academic advising office and decentralized advising by faculty. These two forms represent this academic model of colleges and universities quite well. They emerged either as the traditional model preferred by faculty or as an ad hoc response to more recent enrollment expansion. Because these two approaches to academic advising arose in response to two different sets of demands, they are quite different in structure and in orientation. Such multiple organizational forms in higher education are common. College and university leaders need to find ways to use each approach or both in effective ways in order to maximize the potential positive impact on students.

Boundary Spanning. A basic concept growing out of systems theory is boundary spanning. This concept has been applied primarily to the relationship of an organization to its environment (Adams, 1976). In business organizations, sales and marketing departments lie at the boundary between the organization and its environment, and in colleges and universities it is the planning, development, and institutional research offices that operate at the boundary. This is because the purpose of these offices is to monitor the environment, identify the portions of the environment bearing on the organization, and interpret the environment for the organization. During times of decline and resource scarcity, the environment takes on greater potential importance for the organization. By properly scanning the environment, the organization can adapt to new circumstances. In higher education, community colleges are especially effective boundary spanners because of their adaptability, their capacity to alter programs to changing student demand, and their effectiveness at responding to new labor market conditions.

Boundary spanning can be utilized *within* organizations as well as between the organization and the environment. Of the four generic types of organizations depicted in Table 1, the concept of internal boundary spanning may be most relevant to academic or professional organizations. In academic organizations, in contrast to the other three types of organizations, goals tend to be more diffuse, the social structure tends to be more fragmented, and individual participation tends to be oriented more to temporal concerns. As a result, the internal social structure of the organization can be loosely coupled. In organizations dominated by loose coupling, temporary structures may accomplish organizational tasks and achieve purposes. The means to do this may include committees, task forces, and study groups. These temporary organizational structures are very common in colleges and universities.

Organizational structures of this type are linked to other parts of the organization by individuals, groups, or others serving as internal boundary spanners.

Few people in organizations have, as a part of their major role, the function of boundary spanning. An exception to this rule is academic advisors who "represent classic models of expanded boundary spanning" (Fitzgerald, 1981, p. 10). In fact, academic advisors span boundaries in at least two distinct ways. They serve as boundary spanners because they link full-time teaching faculty with support staff within the institution. These support staff include a broad range of service professionals in such areas as academic support services, student services, counseling, vocational and career placement, and financial aids. Academic advisors serve as a link for students, thus extending beyond the boundary of both academic discipline and support service. Advisors also serve as a link between the institutional mission statement and its official goals, as well as the actual instructional programs and the operational goals and objectives occurring at a lower place in the hierarchy (Kramer, 1981). Academic advisors thus serve as a dual link in the institution.

Differentiation and Integration. Differentiation and integration are two basic, dynamic processes occurring concurrently. Far more crucial than merely considering characteristics like size, span of control, and organizational charts, differentiation is the process by which organizations internally segment in order to respond effectively to the environment (Lawrence and Lorsch, 1967). Differentiation occurs both vertically and horizontally. Vertically, differentiation determines the number of levels and the "shape" of the hierarchy in the organization. Differentiation is a layering device that deals with line and staff, rank of organizational officials, and communications channels in the chain of command. Horizontally, differentiation occurs by departmentalization, commonly according to function, location, or product (Kast and Rosenzweig, 1979). Academic advisors and the advising process simultaneously serve as function, location, and product. Advising is one of several major institutional functions in the area of academic and support services. Advising centers are organized according to location. The result of academic advising is a better-informed student who, as a "product" of advising, is more capable of autonomous decision making.

Integration is critical to administrators because it is the process by which coordination and control are achieved within the organization. Integration is achieved through both structure and personnel. While the administrative hierarchy helps achieve integration, there must be more than simply structure involved; otherwise, integration might be enhanced simply by adding another administrative layer. Instead, integration is achieved by the extent to which components of the organization are synthesized in meaningful ways. Because academic advisors are internal boundary spanners, they are in ideal positions to help achieve integration in academic institutions.

Academic advisors help students achieve greater understanding of the college or university as an academic organization and of career choices that are congruent with individual strengths, abilities, and interests. In this way, advisors are facilitators—developmental specialists who help integrate students with the institution.

Outcomes and Productivity. The concepts of educational outcomes and productivity appear to be of an order different from organizational structure, boundary spanning, differentiation, and integration. The reason for this is that much of the literature on management and administration deals with initial or entry-level characteristics and process dimensions. Consequently, assumptions are made about the extent to which input characteristics will be associated with such outcomes as student satisfaction, the contribution of education to work, higher lifetime earnings, or more involved citizens. However, there is a dearth of research on educational outcomes and the productivity of institutions.

A major emphasis in American education has been on access. Along with this orientation to educational opportunity came policies and procedures designed to help those not qualified, using narrower, more traditional measures. There were remedial and compensatory education, increased counseling, open-door admissions, and a new phenomenon in higher education known as the temporary dropout or "stop out." As the 1980s began, a shift in values occurred in the United States. Manifested in the landslide victory of Ronald Reagan in the 1980 presidential election, there were other signs of a shift toward conservatism. These signs included emphasis upon basic skills, criticism of nonacademic subjects in schools, re-examination of student aid by the federal government, and increased attention to admissions standards in institutions such as public colleges and even in community colleges having open access.

Watchwords of the current decade are quality, excellence, outcomes, and productivity (Finn, 1983). Cycles of reform are not unknown in education, and it is not at all clear exactly what the reform movement includes. It is safe to say that such items as merit pay, admissions standards, and performance criteria for graduation will continue to exist.

One of the implications of a shift toward educational outcomes and personnel productivity is that functions such as academic advising have become increasingly more important to colleges and universities. The growth of literature and research dealing with academic advising is noteworthy. There is more information on academic advising in the Educational Resources Information Center (ERIC) since 1980 than all previous years combined, and in 1981 "academic advising" began to be used as a separate descriptor in ERIC. Academic advising is an increasingly popular topic for doctoral dissertations. There are now presentations on advising on the programs of virtually every major conference in higher and postsecondary education.

The primary implication for academic advising of the recent emphasis on outcomes and productivity is in the area of the management of advising and research dealing with the impact of advising. Academic advising managers, administrators, and coordinators must be attuned increasingly to the outcomes and impact of advising. At a time when less than 40 percent of the college seniors are satisfied with academic advising and not quite half of the college sophomores are satisfied with advising (Watkins, 1983), serious attention must be given to this area. More empirical research is needed on the topic, including the impact of academic advising, levels of student satisfaction with advising, the centralized advising of new students and undeclared majors, the impact of faculty who demonstrate interest in advising versus those who must advise due to job assignment, and the relationship between advising and retention. Retention research has great potential utility for generating data that will answer these questions. There are many who claim that effective advising will enhance retention (Creamer, 1980; Crockett, 1978; Habley, 1981; Lenning, Sauer, and Beal, 1980; Lewis, Leach, and Lutz, 1983; Noel, 1976), but to date there is insufficient empirical research on the topic. Nevertheless, studies by Farmer and Barbour (1980) and by Schotzinger, Lubetkin, and Rynearson (1978) show that student retention was improved substantially by academic advising. And, as shown by the work of Enos (1981), even though student satisfaction with advising may increase, a corresponding increase in student retention may not result. If academic advising remains primarily a singular event during which a student obtains a faculty signature for registration, then academic advising may be relegated to the undistinguished category of a "solution without substance" as a way to improve student retention (Green, 1983).

Institutional Characteristics

Five institutional characteristics have been identified and analyzed, according to their implications for the design of academic advising systems. These institutional characteristics include *size, control, type, residential or nonresidential,* and *program mix.*

Size is a deceptive variable. Negative consequences have been imputed to size as an institutional characteristic, with little empirical evidence offered in support. While size has been found to be related to the complexity of the organizational structure and to the extent of organizational differentiation (Meyer and Associates, 1980), size is not related causally to measures of outcome or effectiveness (Ecker, 1979; Lazarsfeld and Thielens, 1958).

Colleges and universities of large size are a fairly recent phenomenon in American higher education. Only 9 percent of the private institutions enrolled more than 20,000 students as of 1977, while over 26 percent of the public institutions enrolled more than 20,000 students (Carnegie Council on Policy Studies in Higher Education, 1980). On the other hand, three quarters of all private institutions enroll from 500 to 9,999 students, and another 6 percent enroll less than 500 students each. In the public sector, only .2

percent enroll less than 500 students, while nearly 45 percent enroll from 500 to 9,999 students. The growth in the size and number of institutions has been largely an occurrence of the two-decade period from 1950 to 1970, particularly in the public sector. It was in this sector that community colleges grew at the rate of nearly one new college per week during portions of the 1960s, and comprehensive colleges and universities, including former teacher's colleges and regional state universities, grew in size and in number during this same period.

Centralized advising offices tended to emerge in larger institutions, especially in public colleges and universities and in community colleges. As a structural variable, therefore, larger institutional size is associated with centralized advising offices. Centralized academic advising is more efficient in larger institutions. Whether or not centralized academic advising is more effective and results in higher student retention is a potentially fruitful topic for research.

In regard to control and type as institutional characteristics, it is common to find them used as dichotomous variables. *Control* is a means to group institutions into public or private colleges, and *type* is a variable used to separate four-year from two-year colleges. Each of these dichotomies masks a more complex reality. In control referring to the source of authority over institutional governance and policy making, institutions can be either public or private. Within the public group, institutions can be federal, state, or local, with state-controlled institutions being the most common and numerous. Within the private college group, there are private, independent institutions as well as sectarian colleges representing a wide range of religious organizations and orders. Institutional type refers to four-year as well as two-year colleges. Four-year colleges include research universities, comprehensive colleges and universities, and liberal arts colleges, to use the Carnegie classification; there are also specialized institutions such as engineering schools, technical colleges, and special-purpose institutions. Two-year colleges include comprehensive community colleges, two-year technical institutes, and private two-year or junior colleges.

It was during the 1960s that advising grew as a function in importance and in size. Advising became an important function simply because there were large numbers of students, many of whom were uncommitted as to a major field of study for up to two years of their college experience. In community colleges, for instance, much of the academic course and schedule planning had to take place during the summer months prior to the beginning of the academic year, because students would only be on campus for two years and their programs of study were, in many cases, tightly prescribed. Therefore, academic advising became an important part of the summer counseling duties of nonteaching staff in community colleges. A logical structure created to serve these students was the advising center. Centralized in a location accessible to students, advising centers grew rapidly in number in the 1960s. Advising centers also began to be used in the rapidly growing comprehensive colleges and universities and in the major state universities as a means to accommodate the large influx of new students (Grites, 1979a).

An important institutional characteristic for the design of academic advising delivery systems is whether or not the campus is *residential*. Predominantly commuter or *nonresidential* campuses, of course, include most community colleges and many institutions located in or near urban areas. Predominantly residential campuses include many universities, colleges, and some two-year institutions. Obviously, a large number of universities and colleges are neither predominantly commuter nor residential but some combination of both. This characteristic will be a useful indicator of where the advising center might be located, as well as an indicator of who might be potential advisors and allied or paraprofessional staff.

For campuses having residence halls, there are several important implications for advising. The growth of the size and number of comprehensive colleges and universities and the growth of major state universities included expansion of residence hall systems to what approximates medium-sized cities in many instances. Given the fact that research has demonstrated the importance of residence halls to student life and development (Astin, 1977; Blimling and Schuh, 1981), the on-campus living experience becomes a potentially important contributor to campus and organizational climate. This is the first major implication for advising. Residential institutions have unique organizational climates that can exert powerful influences upon students. The second implication for advising is that professional and student staff in residence halls are potential adjuncts to advising. They may serve as allied and paraprofessional advisors. The full-time residence hall staff members are an information source, and they may be able to function as part-time academic advisors as well as student affairs professionals (Abel, 1981). The residence halls themselves may offer a physical setting in which academic advising can take place (Gelfand, 1980). At a time when campus space may be at a premium or creating new space for an advising center may be impossible, residence halls—by definition in accessable locations—may hold considerable promise for serving as locations for advising centers.

It might appear as if *program mix* would be more of an indirect correlate than a direct determinant of an academic advising delivery system. However, program mix can literally offer the key as to what type, where, and whom to involve in an academic advising system. Program mix includes the scope and the depth of academic programs by major area. The proportion of liberal arts students, in comparison with professional schools, the allied professions, and preprofessional programs, provides direction to leaders wishing to design the most appropriate academic advising system. The advising staff must reflect a congruent balance of disciplinary and professional field orientations, similar to that found in the configuration of academic programs on campus. If the campus has strong preparation programs for business, medicine, and law, then the academic advising system should reflect that emphasis. If all first-year students are "undeclared majors" by definition, then centralized advising centers are probably in order.

Delivery System Design for Academic Advising

There are three major sets of variables to consider in designing a delivery system for academic advising. Two variable sets have already been reviewed in this chapter—the organizational context of academic advising and the more specific characteristics of the college or university in question. The third variable set pertains directly to the academic advising delivery system, and there are five components to be considered. These components include the students, the advisors, the organizational structure of academic advising, the budget, and the facilities. The delivery system consists of more than merely advisors. It must include the context in which advising is to be accomplished, who is offering the advising, and the students as the recipients of advising.

Students. In the literature, one might suspect that student clients are a generally undifferentiated group. On the contrary, they are a complex and highly individualized group of men and women. Academic advisors recognize that students differ in a number of potentially significant ways. There are many contextual, precollege, and demographic characteristics that need to be taken into account as an advising relationship is established. Students' intended goals and aspirations need to be considered, and these include their career plans and levels of commitment to the institution. Any of these individual areas can be potent motivators for students.

In addition to career intent and institutional commitment, there is the matter of the individual student's current situation and anticipated short-range circumstances. For purposes of academic advising, the students may be regarded as being in one of five categories: *declared majors, new students and undeclared majors, preprofessional students, students with special needs,* and *prefreshmen.*

So-called traditional academic advising using faculty as advisors has tended to focus on declared majors. These are the students largely within the confines of specific academic departments, the students committed to a particular major field, and the students who because of their declared major are worthy of attention by a specific faculty. In size, the number of declared majors may be extremely large, easily in excess of 10,000 or 15,000 students in the largest universities. These students never present the institution with a problem similar in magnitude to their size. This is because declared majors are usually departmentally bound. In a large institution with 100 separate academic departments, this huge number of students becomes quickly dispersed throughout the university. It is in the academic departments where academic advising is done by faculty. However, recent experience has shown that it is also in the academic departments or in college units where centralized academic advising offices have been used with considerable success. This may be an organizational form characterizing academic advising of the future (Higbee, 1979; Johnson and Sprandel, 1975; Polson and Jurich, 1979, 1981; Spencer, Peterson, and Kramer, 1982).

Academic advising centers have tended to concentrate on new students and undeclared majors, often the largest undifferentiated student group on campus. In major state universities, the size of this single student group can exceed 5,000 students. While this is not as sizable as the overall number of declared majors, the 5,000 new students and undeclared majors constitute a group having a similar characteristic—students without a major field of study. These uncommitted students are operating in a searching, exploratory mode. They are the group most likely to need an entire range of student affairs and academic support services, including testing, academic advising, career counseling, even personal or therapeutic counseling, and the time and individual freedom to explore academic and career options (see Chapters Five, Six, and Seven). This is more difficult to do after a major field is chosen, and academic departments are less tolerant than are academic advising centers of students who need time for exploration.

Preprofessional students and students with special needs are other important student groups who are potential users of academic advising services. Preprofessional students, as the name would imply, are targeted to specific career goals oriented largely to entering such professional schools as law and medicine. While the professional school has been the focus of some well-known research studies, preprofessional training largely has been untouched by researchers. The conferences of the National Academic Advising Association (NACADA) have begun to include a number of sessions with a focus on advising preprofessional students, however, and this should stimulate more empirical research on the topic.

Students with special needs have provided the opportunity for research and have been the focus of institutional policy concern for some time. These include underprepared students, students with academic deficiencies, and, more recently, students with physical and other handicapping conditions. These students provided the impetus for special student affairs programs that grew in both size and number in the 1960s and 1970s. Many of these services were organized as outreach efforts of counseling and student affairs offices, and many of them expanded to offer academic and career guidance. As a student group, students with special needs are no different from other students, with the exception of their having some extraordinary need, condition, or circumstance justifying intervention either prior to or concurrent with academic advising. Students with special needs present an opportunity for linkage and outreach efforts involving academic advisors and counselors working in special program areas. (See Chapters Ten and Eleven for more information about the needs of these students.)

The final category of students to be discussed is prefreshmen. This is an elusive group, but it presents the institution with opportunities for involvement and advising. Prefreshmen essentially are a nongroup seldom aggregated as a definitive student group until they arrive on campus. Obviously, by the time this event occurs, the students have become freshmen and are affected by on-campus activities provided for new students. One reason why prefreshmen are important is that a substantial percentage of those who eventually withdraw or drop out develop their initial thoughts about leaving during this prefreshman period (Cope and Hannah, 1975). Another reason is that the prefreshman period may involve a considerable length of time, certainly longer than a single summer season. It is during this period when uncertainty occurs and self-doubt can begin. There are a number of possibilities for positive intervention involving prefreshmen. Grites (1979b) described this prefreshman period as "a void" and suggested that both secondary school counselors and college advisors could target programs, activities, and communications to these students. McDaniel, Faulkner, and Powell (1981) described a one-hour workshop offered in "primary feeder high schools" that focused on advising, scheduling, and registration. Feike, Looney, and Sanford (1981) were part of an intensive two-day "preview" program for prefreshmen and transfer students in the summer months during which students registered for fall classes. It is common for community colleges to offer summer registration periods for incoming freshmen. The emerging literature on retention and attrition indicates that this period between acceptance to college and completion of the first semester is a time of anxiety and indecision. The academic advising literature is beginning to provide useful data in this area for advisors and administrators (see Chapter Three).

After new students have arrived on campus, there are a number of potentially significant ways to extend beyond information dispensing and social activities. As explained by Higginson, Moore, and White (1981), freshmen themselves report that their greatest needs are academic in nature; orientation presents a key opportunity to begin retention efforts, and the authors suggested a number of specific activities: a personal interview with an advisor, planning for course scheduling, simulated registration, and follow-up sessions for personal counseling and learning survival skills. Courses can be offered that help integrate freshmen into the institutional mainstream. These courses may be offered with or without academic credit. They may be led by a single faculty member or teams involving faculty or faculty-student affairs professional combinations. Despite conservative reactions to such experiences as not being rigorous, the research reported on the outcomes of these courses would indicate that careful consideration should be given to including them. The experience of one university in a freshman-faculty mentoring program lends support to the potentially positive effects of early intervention by institutional representatives (Kramer and White, 1982; see Chapter Seventeen).

It is not possible to discuss different categories of students without giving attention to their developmental needs. Developmental needs of students vary across and within the five categories of students outlined in this section. The basic thesis of this book is that academic advising can usefully be conceptualized as a developmental process. A number of academic advising models have been described using developmental constructs. These basic approaches have been identified elsewhere and will not be reviewed here (Crookston, 1972; Ender, Winston, and Miller, 1982; Grites, 1979a; McLaughlin and Starr, 1982; Polson and Cashin, 1981). These models are variations on a developmental theme; what is important is to consider the specific constructs involved in each model and to assess their utility to particular campus circumstances. Miller and McCaffrey (1982), for instance, advanced the "SPICE of Developmental Life" notion including the self, the physical, the interpersonal, the career, and the educational aspects of human development. Sample tasks involved in each of three major life cycle phases from late adolescence to young adulthood to mid-life transition were identified along with appropriate responses of academic advisors. Potter (1980) conceptualized a four-part functional advising model, consisting of information, clarification, insight, and self-acceptance, and posited that advisors could serve to help students gain insight while other professionals, such as counselors and administrative assistants, could be utilized more appropriately in the other functions. Shane (1981) differentiated advising, counseling, and psychotherapy. Shane reasoned that advising included four basic types—informational, explanatory, analytical, and therapeutic—but that counseling and psychotherapy extended beyond these advising functions to embrace areas such as crisis intervention, personal developmental issues, and adjustment problems. Shane noted that advising sessions tended to be either informational or analytical in nature. Research is needed to examine the developmental conditions of students at each discrete stage of the college experience in relation to the type of academic advising provided by institutions. It may be, for instance, that undeclared majors tend to need both informational and therapeutic advising, while declared majors and upperclass students need explanatory and analytical advising. On the other hand, it may be that these functional types of advising can be arranged in a hierarchy of prepotency from informational advising on the most elementary level to therapeutic advising on the most advanced level. Conclusive research results from definitive studies would go far in providing the type of data base with which to design the most effective academic advising delivery system.

Advisors. A major component in the delivery of academic advising services is the advisor. Type of institutional relationship or appointment is one consideration, with the primary difference being among faculty or teaching staff, administrators or support staff, and students. Teaching positions are not only full- or part-time but also tenured or permanent appointment, tenure-seeking (also known as "tenure track"), and temporary or adjunct. Review of the literature indicates clearly that the traditional advisors are faculty; they still are the predominant type of advisors, as shown in the 1982 national survey (Chapter Two), and in most institutions faculty will continue to be the major means of delivery of advising to the students. At the same time, there continue to be substantial problems with faculty advising. There is a pervasive view that student dissatisfaction with faculty advising is more widespread and intense than it should be (see Chapter One). There are reasons why faculty cannot, and will not, be effective and motivated advisors. To be sure, there are exceptions, and those faculty interested in and motivated by advising continue to offer potential for meaningful impact on students. At the present time, however, the rewards for advising tend to be intrinsic. As long as faculty are expected to advise as part of their on-load assignment while little institutional attention is devoted to improving advising, then academic advising is likely to remain an item of lesser importance for faculty. In fact, in the present system on many campuses, there is a disincentive for advising, lest effective advising be interpreted by more senior professors as a move by the young and the disenfranchised for popularity, power, and student esteem. Perhaps the real issue is not whether or not faculty should advise but how to enhance the effectiveness of advising by involving faculty who desire to advise and for whom advising is an important professional activity (see Chapter Fifteen). Grites (1979a) said it cogently, "One must be cautious not to generalize about the inadequacy of faculty advising. The age-old concept has yet to be shown intrinsically ineffective and should not be discarded; rather, faculty advising should be considered for its effectiveness, especially as it is coordinated with other delivery systems" (p. 13).

While faculty remain the largest group of advisors and faculty advising is the traditional mode in higher education, full-time professional advisors are a major means by which advising delivery services are structured. The notion of full-time advisors is difficult to differentiate from centralized advising offices because the two appeared concurrently and continue to be used together. At the institutional or major college level, having a centralized advising office means that either there is a full-time office director or advising coordinator or that there is a staff of professional advisors along with a full-time director. The issue of having a full-time director is essentially the matter of institutional commitment. The importance of a positive and visible commitment to advising by the

institution is well reported in the literature. Commitment is translated into resources, resulting in a person whose full-time responsibility is devoted to academic advising. Having full-time leadership
in academic advising, most frequently seen in hiring an advising
director or coordinator, is virtually a precondition for effective
advising (see Chapters Two and Thirteen for elaboration).

The issues of having a staff of full-time academic advisors,
employing both professional and faculty advisors, assigning faculty
to a centralized advising office, and hiring students as advisors and
paraprofessional advisors are matters left up to the discretion of the
leadership for advising, the availability of institutional financial
resources, and the flexibility with which personnel decisions can be
made. One can locate a small but growing information base on each
of these four issues. There are no definitive findings presently
existing that would lead to an absolute conclusive recommendation
on any of these for all institutions. There is far too much variability
within and among institutions in areas influencing decision making on each of these points. A possible exception to this might be
in the areas of utilizing students as advisors and using paraprofessional advisors. The existing research indicates that students and
paraprofessionals can be effectively used in an advising capacity
(Barman and Benson, 1981; Habley, 1978; Murry, 1972; Upcraft,
1971), but that these individuals may provide an important supplement to, rather than a substitute for, academic advising by faculty
(Goldberg, 1981; Hutchins and Miller, 1979) (see Chapter Sixteen
for more details).

Organizational Structure of Advising. Although the organizational structure for an advising delivery system is a vital consideration, it must not be ascribed an excessive degree of importance
to structure as an independent variable or element of causation in
areas such as the effectiveness of academic advising, the degree of
satisfaction, or the association between academic success and the
structure of the advising system. It is common to make erroneous
assumptions about the importance of organizational structure. In
fact, structure is more of a dependent or moderating variable than
it is an independent variable. Organizational and administrative
structure tends to reflect the dominant modes of organizational
behavior, the values and preferences of the chief administrators and

policy makers, and the particular context and evolution of the college or university as an organization. Organizational structure alone does not cause such things as student satisfaction, employee happiness, and academic success. Structure may reflect whether or not the president believed that academic advising was an important activity and whether or not advising would command sufficient institutional resources to support adequate staff and services.

In the design of delivery systems for academic advising, there are a number of major areas requiring policy decisions by institutional leaders. In the literature, the design components of organizational structure and the identity of the advisors appear to be most important. Any assumption that these are the two most vital components is mistaken. As explained previously, organizational structure may be more reflective of the institution's history, evolution, and whether or not advising was given a priority. By the same token, arguments about whether faculty advising is more effective than advising by full-time professionals are specious and counterproductive.

In this analysis, the position is taken that virtually all colleges and universities have legitimate need for integrated academic advising along a continuum going from decentralized to centralized structures. In the design of integrated academic advising, there will be the need for some combination of faculty advisors and full-time professional advisors. The exact number of each, along with the extent to which advising will be centralized, will depend upon particular institutional circumstances. A college may choose a centralized advising office headed by a full-time director and a small number of full-time professional advisors who are the primary delivery system for new students, including transfers, and for undeclared majors. Some institutions have utilized this centralized office effectively at the institutional level, and some have chosen to locate centralized offices in each college or major institutional division. After students choose major fields, they may then be assigned to departmentally based faculty. In some instances, departments of larger size have developed their own central advising offices within the department. Other departments will utilize the services of a centralized college advising office.

Budget and Facilities. The final two components to be included in the design of a delivery system for academic advising are budget and facilities. A centralized advising office requiring a separate line item in the college or university budget is clearly an issue of fiscal consequence. If the centralized advising office has a number of full-time academic advisors accounted for in the advising budget, the entire operation may exceed $100,000 annually, and in larger institutions the academic advising budget may approach a quarter of a million dollars in an annual operating budget. In private institutions, especially, it does not take long for this amount to be equaled in tuition revenue if tuition and fees exceed $7,500 annually. Even in public institutions, tuition revenue is of note, especially if one compounds that revenue over the number of terms remaining until graduation. If effective academic advising is associated with higher retention rates, the tuition revenue alone will compensate for the institution's investment in academic advising as a separate and distinct budget item.

Where advising is not a separate institutional function, one tends to find the more traditional approach of diffusing advising among faculty. In that instance, advising is decentralized and often tends to be found in smaller institutions. This approach works well with upperclass and preprofessional students, and the advisors tend to be faculty who are assigned on-load, where advising is part of a faculty member's basic job responsibility. In such instances, advising may tend to use existing facilities. On the other hand, in larger institutions advising has been centralized in offices having full-time professional advisors who serve as the primary delivery for new students and undeclared majors. In these larger institutions, advising will usually be budgeted in separate categories within the institution, and there probably will be an identified and separate advising office.

Summary and Conclusion

It is the conclusion of this analysis that most institutions should consider developing a delivery system for advising using both faculty advisors and full-time staff. The exact configuration of advising will grow out of the organizational context, institutional characteristics, and the delivery system components deemed appropriate for that institution as interpreted by the institutional leadership. There are many particular configurations possible. Habley (in press) offers seven analytically distinct organizational structures for academic advising, although most options involve some combination of both faculty and professional advisors.

Finally, there are other critical issues to consider in organizing an academic advising system. These issues go beyond questions of structure and personnel to process considerations. The effectiveness of academic advising may well depend on the soundness of the conceptual approach to advising chosen on that particular campus. As identified by Wilder (1981) and described in a case study of how advising was reformulated and improved on one campus (Steppanen, 1981), the elements of the conceptual model likely will include advisor selection, the ongoing advisor training program, evaluation of advisors as well as the advising system, and the extent to which advising is recognized as a legitimate and important function at the institution.

References

Abel, J. "Residence Hall Coordinators: Academic Advising for 'Undecided' Students." *National Academic Advising Association (NACADA) Journal*, 1981, *1* (2), 44–46.

Adams, J. S. "The Structure and Dynamics of Behavior in Organizational Boundary Roles." In M. D. Dunnette (Ed.), *Handbook of Industrial and Organizational Psychology*. Chicago: Rand McNally, 1976.

Astin, A. W. *Four Critical Years: Effects of College on Beliefs, Attitudes, and Knowledge*. San Francisco: Jossey-Bass, 1977.

Baldridge, J. V., Curtis, D., Ecker, G. P., and Riley, G. L. "Alternative Models of Governance in Higher Education." In G. L. Riley and J. V. Baldridge (Eds.), *Governing Academic Organizations*. Berkeley, Calif.: McCutchan, 1977.

Barman, C. R., and Benson, P. A. "Peer Advising: A Working Model." *National Academic Advising Association (NACADA) Journal*, 1981, *1* (2), 33–40.

Blau, P. M., and Scott, R. A. *Formal Organizations: A Comparative Approach*. San Francisco: Chandler, 1962.

Blimling, G. S., and Schuh, J. H. (Eds.). *New Directions for Student*

Services: Increasing the Educational Role of Residence Halls, no. 13. San Francisco: Jossey-Bass, 1981.

Carnegie Council on Policy Studies in Higher Education. *Three Thousand Futures: The Next Twenty Years for Higher Education.* San Francisco: Jossey-Bass, 1980.

Cohen, M. D., and March, J. G. *Leadership and Ambiguity.* New York: McGraw-Hill, 1974.

Cope, R. G., and Hannah, W. *Revolving College Doors: The Causes and Consequences of Dropping Out, Stopping Out, and Transferring.* New York: Wiley, 1975.

Creamer, D. C. "Educational Advising for Student Retention: An Institutional Perspective." *Community College Review,* 1980, 7 (4), 11-18.

Crockett, D. S. "Academic Advising: A Cornerstone of Student Retention." In L. Noel (Ed.), *New Directions for Student Services: Reducing the Dropout Rate,* no. 3. San Francisco: Jossey-Bass, 1978.

Crookston, B. B. "A Developmental View of Academic Advising as Teaching." *Journal of College Student Personnel,* 1972, *13,* 12-17.

Dressel, P. "Advising Students About Programs and Courses." Presented at the 5th National Conference on Academic Advising, Indianapolis, Ind., Oct. 1981.

Easton, D. *A Systems Analysis of Political Life.* New York: Wiley, 1965.

Ecker, G. "The Relationship of Institutional Size and Complexity to Faculty Autonomy: A Reconsideration and Caution." *Research in Higher Education,* 1979, *11,* 295-307.

Ender, S. C., Winston, R. B., Jr., and Miller, T. K. "Academic Advising as Student Development." In R. B. Winston, Jr., S. C. Ender, and T. K. Miller (Eds.), *New Directions for Student Services: Developmental Approaches to Academic Advising,* no. 17. San Francisco: Jossey-Bass, 1982.

Enos, P. B. "Student Satisfaction with Faculty Academic Advising and Persistence Beyond the Freshman Year in College." Unpublished doctoral dissertation, University of Iowa, 1981.

Farmer, R. L., and Barbour, J. R. "Attrition Reduction Through

Academic Advising." Presented at the 4th National Conference on Academic Advising, Asheville, N.C., Oct. 1980.

Feike, E., Looney, S. C., and Sanford, J. L. "Developmental Advising: Theory into Practice." Presented at the 5th National Conference on Academic Advising, Indianapolis, Ind., Oct. 1981.

Finn, C. E., Jr. "The Drive for Educational Excellence: Moving Toward a Public Consensus." *Change,* 1983, *15* (3), 14-22.

Fitzgerald, L. F. "Academic Advisors: The Boundary Spanners." Presented at the 5th National Conference on Academic Advising, Indianapolis, Ind., Oct. 1981.

Gelfand, A. R. "Developing a Freshman Advising Center in the Residence Halls." Presented at the 4th National Conference on Academic Advising, Asheville, N.C., Oct. 1980.

Goldberg, L. G. "Peer Advising: A Supplement to, but Not a Substitute for, Faculty Advising." *National Academic Advising Association (NACADA) Journal,* 1981, *1* (2), 41-43.

Goodman, P. *The Community of Scholars.* New York: Random House, 1962.

Green, K. C. "Retention: An Old Solution Finds a New Problem." *American Association for Higher Education (AAHE) Bulletin,* 1983, *35* (8), 3-6.

Grites, T. J. *Academic Advising: Getting Us Through the Eighties.* Washington, D.C.: American Association for Higher Education– Educational Resource Information Center (AAHE-ERIC)/Higher Education Research Report No. 7, 1979a.

Grites, T. J. "Between High School Counselor and College Advisor— A Void." *Personnel and Guidance Journal,* 1979b, *58,* 200-204.

Habley, W. R. "Advisee Satisfaction with Student, Faculty, and Advisement Center Academic Advisors." Unpublished doctoral dissertation, Illinois State University, 1978.

Habley, W. R. "Academic Advisement: The Critical Link in Student Retention." *National Association of Student Personnel Administrators (NASPA) Journal,* 1981, *18* (4), 45-50.

Habley, W. R. "Organizational Structures for Academic Advising: Models and Implications." *Journal of College Student Personnel,* in press.

Higbee, M. T. "Student Advisement Centers: A Timely Idea." *Improving College and University Teaching,* 1979, *27* (1), 47-48.

Higginson, L. C., Moore, L. V., and White, E. R. "A New Role for Orientation: Getting Down to Academics." *National Association of Student Personnel Administrators (NASPA) Journal*, 1981, *19* (1), 21-28.

Hill, J. E. "Academic Advising: Contributions to One College's Survival." *National Association of College Admissions Counselors (NACAC) Journal*, 1979, *23* (4), 35-38.

Hutchins, D. E., and Miller, W. B. "Group Interaction as a Vehicle to Facilitate Faculty-Student Advisement." *Journal of College Student Personnel*, 1979, *20*, 253-257.

Johnson, J., and Sprandel, K. "Centralized Academic Advising at the Department Level: A Model." *University College Quarterly*, 1975, *21* (1), 16-20.

Kast, F. E., and Rosenzweig, J. E. *Organization and Management: A Systems and Contingency Approach*. New York: McGraw-Hill, 1979.

Kramer, G. L., and White, M. T. "Developing a Faculty Mentoring Program: An Experiment." *National Academic Advising Association (NACADA) Journal*, 1982, *2* (2), 47-58.

Kramer, H. C. "The Advising Coordinator: Managing from a One-Down Position." *National Academic Advising Association (NACADA) Journal*, 1981, *1* (1), 7-15.

Lawrence, P. R., and Lorsch, J. W. *Organization and Management: Managing Differentiation and Integration*. Boston: Harvard University Press, 1967.

Lazarsfeld, P. F., and Thielens, W., Jr. *The Academic Mind*. New York: Free Press, 1958.

Lenning, O. T., Sauer, K., and Beal, P. E. *Student Retention Strategies*. Washington, D.C.: American Association for Higher Education, 1980.

Lewis, C. T., Leach, E. R., and Lutz, L. L. "A Marketing Model for Student Retention." *National Association of Student Personnel Administrators (NASPA) Journal*, 1983, *20* (3), 15-24.

McDaniel, M., Faulkner, E., and Powell, P. "A Nontraditional Approach to Pre-College Counseling." Presented at the 5th National Conference on Academic Advising, Indianapolis, Ind., Oct. 1981.

McLaughlin, B. M., and Starr, E. A. "Academic Advising Literature

Since 1965: A College Student Personnel Abstracts Review." *National Academic Advising Association (NACADA) Journal,* 1982, *2* (2), 14-23.

Meyer, M. W., and Associates. *Environments and Organizations: Theoretical and Empirical Perspectives.* San Francisco: Jossey-Bass, 1980.

Miller, T. K., and McCaffrey, S. S. "Student Development Theory: Foundations for Academic Advising." In R. B. Winston, Jr., S. C. Ender, and T. K. Miller (Eds.), *New Directions for Student Services: Developmental Approaches to Academic Advising,* no. 17. San Francisco: Jossey-Bass, 1982.

Murry, J. P. "The Comparative Effectiveness of Student-to-Student and Faculty Advising Programs." *Journal of College Student Personnel,* 1972, *13,* 562-566.

Noel, L. "College Student Retention: A Campus-Wide Responsibility." *National Association of College Admissions Counselors (NACAC) Journal,* 1976, *21* (1), 33-36.

Pfeffer, J. *Power in Organizations.* Marshfield, Mass.: Pitman, 1981.

Polson, C. J., and Cashin, W. E. "Research Priorities for Academic Advising: Results of a Survey of NACADA Membership." *National Academic Advising Association (NACADA) Journal,* 1981, *1* (1), 34-43.

Polson, C. J., and Jurich, A. P. "The Departmental Academic Advising Center: An Alternative to Faculty Advising." *Journal of College Student Personnel,* 1979, *20,* 249-253.

Polson, C. J., and Jurich, A. P. "The Impact of Advising Skills Upon the Effectiveness of the Departmental Academic Advising Center." *National Academic Advising Association (NACADA) Journal,* 1981, *1* (2), 47-55.

Potter, E. B. "Functions of Advising." Presented at the 4th National Conference on Academic Advising, Asheville, N.C., Oct. 1980.

Rudolph, F. *The American College and University.* New York: Random House, 1962.

Schotzinger, K., Lubetkin, A. I., and Rynearson, R. C. "Advising Can Reduce Attrition: A Comprehensive Continuing Orientation Program." Presented at the 2nd National Conference on Academic Advising, Memphis, Tenn., Oct. 1978.

Shane, D. "Academic Advising in Higher Education: A Developmental Approach for College Students of All Ages." *National Academic Advising Association (NACADA) Journal*, 1981, *1* (2), 12-23.

Simon, H. *Administrative Behavior*. New York: Macmillan, 1957.

Spencer, R. W., Peterson, E. D., and Kramer, G. L. "Utilizing College Advising Centers to Facilitate and Revitalize Academic Advising." *National Academic Advising Association (NACADA) Journal*, 1982, *2* (1), 13-23.

Steppanen, L. J. "Improving College Advising Systems." *National Association of Student Personnel Administrators (NASPA) Journal*, 1981, *19* (2), 39-44.

Thompson, J. D. *Organizations in Action*. New York: McGraw-Hill, 1967.

Upcraft, M. L. "Undergraduate Students as Academic Advisors." *Personnel and Guidance Journal*, 1971, *49*, 827-831.

Watkins, B. T. "Students Like Classes, Dislike Campus Services." *Chronicle of Higher Education*, July 27, 1983 p. 3, and "Correction," August 3, 1983, p. 3.

Weick, K. E. "Educational Organizations as Loosely Coupled Systems." *Administrative Science Quarterly*, 1976, *21*, 1-19.

Wilder, J. R. "A Successful Academic Advising Program: Essential Ingredients." *Journal of College Student Personnel*, 1981, *22*, 488-492.

13

Administering Advising Programs: Staffing, Budgeting, and Other Issues

David W. King

Effective administration of advising programs in most colleges and universities entails not only managerial and organizational skills in the usual sense but also requires a variety of other qualifications. The advising administrator must have broad credibility with faculty, professional staff, students, and other administrators. The task requires political astuteness, breadth of perspective, and experience, preferably in teaching, administration, and student services. To develop and enhance institutional advising services, the person or persons primarily responsible for the advising functions must be skilled at innovation and facilitation and must have a broad knowledge of the institution and its services. This chapter provides those who have responsibility for administering academic advising services with guidelines on a number of issues that can help improve institutional advising systems.

The first premise of this chapter is that there must be an advising "system" per se; it cannot be an ad hoc arrangement. The advising service may be organized as a centralized delivery system for the whole institution, school, department, or other subunit. This usually entails one or more persons designated with the responsibility for directing the service. Often this kind of service is offered in a central location with a professional staff of trained advisors and other support staff (for example, secretaries, records clerks, and receptionists). There are a wide variety of organizational models for centralized delivery systems used at different colleges and universities (Peabody, Metz, and Sedlacek, 1983; Johnson and Sprandel, 1975).

Decentralized advising systems often provide services delivered in several different places, such as specific academic departments, schools, or other programmatic units. These types of systems often have decentralized control as well. Sometimes a person (or persons) is designated to have responsibility for directing academic advising for a particular academic department, program, academic class, major, or some other specified subgroup of the student population, such as undeclared students, transfer students, adult learners, and so on.

Either the centralized or decentralized type of advising delivery systems may be staffed by professionally trained academic advisors or counselors, faculty advisors, or such paraprofessionals as peer advisors or trained clerical staff. "In general, institutions are traditional in their reliance on faculty to dispense information through the academic advising 'process'" (Carstensen and Silberhorn, 1979, p. 15). Approximately 80 percent of the advising services at four-year colleges and universities is delivered by faculty advisors (see Chapter Two); about 4 to 7 percent is done by professional counselors or advisors. At two-year colleges, about 58 percent of the advising is done by faculty and about 35 percent is done by professional counselors.

It is not meaningful to advocate one system over another. Each has merits and each component may be utilized very effectively to meet different needs, even in the same college or university. Ultimately, that judgment must be made by the advising administrators to meet institution or program-specific needs.

The second premise of this chapter is that the goal of the academic advising administrator is to maintain an advising system that will maximize the quality of the information and assistance provided by advisors to students. Regardless of the type of advising system used, administrators should attempt to create an advising environment in which the advisor will be able, whenever possible, to build a "mentoring" relationship with each student for whom he or she is responsible. A *mentor* in this context is not a colleague but rather a wise and trusted counselor with whom the student can discuss and seek guidance for a variety of problems and needs.

A "mentoring" relationship is designed to facilitate *both* the personal and academic development of the student. McCaffrey and Miller (1980) also advocate a mentoring approach to academic advising. In their work, "mentoring, viewed as mature advisement, is seen as an ongoing process that provides students with a significant and trusted guide or consultant to assist them in achieving maximum benefit from the higher-education experience" (p. 187). Mentoring encompasses the roles of consultant, referral agent, teacher, counselor, administrator, researcher, evaluator, and liaison with other people and services of the institution. More significantly, "the mentor is a significant and concerned person who effectively facilitates self-responsibility, self-directedness, and developmental task achievement in students" (p. 192). Kramer and White (1982) present a different model for an experimental freshman mentoring program at Brigham Young University. The advisor who aspires to be a mentor is not simply a person who helps students schedule their courses. Rather the advisor becomes the student's entrée to the complex questions associated with educational, career, and personal decision making.

Keeping in mind these two basic premises—that a "system" of advising exists and that the goal of advising is to create a mentoring relationship—several specific issues that are of concern to administrators of advising programs will now be discussed.

Leadership Styles

One of the major challenges facing an advising administrator is described by Kramer and Gardner's (1978, p. 1.116) contention that "your own dilemma is how to manage advising without being perceived as a manager and how to carry out managerial functions in a nonmanagerial manner." Their work is one of the most comprehensive studies of the management of faculty-based advising systems. Kramer and Gardner's thesis, however, assumes a rather aggressive management style that may be viewed as anathema by many academics. A more viable role of the advising administrator would be to concentrate on orchestrating resources and developing staffing in ways that will not antagonize people but will enhance the quality and overall effectiveness of the advising system. In many colleges and universities where faculty do most of the academic advising, the advising administrator is more realistically an enabler or facilitator rather than an aggressive manager. In many centralized advising systems that rely primarily on professional staff advisors, managing and directing resources and staff can be done in more overt ways.

The administration of advising services requires a variety of leadership styles and the administrator, to be effective, must rely on diverse management strategies to achieve objectives. However, advising administrators who work with faculty must frequently rely on collegial modalities or risk an uncooperative response from faculty who are usually not accustomed to aggressive, highly directive leadership styles. The leadership of faculty advisors, therefore, presents some serious challenges. In many postsecondary institutions, the department chair is viewed as the first among equals, unless that person has been ensconced in a power position for years by reason of stature or lengthy tenure. Even deans and provosts are often viewed as "supervisors" only with reluctance and considerable trepidation on the part of their colleagues. Those charged with responsibility for academic advising are often not in the mainstream of academic authority; this compounds their leadership dilemma. How can one establish credibility with faculty who must advise? How can one hope to "train" faculty advisors to enhance their skills?

The supervision and training of "professional" staff advisors are not usually an overwhelming challenge if an appropriate advising model is adopted and reasonable management skills are employed. As noted earlier, Kramer and Gardner (1978) postulate a very assertive style of management that in many respects may be too directive for a faculty-based advising system. Providing leadership for and enhancing the quality of advising services delivered by faculty advisors does, however, require some rather sophisticated management skills, a more indirect approach as a change agent, and considerable flexibility in advancing toward the desired objectives.

Kramer (1981) discusses some of the managerial frustrations that advising coordinators must face, particularly in working with faculty advisors. Leadership of a centralized advising system or one that utilizes professional or paraprofessional advisors poses other types of challenges. The point is that in any combination of structures within advising systems, different leadership styles may be required and various styles may be required by the same person to respond to different types of problems.

There are a number of helpful works on leadership styles in educational settings. One of the most useful is developed by Reddin (1970, pp. 205–250), who describes eight managerial styles related to each other through four basic categories of leadership styles. The first leadership style he calls the "Separated Manager"; this manager is cautious, orderly, precise, and prefers paperwork and established procedures. Because of the complex interpersonal and diplomatic skills, as well as the political sensitivity needed to weld together a good advising system, this style is generally not appropriate for administrators of advising systems. The spectrum of this "Separated" style includes the least effective "Deserter" type, who is uncreative, hinders others, and avoids responsibility, cooperation, and commitment. This approach is disastrous. The more effective "Separated" style, whom Reddin calls the "Bureaucrat Manager," likes to follow orders, is reliable and efficient, and can maintain an existing system. This style is useful if you have an efficient advising system in existence. Obviously it is not a viable approach if the institution needs an innovative person to create a new system or reorganize an existing one.

The second leadership style Reddin labels the "Related Manager"; this style emphasizes personal development and is approving, empathetic, and generally people oriented. This type of administrative style is fine if it is active rather than passive. The passive type, called the "Missionary Manager" by Reddin, goes to great lengths to avoid conflict, avoids initiative, is unconcerned about productivity, and worries mainly about acceptance. This kind of dependent, "lay-back" approach to problem solving will usually not work in a situation that should view the advisor and the advising administrator as a change agent. At the more productive end of the "Related" style is the "Developer Manager," who promotes communication and mutual trust, and works to develop the talent of others. This style is useful for the advising administrator to build an effective team relationship between advisors and referral services. It also helps to facilitate needed cooperation among the diverse elements of the institution that should be involved in the advising process. This style makes for good bridge building.

The third leadership style described by Reddin is the "Dedicated Manager," who is more confident, aggressive, self-reliant, and independent than the other leadership styles. This type of leader usually will take the initiative to define tasks and set responsibilities and standards. This person establishes the rules and procedures and does not just follow them. This style is very advantageous if you are developing a new advising system or reorganizing a chaotic or ineffective advising arrangement. There are also two subtypes within this style, according to Reddin. The "Autocrat Manager" is very intimidating, instills fear, demands obedience, and suppresses disagreement. This Machiavellian type makes all decisions and thereby discourages growth of other team and staff members. This approach is useful only temporarily if you are trying to clean up the chaos caused by warring interest groups or similar problems. Frankly, the "Benevolent Autocratic" type is more appropriate for this sort of situation. This type of leader is decisive, committed, works hard, and gets the job done.

Reddin advocates what he defines as the fourth leadership type—the "Integrated Manager." This type of administrator defines goals, stresses participation and integration within the organization, and emphasizes shared objectives and responsibilities. This style has enormous advantages in working with the complex forces and procedures involved in advising, which is both an interpersonal and an intra-institutional process. The weaker form of this type of leadership, called the "Compromiser Manager," is too accommodating, avoids closure, is too idealistic and ambiguous, and relies too much on participation. One needs cooperation and consensus in building an advising system, but too much reliance on a consensus approach will probably sabotage the effort. The preferred approach is the "Executive Manager," who effectively coordinates all elements, relies on team decision making and reasonable consultation, and then induces commitment. This general strategy is likely to produce more satisfactory results over a longer period of time.

In summary, all of these leadership styles are useful in some ways under some circumstances. The most viable approach would seem to be to select different types of people to do specific jobs, as the administrative needs dictate certain leadership styles. The person with the broadest administrative responsibility needs to possess some of the attributes of the "Benevolent Autocrat" and the "Executive Manager" styles. Those with lesser responsibility may generally be selected from the "Bureaucratic" or "Developer" leadership types. It is probably not possible to generalize about the styles most useful in working with professional advisors, faculty advisors, paraprofessionals, or centralized versus decentralized types of systems. The appropriateness of the leadership style will obviously depend on the specific circumstances prevailing in a particular school, department program, or other organizational unit. Sometimes more directive approaches are needed rather than nondirective. Under some circumstances the administration must cultivate a collegial relationship, in others a hierarchical line of authority.

In general, advising administrators must possess or cultivate responsive, flexible leadership styles. Authoritarian administrators are likely to antagonize and alienate the very people who need to be integrated into an interactive network of services. Passive paper shuffling also will not be as effective as a proactive stance tempered by skilled diplomacy. As frustrating and tedious as the process may be, the most viable programs in academe are usually achieved by consensus. Many times one needs to cultivate and utilize a variety of flexible approaches in order to get the job done. Sometimes one must plant and nurture the seeds by conveying the impression that the idea originated with others. There is great value in studying the literature on leadership styles in administration in higher education and in knowing how to use different approaches at different times to achieve different goals.

Principles of Advising Administration

It is important that an institution's advising program be organized in a systematic fashion. This section identifies twelve basic organizational principles and discusses them in light of their applicability to advising practice.

Formulate Institutional Advising Policy and Commitment. The first principle for effective administration of any academic advising system assumes the formulation of a comprehensive institutional policy on academic advising and a commitment to a holistic and developmental advising philosophy. Carstensen and Silberhorn (1979, p. 15) found that "generally, institutions have no comprehensive statement of policy regarding the delivery of academic advising. This may be indicative of a lack of a clear sense of institutional mission in delivering this service." (There seems to be some improvement here; see Chapter Two.) However, a good deal of research in higher education has reinforced the value of a good advising program in satisfying a variety of student needs (Astin, 1975; Winston, Ender, and Miller, 1982). Advising is also a key element in any student retention strategy—a matter of grave concern for many colleges and universities in the 1980s (Beal and Noel, 1980; Habley, 1981). An advising administrator should give first priority to the formulation of a significant administrative commitment to a quality advising program evidenced by adequate budgetary support, staffing, and resource allocation. A truly viable advising service of any kind requires a major institutional commitment affirming the importance of advising through supportive statements by such key administrators as the president, vice-presidents, deans, and others. The institution must also demonstrate commitment to advising by making the quality of advising a significant part of the reward system—an integral part of promotion, tenure, and merit criteria. This point will be discussed in more detail later.

To make a case before the administrative leadership, it is helpful to use national research data such as Astin's (1975) *Preventing Students from Dropping Out,* the wealth of data available through the American College Testing Program (ACT) seminars on academic advising and student retention, or the publications and conferences sponsored by the National Academic Advising Association (NACADA). A local survey designed to solicit student views on the quality of institutional advising services can also be useful and illustrative in making a case for the necessity of a significant institutional policy commitment to upgrade the quality of academic advising.

Designate Administrative Responsibility for Advising. In addition to the question of how to elicit institutional commitments, it is important to consider ways of measuring and demonstrating that commitment. The second principle is that at least one person must be officially designated as responsible for administering advising services for the institution and all of its major organizational subunits, such as the school, department, or degree program. All too often advising is perceived as a tangential responsibility and is treated as secondary or ancillary to the major responsibility of faculty or professional staff people. The leadership of the institution, through its policy formulation, pronouncements, and professional development programs, must communicate to all campus constituencies that academic advising or "mentoring" is an integral part of its educational service to students. The leadership should also stress that advising is a key element in an institutional student retention strategy (Crockett, 1978).

If at all possible, the person primarily responsible for administering advising services should report to a key administrator, such as the chief academic or student affairs officer. This affiliation with a major line officer provides visibility and credibility for the advising administrator and easier access to an administrator with control over budget and staffing resources. Most institutions can benefit from the establishment of a hierarchy of persons charged with responsibility for advising from the institutional coordinator's level through administrators at the college, school, department, program, or other appropriate subunit level. In addition, it may be advisable to delegate responsibilities to designated persons for administering advising services to various student subgroups, such as freshmen, transfer students, adult learners, nontraditional students, veterans, various preprofessional students, and others. Each of these groups has different types of needs that require different types of advising skills. Not all advisors, even professional advisors, are qualified to work effectively with all types of students and all kinds of problems. This is the main reason why *all* academic advisors—faculty, professionals, or paraprofessionals—need to be trained to serve specific clienteles. The importance of advisor training will be developed in a later section of this chapter. No one is innately qualified to advise students, especially if it is the institution's goal to enrich the advising process and create a true "mentoring" relationship between the academic advisor and the student.

Provide Distinct Staffing and Budgetary Commitments. The institutional administrator for advising services needs to resolve several very basic issues in order to establish credibility and ensure broader impact. The third basic principle is that there must be distinct staffing and budgetary allocations for either the advising services per se or for staffing those services. This might entail the allocation of funds plus the assignment of full-time or part-time administrative appointments and/or professional staff appointments to deal with advising. Faculty who are designated to have administrative responsibility for advising within schools, academic departments, or programs may be appointed on a released-time basis. Another option is to pay them extraservice compensation or reward them in other ways. Most American higher educational institutions are confronted with major fiscal constraints and are being challenged to do more with less. Fortunately, there are ways to use and develop staff and material resources imaginatively to produce quality advising services at relatively low cost. These and other options are explored later in this chapter. The crucial consideration here is that administration of advising should *not* be simply an add-on, unrewarded responsibility in the institution. If it is, then advising will be perceived as relatively unimportant and the quality will be poor. As a consequence, the institution is likely to reap a harvest of greater student frustration and dissonance, and a higher student attrition rate.

Clarify Reporting Lines. Another principle is that the advising administrator must ensure that there are clear reporting lines for all those involved in advising. This is the major rationale for designating specific persons at each level in each subunit with responsibility for advising. This approach helps ensure that the job is accomplished and aids in assessing the strong and weak elements of the advising system. Clear reporting lines also facilitate dissemination of information to all advisors and provide a feedback loop for problems and inquiries. This hierarchy of responsibility for advising also provides students with a route for seeking additional assistance or for appealing grievances with advisors. Clearly delineated lines of authority and responsibility for advising services will provide greater accountability both to students and to the principal administrators at the institution.

Carefully Define Goals. It is necessary to formulate clearly defined goals and tasks for those who have administrative responsibility for advising, as well as for those who actually advise students. In a collegial setting, particularly in working primarily with faculty advisors, the advising administrator must set reasonable goals for delivering and improving advising services. Advising administrators with centralized and professional advising services can usually exercise more direct control over the definition and implementation of goals. Goal setting in faculty-based advising systems may require more patient education of the faculty and academic leadership regarding the importance and value of good advising. In any kind of advising organization, however, the important point is that everyone involved needs to know precisely what their goals are and how they are to be implemented. Careful planning of goals is likely to enhance the prospects for success in any advising program.

Promote Incremental Change. Patience is another significant qualification for those who would administer and hopefully improve the quality of advising, but patience needs to be combined with persistence. This sixth principle assumes that the advising administrator needs not only to be "proactive" in developing and delivering advising services but also needs to set incremental goals for formulating or improving those services, as few things in higher education are changed overnight. At times, the tasks may require the patience of Job because the commitment to change will probably be challenged again and again.

Be Committed to Developmental Advising. It is imperative that advising administrators do more than study management science. Administrators must also be able to empower advising practitioners with the understanding that the major goal of advising is to create a "mentoring" relationship between the advisor and the student. Research on advising by Crockett (1978) and Astin (1975) has demonstrated that one of the most significant factors affecting success of students in college is the quality of their association with a responsible, mature adult person in the institution. Perry (1975) emphasizes that the advisor occupies the critical space between students and the institution.

In order to build better advising environments, the advising administrator needs to study student development theory. Insights from this study need to be shared in professional development workshops for advisors. Crookston (1972) presents a developmental view of academic advising as a form of teaching. He points out that advising has traditionally been a prescriptive relationship in which the advisor is viewed as the authority figure, and the student simply acts on the advisor's advice. Crookston urges an interactive relationship between the advisor and the student. In a developmental advising relationship, Crookston says the advisor and the student "differentially engage in a series of developmental tasks, the successful completion of which results in varying degrees of learning *by both parties*" (p. 13). The goal of developmental advising is "toward openness, acceptance, trust, sharing of data, and collaborative problem solving, decision making, and evaluation" (p. 16). Advisors therefore need to be committed to a high degree of caring (not coddling), as defined in the concept of "mentoring." In fact, advising can be a major catalyst in the student's maturation process. The advisor needs to understand the student, wherever he or she *is* developmentally, and be prepared to help that person achieve the fullest possible growth.

Advising communication must be dealt with, not just as an organizational problem but also as a growing challenge brought about by the increasingly heterogeneous student bodies at many of our colleges. Advisors must learn to hear and respond to their different voices and needs (see Chapter Ten). This point is another manifestation of the need for developmental approaches to academic advising. Browning (1973) speaks of "generativity"—each generation's obligation to provide for the well-being of the next generation. To promote generative advising relationships, the advising administrator must try to create an atmosphere of "mutuality" in which both the advisor and the student actively listen to each other. On the subject of "mutuality," Erikson (1964, p. 233) wrote: *"Truly worthwhile acts enhance a mutuality between the doer and the other—a mutuality which strengthens the doer even as it strengthens the other.* Thus, the 'doer' and 'the other' are partners in one deed. Seen in the light of human development, this means that the doer is activated in whatever strength is *appropriate to his age, stage, and condition,* even as he activates in the other the strength appropriate to *his* age, stage, and condition."

One of the most provocative applications of cognitive development theory to advising has been made by Perry and Knefelkamp. Perry's work (1970, see Chapter Four) on the intellectual and ethical development of college students postulates nine positions of cognitive/ethical maturation: dualism, several levels of multiplicity, contextual relativism, temporizing, initial commitment, competing commitment, and finally ethical development. Most freshmen enter with a very conventional, realistic orientation at the lower levels. Upperclass students may graduate at the middle developmental level of contextual relativism, meaning they accept uncertainty, are more independent in their thinking, but seek context nonetheless. Perry and Knefelkamp, in various unpublished speeches, have stressed the importance of colleges adjusting to the needs of the students being served. This applies to both the learning environment in the classroom and that of the advising relationship. Advisors must understand and recognize the existence of these developmental steps and be able to relate appropriately to the developmental needs of each stage. Knefelkamp's research has demonstrated, for example, that many adult learners coming to higher education are developmentally at the lower levels of Perry's cognitive model, even though they are older. Knefelkamp's point is that advising environments must reflect the developmental stages of the students. Many of the "new students" on our campuses, who represent the lower one third of aptitude and development, seek conventional and realistic choices and have no tolerance for ambiguity. Many advisors, especially faculty, have little appreciation for this because they tend to function developmentally at more advanced stages.

Understand the Relationship Between Student Development Theory and the "New Student." The eighth principle entails a challenge facing advising systems in the 1980s resulting from the advent of the so-called new student on campuses. These students, who are entering four-year colleges in large numbers, possess some characteristics quite different from the majority of more "traditional" students who populated campuses in the 1960s and the early 1970s. They are often not motivated by learning so much as by the prospect of career mobility. They tend to have very practical career-related goals and little patience for or interest in the other amenities afforded by a college education. These values represent a major dichotomy with those of many faculty who are responsible for teaching and often for advising them. The faculty and professional staff often cherish much more traditional values regarding the worth of higher education. Perry, Knefelkamp, Chickering, Cross, and others have studied the characteristics of this new segment of the student population.

Cross (1971) analyzes the cognitive, social, academic, and attitudinal characteristics of the new students. Her major thesis is that there are large numbers of new students in higher education with different expectations and often with lower levels of academic achievement. She concludes, based on four national research studies, that institutions of higher education are generally not prepared to educate this new clientele. Colleges tend to maintain traditional services, curricula, and attitudes, even though they are now admitting and attempting to serve many students who do not hold those same values or expectations. In the comprehensive study *The Modern American College,* Chickering and Associates (1981) analyze the characteristics of today's students and then consider the implications for curriculum change, teaching/learning styles, student services, and administration. Newton and Ender (1980) present a compilation of student development strategies that can be applied to various programs and services in higher education designed to facilitate the social, emotional, ethical, and intellectual growth of college students. Abel (1978, p. 104) contends that advising is an extension of teaching and that "the academic advising administrator can be one of the most valuable middle managers in integrating student development concepts throughout the institution." Hence, the advising administrator faces an even greater challenge in trying to relate many services to the diverse needs of this new student population.

Among other characteristics, these new students seek very concrete experiences and require immediate gratification; they are also very prone to attrition. What can an institutional advising system do to respond to these students' demands, using advising practitioners who often hold antithetical values? Perry (1975) and Knefelkamp (1980) suggest that just as college teachers should study cognitive and student development theory, so must advisors and advising administrators. If they don't, they are not going to be able to serve many of the students now being admitted. The advising system, like the rest of the college, must adjust to the needs of the new students now being admitted. This leads us to the critical role of integrating services designed to relate to the needs of the "whole" student.

Holistic Approaches to Student Development. The ninth principle postulates that the basic operational philosophy of a good advising program, if it is to be viable and effective, must be founded on holistic as well as developmental approaches to the delivery of advising services. *Holism*, as defined by Caple (1980), denotes a theory that "whole entities of human beings possess an existence and a reality greater than the sum of their parts. The whole can never be fully understood separate from its parts. . . . Holism includes the cognitive and emotional self; it includes the physical self and the mental self, and it means much more than simply taking care of all the various components that make up the whole being. It is the unique being that results from the special blend of the spiritual, the natural, and the social self" (p. 208).

Advising should therefore be responsive to the needs of the whole student, not just to institutional needs or the concerns with which advisors feel "comfortable." The very scope of student needs means that advising services cannot be parochial. A dynamic advising system must incorporate a comprehensive response system.

These elements are explored in the context of the Perry model of student development by Hillman and Lewis (1980) and by Miller and McCaffrey (1982). Ender, Winston, and Miller (1982) focus on the importance of educating the whole person, not just the student's mind. They argue that student development principles must be incorporated into all aspects of the institution's mission, curricula, and services, including advising.

The advising function stretches across many aspects of the student's life encompassing educational goals, academic needs, skill development, social adjustment, personal counseling, career planning, and many other facets. No one advisor can probably help the student resolve all of these "life concerns," but the advisor at a minimum should be able to help the student find out how to deal with these needs. One should never leave a student suspended with the response "I don't know" or "I don't feel comfortable dealing with that question." The advising system should promote a good referral network.

Holistic theories of student development such as Heath's (1968) emphasize the importance of focusing institutional services on all elements of a student's experience. Heath contends that students cannot be treated as if they can be separated into small parts. All aspects of the student's life bear upon the learning experience. The classroom is only one dimension of the student's total experience. In summary, Heath urges educators to move away from fragmenting services to deal with the needs of the whole student.

Chickering (1981) contends that colleges need to focus more attention on the role of translation and integration in the advising and teaching processes. Viable advising systems need to integrate advising, career development, and intellectual development. Advisors need to create more empathetic environments to better understand how students think and make meaning of the world. The advisor needs to communicate that understanding. The advising administrator must understand that in the translation from holistic developmental theories to practice, theory needs to inform practice, and practice needs to inform and modify theory. Grites maintains that the "advising process becomes one of total institutional integration, and its outcomes are shared by all the participants. With such integration institutions foster a 'developmental' milieu in which all elements of the institution serve common goals" (1979, p. 39).

Facilitate Interservice Cooperation. The scope and diversity of student needs and the necessity of a holistic institutional response to those needs mean that all institutional advising services must encompass and facilitate cooperation among many elements of the institution. All types of student affairs offices, faculty, academic departments, and academic and business service offices must be encouraged to cooperate effectively in delivering services to students. This is particularly true of academic advising, which is heavily dependent on a good referral network if it is to be a meaningful experience. This principle is true even though it means that traditionally difficult or even abrasive relationships have to be bridged between academic affairs, student affairs, and business affairs people. For example, faculty members *must* be encouraged to communicate with residence hall staff, academic administrators, the registrar's staff, librarians, or campus security as needed. The reverse relationship must also be facilitated. It is the difficult responsibility of the advising administrator to create procedures, forms, and lines of communication for *all* of these people to come together in the institution to better serve legitimate student needs. This principle may be perceived to be more applicable to the mission of two- and four-year undergraduate colleges, but to an even greater degree it also applies to the needs of students in large research-oriented universities.

In summary, if student needs are diverse and extensive, then the advising response system must also be comprehensive and facilitate cooperation among many campus offices and people. This means that people and offices who may function in different vertical reporting lines must be brought together through horizontal channels of communication and cooperation within the organizational hierarchy. Too frequently administrative services are organized in hierarchies to deal with problems in ways that inadvertently impede the effective delivery of those services. Often the institutional organization chart focuses too much on administrative convenience rather than on the needs of the users—in this case, the students.

Provide for Referral Procedures. This advising organizational model also postulates the need for an active, outreach-oriented operational philosophy among all student, academic, and business service areas that relate to the academic advising process. Passive approaches dependent on waiting for the student to come to the service are less desirable in this approach. If the advising system should be defined as much as possible by the needs of students, rather than by the insular proclivities of advisors and service offices, how then can the advising administrator deal pragmatically with all the real strengths and weaknesses of the elements that make up a comprehensive advising network? The administrator has the seemingly overwhelming challenge of reconciling a wide variety of student needs and often divergent response services.

In his assessment of the critical role of academic advising in helping students to maximize the value of their liberal education, Grites (1981) focuses on a good referral system as a key element. He says, "The advisor serves as a facilitator of communication, a coordinator of learning experiences, and a referral agent" (p. 2). Referrals, he contends, afford the advisor with an opportunity to "extend the advising process . . . to other service offices available on the campus" (p. 3).

This leads to the critical responsibility of building a good referral network and response system. Student satisfaction, success, and retention are often directly affected by the quality of the referral process. Obviously, many students do not perceive their problems in neat, functional administrative units, such as personal counseling, course scheduling, career counseling, or academic advising. As has been already asserted, no single advisor or other professional person in the residence hall, counseling center, placement office, or registrar's office can provide all services to a student. The advising administrator, in cooperation with other student affairs administrators, however, needs to consciously orchestrate a referral system for *all* academic, student, and business services so that the system and those who work within it are capable of at least an initial helpful response to all kinds of student needs. The major complaint of students on many campuses is the "runaround" they receive from many faculty, advisors, and student affairs staff people. The challenge is to build a service referral system that does not bounce students around like so many Ping-Pong balls.

This goal assumes the necessity of an ongoing referral training program for *all* those who work with students. The programs would help all staff to become more knowledgeable about the kinds of services that exist on campus. All "service" people, from custodians to deans, need to develop appropriate communication and referral skills.

Build Student Retention Policies. This principle focuses on the relationship of a holistic and cooperative approach to academic advising and the success of an institution's student retention policies. Quality advising services are critical components of an institutional student retention program. Astin's (1975) research presents relevant data based on his national research. His study provides compelling evidence to convince those who doubt the merit or necessity of campus-wide retention efforts. He points to the value of better counseling and advising to help students plan their program of study more carefully, organize their time and activities more efficiently, get more positively involved in campus life, and recognize the value of part-time employment, among other factors. In discussing the advisors' role in minimizing student attrition, Astin says, "Counselors or advisors who wish to identify potential dropouts should be alert to certain patterns of behavior strongly related to attrition. . . . In short, counselors and advisors should look for behavioral or environmental changes that suggest declining commitment to or involvement in the campus community" (pp. 153–154). These kinds of attrition/retention concerns can be effectively addressed in the student and advisor handbooks, in good referral services, by prompt response to observed student problems, and in a broad, comprehensive campus-wide program to reduce student attrition.

Integrate the Twelve Principles of Advising Administration. Reviewing all twelve principles, several generalizations can be made. From an administrative perspective, one of the essential elements of any successful advising system is the promotion of extensive cooperation among the various offices in student affairs, academic affairs, and business affairs that serve students. Unfortunately, on many campuses, there is a history of barrier building and a nurturing of "we-they" mentalities mitigating against cooperation. In an era of declining enrollments and growing concerns about student attrition, advising administrators need to raise the level of awareness of chief administrators about the need to overcome old barriers. The welfare of students and institutions is at stake. Various types of services to students are often divided up among several administrative units of the college or university. The emphasis on vertical reporting lines may be helpful to administrators, but it often has little relationship to student needs or to the efficient delivery of integrated services.

It is also important to consider some of the strategies for promoting interdivisional and interoffice cooperation in delivering advising services. Our basic premise herein is based on student development theory and a holistic philosophy for serving students. It assumes that advising is a comprehensive set of tasks incorporating program planning, scheduling, career planning, goal clarification, personal counseling, policy clarification, and study skills, among others. It also means that referral to a wide range of other more specialized services must be facilitated. Since persons working in one set of vertical reporting lines seldom meet frequently with persons functioning in another set of vertical reporting lines, one major challenge for advising administrators is to create opportunities for professional staff from diverse service areas to meet and discuss policies, procedures, and problems of common concern. Advising administrators have the responsibility to be catalysts in promoting lines of communication that might not evolve otherwise. Surely a major key to cooperation is communication.

Coordination via regular avenues of communication is also essential for advisors and all those responsible for advising services. Regular meetings with carefully planned agendas should be scheduled to ensure the circulation of information and coordination of policies and procedures to better serve students. Cooperative workshops that cut across divisions or offices can be utilized as meaningful professional development experiences to improve the skills of advisors and advising coordinators.

Ideally, the advising administrator needs a fertile climate in which to promote this unique enterprise. There must be incentives and rewards for these cooperative efforts. Supervisors and department heads must stimulate and encourage such outreach initiatives. And finally, the value of these bridge-building and retention efforts must be spearheaded whenever possible by the institution's chief administrative officers who affirm that improved advising is a major campus commitment, entailing broad cross-institutional cooperation.

Managing the Resources of an Advising System

The development of an effective advising system requires careful planning of resource allocation and clarification of realistic goals within a specific time frame. In order to sell an advising scheme to the campus leadership, the advising administrator must allocate resources guided by institution-based research designed to better understand student advising needs. This assessment of advising needs must then be analyzed in conjunction with a study of available staff and budgetary resources. Then there must be a study of what is required to build an operative interactive referral system for advising. In addition, any plan to develop or redeploy advising resources is more likely to be endorsed or successfully implemented if the advising administrator employs an incremental timetable for its implementation.

Resource Management Strategies. One of the major challenges confronting advising administrators, like other leaders in higher education, is the problem of how to accomplish more with less and still make the advising system work. Many of the people designated to administer advising programs may have either academic or student affairs backgrounds with little formal preparation in the area of resource allocation and management. Persons without this training need to pursue it through course work available from various graduate institutes in administration in higher education or through workshops provided by various professional associations. There are several basic responsibilities incorporated under the rubric of resource allocations and management. They include fiscal resource management, budget strategies and priorities, allocation of all staff resources, cost-effective options, technical support systems, adequate physical facilities, and some others.

As indicated earlier, it is highly desirable to seek a specific budgetary allocation for advising services, materials, publications, staff support, and other needs. This ensures a greater degree of autonomy and flexibility. Like a clearly defined job description for advising administrators, a budget demonstrates institutional commitment to advising. Fiscal independence has numerous advantages but also entails a variety of responsibilities and accountability. Budgetary priorities must be established carefully. Budgetary management of an advising system may involve complex negotiations with other sectors of the campus regarding shared resources, staffing, and materials. Various strategies may need to be employed to stretch fiscal resources. Staff exchanges, trade-offs, released time, equipment sharing, and other measures may help to do more with less.

Managing the Human Resources. Another of the major problems confronting advising administrators at some institutions is the deficiency of qualified advising practitioners and heavy advising loads. There are some good, relatively low-cost alternatives for recruiting qualified advisors. Consider using trained volunteer faculty or staff advisors to work with specific target clientele, or released time for faculty or staff advisors to carry heavier advising loads. One could also employ faculty or staff reassignment, student peer advisors on the work-study payroll, or credit-bearing, supervised advising internships utilizing trained undergraduate or graduate students. Any consideration of resources in staffing an advising system must carefully consider the relative value of all staffing options. One might also consider recruiting and training nontraditional practitioners, such as librarians, administrators, residence hall staff, and others, to advise selected student populations. Secretarial and clerical staff in academic departments and those in academic or student affairs offices also do a great deal of de facto advising. In order to perform these advising services effectively, they need to be properly trained and assigned appropriate tasks. All too often administrators responsible for advising neglect the important role of clerical staff who are in reality usually the first contact that students have when they seek help from a service office. The advising operation also needs adequate secretarial and clerical staff to carry out assigned tasks, answer basic questions, and provide information in a timely and helpful fashion.

Managing Information. Among the critical supporting resources necessary for a good advising system is the formation of a comprehensive student information system founded on an institutional data base. Many institutions are beginning to build adequate data bases, but easy access to accurate and current academic and demographic information about students is an absolutely essential resource in the advising delivery system. An interactive data base, reliable record keeping, and adequate computer support are imperative. Ancillary services like telephones, copying, mailing, and appropriate equipment must be carefully assessed. Probably the most important technological support for an advising system is access to computer time—for record keeping and assistance in advising (see Chapter Nine).

Managing Physical Resources. Another consideration frequently ignored by advising administrators is the value of appropriate physical facilities. Substantive advising or counseling cannot occur in public areas. Privacy and confidentiality must be guaranteed, yet advising services should be easily accessible and centrally located. Don't burden access to advising services with a lot of physical impediments that militate against the very goals of the service. Advising services and other primary referral services for students should be located in close physical proximity to each other whenever possible. This relates to the operational principle of facilitating cooperation noted earlier.

Components of an Effective Advising System

The components of an effective advising system need careful consideration. This will involve determination of who should do the advising, how to organize the advising services, and exactly what advisors should do.

Organization of Advising Services. As noted earlier, one of the major managerial considerations involved in the organization or improvement of any advising system is the necessity of identifying a person or persons in the institution with overall responsibility for administering advising services, as well as designating an advising administrator or coordinator in each appropriate subunit within the institution. It may be appropriate to employ centralized advising services with "professional" advisors in some programs and decentralized advising with trained faculty or peer advisors in other areas. Extensive discussions of delivery systems may be found in Crockett (1982) and Chapter Twelve; detailed examples are given in Chapter Seventeen.

Differentiated Advising Services. Since all students do not have the same advising needs and therefore cannot be advised in the same way, advising services must be provided through a differentiated delivery system that targets the needs of particular student populations, such as freshmen, transfers, minorities, women, adults, preprofessional, nontraditional, part-time, and others. There are advising needs common to all of these groups, but there are also needs distinct to each. For a detailed discussion of the unique needs of many of these groups, see Chapters Four and Ten.

Another concern is that advising must be delivered in different ways to different people. For example, an advisor should not work with an eighteen-year-old person in the same way he or she would advise a sixty-five-year-old person or a working mother. The advising administrator must construct and maintain a system that is flexible and responsive to the different needs of increasingly diverse student populations at many institutions.

Communication. A good communication network is the lifeblood of a truly viable advising system. Among the major responsibilities of the advising administrator are the facilitation of regular communication among all components of the advising system and the provision of accurate information and access to information for all advisors. A number of these avenues of effective communication are discussed in other sections—advising resource publications, referral charts and procedures, regular meetings for advisors and advising service coordinators, professional development workshops, and other means for sharing information and promoting dialogue.

In addition, there are several other communication-related considerations. Publicizing advising services and accomplishments will heighten visibility on campus and improve prospects for success. Regular communication about changes in the referral network is essential. The quality of advising is based on substantive communication and access to accurate and up-to-date student records and information. The advising administrator could benefit from the study of both organizational and interpersonal communication skills. One useful study is Villeme's (1982) discussion of the mechanics of advising communication and some ways of dealing with communication barriers in advising relationships.

A major part of a good advising communications system should be the publications used to help advisors and students improve the quality of the advising experience. Whenever possible, as part of the cooperative effort inherent in a comprehensive advising system, the advising administrators should bring together representatives from different student, academic, and business affairs areas to discuss development of advising publications. Periodic, regularly scheduled, intra-institutional discussions can also be helpful in updating, coordinating, and generally improving publications. The production of advising publications is an appropriate cooperative effort that can create comprehensive advising resources for students and advisors. Grites (Chapter Eight) discusses the creation of handbooks, calendars, and other publications that can enhance the communication flow.

Professional Development Programs and Advisor Training. It is not appropriate here to detail advisor training programs but rather to emphasize the necessity of training all advisors, regardless of their background—faculty, professionals, clerical staff, peer advisors, and anyone else (see Gordon's discussion in Chapter Sixteen). Walsh (1979, p. 449) contends that "unless training is a formal and regular element, new advisors will not absorb the philosophy and skills needed for advising. In addition, people tend to be more involved in an activity if they know they are competent. . . . The person who coordinates advising for a college should have training as a job responsibility." In a survey of advising administrators conducted by Carstensen and Silberhorn (1979) for ACT, the number one need identified in the national survey was for additional advisor training procedures and materials.

Formulation of professional development programs for advisors and support staff should not only help to enhance developmental advising skills but should also convey the idea that the advising program is a common effort striving toward common goals. Professional development workshops should be scheduled on a regular basis, just like intraoffice and interoffice staff meetings.

These forums help to create mutual support groups and facilitate communication.

At State University of New York at Oswego, the differentiated delivery system for advising services encompasses specialized training for volunteer faculty advisors who work through the Student Advisement Center with undeclared students, mini-advising workshops for faculty advisors in each academic department, advisor training workshops for new faculty, and regular workshop meetings of academic department advising coordinators. Peer advisors are given rather extensive training to work with majors through advising centers in several large departments. Peer advisors who work in the Office of the Dean of Arts and Sciences are trained to deal with the intricacies of the curriculum, referral services, basic counseling skills, and other relevant concerns. The professional advisors in the Student Advisement Center are trained counselors who then receive intensive in-service training to deal with the complex programs, procedures, and problems of the institution and the students. A very successful workshop for clerical, maintenance, and secretarial staff has also been conducted, focusing on the role of support staff in delivering services to students and in student retention.

Advising administrators should be committed to efficient and realistic developmental approaches for delivering advising services. Great quantities of scarce resources can be wasted if those assigned to certain advising tasks are not properly trained. The consequence is that no meaningful learning or development takes place. Less "talking at" students and more "communicating with" students is needed. The student is not just a "receiver" of information or guidance. Quality academic advising reflects a reciprocal relationship based on interactive processes occurring between the advisor and the student, and with other elements of the campus. Advisors are not charged with making the decisions for students but with creating an informed atmosphere in which the student can make meaningful decisions. Through reading, role playing, workshops, and modeling, the advising administrator assists advisors in developing the requisite helping skills. A commitment to developmental advising requires a great deal of professional development programming for the advising administrator, the faculty and staff advisors, and even the students who must learn to take advantage of advising services in more assertive ways.

Evaluating Advising. All practitioners involved in delivering advising should be evaluated at regular intervals. But the advisors need to know what criteria are being used to evaluate them. A common error that can devastate morale and lead to some highly counterproductive outcomes is the absence of mutually understood criteria for evaluation. The practitioners should be involved in the development of these criteria. Whenever possible, there should also be evaluation of control groups in order to get a more accurate perspective on the relative outcomes of the services being delivered.

Unfortunately, most institutions do not evaluate academic advising and many of those that do are doing it poorly. Carstensen and Silberhorn (1979, p. 15) concluded, based on their national survey of academic advising, that "there are few effective systems in place for the evaluation of academic advising and little reward or recognition attached to its successful delivery." Based on a survey of advising services at twenty-nine public institutions in Maryland, Peabody, Metz, and Sedlacek (1983, p. 84) reported that at the survey institutions "professional advising staff were more often judged by specific criteria than were faculty members. Respondents most often said that if faculty were advisors, they were not chosen to be advisors by criteria because advising was then assumed to be within the role of being a faculty member." Given these problems, there are still reasonable criteria that can be employed to evaluate advising.

Kapraun and Coldren (1980) describe a ten-criteria questionnaire used at one campus of Penn State University that provides useful formative and summative evaluation of advisors based on each student's perceptions of the quality of the advising service delivered by his or her own advisor. A more comprehensive scheme for evaluating the effectiveness of institutional advising services is outlined by Crockett (1972). Crockett (1978), in turn through the American College Testing Program's seminars on academic advising and their *Academic Advising: A Resource Document,* has provided extensive and varied tools for evaluating advising that can be adapted to a wide variety of institutional types and needs.

More recently, Brown and Sanstead's (1982) work on evaluating advisor effectiveness offers additional perspectives. They stress the importance of focusing on the advising process in any really effective system of evaluating academic advising: "The primary evaluation role is providing information that is useful for decision making about academic advising programs. The information should help decision makers improve the advising system and determine whether some dimension or component of the program should be retained, expanded, or terminated" (p. 56). In their analysis of evaluating the advising process, they focus on the assessment of advisor commitment, advising program goals, plus student and faculty expectations. Brown and Sanstead argue for more formative evaluation to improve advising services, not just summative evaluation. Once an evaluation system is in place to assess the quality of the process and the effectiveness of the advisors, then there should also be attention given to a reward system for "good advising."

Reward Systems. Too frequently, good advising is not recognized in tangible ways by traditional institutional reward systems. Carstensen and Silberhorn's (1979, p. 15) survey drew the same conclusion: "Generally, academic advising has been and still is perceived by administrators as a low-status function." In another survey, Larson and Brown (1983) study the perspectives of faculty advisors and chairs regarding the role of advising performance in their reward system. Generally, they conclude that rewards for good advising depend on the existence of an evaluation system.

On many campuses advising is not a significant criterion for personnel or salary consideration. If, as the literature on advising demonstrates, the advisor occupies a critical space between the student and the institution, how can advising achieve more recognition? The chief advising administrator must convince the leadership of the institution that advising is central to student success and retention. It therefore must be built into the institutional reward system, preferably in all promotion, tenure, and merit decisions. It is somewhat easier to accomplish this change with the performance programs and job descriptions of professional and clerical staff. Only then will faculty and staff people be convinced that the institution is willing to put money behind its stated priorities. The granting of sabbatical and retraining leaves could be used as a means of recognizing and helping people improve their skills in advising or their work as advising administrators. Released time is another possible incentive or reward to facilitate improved advising. Award certificates or plaques can be utilized to recognize good advising. The institution could present an "advisor of the year" award or give an appreciation luncheon or reception to recognize those who have made unique contributions to advising. This would parallel the rationale for the "outstanding teacher" or "outstanding researcher" awards presented in many colleges and universities.

Research, Planning, and Reassessment. It is impossible to overemphasize the importance for the advising administrator of continuous advising research, long-range planning, reassessment of goals, and appropriate modification of the advising systems. The student population, the advisors, and the institution are not static; thus the advising delivery system must be flexible, dynamic, and responsive. Permanent solutions to problems and needs do not exist in this context. Any potentially successful advising program must be based on adequate research focusing on the needs of the clientele to be served, the value of various kinds of advising delivery systems, and the types of practitioners needed. Constant assessment is crucial in monitoring who is being served, how well, how frequently, in what ways, by whom, and so on. The advising system and the preparation of practitioners would then have to be modified to respond to these kinds of changes.

The institutional master plan for advising should therefore be reviewed at regular intervals. The planning should be a continuous process that defines specific goals and sets a timetable for completion of those goals. Dynamic planning, comprehensive evaluation, and a meaningful reward system for advising are important in overcoming the ambiguity and confusion that advisors often feel because of unclear goals, conflicting perceptions, and ambivalent leadership.

Summary

In summary, there are several principles that advising administrators should consider if they hope to develop a truly effective advising system. There must be an institutional commitment to advising substantiated by the allocation of budget, staffing, and other resources. Advising must be publicly presented as a high-priority concern on campus. A person should be designated as the institutional director of advising services, and other specific persons should be assigned responsibility for advising in each appropriate subunit within the institution. This will facilitate communication, coordination, and accountability. The advising delivery system, in almost every instance, should be differentiated to make the system more responsive to the specific needs of various types of students.

Advising practitioners must be carefully selected and trained to enhance their effectiveness. Since student needs are comprehensive, the advising system should be based on a holistic philosophy for delivery of services to students. This is accomplished both in the way advisors advise and through the effective use of a carefully constructed, comprehensive referral system. These approaches will encourage cooperation within the referral network. Advising services should be delivered developmentally so that the students will be actively involved in the learning and decision-making process. The goals of the advising system, like the goal clarification done with students, should be realistic and achievable. "Pie-in-the-sky" objectives often lead to disillusionment, bitterness, and failure. Some students need to build self-confidence; others need to be assisted in confronting reality if there is a major dichotomy between their educational goals and their aptitude. An accurate and efficient student information system is very important in good advising. Advisors need to keep accurate records and work within a facilitative communication system. Incentives can be provided through opportunities for recognition, as well as monetary and other rewards.

The successful advising administrator needs to be politically astute in order to achieve and maintain support from key administrators and faculty leaders. Cultivation of the art of diplomacy is another vital skill that must be employed frequently in negotiating advising plans with various departments and service offices.

The development of a viable institutional advising program that truly promotes student development is no easy task. It is a challenging opportunity to create new programs, initiatives, and linkages that do not develop naturally in most academic settings. To do this, the advising administrator must carefully build credibility and cooperation among many elements of the campus. The results can bring great personal and professional satisfaction for advisors and the prospect of enriching the educational experience for many students.

References

Abel, J. "Academic Advising Administrators: Contributors to Student Based Management Practices." *Journal of the National Association of Women Deans, Administrators, and Counselors,* 1978, *41,* 102–105.

Astin, A. W. *Preventing Students from Dropping Out.* San Francisco: Jossey-Bass, 1975.

Beal, P. E., and Noel, L. *What Works in Student Retention.* Iowa City, Iowa: American College Testing Program and National Center for Higher Education Management Systems, 1980.

Brown, R. D., and Sanstead, M. J. "Using Evaluation to Make Decisions About Academic Advising Programs." In R. B. Winston, Jr., S. C. Ender, and T. K. Miller (Eds.), *New Directions for Student Services: Developmental Approaches to Academic Advising,* no. 17. San Francisco: Jossey-Bass, 1982.

Browning, D. S. *Generative Man: Psychoanalytic Perspectives.* Philadelphia: Westminster Press, 1973.

Caple, R. B. "Holistic Counseling: A More Complete Perspective." In F. B. Newton and K. Ender (Eds.), *Student Development Practices: Strategies for Making a Difference.* Springfield, Ill.: Thomas, 1980.

Carstensen, D. J., and Silberhorn, C. A. *A National Survey of Academic Advising, Final Report.* Iowa City, Iowa: American College Testing Program, 1979.

Chickering, A. W., and Associates. *The Modern American College: Responding to the New Realities of Diverse Students and a Changing Society.* San Francisco: Jossey-Bass, 1981.

Crockett, D. S. "How Good Is Your Advising Program? A Self-Inquiry Technique." *Southern College Personnel Association Journal,* 1972, *1,* 33–40.

Crockett, D. S. (Ed.). *Academic Advising: A Resource Document.* Iowa City, Iowa: American College Testing Program, 1978.

Crockett, D. S. *Academic Advising: A Resource Document—1979 Supplement.* Iowa City, Iowa: American College Testing Program, 1979.

Crockett, D. S. *Advising Skills, Techniques and Resources.* (Rev. ed.) Iowa City, Iowa: American College Testing Program, 1982.

Crookston, B. B. "A Developmental View of Academic Advising as Teaching." *Journal of College Student Personnel,* 1972, *13,* 12-17.

Cross, K. P. *Beyond the Open Door: New Students to Higher Education.* San Francisco: Jossey-Bass, 1971.

Ender, S. C., Winston, R. B., Jr., and Miller, T. K. "Academic Advising as Student Development." In R. B. Winston, Jr., S. C. Ender, and T. K. Miller (Eds.), *New Directions for Student Services: Developmental Approaches to Academic Advising,* no. 17. San Francisco: Jossey-Bass, 1982.

Erikson, E. H. "The Golden Rule and the Light of New Insight." In E. H. Erikson, *Insight and Responsibility: Lectures on the Ethical Implications of Psychoanalytic Insight.* New York: Norton, 1964.

Grites, T. J. "Academic Advising: Getting Us Through the Eighties." *American Association for Higher Education/Educational Resources Information Style Higher Education Research Report No. 7.* Washington, D.C.: American Association for Higher Education, 1979.

Grites, T. J. "Academic Advising: An Atlas for Liberal Education." *Forum for Liberal Education,* 1981, *3* (4).

Habley, W. R. "Academic Advisement: The Critical Link in Student Retention." *National Association of Student Personnel Administrators (NASPA) Journal,* 1981, *18,* 45-50.

Heath, D. H. *Growing Up in College: Liberal Education and Maturity.* San Francisco: Jossey-Bass, 1968.

Hillman, L., and Lewis, A. "Using Student Development Theory as a Tool in Academic Advising." Unpublished paper, University of Maryland, 1980.

Johnson, J., and Sprandel, K. "Centralized Academic Advising at the Department Level: A Model." *University College Quarterly,* 1975, *21,* 16-20.

Kapraun, E. D., and Coldren, D. W. "An Approach to the Evaluation of Academic Advising." *Journal of College Student Personnel*, 1980, *21*, 85-86.

Knefelkamp, L. L. "Designing Developmental Advising Environments." Paper presented at the National Academic Advising Association Conference, Asheville, N. C., 1980.

Kramer, G. L., and White, M. T. "Developing a Faculty Mentoring Program: An Experiment." *National Academic Advising Association (NACADA) Journal*, 1982, *2* (2), 47-58.

Kramer, H. C. "The Advising Coordinator: Managing from a One-Down Position." *National Academic Advising Association (NACADA) Journal*, 1981, *1* (1), 7-15.

Kramer, H. C., and Gardner, R. E. "Managing Faculty Advising." In D. S. Crockett (Ed.), *Academic Advising: A Resource Document*. Iowa City, Iowa: American College Testing Program, 1978.

Kramer, H. C., and Gardner, R. E. *Advising by Faculty*. (2nd ed.) Washington, D.C.: National Education Association, 1983.

Larson, M. D., and Brown, B. M. "Rewards for Academic Advising: An Evaluation." *National Academic Advising Association (NACADA) Journal*, 1983, *3* (2), 53-60.

McCaffrey, S. S., and Miller, T. K. "Mentoring: An Approach to Academic Advising." In F. B. Newton and K. L. Ender (Eds.), *Student Development Practices: Strategies for Making a Difference*. Springfield, Ill.: Thomas, 1980.

Miller, T. K., and McCaffrey, S. S. "Student Development Theory: Foundations for Academic Advising." In R. B. Winston, Jr., S. C. Ender, and T. K. Miller (Eds.), *New Directions for Student Services: Developmental Approaches to Academic Advising*, no. 17. San Francisco: Jossey-Bass, 1982.

Newton, F. B., and Ender, K. L. *Student Development Practices: Strategies for Making a Difference*. Springfield, Ill.: Thomas, 1980.

Peabody, S. A., Metz, J. F., Jr., and Sedlacek, W. E. "A Survey of Academic Advising Models (Used by Maryland State Public Institutions of Higher Education)." *Journal of College Student Personnel*, 1983, *24* (1), 83-84.

Perry, W. G., Jr. *Forms of Intellectual and Ethical Development in the College Years: A Scheme.* New York: Holt, Rinehart & Winston, 1970.

Perry, W. G., Jr. "On Advising and Counseling." In *Annual Report of the Bureau of Study Counsel, Harvard University, 1974-75.* Cambridge, Mass.: Harvard University Press, 1975.

Reddin, W. J. *Managerial Effectiveness.* New York: McGraw-Hill, 1970.

Villeme, M. G. "Overcoming Communication Barriers in Advising." *National Academic Advising Association (NACADA) Journal,* 1982, 2 (2), 70-73.

Walsh, E. M. "Revitalizing Academic Advisement." *Personnel and Guidance Journal,* 1979, 57, 446-449.

Winston, R. B., Jr., Ender, S. C., and Miller, T. K. *New Directions for Student Services: Developmental Approaches to Academic Advising,* no. 17. San Francisco: Jossey-Bass, 1982.

14

Legal Issues
in Academic Advising

᪥ᨾᨭ.᪥ᨾᨭ.᪥ᨾᨭ.᪥ᨾᨭ.᪥ᨾᨭ.᪥ᨾᨭ.᪥ᨾᨭ.᪥ᨾᨭ.

Donald D. Gehring

Education is considered to be an important prerequisite for a productive life in modern American society. Students have recognized this fact and have become increasingly consumer oriented, using external agencies to remedy alleged wrongs on campus (Levine, 1980). Questions and grievances once resolved within the institution are now being framed as legal rights and responsibilities and are being presented to the courts for resolution (Gehring, 1978). Academic advising, which is at the very core of every educational delivery system, has often been the subject of student-initiated litigation. Aggrieved students who are successful in showing that they have been damaged by the actions of their institutions or their representatives may be awarded financial compensation in order to be "made whole" again. These financial awards are assessed against those individuals whose actions caused the students to suffer. The central position of academic advisors in the educational process demands that they understand the different legal relationships that exist between the student and the institution. Developing an understanding of these relationships and the multitude of legal issues that arise in the advising process will help the advisor to avoid potential institutional and personal liability, as well as to retain control of the advising process without judicial interference.

The U.S. Supreme Court has recognized that "education has a fundamental role in maintaining the fabric of our society" (*Plyler*, 1982, p. 22), but generally the judiciary has exercised a great deal of restraint with respect to entering the academic arena. Courts consistently have stated that they are not qualified to make academic decisions and will not do so, preferring to leave those decisions to educators (*Connelly*, 1965). The courts, however, have said very clearly that they will intervene where academic decisions are obviously arbitrary, exhibit an abuse of discretion, violate the terms of a contract or statute, or abridge protected rights. Thus, in order to avoid liability, prevent judicial interference, and retain control of the academic advising process, advisors must understand the rights and responsibilities flowing from the different relationships that exist among themselves, their students, and their institutions.

This chapter provides an introduction to the primary legal relationships that impinge upon the advising process and the rights and responsibilities of the parties involved in those relationships. The advising process involves constitutional parameters, contractual obligations, statutory mandates, and the right of students to be free from damage to their persons, property, and reputations. Therefore, each of these relationships will be discussed in the context of educational advising. The relationships discussed are presented as they have been interpreted by the courts. The facts of specific cases are often provided to enhance the understanding of the issues involved in academic advising. Also, actual language of the courts is used to give the advisor a flavor for the way in which courts view these issues. The case law discussed is designed to be instructive but should not be considered an exhaustive listing. Academic advisors who understand these relationships will be better able to detect the legal issues that arise every day in the advising process.

Advisors who are able to identify the issues confronting them will be prepared to respond in ways that should minimize litigation and liability.

A word of caution is in order, however. Most institutions employ in-house or retained counsel. These individuals are trained experts and their opinions should be sought whenever the advisor must confront a situation involving complex legal issues. Acting on advice of counsel, in some cases, may even shield the advisor from potential liability.

Constitutional Relationships

Students at public institutions enjoy the protections of the U.S. Constitution (*Tinker*, 1969). The rights guaranteed under the Constitution, however, generally do not accrue to students at private colleges and universities, unless the private institution is so entwined with the state as to make its actions essentially those of the state. Generally, this concept of "state action" has not been applied to private colleges except where racial discrimination has existed. Courts will examine each situation on its own merits to determine if state action is present (*Burton*, 1961); however, the receipt of state funding alone is usually insufficient (*Grafton*, 1973).

Most of the personal rights guaranteed under the Constitution are found in the amendments. The First (freedom of speech, press, assembly, religion, and the right to petition for redress of grievance), the Fourth (search and seizure), and the Fourteenth (due process and equal protection) Amendments are generally more applicable to the social context in higher education than they are to the academic advising process. However, academic advisors must understand that students are protected by the U.S. Constitution in expressing their personal views "no matter how offensive to good taste . . . [and the dissemination of these views] may not be shut off in the name alone of 'conventions of decency'" (*Papish*, 1973, p. 1199). The freedom of speech clause not only protects students in expressing their views but also protects advisors. A faculty advisor who was denied tenure because he counseled a student to seek legal advice concerning his suspension from the college was reinstated by a trial court. The college characterized the faculty member's advice as being given "in a cavalier or immature fashion" (*Stern*, 1983, p. 46), but the court held that it was protected speech. The Third Circuit Court of Appeals affirmed the fact that the advice constituted protected speech since it did not disrupt the operation of the institution, create disharmony among co-workers, or undercut the disciplinary process (*Stern*, 1983). Advice given in good faith to students in the fulfillment of the advisor's responsibilities that is neither designed to disrupt the educational process nor to incite students to imminent lawless action would be constitutionally protected. A public institution may not discipline for the exercise of a constitutionally protected right.

The equal protection rights contained in the Fourteenth Amendment can also create legal issues for the academic advisor. There are no absolute rights and the equal protection clause does not mean that everyone must be treated equally. However, if individuals are to be treated differently, then some rational relationship must exist between the legitimate interests of the state and the rule creating the disparate treatment. For example, a regulation that prohibits freshman medical students from being employed but allows students in other classes to hold outside employment would probably be upheld by the courts, based upon the legitimate interest of the state in retaining students since medical education is so expensive for the state to provide and freshman attrition rates are high. On the other hand, the same rule applied only to freshman female students would probably not be upheld. It is doubtful that there would be a legitimate state interest to be served by treating women differently. Rules that create "suspect" classes—those based on race or alienage—or those that deprive individuals of a fundamental right require a much higher standard to support the different treatment. Education per se has not been held to be a fundamental right (*Plyler*, 1982); however, advisors who confront equal protection issues should consult institutional counsel before taking action. For example, it would be best to consult counsel before initiating a regulation that waived co-op requirements for international students but did not apply the same waiver to American students. Unless there was a "compelling state interest" to be served, such a regulation might violate the Constitution.

Advisors at public institutions who abridge the constitutional rights of students could be liable for damages under the provisions of an old civil rights law (42 *U.S.C.* 1983). When damages have been awarded under this act, however, the courts have only ordered a nominal amount of one dollar unless the individual can show an actual loss or injury (*Carey*, 1978). Thus, advisors need to be sensitive to the constitutional rights of students and respect them. Remember, the Supreme Court has said that students do not shed their constitutional rights at the schoolhouse gate (*Tinker*, 1969).

Contractual Relationships

The contractual relationship, defining the rights and responsibilities of students and the institution, affects the advising process more than any other relationship. Thus, it is most important that advisors understand this relationship. In very general terms, the institution states that if students abide by all reasonable regulations, including paying all tuition and fees, and maintain a certain academic average for a prescribed curriculum, then a degree will be awarded. By matriculating, students agree to abide by the rules and regulations and pay their tuition and fees. Courts consistently find this type of contractual arrangement to define the relationship between students and their institutions (*DeMarco*, 1976; *Greene*, 1967; *University of Texas Health Science Center*, 1982).

The terms of the contract are contained in the various catalogues and other documents of the institution unless there is a specific statement to the effect that the material does not constitute part of the contract. There are also terms and conditions that are implied rather than expressed, and under certain circumstances the contract may be changed. Courts are sensitive to the special nature of the academic environment and do not apply contract law rigidly when interpreting institutional contracts. However, institutions are required to follow their own rules and promised services that are not delivered may result in a suit based on breach of contract, specific performance, or even *fraud!*

Entering into the Contract. The first question to be addressed in understanding the contractual relationship is "When does the contract become effective?" In other words, at what point do the student and the institution enter into a contract? The Supreme Court of Illinois found that a medical school entered into a contract with a prospective student when it accepted the student's application and the requisite fee (*Steinberg*, 1977). A good understanding of how the contract comes about can be obtained from the words of the court when it stated, "Here the description in the brochure containing the terms under which an application will be appraised constituted an invitation for an offer. The tender of the application, as well as the payment of the fee pursuant to the terms of the brochure, was an offer to apply. Acceptance of the application and fee constituted acceptance of an offer to apply under the criteria defendant had established" (p. 639). Other courts have relied on this decision to find that brochures describing programs and services also form the basis for the contract once a student has been enrolled (*Yakin*, 1981). Thus, advisors must understand that after students have matriculated, they are legally entitled to those services and facilities promised by the catalogue and brochures of the institution. Failure to provide promised services, including the availability of advisors to students, could result in a suit for breach of contract.

Students, too, are bound to abide by the rules and regulations contained in the official documents of the college. For example, where the catalogue states that students are responsible for knowing and complying with the deadlines published in official bulletins, if students miss the course drop deadline, their arguments blaming their advisors for not informing them of the date would be legally very tenuous. Whether students have had notice of the rules is another question. At least one court has held that giving students a copy of the handbook containing the rules and regulations constituted actual knowledge of the rules (*State Board of Regents of University*, 1978). However, a New York court has said that students should be given notice of the salient sections of the catalogue before they are held to every word of its contents (*Drucker*, 1968). If an institution published the fact that students are required to keep it informed of their current address, then mailing students a notice of academic regulations or other information to the last known address would satisfy the notice requirement (*Wright*, 1968).

Statements of Advisors as Part of the Contract. Catalogues and brochures are not the only basis for the contract. Sometimes statements made by officials authorized to do so create terms or promises the institution must fulfill. A student disciplinary case provides a good illustration of how such a verbal contract is created. During an investigation at the U.S. Merchant Marine Academy, federal narcotics agents promised several students impunity if they spoke freely about their use of drugs. The students were suspended after they admitted their use of marijuana. In reinstating the students, the federal court said that a contract existed that was breached by the academy. "As agents, the questioners were authorized to make promises to the students concerning the use of their statements. They told plaintiffs [students] that if they spoke freely nothing they said would be used against them. Plaintiffs, by speaking freely, accepted this offer, and a contract was made. The Academy is bound by this agreement" (*Krawez*, 1969, p. 1235).

A similar analysis was made with respect to the statements of faculty in advising a student about the courses he needed in order to graduate. A student enrolled at Brooklyn College was advised by several faculty members that a particular course of action would fulfill the requirements for his degree. This advice included taking two courses on an independent basis without attending classes. The student successfully fulfilled all requirements but the dean of faculty withheld the degree because the two courses were not taken "in attendance." In ordering the college to award the degree, the court noted that the student had "acted in obvious reliance upon the counsel and advice of members of the staff of the college administration to whom he was referred and who were authorized to give him such counsel and advice" (*Blank*, 1966, p. 802). Having determined that fact, the court held that "the Dean of faculty may not escape the binding effect of the acts of his agents . . . and the consequences that must equitably follow therefrom" (p. 803). Since the statements of advisors may become part of the legally enforceable contract, caution should be exercised by advisors in making promises to students. Young (1982) has suggested that advisors keep notes of their discussions with students to avoid disputes over what was or was not promised.

The courts, however, require evidence to support the fact that statements have been made that alter the contractual terms contained in the catalogue. The uncontroverted statements of students have not been held to be sufficient to support a waiver of degree (*Holloway*, 1978) or retention (*Hines*, 1981) requirements found in the catalogue. For example, a student at the University of Montana was denied his master's degree in business administration (M.B.A.) because he failed to obtain a C in a 600-level course as required by a rule published in the catalogue. The student alleged that his advisor had verbally waived the requirement (*Holloway*, 1978). The advisor testified that he had no recollection of ever having waived the requirement for this student and that he had never done so for any other student. The advisor also stated that the business school had a procedure for handling waivers and he had not forgotten to use it in this instance. The Supreme Court of Montana upheld the denial of the degree saying, "The record afforded sufficient evidence that no waiver had been granted without any finding necessary as to the truth of Holloway's [the student's] testimony" (p. 1269).

The highest state court in New York refused to interfere in a situation where a faculty member had actually misinformed graduate students about the requirements for passing a comprehensive exam. The student who failed the exam claimed that he studied based on the statements made to him by the professor. The college offered the student another opportunity to take the exam, but he declined and asked the court to award him the degree since he had passed the exam under the criteria set forth by the professor's statements. The court, while noting that a principal is not held to answer for the misstatements of his agents (the advisor), said that the contract between the student and the college was met by the good faith offer for another exam that would allow the student to demonstrate his academic competence without judicial interference (*Olsson*, 1980).

Implied Aspects of the Contract. Written documents and statements by officials of the institution are not the only contractual conditions. There are also implied terms that define the contract. Advisors need to know that courts have held one of the implied terms of the contract to be a student's reasonable expectation of being able to complete a program once it is started. A federal district court ordered the state of Montana to pay damages to students whose program was discontinued (*Peretti*, 1979). In Ohio, a state court went a step further, saying that in a program leading to professional license, it is *implied* that the program "has been accredited by the appropriate accrediting agency" (*Behrend*, 1977, p. 620).

Changing the Terms of the Contract. The advisor also needs to understand the parameters involved when the institution changes the terms or conditions of the contract after the student has matriculated. The parameters depend upon the type of change being made and how it is made. If the change is insignificant or has no real impact on students, it will not usually be considered a breach of the contract. The constitution of the student government association at Vassar College gave students the authority to enact social rules. When the students liberalized the residence hall visitation policy and the college president approved the change, the mother of a student challenged the change as a breach of contract. A lower state court dismissed the complaint, applying the "rule of reason" and finding that no significant harm to the student resulted. The court said that the institution must be free to govern itself and the mere speculation of what might ensue from the liberalized visitation rules was insufficient to justify judicial interference (*Jones*, 1969). Changes made by institutions that are designed to fulfill their educational responsibilities, that are not arbitrary, and that do not cause significant harm to the student have also been upheld. The school of education at Georgia State University added a comprehensive exam to the requirements for the master's degree after a graduate student had enrolled in the program. The student was given ample notice of the requirement and was offered a special tailor-made program to prepare for the exam. The Fifth Circuit Court of Appeals held that the student had not been treated arbitrarily or capriciously and that "implicit in the student's contract with the university upon matriculation is the student's agreement to comply with the university's rules and regulations, which the university clearly is entitled to modify so as to properly exercise its educational responsibility" (*Mahavongsana*, 1976, p. 450).

Arbitrary changes that do not further an institution's educational responsibilities, however, will not be tolerated. For example, in a graduate program a student alleged that he had been singled out to complete special requirements not mandated for others. He had been required to meet an additional section of a practicum, to be graded and evaluated by his fellow graduate students. In finding that the student had stated a cause of action, the California court articulated the standards to be used in changing academic requirements. The court said, "We are not unmindful, however, that various considerations, in addition to academic factors, may provide justification for a school's fashioning special requirements for an applicant for an advanced degree—requirements which are neither arbitrary nor capricious—but are founded on the university's familiarity with the student involved, and the judgment of teachers whose responsibility it is to prepare the student for professional life. But what is not legally permissible is for a university or its faculty to pursue an unreasonable or a punitive course with a student for reasons that have nothing to do with his qualifications for an advanced degree" (*Shuffer*, 1977, p. 534).

Once a student successfully completes the requirements for a degree as set forth in the institution's documents or as outlined by authorized officials, the college or university may not arbitrarily impose additional requirements. A two-year college student who took certain courses after being advised by the dean, the director of admissions, and the school's counselor was refused a degree because he lacked the proper credits within a concentration. A New York court held that additional requirements could not be imposed after he had already completed those outlined to him (*Healy*, 1971). A similar situation involved a Ph.D. candidate who completed his written and oral exams as administered by his thesis committee. He was later informed that his committee had never been approved by the graduate college and he would be required to be totally reevaluated. This action by the university was found to be arbitrary and in bad faith (*Tanner*, 1977).

Many institutions include statements in their catalogues to the effect that the university reserves the right to make changes to the catalogue upon notice to students. Courts have given considerable deference to such statements when institutions have raised tuition (*Basch*, 1977; *Eisle*, 1978) or eliminated specific services (*Abbariao*, 1977). Even when academic requirements were added as a requirement for a degree in *Mahavongsana* (1976), the court was aware that the university had included a statement in its catalogue that "a student will normally satisfy the degree requirements of the catalogue in effect at the time of entrance. . . . for graduate degrees a minimum average grade of B is required. Additional regulations pertaining to standards of performance may be presented by the respective schools" (*Mahavongsana*, 1975, p. 383).

However, if an institution states explicitly that students may elect to complete their degree under the requirements set forth in the catalogue in effect when they entered the institution, then the institution is bound by that agreement and may not require students to conform to subsequent unilateral changes (*University of Texas Health Science Center*, 1982).

Failing to follow one's own rules provides yet another condition justifying judicial interference in the academic process. Once the terms and conditions of the contract have been published, they must be adhered to—especially where deviation from them will cause the student injury. A student who was suspended for disciplinary reasons was reinstated by the highest state court in New York, which held that "whether by analogy to the law of associations, on the basis of a supposed contract between university and student, or simply as a matter of essential fairness in the somewhat one-sided relationship between the institution and the individual, we hold that when a university has adopted a rule or guideline . . . that procedure must be substantially observed" (*Tedeschi*, 1980, p. 764).

Other federal and state courts have arrived at similar conclusions with respect to academic matters (*Clayton*, 1981; *Heisler*, 1982). Failure to follow one's own rules or to provide services promised could result in voiding the contract (*Delta School of Business*, 1981) and relieving students of their obligations or nullifying institutional action (*Tedeschi*, 1980).

Furthermore, if it appears that promises of services are made without due regard for whether they can be provided, then the individuals making such promises could be sued for fraud. A public two-year college was sued successfully for $12,500 when it promised an individual that specific lab equipment would be available but the equipment was never provided during his tenure as a student (*Dizick*, 1979). The Oregon Supreme Court found that this action constituted an inducement to enroll, rather than a discretionary decision of administrative officials. Actual fraud was found in another instance where a very poorly prepared student was advised that he could qualify for a $10,000 job in data processing or computer programming and that the school would place him in a job when he completed his course of study. Five years after completing his course of study, he was still unable to pass any employment tests and was unable to find employment. Based upon the institution's deceptive practices and their fraudulent inducement to enroll, the student was awarded punitive damages (*Joyner*, 1978).

Interpretation of the Contract. Because of the special nature of the academic setting, courts have not applied rigid commercial contract law to the contractual relationship that exists between the student and the institution (*Abbariao*, 1977; *Lyons*, 1977). Rather, the courts have used the common meanings of words, the "rule of reason," and interpreted what they consider was the institution's intent in constructing the rules and regulations.

Where an institution publishes a statement that it is "desirable" for students to be apprised of their progress, the term was interpreted to be an unenforceable expression of desire and not a mandate (*Abrams*, 1979). However, where state regulations "required" that students be informed of their progress and remaining obligations, the word was considered a mandatory condition of the contract and failure to inform the student breached the contract (*Kantor*, 1979).

Many institutions include a statement that students are responsible for their own academic programs. These institutions still offer students the assistance of advisors to help in the educational planning process. Meeting with one's advisor is usually recommended, however. A student who never saw his advisor every term was informed by the advisor that he had to repeat two D's in order to graduate. The court found that since the bulletin of the college only "recommended" that students see an advisor and since the fact that the D's had to be repeated was contained in the catalogue, there was notice. "Any obligation of Illinois Benedictine College (IBC) [the institution involved] or its agent to notify Wilson of a deficiency which he wishes to infer from the bulletin lacks support" (*Wilson*, 1983, p. 908). Another court has said that with regard to advising graduate students, "the possibility of academic failure is implicit in the nature of the educational contract between a student and a university. A graduate student seeking admission to a university knows a certain level of performance is necessary to obtain a degree. It is unreasonable to require the university to warn applicants of the obvious" (*Maas*, 1980, p. 108).

Summary. The fundamental relationship that exists between students and their institutions is contractual. Advisors should be aware of this contractual relationship, which becomes effective when the student matriculates; its terms and conditions are expressly set forth in the catalogue and other documents of the institution. Services that are promised should be delivered and those that cannot be provided should not be promised. Not meeting the terms of the contract could result in a suit causing unwanted judicial interference, a loss of time, and possibly monetary damages. Thus advisors, as agents of the institution, need to be careful of what they commit the institution to, since their statements may also bind the college or university. The courts have not applied strict commercial law to the contractual relationship between students and their institutions. Rather, the courts have been sensitive to the special nature of educational institutions and have allowed unilateral changes to be made to the terms of the contract where such changes further the institution's educational responsibilities and proper notice is given. The judiciary recognizes that it is not qualified to make academic decisions and prefers not to substitute its judgment for that of qualified faculty. However, the courts will not permit arbitrary changes to be made or actions taken that damage students and that are not designed to fulfill the educational responsibilities of the college or university. Once a student completes the requirements, a degree must be awarded.

An illustration that includes many of the concepts discussed in this section is provided by the case of a medical student who was denied a degree (*DeMarco*, 1976). The student stated on his application that he had not attended any other medical schools when in fact he had. His response was based on his belief that the question concerned his desire to transfer credits from another medical school. This fact was discovered six weeks before he was to graduate and he was dismissed. He was also informed that he was the only student in his class who had not fulfilled his financial pledge to the college.

He was later readmitted after he pledged $40,000 and paid $20,000. His readmission was conditioned on completing certain work and taking the National Board Exams. He completed the required work and received favorable evaluations but failed one part of the National Board Exams. Passing the exams was not a requirement when he entered the institution. The state court in Illinois ordered the institution to award the student his degree stating, "The 1941 contract provided for the issuance of a diploma at the successful completion of their academic program as stated in their catalogue. The evidence established the plaintiff [the student] earned the degree, and it was proper for the court to order the mandatory injunction" (DeMarco, 1976). The court found that the school's primary concern seemed to be financial contributions, "which caused it to act in an arbitrary and capricious manner" (p. 364). The court pointed out that "the 1970 requirement whereby the plaintiff was required to demonstrate current knowledge of medicine by passing Parts I and II of the National Boards was not responsive to the injustice done to him in 1944 when he was dismissed or in later years when he was denied readmission and reflects the inequitable use of power by the school. The extra requirement of demonstrating current medical knowledge was arbitrary and unreasonable, in light of the fact the examinations have never been required for a degree, then or now. It is recognized that a school is entitled to enter into a special degree program with a student with whom there has been no previous history of bad faith; however, in this case the school admittedly acted in bad faith. . . ." (p. 364).

Statutory Relationships

In addition to the constitutional and contractual relationships that exist between students and their institutions, advisors also need to be aware of the rights students derive from various federal and state statutes. Each state has different laws governing the ways in which state institutions relate to students. This chapter cannot address statutes in each of the fifty states and the various territories, but it should be recognized that these state statutes may impinge directly on the obligations of advisors. In Kantor v. Schmidt (1979), New York state regulations "required" that students be kept informed of their progress. This regulation therefore mandated action that must be taken by an institution. Advisors must know if state mandates have been delegated to them to perform.

There are several federal laws that specifically relate to the educational advising process. These laws and their implementing regulations stem from the civil rights movement of the 1960s and are directly focused on colleges and universities and the various activities that take place in those institutions. Generally, these laws prohibit different forms of discrimination. The penalty for the institution, if there is a failure to comply, is a loss of federal funds, and individual advisors who violate federal laws could be personally liable for damages. The laws generally apply to educational institutions that receive federal funds; having at least one student who receives federal financial aid is enough to require institutional compliance (*Bob Jones University*, 1974; *Hillsdale College*, 1982).

The laws and regulations that affect the advising process are very detailed and complex. There is no easy way to learn them; however, the Appendix at the end of this chapter includes the salient provisions of the laws as they relate to advising as well as implications of those provisions for advisors. If doubts arise, and they are bound to in this complex area, the advisor should consult institutional counsel. Judicial interpretations are also provided to help the advisor understand how these laws are being translated into practice.

Prohibition Against Discrimination on the Basis of Race, Color, or National Origin. Title VI of the Civil Rights Act of 1964 prohibits discrimination on the basis of race, color, or national origin. The Supreme Court has held that programs that set aside a specific quota of spaces based on a student's race would be in violation of Title VI (*Regents of the University of California*, 1978). Title VII of the same act prohibits discrimination in employment on the basis of race, color, sex, national origin, or religion. There are guidelines issued under this law prohibiting sexual harassment (29 *C.F.R* 1604.11). Title VII would protect the advisor and would, for example, require that advising loads be equitably distributed and that there not be any disparity in salary based solely on sex or race. There are also guidelines under Title VII for accommodating

an individual's religious practice (29 *C.F.R* 1605). The observance
of religious holidays is a protected practice under Title VII and
requires employers to provide reasonable accommodations to such
observances (*Trans World Airlines,* 1977; *Rankins,* 1979).

    Prohibition Against Discrimination on the Basis of Sex.
Title IX of the Education Amendments of 1972, which was modeled
after Title VI, prohibits discrimination in educational programs or
activities on the basis of sex. Sections 86.34 and 86.36 of the
implementing regulations of this law specifically relate to the
educational advising process. With certain exceptions, Section 86.34
prohibits courses segregated on the basis of gender. Section 86.36
states that "a recipient shall not discriminate against any person on
the basis of sex in the counseling or guidance of students or
applicants for admission." The section also prohibits the advisor
from using sex-biased appraisal and counseling materials. While
the sexual harassment of students is not specifically mentioned in
Title IX, it has been held to protect students against such abuse
(*Alexander,* 1980).

    *Prohibition Against Discrimination on the Basis of Han-
dicap.* Section 504 of the Rehabilitation Act of 1973 addresses
discrimination on the basis of one's handicap. The implementing
regulations make it clear that both mental and physical impair-
ments are included within the rubric of *handicapped.* The regulations do not require that buildings be accessible per se but rather
that programs and services be made accessible to handicapped
students (34 *C.F.R.* 104). Reasonable accommodations by the institution might be required and students should be permitted to use
auxiliary aids such as tape recorders (*Littsey,* 1981) or have sign-
language interpreters (*Camenisch,* 1980) to assist them in class and
for exams. Advisors interested in helping their students obtain sign-
language interpreters should know that the courts have recently
been placing that obligation on state departments of vocational
rehabilitation (*Jones,* 1982; *Schornstein,* 1981).

    Advisors should be aware, however, that handicapped per-
sons under this act are those who are qualified in spite of their
handicap (*Southeastern Community College,* 1979), and the courts
will allow educators a great deal of leeway in determining if an
individual can meet the academic and professional standards with-

out undue risk to the individual or to others (*Doe*, 1981). In *Doe* v. *New York University* (1981) a student who had made several attempts to take her own life was withdrawn from a medical school. She subsequently received psychiatric treatment and completed a master's program at Harvard but the medical school, on the basis of its own psychiatric examination, decided that if the student were placed under the stress of a program of medical education, she would suffer a high risk of personality disorganization. The Second Circuit Court of Appeals upheld the institution saying that in their view, "she would not be qualified for readmission if there is a significant risk of such recurrence. It would be unreasonable to infer that Congress intended to force institutions to accept or readmit persons who pose a significant risk of harm to themselves or others even if the chances of harm were less than 50 percent" (p. 777).

In making decisions concerning whether handicapped students may take part in activities, advisors should be aware of the risk of harm but should not be paternalistic toward handicapped students. A university was enjoined by a federal court in its attempt to prohibit a student, who was only sighted in one eye, from participating in intercollegiate football (*Wright*, 1981). The court noted that it was this type of paternalization that was prohibited by Section 504.

Students' Right to Access Their Records and Privacy of Records. One of the most important statutes for an advisor to be aware of is the Family Educational Rights and Privacy Act (F.E.R.P.A.). This federal law is popularly known as the Buckley Amendment and generally gives students a guaranteed right to inspect most of their records. The law also prohibits disclosing information from a student's record without first obtaining the student's written consent. Educational records are defined by the law's implementing regulations as "records which: (1) are directly related to a student, and (2) are maintained by an educational agency or institution or by a party acting for the agency or institution" (34 *C.F.R.* 99.3).

There are several exceptions to the general provisions of the law. Educational advisors, however, would be most concerned about the "personal notes" exception. If an advisor keeps personal notes about a student, which are in the advisor's sole possession and are not shared with anyone else except a short-term substitute, then those notes are not open to student inspection. In addition, medical and psychiatric records are not open to a student's inspection unless the student is qualified to interpret them; however, the student has a right to have a qualified professional inspect the records and interpret them. Institutional officials with legitimate educational interests may also inspect student records without the consent of the student. Institutions are not precluded from providing information in a student record to the student's parents without prior consent if the student is a financial dependent of his or her parents. Financial dependence is determined by whether the parents claimed the student as a deduction on their federal taxes. On the other hand, the institution is not required to disclose information to parents and may develop its own institutional policy with respect to such disclosure. Information from the records of financially independent students cannot be disclosed to parents any more than they can be to any other individual without the student's prior written consent. Directory-type information, however, may be disclosed to anyone without prior consent if it is the institution's policy to do so, and the institution has complied with the Buckley Amendment rules for such disclosure. Directory information includes such items as years of attendance, address, phone number, major, participation in athletics or other recognized activities, and awards. Information pertaining to a student also may be disclosed in a health or safety emergency.

The college or university is required by law to have a policy available that, among other things, outlines a student's rights under the law, the location of records, who the institutional officials are, and what constitutes a legitimate educational interest. *Advisors should have a personal copy of this policy and should be familiar with its contents.* Most institutions have designated one individual on the campus to process all requests for information from students' records. Advisors should refer *all* requests for information to this individual. There may also be a specific state law protecting the privacy of student records. For instance, Kentucky provides for the confidentiality of students' academic records (*K.R.S.* 164 283). With certain exceptions, this state law requires a student's written authorization before academic records may be released.

There is also a federal Privacy Act that should be of interest to advisors. The act generally applies to federal agencies, but one section prohibits state or local government agencies (public colleges and universities are considered to be state or local governmental agencies) from requiring any person to disclose their social security number (5 *U.S.C.S.* 552a). However, if the institution maintained a system of records that required disclosure of the social security number under a law or regulation enacted prior to 1975, then that system is exempt from the prohibitions of the act (5 *U.S.C.S.* 552a note).

Violations of Federal Law. Generally, if one violates any of the laws just outlined, there would be attempts by the responsible federal agency to rectify the situation. If the institution continues to disregard the law, proceedings would be initiated to cut off federal funds. More important to the advisor, however, is the possibility of a suit for damages under the Civil Rights Act of 1971 if the advisor violates rights guaranteed by federal laws (*Maine*, 1980). As mentioned earlier, the courts have only awarded nominal damages unless an actual injury can be shown (*Carey*, 1978). While most advisors can afford nominal damages of one dollar, the time and energy expended in a lawsuit can be more costly. In addition, if a student successfully vindicates a statutory or constitutional right and is the prevailing party in the suit, then the student's legal fees could be assessed against the offending party (42 *U.S.C.S.* 1988). Generally, however, if advisors act in "good faith" in making decisions within the scope of their employment, then they can avoid liability. An advisor who is aware of the constitutional and statutory rights of students will be able to see that a particular situation may involve legal issues. Once that determination is made and the advisor is unsure of what action to take, seeking the advice of superiors or university counsel generally would be considered a "good faith" effort.

Torts: The Twisted Relationship

Advisors are expected to act as reasonable persons and not injure the person, property, or reputation of others. If an advisor does commit such a civil wrong, the courts will provide a remedy

to the injured student in the form of damages. Such civil wrongs
are called torts. The term is derived from a Latin word meaning
twisted. Because of the nature of their work, advisors should mainly
be concerned with the torts of negligence and defamation.

Negligence. Negligence results when a duty is breached and
an injury is caused by that breach. If there is no duty, there can be
no breach and, thus, no negligence. In institutions where students
are *required* to attend advising sessions and obtain approval for a
program of study, a student might allege negligence if he or she
were misadvised and, as a result, suffered an injury. In such a case,
by requiring students to attend advising sessions, the institution
creates a duty to provide advising. If the advice given is inaccurate
(breach of the duty by commission) or the advisor is totally
unavailable (breach of the duty by omission) and the student must
spend an extra term completing requirements as a result (injury
caused by the breach), then a finding of negligence could result.
Faculty are generally held by the courts to a standard of providing
proper supervision, maintaining equipment in a reasonable state of
repair, and providing proper instruction. The latter duty would
probably also be required of advisors.

Privileged Communications. Much of an educational advisor's activities involve conversations with students. There is often
confusion between what is legally termed "privileged communications" and what advisors refer to as "confidential communications." A privileged communication is created by state law and the
disclosure of privileged information generally may not be com-
pelled. Advisors generally do not enjoy absolutely privileged communication in the same way that physicians and lawyers do. Most
states do not even grant an absolute privilege to college or university
counselors (Knapp and Vandecreek, 1983). A confidential communication, on the other hand, would refer to information that the
advisor would not disclose except under compulsion of law or some
emergency. The term *confidentiality* usually refers to an obligation
or duty created by an ethical code of conduct. An advisor may
choose not to disclose anything a student says in an advising session
(keep it confidential), but if the advisor does not enjoy a statutorily
created privilege, a court may demand the disclosure under penalty
of law.

Educational advising sessions often include information of a very personal nature. Regardless of an advisor's intention to keep this information confidential, there may be a legal duty to disclose information gained in an advising session. If, during advising sessions, a student indicates an intent to commit serious personal injury, injure others, or destroy property, the advisor may have a legal duty to warn the intended victim or other appropriate authority. The legal duty is created by the "reasonable forseeability" of injury (Gehring, 1982). *Remember that breaching a duty that results in an injury is negligence.*

Advisors are often called upon to provide information about the qualifications of their students to enter particular programs or to be employed in certain positions. Generally, such communication enjoys a qualified privilege. In other words, advisors would not be held liable for communications provided within the official sphere of their responsibility when such communications are made without malice. However, advisors should be aware that malicious statements, or those not within the sphere of the advisor's responsibilities, could constitute the tort of defamation if the student's reputation were injured. Defamation includes libel (written) and slander (verbal) and results when one individual makes a false statement about another individual to a third party. There must also be some injury suffered, such as subjecting the person about whom the statement was made to scorn or ridicule. Thus, the best defense is to speak and write only those things that are factual. Hence, in offering information to prospective employers or others, advisors should state facts without making assumptions. For example, there is a great deal of difference between stating that a student "has been very irresponsible this term" and stating that the "student did not attend advising sessions." Advisors should also remember that generally under the Buckley Amendment, information from a student's record cannot be transmitted without the student's written consent and students have a federally protected right of access to communications that are made about them.

Several cases will help to illustrate the difference between those communications that enjoy a qualified privilege and those that do not. In one instance, a professor was asked by the university ombudsman about the qualifications of a former student to pursue her doctorate after she had twice failed her qualifying exams. The professor responded by stating that the student's performance on one of her exams had been "totally inadequate; . . . [and] she was never considered one of the star students in our department" (*Beckman*, 1980, p. 586). The professor also indicated that it would be totally unacceptable if she were to be granted a doctorate. The Pennsylvania Superior Court found the professor's remarks to be directed to a limited audience within the university and to constitute his opinion of the student's qualifications to continue. Thus, the communication was privileged (*Beckman*, 1980). In another instance, the dean of students wrote to the mother of a female student stating that she had contracted a venereal disease. When the mother brought suit against the dean for libel, the court found the statement to be privileged (*Kenney*, 1923).

Another professor who accused a graduate student of being a thief and a liar and of having problems with the Internal Revenue Service (I.R.S.) was held to have defamed the student and was assessed $200,000 in damages (*Melton*, 1978). The professor made these statements both in writing and verbally during a theft investigation; after it was concluded, the student was shown not to be involved. The Supreme Court of Georgia held that there was malice present and this was enough to overcome the professor's qualified privileged communication.

To be personally liable, an advisor must personally commit the tortious act or must be involved in some close causal way. Advisors employed at state institutions who are sued in their personal capacity for committing a tort are not usually protected by the doctrine of "sovereign immunity." If the tort results from performing a discretionary act (such as making a policy decision) that is within the advisor's assigned duties, then the advisor may be able to claim an "official immunity" defense. For at least this reason, it would be a good idea for advisors to have specific position descriptions detailing their duties. Position descriptions for advisors may be included in an advising handbook. The best defense for advisors to limit their liability, however, is to act as reasonable individuals and in the best interest of their students.

Summary

There is a great deal to know about the legal rights and responsibilities of an academic advisor. Generally, however, the courts will not interfere in academic matters unless it can be shown that students were treated arbitrarily or capriciously, that students had their constitutional, statutory, contractual, or other rights abridged, or that there is a clear abuse of discretion. Thus, advisors should have a basic familiarity with those rights and have some understanding of actions the courts have found to be arbitrary or capricious, or to constitute an abuse of discretion. This chapter has presented that information. The twenty statements listed below summarize the knowledge advisors require to avoid potential liability and thereby retain control of the advising process by the university or college.

1. Students at public institutions enjoy the rights and privileges afforded by the Constitution in their relationship with educational advisors. Students at private institutions may enjoy similar privileges if their institution is acting under "color of state" law. Advisors at public institutions also enjoy the liberties granted under the Constitution as they carry out their responsibilities.

2. Neither students nor advisors may be restrained in the exercise of their constitutional rights, nor may they be disciplined for exercising such rights.

3. There are no absolute rights, but advisors should contact legal counsel before acting in ways that might infringe on a student's right to freedom of speech, expression (written, verbal, or symbolic), assembly, association, the exercise of their religion, or their right to petition for redress of grievances. Whether carrying out institutional policies or acting on their own, advisors may not abridge students' constitutional rights.

4. Advisors should not promise students anything unless it can be provided. The statements of advisors may be binding upon the institution. Advising procedures should be stated clearly.

5. It would be beneficial to have an advising handbook that included the position description for advisors. Position de-

scriptions should include the duties and responsibilities of advisors and to whom they report.

6. There should be a clear statement of the advising policy in the catalogue and the advising handbook, including students' and advisors' rights and obligations. The policy should also detail the process by which students are assigned advisors, procedures for changing advisors, and grievance procedures.

7. Once the standards for advising have been established, the advisor must adhere to them.

8. Advisors should keep anecdotal notes of their advising sessions. If not shared with anyone else, these notes are private and students do not have a Buckley Amendment right of access to them.

9. Changes in degree or other academic requirements should be made only where the change is educationally justifiable, and students should be provided adequate notice of the change.

10. Advisors should not differentiate between students in providing advising or educational services based upon the student's race, color, sex, or national origin.

11. Advisors should be aware that every program operated by their institution must be accessible to handicapped students (assuming federal funding), and handicapped students who can meet the qualifications for the program in spite of their handicap may not be denied entry to that program.

12. Students have a general right to inspect the records an institution keeps on them. They also have a general right to decide to whom those records are released.

13. Students do not have a general right to inspect an advisor's personal notes if the advisor does not share the notes with anyone else.

14. All requests for information from a student's record, either by the student or others, should be referred to an individual on campus familiar with the Family Educational Rights and Privacy Act (F.E.R.P.A.), state law, and the institution's policy.

15. The duties defined for the advisor in the institution's advising policy must be fulfilled. A failure to do so could result in injury to a student and a possible negligence suit.

16. Advisors usually do not enjoy a statutorily created absolute privilege in their communications, and thus judicial bodies may compel disclosure of such communications. Advisors should not otherwise divulge information gained in advising sessions unless an emergency exists where there is a reasonable forseeability of injury to the student, others, or property.

17. Whenever providing information about a student, the advisor should state facts.

18. If advisors offer information about students in good faith, with the consent of the student, and in fulfillment of their duties as an advisor, that information would generally enjoy a qualified privilege and the advisor could not be held liable for what was communicated.

19. Advisors should act in the best interest of the student at all times.

20. Whenever in doubt, contact institutional counsel or other appropriate authority.

Appendix: Federal Statutes and Regulations Affecting Academic Advising.

Statute	General Provisions of the Statute and Implementing Regulations	Implications for Advisors
Title VI of the Civil Rights Act of 1964 (42 *U.S.C.* 2000d) with regulations at 34 *C.F.R.* 100 and 45 *C.F.R.* 80	This law prohibits discrimination on the basis of race, color, and national origin in programs or activities receiving federal financial assistance.	Advisors should not treat students differently on the basis of their race, color, or national origin. Students, regardless of their race, should be given an equal opportunity to participate in all the courses, programs, or activities of an institution. Advisors should be familiar with the grievance procedures in order to advise students how to proceed if they believe they have been discriminated against.
Title VII of the Civil Rights Act of 1964 (42 *U.S.C.* 2000e–2) with regulations at 29 *C.F.R.* 1601; sexual harassment guidelines at 29 *C.F.R.* 1604.11	This law prohibits discrimination in employment on the basis of race, color, sex, national origin, or religion. The law is interpreted to prohibit sexual harassment also.	Advisors cannot be discriminated against on the basis of specified criteria in employment, including the terms of their working conditions (includes office space, course or student load, location, and so on), salary, benefits, or services. Sexually intimidating or offensive environments are prohibited also, and grievance procedures should be available to resolve such problems.
Title IX of the Education Amendments of 1972 (20 *U.S.C.* 1681) with regulations at 34 *C.F.R.* 106 and 45 *C.F.R.* 86	The law prohibits discrimination on the basis of sex in educational programs and activities receiving federal financial assistance. The regulations specifically address discrimination in scheduling students in classes, advising them in finding employment, the use of appraised materials, counseling, and providing other benefits and services.	Traditional sex role stereotypes must be eliminated. Students have a right to register for any course or program of study for which they are qualified. Materials that cast individuals in stereotypical roles may not be used.
		Unless pregnant students voluntarily request to participate in a separate program or activity, they should not be treated differently.
	Discrimination in employment—of advisors, students, or others—is included under this law and	If advisors assist students to obtain jobs, they must be sure that the organization with which the student

partial status, and preemployment
inquiries.

then unless there is a bona fide occupational qualification for a position, members of a specific sex should not be employed to perform specific tasks. Remember that students of both sexes can type, carry books, and help advise students of the same or the opposite sex.

Advisors should become familiar with the procedure for handling grievances alleging sex discrimination.

Section 504 of the Rehabilitation Act of 1973 (29 *U.S.C.* 794) with regulations at 34 *C.F.R.* 104 and 45 *C.F.R.* 84

Prohibited under this law is discrimination against otherwise qualified handicapped persons in programs or activities receiving federal financial assistance. The regulations provide a broad definition of what constitutes a handicap, including anyone who has, has a record of, or who is regarded as having a handicap that limits a major life activity. While the regulations do not require all buildings to be accessible to handicapped students, they do mandate that *all* programs be accessible. Qualified handicapped students may not be denied access to a program based solely on their handicap and academic requirements that discriminate against otherwise qualified handicapped students must be modified. This might include scheduling, testing, or the way specific courses are taught. Handicapped students are also to be provided with and permitted to use devices and persons to assist them such as readers, interpreters, recorders, and similar auxiliary aids.

Services and benefits must be provided to handicapped students without discrimination. This specifically includes counseling, educational advising, and placement services.

Advisors need to be aware that they may be assigned handicapped students and these individuals are entitled to enroll in any course or program for which they are qualified. Do not assume that handicapped students cannot perform because of their handicaps.

Classes must be made accessible to handicapped students, regardless of their traditional location. Advisors must also be accessible to handicapped students, as must all other services at the institution.

Advisors should be aware of handicapped student services on the campus so that they may direct handicapped students to those services. Advisors may also want to take advantage of such services in assisting their students. For example, an advisor may wish to use a sign-language interpreter to discuss career ob-

Appendix: Federal Statutes and Regulations Affecting Academic Advising. (cont'd)

Statute	General Provisions of the Statute and Implementing Regulations	Implications for Advisors
Family Educational Rights and Privacy Act of 1974 (20 U.S.C. 1232(g)) with regulation at 34 C.F.R. 99; popularly known as the Buckley Amendment	Generally, this law requires that institutions allow students access to their educational records and that those records not be shared with anyone without the student's signed, written consent. There are a variety of exceptions to the access and the transmission requirements. Educational records are defined as those records that are directly related to a student and that are maintained by the institution. The institution must have a policy related to access, transmission, and challenging of records. Students must be informed annually of their rights under the law and the location of the policy.	jectives with a hearing impaired student or have advising instructions read on a tape for a visually impaired student. As a general rule, do not provide information over the telephone. Advisors may not share information about students with anyone unless that individual is a "school official" with a "legitimate educational interest" as defined by the institution's policy. Since there are so many exceptions and conditions to this law, advisors should refer all requests for information—either by the student or others—to university counsel, the vice-president for academic affairs, the vice-president for student affairs, or other institutional officials designated to receive such requests. Letters of recommendation should not be sent without a written, dated request from the student indicating a desire for the letter to be written and to whom it should be sent. This may either be a standard form or a handwritten note. Verbal requests from students should not be honored. Keep the written request with a copy of the letter. If students are used as peer advisors, they should have a specific informed consent from the students they are advising giving them permission to have access to particular records that might be required to

Cases Cited

Abbariao v. *Hamline University School of Law*, 258 N.W.2d 108 (Minn. 1977).

Abrams v. *Illinois College of Podiatric Medicine*, 395 N.E.2d 1061 (Ill. App. 1st Dist., 4th Div. 1979).

Alexander v. *Yale University*, 631 F.2d 178 (2d Cir. 1980).

Aronson v. *North Park College*, 418 N.E.2d 776 (Ill. App. 1st Dist., 1st Div. 1981).

Basch v. *George Washington University*, 370 A.2d 1364 (D.C. Ct. App. 1977).

Beckman v. *Dunn*, 419 A.2d 583 (Sup. Ct., Pa. 1980).

Behrend v. *State*, 379 N.E.2d 617 (Ohio App., Franklin Cty. 1977).

Blank v. *Board of Higher Education of City of New York*, 273 N.Y.S.2d 796 (S. Ct. Sp. Term, Kings Cty. 1966).

Bob Jones University v. *Johnson*, 396 F. Supp. 597 (D.S.C. Greenville 1974).

Burton v. *Wilmington Parking Authority*, 365 U.S. 715 (1961).

Camenisch v. *University of Texas*, 616 F.2d 127 (5th Cir. 1980).

Carey v. *Piphus*, 98 S. Ct. 1042 (1978).

Clayton v. *Trustees of Princeton University*, 519 F. Supp. 802 (D.N.J. 1981).

Connelly v. *University of Vermont and State Agricultural College*, 244 F. Supp. 156 (D. Vt. 1965).

Delta School of Business, Etc. v. *Shropshire*, 399 So.2d 1212 (La. App. 1st Dist. 1981).

DeMarco v. *University of Health Sciences*, 352 N.E.2d 356 (Ill. App. 1st Dist., 4th Div. 1976).

Dizick v. *Umpqua Community College*, 599 P.2d 444 (Ore. 1979).

Doe v. *New York University*, 666 F.2d 761 (2d Cir. 1981).

Drucker v. *New York University*, 293 N.Y.S.2d 923 (Civ. Ct., Queens Cty. 1968).

Eisle v. *Ayers*, 381 N.E.2d 21 (Ill. App. 1st Dist., 3rd Div. 1978).

Grafton v. *Brooklyn Law School*, 478 F.2d 1137 (2d Cir. 1973).

Greene v. *Howard University*, 271 F. Supp. 609 (D.D.C. 1967).

Healy v. *Larsson*, 323 N.Y.S.2d 625 (S. Ct. Sp. Term., Schenectady Cty. 1971).

Heisler v. *New York Medical College*, 449 N.Y.S.2d 834 (S. Ct., Westchester Cty. 1982).

Hillsdale College v. *Department of Health, Education and Welfare,* 696 F.2d 418 (6th Cir. 1982).

Hines v. *Rinker,* 667 F.2d 699 (8th Cir. 1981).

Holloway v. *University of Montana,* 582 P.2d 1265 (Mont. 1978).

Jones v. *Illinois Department of Rehabilitation Services,* 689 F.2d 724 (7th Cir. 1982).

Jones v. *Vassar College,* 299 N.Y.S.2d 283 (S. Ct., Dutchess Cty. 1969).

Joyner v. *Albert Merrill School,* 411 N.Y.S.2d 988 (Civ. Ct., N.Y. Cty. 1978).

Kantor v. *Schmidt,* 423 N.Y.S.2d 208 (S. Ct. App. Div., 2nd Dept. 1979).

Kenney v. *Gurley,* 95 So. 34 (Ala. 1923).

Krawez v. *Stans,* 306 F. Supp. 1230 (E.D. N.Y. 1969).

Littsey v. *Board of Governors of Wayne State University,* 310 N.W.2d 399 (Mich. App. 1981).

Lyons v. *Salve Regina College,* 565 F.2d 200 (1st Cir. 1977).

Maas v. *Corporation of Gonzaga University,* 618 P.2d 106 (Wa. App. Div. 3, Panel 1 1980).

Mahavongsana v. *Hall,* 401 F. Supp. 381 (N.D. Ga. Atlanta 1975).

Mahavongsana v. *Hall,* 529 F.2d 448 (5th Cir. 1976).

Maine v. *Thiboutot,* 100 S. Ct. 2502 (1980).

Melton v. *Bow,* 247 S.E.2d 100 (Ga. 1978).

Olsson v. *Board of Higher Education of City of New York,* 426 N.Y.S.2d 248 (1980).

Papish v. *Board of Curators of University of Missouri,* 93 S. Ct. 1197 (1973).

Peretti v. *State of Montana,* 464 F. Supp. 784 (D. Mont., Missoula Div. 1979).

Plyler v. *Doe,* 457 U.S. 202 (1982).

Rankins v. *Commission on Professional Competence of Ducor Union School District,* 593 P.2d 852 (Ca. 1979).

Regents of the University of California v. *Bakke,* 98 S. Ct. 2733 (1978).

Schornstein v. *New Jersey Division of Vocational Rehabilitation Services,* 519 F. Supp. 773 (D.N.J. 1981).

Shuffer v. *Board of Trustees of California State University and Colleges,* 136 Cal. Rptr. 527 (Ct. App. 2nd Dist., Div. 4 1977).

Southeastern Community College v. *Davis*, 99 S. Ct. 2361 (1979).

State Board of Regents of University v. *Gray*, 561 S.W.2d 140 (Tenn. 1978).

Steinberg v. *Chicago Medical School*, 371 N.E.2d 634 (Ill. 1977).

Stern v. *Shouldice*, 706 F.2d 742 (6th Cir. 1983).

Tanner v. *Board of Trustees of University of Illinois*, 363 N.E.2d 208 (Ill. App. 4th Dist. 1977).

Tedeschi v. *Wagner College*, 427 N.Y.S.2d 760 (1980).

Tinker v. *Des Moines Independent Community School District*, 393 U.S. 503 (1969).

Trans World Airlines, Inc. v. *Hardison*, 97 S. Ct. 2264 (1977).

University of Texas Health Science Center v. *Babb*, 646 S.W.2d 502 (Tex. App. 1st Dist. 1982).

Wilson v. *Illinois Benedictine College*, 445 N.E.2d 901 (Ill. App. 2nd Dist. 1983).

Wright v. *Columbia University*, 520 F. Supp. 789 (E.D. Pa. 1981).

Wright v. *Texas Southern University*, 392 F.2d 728 (5th Cir. 1968).

Yakin v. *University of Illinois, Etc.*, 508 F. Supp. 848 (N.D. Ill. E.D. 1981).

References

Gehring, D. D. "Students." In D. P. Young (Ed.), *The Yearbook of Higher Education Law*. Topeka, Kans.: National Organization for Legal Problems in Education, 1978, pp. 116-209.

Gehring, D. D. "The Counselor's Duty to Warn." *Personnel and Guidance Journal*, 1982, *61*, 208-210.

Knapp, S., and Vandecreek, L. "Privileged Communications and the Counselor." *Personnel and Guidance Journal*, 1983, *62*, 83-85.

Levine, A. *When Dreams and Heroes Died: A Portrait of Today's College Student*. San Francisco: Jossey-Bass, 1980.

Young, D. P. "Legal Issues Regarding Academic Advising." *National Academic Advising Association (NACADA) Journal*, 1982, *2* (2), 41-45.

15

Improving Advising
Knowledge and Skills
Through Faculty Development

❧❧❧❧❧❧❧❧

Howard C. Kramer, Robert E. Gardner

Academic advising should be designed to facilitate the educational mission of the institution and to assist students in achieving personally relevant academic objectives. This chapter explores means by which the advising program may be linked with another institutional program, faculty development.

The term *faculty development* has become a common part of educational lexicon as institutions have recognized that special programs are necessary to assist change and spark faculty interest and productivity. Since faculty are trained in graduate schools largely to perform research in their disciplines, they have little cross-disciplinary background, inclination, and understanding; little training in the pedagogical nuances needed in teaching; and inadequate awareness of skills in the organizational and administrative techniques and requirements of other parts of their roles

(Bess, 1982b). Given the emphasis on instruction, it is not surprising that most faculty development efforts have centered on the teaching function. This head-on approach is not without difficulty: Some faculty do not feel the need to be developed, some believe that teaching is an art not easily enhanced, and still others feel that classroom interactions are sacred rites not open to improvement from the outside. For these reasons, it may be that more positive results can be obtained from a subtle approach, producing the desired results by exploring areas not directly seen as teaching. As Lewis and Becker (1979) pointed out, when there is interest in having faculty acquire new skills, there is utility in examining the characteristics of desired faculty activities that can bring satisfaction and in creating situations in which satisfactions can be found more readily. Because there are many parallels between advising and teaching, and indeed because developmental advising incorporates many concepts relevant to teaching, there is reason to suggest that a developmental advising program might address the same issues and be an integrated part of a faculty development program. The fact that the connection is not immediately obvious to faculty may well prove to be a significant advantage.

A number of assumptions are made in this chapter that lay a foundation for what follows. First, it is assumed that the institution is committed to quality academic advising and the delivery of advising through faculty members who are involved in teaching and research. In this context, one ought not to forget that Dornbush (1979) discovered that faculty wanted to direct their efforts toward those tasks whose evaluations were more influential. Such commitment should find expression through funding and through assigning responsibility for this activity to one person, the advising coordinator. Second, it is assumed the institution is committed to faculty development and that this commitment is expressed in a similar, realistic manner. Third, it is assumed that the person responsible for academic advising has an interest in weaving the two functions together as an approach for improving the academic advising program of the institution.

Throughout the chapter, teaching and advising are treated as synonymous terms, in that both are variants of the same theme—instruction. Furthermore, each should be viewed as having a conceptual framework that may be used to provide structure and meaning to the activity. In addition, each may be discussed in terms of goals, objectives, methods, and outcomes that accrue when the conceptual framework is used as a guide to application in practice. This linkage between the two functions is especially important for it allows faculty to view advising as an extension of the teaching role rather than as an addition to it.

Also, throughout the chapter, the role of advising coordinator is a prominent one. This position refers to the person charged by the institution to manage, coordinate, monitor, or direct some portion of the advising program. In many colleges and universities, the program is designed for students in the freshman and sophomore classes. In large-enrollment institutions, the advising program may be designed for students who have not declared an undergraduate major. In any event, in every institution there should exist some person who may be described as the advising coordinator. This chapter, then, is directed at the theoretical conceptions, planning activities, and operational duties that are part of the role of the advising coordinator.

Faculty Development as a Foundation

One critical task for the coordinator is to take the need for faculty development and meet it through a developmental advising program, rather than via a head-on approach in workshops on teaching. The stated objective is to develop faculty through the advising program. Another prominent task is to use faculty development to establish a developmental advising program, for this will accomplish the stated objective, as well as benefit students. Getting such a scheme off the ground will require selling the idea to influential persons, both faculty and administration, who are identified as opinion formers on campus, particularly if advising is a low priority in the community. It is not a task that can best be done by submitting a proposal because few know what developmental advising is, and the result will be that the idea will be rejected out-of-hand. It is better done by identifying the critical opinion formers, particularly on the faculty, and talking to them about conditions in education and the need for programs to increase the value of faculty to the institution. In an informal atmosphere, it will be easy to brainstorm ways the desired faculty development might be attained, with one idea being use of the advising system. One way to get this idea on the table is to think by analogy, that is, of teaching situations that occur outside the classroom, particularly one-on-one, that involve the exchange of information and foster intellectual development and critical thinking. Advising, one can argue, is one such situation.

This person-to-person scenario by the coordinator could be repeated with all persons on campus who are in a position to be supportive of improved faculty development, with different analogues used in the brainstorming sessions with different individuals. For example, administrators may want to think of ways to cut costs by accomplishing two goals with the same program and may therefore find the idea of incorporating faculty development and advising an attractive one. Or department chairpersons who are concerned about the quality of teaching in their departments may be sensitive to the need to improve the quality of advising; they may find an approach that addresses both concerns more attractive than one that meets them separately. Furthermore, the persons responsible for faculty development may be in search of stimulating programs that will increase the stature and power of their particular area of responsibility and also give them an increased role in the institution. The point is simple: Touch base with everyone of stature on campus who supports faculty development and gently encourage them to think about advising as a possible way to achieve the desired goals.

At the same time, it is prudent to discover those who are opposed to faculty development programs, to assess their strength on campus and to understand the reasons behind their opposition. Is there a chance they might be supportive of a program that does not directly threaten them, where they would not support a program focusing on an activity like teaching (that they assume they have mastered)? Since few would claim to have mastered advising or even to have considered it important, would they be more willing to consider a training program designed to improve their advising skills, rather than one aimed at improving their teaching skills? If the answer is yes, a potential opponent becomes an advocate. Many faculty opposed to faculty development (when this means an emphasis on teaching) are not opposed to similar efforts in advising, and they can be added to those who support faculty development for our particular effort. For this reason, it is important to talk with those who oppose faculty development per se, as well as those who support it.

The process just described is what Kurt Lewin (1951) called the force-field analysis. He proposed that any given level of behavior is a situation of a quasi-stationary equilibrium in a field of forces. A balance exists because the driving forces that exert pressure toward changing are countered by restraining forces that exert pressure against changing. By charting the results of discussions with those supportive of faculty development and those opposed to it, the coordinator is creating an analysis of forces for and forces against such efforts. In short, a force-field analysis of faculty development or advising may be completed.

In all these activities designed to promote developmental advising, it may be useful to talk about the reason for thinking about advising. Specifically, it may be worth mentioning that the reason is not only to improve service to students but also to improve the skills of the faculty. Too often advising is promoted as a student service when, in fact, the primary reason for undertaking advising is a selfish one for both the faculty member and the institution. Although effective advising is important for students, it also assists faculty and helps develop the institution and its program. This is important to stress because many faculty have not thought of advising in this way before. One basic reason for advising by faculty, as opposed to advising provided by students or professional advisors, is the desirable impact of this activity on the faculty who offer the service.

Once the groundwork has been laid and the notion that developmental advising might be used as a vehicle for faculty development is accepted as a legitimate possibility, it is time to organize selected supporters in a "planning group" to study the issue more closely. This can be done by selecting a series of books or articles for discussion in weekly sessions, perhaps with each person taking responsibility for one session per term. Outside speakers who are familiar with developmental advising might be invited to campus for a seminar or a colloquium or be asked to comment on a specific topic. Members of the group might seek funds to visit another campus where a developmental program is in place in order to determine the views of the faculty, students, and administration about the scheme. Once familiarity with the basic ideas is achieved, the group should draw up a "plan" for the institution: If developmental advising were to be implemented as part of the faculty development program, what would it look like? What would it cost? What kinds of training would be necessary? How would start-up be achieved? Steady state maintained? If the group has been drawn from opinion formers who support development for the faculty and if a reasonable amount of research on developmental advising was carried out, there is an excellent chance of having the plan approved. It is understood, of course, that the level of administrative acceptance of the plan and its probability of success are positively correlated. That is to say, the greater the degree of plan acceptance by the administrative hierarchy, influential committees, and powerful opinion leaders in the academic community, the greater the chance of plan implementation and acceptance.

Planning and Building Support

Following the acceptance of the plan by institutional leaders, the coordinator must go about the initial steps of building support for the plan within the institution. Academic institutions, like factories, have particular patterns of beliefs, values, and practices shared by all who teach there (Sanford, 1982). This culture heavily influences what professors do; hence efforts to alter institutional practices regarding advising must acknowledge and build upon existing institutional mores. A simple approach to finding out what faculty think is to ask them. A program of informal visits and discussions about advising with a small sample of junior and senior faculty, department heads, college officials, and students can do wonders in creating a mosaic of the institution's present perspectives on advising. This activity of the advising coordinator literally moving about campus talking to persons about their views of advising provides not only information but plants seeds for an emerging advising network as well. This interview intervention, across the many boundaries between subsystems in the institution, begins to treat advising for what it is, both a problem and an opportunity for the institution. Interviewing serves to open boundaries, to broaden the range of allowable experience and behavior, and to enlarge and enrich people's perceptions of others (Sanford, 1982).

No faculty development program can take place unless faculty members themselves want it (Freedman, 1979). Following the interviews, it is necessary to create conditions that will stimulate faculty members to think about their institutional situation, the arena of advising, and their own development. The next step in building social support structures for the discussion of advising is a systematic discussion of the interview results with those who were interviewed. The advising coordinator should analyze the interviews, distribute a draft interpretative report to the participants, and give them an opportunity, in groups of ten or so persons, to discuss the findings. The discussion session should center on the educational issues pertaining to the advising issue yet, concurrently, should provide ample opportunity for personal reflection and response. Herein lies the opportunity for faculty members to discover common points of view and the fact that advising is a complex challenge that requires improved performance.

Because organizational climates have a powerful influence on people's feelings (Nord, 1982, p. 50), a companion activity to the interviews must be fostering a positive institutional climate. This translates into the nature of the physical facilities used for the group meetings to the type of announcements, communiques, or reports about these events. After all, if advising is to become an important component within the institution, then treat it as such by meeting in the best location the institution has to offer. Conversely, meeting in some third-rate (that is, small, crowded, hot) seminar room only serves to convince observers that advising is another area of the institution in which there is a discrepancy between talk and action.

Similarly, according to Nord (1982), in all phases of communication—letters and publications, interactions with large groups, and one-on-one sessions—large numbers of stimuli that elicit emotions are present. Before, during, and following the interviews, the coordinator and other institutional officials can use communication not only to accomplish the short-run goal of information transmission but as an opportunity to present stimuli that evoke the feelings they wish to develop that contribute to the "motivation" to advise. For example, clear and consistent use of terms such as *excellence, opportunity,* and *creative,* in contrast to *routine, difficult,* or *required,* evoke quite different feelings about advising in the listener. Care given to the use of language about advising requires not only an understanding of the current attitude of the institution about advising but it also requires a conceptual map, expressed in behavioral terms, of the outcomes the coordinator wishes to achieve.

A third action designed to gather support for the advising program centers on the use of ceremonies, rituals, and symbols. The coordinator should encourage persons in the institution to take advantage of opportunities, or to create new ones, to elicit emotions that encourage advising excellence by the faculty and a demand for advising excellence by the students. According to Nord (1982), the search for ways to schedule and utilize ritualistic activities and ceremonies as opportunities to "work up the group to prepare faculty to be responsive" seems very worthwhile (p. 51). Within every institutional calendar, such events as the advent of summer visitations by prospective students, orientation programs for new students, beginning of term convocations, faculty meetings, board of trustee events, and special programs scheduled during the academic year offer opportunities to engage the audience by appealing to the past successes and shared values, as well as to raise expectations of what advising is or should be. What is suggested, then, is that opportunities available in the regularly scheduled events of any institution should be used to dramatize the value, and the results, associated with effective advising.

Orientation to the Program

A central concept in sociotechnical theory is that of the *primary task,* which is the task that an organization must perform if it is to survive and prosper. A major objective for the advising coordinator is to orient faculty to the concept that advising is a part of the primary task of the institution. Within orientation program efforts, the coordinator must provide for discussion of three primary tasks related to advising. First, there should be discussion of the *normative* primary task, that is, the advising activity that people in the organization ought to pursue. Second, discussion should focus on the *existential* primary task, that is, the advising activity faculty members believe they are carrying out. Third, discussion should also focus on the *phenomenal* primary task, that is, the advising activity that faculty members are actually engaged in but of which they may not be aware.

It is important that the orientation program be viewed as an organization development effort where the user system, the faculty, has a problem that must be solved. Coordinator efforts to carry out the orientation program serve as a linkage process (Havelock, 1973) to (1) help the client define the problem and (2) put the client (that is, the faculty advisors) in contact with resources appropriate to the situation.

Buhler-Miko (1981) suggests that planning models can assist colleges and universities in the creation of a sense of community and, through this, promote a healthy quality of life for faculty members as well as improved teaching and learning for students. The orientation program, as a planning model, serves as a systematic procedure for engaging the institution in an analysis of advising at the institution.

First, the orientation program as a planning model asks faculty trained in various disciplines and drawn from all parts of the institution to examine *what they think* in regard to advising. A part of this examination is the refinement of ideas based on a model, or models, of how advising affects the education of students—ideas that in themselves are intellectually challenging. Furthermore, the discussion encourages the faculty to examine the values they hold about advising, teaching, learning, their institution, and, indeed, themselves as scholars, thinkers, and persons.

Second, the orientation program requires faculty and administrators to *interact* about the ideas they generate. Notions about the academy as a collegial environment notwithstanding, we are continually surprised at the positive effect generated by workshops that provide opportunities for faculty members to talk seriously about the intellectual pros and cons of various advising ideas and proposals.

Third, the orientation program gives faculty and administrators an opportunity to think about the institution or the advising program as *an entire system*. Since most personnel, either by function or training, have compartmentalized duties within the institution, they rarely have the opportunity to think globally about the institution and its needs. Here, participants gain from the opportunities to share perceptions, assumptions, and facts about the institution and its operation.

Fourth, the orientation program sets the stage for faculty and administrators to begin to *make choices* and to get involved in a complex set of decisions regarding advising. Questions of need, priority, strategy, feasibility, and implementation must be raised, discussed, and resolved.

Finally, the orientation process begins the stepwise progression that encourages faculty and administrators to *take responsibility* and to develop a sense of ownership for the proposals that are finally enacted as procedure. The sense of community developed by the orientation process provides, as suggested by Nisbet (1973), legitimacy to authority and function. Without the sense of community and the sense of ownership created by the orientation process, no advising program, no matter how intricate and sophisticated the planning process, will be legitimated by the institutional community.

McKeachie (1982) suggests that intrinsic satisfactions are derived from such things as satisfying relationships with students and colleagues, from intellectual stimulation, and from a sense of freedom and autonomy in carrying out one's job with a sense of personal control and efficacy. It seems that a properly conceived and implemented program of orientation to advising may be used to help the faculty define the need, determine a course of action, and set in motion those institutional and personal forces that supplement, rather than sabotage, a revitalization in the advising program. This perspective is in accord with Buhler-Miko's (1981) comment that it is of the utmost importance that schools reestablish the basic value of the institution as a community of learners, not only in the way faculty conduct their teaching but also in all the other forms and functions that they, and others, develop on campus. The revival of the advising program as a vital function surely falls within those parameters.

Training Program

McKeachie (1979) has noted that any plan for reassignment needs to include an analysis of the skills required and an opportunity to develop those skills. Training programs provide the mechanism for developing advising skills.

Activities. Metz (1978) has looked at training sessions in depth and arranged the levels of activities identified in the following hierarchy:

1. *academic information:* awareness of policy and practice with the system
2. *process skills:* awareness of decision-making techniques as related to short- and long-range planning; ability to convey process to students
3. *interpersonal skills:* awareness of relating to persons in individual/group settings; emphasis on listening and feedback skills
4. *environmental perspective:* awareness of where the student is "coming from," geographically, socially, culturally, including on- and off-campus environments
5. *developmental perspective:* awareness of cognitive-affective development of adolescents and young adults

Developmental advising issues fall under levels 2, 3, and 5 in this scheme. Metz (1978) has also indicated that the vast majority of programs never get past the first level in the hierarchy; consequently, it is worth noting that in discussing the training sessions for developmental programs, one is often plowing new ground. Current practice in many training programs is to spend most of the time in training on a small amount of material (level 1), leaving little time for the remaining developmental functions and their accompanying material. The goal, of course, is to reverse this allocation of time and resources; the procedure used to accomplish this is to view a training *program* as an ongoing series, not only as a single September start-up episode. (See Chapter Sixteen for similarities related to paraprofessional training.)

In this regard, it is worth making several observations about the scheme suggested by Metz since it can be used as a hierarchical structure for a program at a particular institution. He suggested seven points:

- A training program must take the participants from the first level to the last, but it need not do so in the span of a single year.
- As one moves from 1 to 5, the degree of difficulty for presenter and participants increases, as does the degree of experience and expertise necessary to have a successful session.
- The program stands as a sequence. Each prior program serves as a foundation to the next and it is best not to omit levels or to reverse the order.
- As one moves from 1 to 5, the size of the group should decrease. Sessions on level 1 can be done easily in large groups and require no practice, while later sessions should be attempted in smaller groups with opportunities being made for practice.
- As one moves from level 1 to 5, the threat to the participant increases in terms of competence and self-esteem.
- The sequence parallels the sequence that may develop in an advising relationship, from basic procedural information giving to developmental themes, and thus alerts participants to the evolution of advising interactions.
- The sequence moves from the specific to the general; the first workshop on information is institution-specific. Later modules are applicable to students at all institutions.

From the foregoing, one thing should be obvious: Developmental advising cannot be achieved by "lifting" a few of the training modules relating to developmental issues and plunking them down in an existing faculty development structure. The program must consist of all the levels if success is to be a high-probability event. However, the session could profitably be blended into a faculty development program, particularly by relating two parallel tracks on advising as teaching. A session on the teaching of content in the classroom could be matched with a session on "teaching" the content of advising. This would give additional weight to the idea that advising is a form of teaching and thereby foster the view that developmental advising is closely related to faculty development as it applies to life in the classroom. The two "tracks" come together clearly at the fifth level, when intellectual development becomes the focus.

   Defining Advising as Decision Making. One of the ways it is possible to introduce developmental advising is to begin with the idea that all advising involves a decision in one form or another, or the advising would not take place. In this way, advising can be described as decision making and an advising interaction as an opportunity to teach students decision-making skills. Such a definition lends itself to a discussion of several related observations:

- Decision making is a rational process but it is influenced by nonrational considerations.
- Decision making is a process that is composed of identifiable steps: information gathering, listing alternatives, evaluating alternatives, deciding deadlines for action, and so on.
- Advising is teaching in that decision making can be taught and in the sense that teaching involves listening and facilitating skills.
- Since teaching involves having influence with those being taught, establishing a supportive relationship is a prelude to the teaching of decision making.

Using a decision-making definition of advising (not the only one that could be used), participants can add further observations/ implications to the list. Such items can then be used as an agenda for additional sessions and, at the same time, serve as the structure for working in a developmental view of advising.

   While there are many different definitions of advising, experience has tended to show that it is not wise to use a more developmental definition of advising at the outset of the training program. Advising defined as decision making is an approach that most faculty can agree with: They see themselves as highly rational, they see their function in the institution as teaching students to be rational, and they see decision making as a valuable rational exercise. In contrast, developmental definitions of advising are often viewed as "counseling"—an activity that faculty do not see as appropriate or interesting, or that they see as something that lies outside the domain of faculty and within the domain of professional counselors. Because it is very important not to reduce interest before the program gains momentum, one should begin with a definition that will build common ground and that is not far removed from the overall emphasis on faculty development related to teaching. Chapter One discusses what advising "is not" and then defines it in a way that can be used in this phase of faculty development.

The other advantage to using the concept of "advising as decision making" is that it is a process that is easily understood and taught. While it is difficult to "teach" the advising process to advisors, it is easier to assist them in learning the steps in the decision-making process. In a follow-up workshop to defining advising, one can analyze the steps in a decision-making process that advisors want to teach their students: gathering information, listing options, evaluating choices, assigning time lines, and so forth. These steps can be converted into advising strategies by the participants, often by taking some elementary examples from the first workshop on information giving. "What course should I take?" is a common advising question that can be easily used, by explaining the contrast between advising as providing the answer and advising as viewing the question as an opportunity to teach the decision-making process so the student can find the answer for himself or herself. Such a comparison is useful in later sessions where developmental schemes provide clues for determining which advising strategy to use in a given instance.

Students' Intellectual Development. From the teaching of decision making, it is but a short step to understanding the intellectual development of students, since this governs how they approach rational decision making. Enter here the model of intellectual development offered by William Perry (1970), for Perry's descriptions of the levels of developing relativistic thinking are directly related to such steps as gathering information in decision making. A student operating at position 1 is likely to make a decision based on the authority of the information giver, not on the

assessment of various options, which is characteristic of a student
in the positions of multiplicity. Similarly, a student who has
mastered relativistic thinking may well understand the need to
gather information and carry out a plan of action, a behavior that
is explained quite well using Perry's scheme. Just as it is important
to start with advising as rational decision making to establish
common ground with faculty, so it is important to start with a
developmental scheme that focuses on intellectual development; it
is very difficult for faculty to deny the importance of understanding,
and fostering, intellectual development as part of their role in the
institution. As Perry observes, this fostering can occur through the
challenge of classroom activities or through the guidance and
support of advising activities. The choice may not be if it is done,
but how it is done.

   A discussion of the work of Perry can lead to an understanding of what is meant by a "developmental" scheme or theory and,
in turn, to an investigation of other developmental schemes that
have been proposed to explain the behavior of students. These
schemes could become the focus of additional workshop and
training sessions, they could become the focus of small study
groups, or they could be assimilated through the distribution of
readings. However, it is important to keep in mind that it is not
necessary to fully understand or master any or all of the various
schemes, and it is not wise to get bogged down in the study of details
or exercise all our critical faculties on the minutiae of various
paradigms. The importance lies in the relation of the schemes to the
advising process per se. To accomplish growth in this area, it is
worthwhile studying the applications of developmental training in
the literature and in having faculty advisors use workshop time to
suggest how the scheme might pertain to practice. Chapter Seven
in this book makes an excellent resource for advisors to use as an
introduction.

   One way of getting to this is to draw up a list of common
advising situations, such as course selection, that occur with great
frequency and then to draw up a "course of action" or strategy that
is based on a knowledge of the various developmental schemes. In
this way, a matrix is produced that represents a repertoire of skills
that have their base in sound theory and experience. From this

exercise, it is easy to begin to apply these strategies for practice in role-playing situations. This is best done in small groups, often in "triads," with one person playing the student, another the advisor, and a third being an observer to record and remark upon the interaction. It is safer and easier to use videotape examples prior to role playing, and if one wishes to make them locally, it is easy to write a script and recruit students to provide the action, or one may use some of the tapes and films currently on the market. Whatever the technique used, the critical parts are to have the advisors generate the frequently encountered situations, to use the theory to suggest appropriate courses of action, and to practice the applications in a nonthreatening environment. If a matrix is generated that lists situations down the side and theories or schemes of development across the top, a skills development program for an entire year can easily be generated.

Follow-Up

In the preceding section, the methods employed in a development program involved working with groups of various sizes, from large groups for informational sessions to smaller groups arranged in triads for practicing skills to be used in a developmental advising scheme. This program or activity should be viewed primarily as a way to introduce concepts, principles, applications, and techniques, but it may not represent a method for mastering such activities. Mastery comes with practice and a genuine interest in learning the techniques at hand, and because a high degree of openness is required, it is not likely to occur in a group setting. If one keeps in mind that faculty development is viewed as a desirable, but potentially threatening, activity for faculty, one begins to understand that it is necessary to adopt a different model of interaction if the program is to succeed.

Individual Consultant Model. Experience to date suggests that a consulting model is the most appropriate one. Or to put it in the context of the many parallels this discussion has attempted to stress, the idea is to engage the faculty member in a relationship that is similar to developmental advising with students—only in this case the advising coordinator (or faculty development program coordinator) is the "advisor" and the faculty member is the "student."

The idea, then, is to establish an advising relationship with some of the faculty members in the faculty development program who, concurrently, are also serving as student advisors. Many of the techniques used with students will work equally well with faculty. Such notions as intrusive advising, communications skills, career decision making, and so on are no less valuable because the "student" is older and involved in teaching as well as learning. If the person in charge of the advisor-consulting program has mastered these techniques as they apply to students, there should be little problem in using them in a new interaction. Perhaps even more importantly, any faculty member who has mastered developmental advising skills with students is in a position to serve as a mentor to faculty who have not mastered such skills. After a period of time, the advising coordinator need no longer do all the work but can use the core of trained faculty that come from the first generation of training activity to work with the second generation of advisor trainees.

One drawback to this technique is that the content of this advising process with faculty is different, even though the techniques are much the same, and this occurs because the development of faculty, intellectually and otherwise, is not necessarily the same as the process outlined by Perry for students. Earlier, the point was made that it is important to become familiar with developmental schemes relating to college students and to "translate" this knowledge into strategies delivered through techniques. To work with faculty in an advising relationship suggests that it is equally important to become familiar with "faculty" development models, so that one can reiterate the process to produce relevant strategies.

In his study of the adult development of faculty members, Newton (1983) suggests that the life structure is the overall design of a person's life at a given time, and it evolves over the years. It has central and peripheral components, and these require integration if the life is to be coherent and satisfying. He underscores the importance of this understanding, concluding that "the life structure, in its manner and level of integration and contradiction, inclusiveness and exclusiveness of parts of self and environment, contains the dynamic of its own growth and change, and of change in personality and environment as well" (p. 442). His research led Newton to the view that adulthood, like childhood and adolescence, consists of a sequence of age-linked eras and periods, so that the work of the professor is different at age sixty than at age forty or the mid-twenties, even when the concrete activities are the same.

There are two developmental themes that are relevant here, the first being the variety of developmental models that address the stages of adult development and aging, since faculty are not exempt from normal adult development themes. The second is the specific development of academic professionals that must be interwoven with many issues of adult development generally. Faculty members, for example, who are experiencing middlessence or mid-life crisis (or whatever term one wishes to choose) may also find themselves in the middle stages of an academic career, when the attractiveness of research begins to wane, the hoped-for full professorship is no longer a reality, and the excitement of teaching the same old survey course has long disappeared. Current theories of development of the self suggest that one of the most important aspects of personality for most individuals is a sense of self-competence and self-efficiency. One of the reasons that faculty development programs are particularly important in these critical times for higher education is that if we are to nurture intrinsic satisfaction in teaching, we need to help both young and old teachers develop a greater sense of self-competency and self-efficiency; that is, we need to help them carry out their course planning and their classroom activities with a sense that they are doing them well (McKeachie, 1982, p. 11). Present knowledge of such subjects is meager at best, and it may well be that the career stages vary substantially from one type of institution to another, making the literature less relevant to a particular situation. In any case, it may be sketched in by interviewing persons in a position to know. Most faculty want to talk about their situations, and there is much to be gained by talking with faculty in different stages of their careers to understand the broad general issues they find confronting them.

Some care should be exercised in selecting the faculty members who will be the "advisees" in the faculty development/advising program. Clearly, the set from which they should come is composed of those faculty already part of the overall program who are, presumably, advising students at the same time. Within this group there are a number of options: (1) select a small number of individuals that are likely to be receptive and to help the coordinator learn as the program progresses, acting as advisor or consultant to a few persons from each level of faculty development identified from earlier research; (2) issue a broad invitation to the group as a whole and let those who think they want to be involved opt to do so; (3) using a brief instrument, or available data, arrange the entire group into smaller groups of individuals judged to be at the same developmental level and work with each group; or (4) select one group of individuals at the same level and specialize with this group. If the latter course is chosen, it may be best to work with a group in the advanced stages of their career since one may presume they have been through many of the developmental levels and can share these experiences and because they are in a good position to undertake the same kind of activities with younger faculty members later on. Just as senior students made suitable advisors for freshmen, so trained senior faculty may become "peer" advisors for their younger colleagues. In the developmental scheme, it is easier to teach and to understand if one has experienced the steps firsthand. Schneider and Zalesny (1982) suggest that mentoring in academicians is another career avenue they take, but that such mentoring behavior is likely only in those who have been relatively successful in gratifying their central needs through their academic work, whether that work be teaching, research, or both.

If the consultant mode is elected, then once the individuals have been selected, the next task is to establish a "contract," just as advisors should establish a "contract" with the students they advise. Contract in this sense does not imply a written document or the use of legalistic jargon; it implies a negotiation of the mutual rights and responsibilities of both parties along with a statement of the objectives of the relationship. This step is critical to a smooth relationship and later evaluation of the success of the endeavor. The purpose of this particular contract is to help individual faculty members master developmental advising skills by focusing on faculty development in an individual context, so that the faculty member is working with the coordinator on advising tasks relating to faculty careers or functions. It implies introspective work after each session, to analyze techniques and the degree of success and to identify explicitly those strategies that were involved. In many ways, it is a role-playing exercise "for real," because the content is of vital importance to the faculty member, much as advising content is for any student. If faculty members have trouble with the term *contract*, one may want to draw parallels with the contract, implied or explicit, that all faculty have with students when they teach a particular course.

One of the functions of the contracting exercise is to identify, or have the faculty members seek to identify, areas of need that they would like to work on during the course of the relationship. These should be related to their development as faculty members, and although these involve personal issues as well, it is best to avoid the implication that the exercise is equivalent to therapy. Another function is to have faculty think about their level of professional development and the skills that are most well developed, as well as those skills that are most in need of further development, in view of future roles in the institution, including advising as well as teaching. Needs do not have to relate to skills. One need faculty members may have is to study the literature on adult development and on student development as a way of gaining knowledge about the subject, just as one might advise students about courses that they should take in order to gain knowledge of a particular subject area. However expressed, when the "contract" is completed, both advisor and faculty "advisee" should have a reasonable idea of the territory that will be covered during the coming year.

Working with Groups. It has been increasingly recognized, for example, by the increase in number of programs at national conferences, that there may be productive ways of advising that go beyond the mentor or consultant mode, namely, working with groups. Earlier, a number of options were listed for follow-up programs, including several that involved working with groups of faculty members judged to be at the same stage of development, rather than a series of individuals. One of the advantages of working with groups is that more persons can participate in the program per unit of time. A second advantage is that the members of the group can share their experiences and insights. This is particularly true when using readings related to developmental schemes and other topics that might be covered in a manner similar to ways one structures a seminar. There are also many advantages to working with a group in teaching and practicing skills, since the strategies can find expression in many different ways. One of the disadvantages is that many faculty and staff are typically more skilled in working with individuals, having practiced this interaction in advising students on many occasions, than they are in working with groups. Groups have a life of their own and one ought to be a student of groups before attempting to lead them, especially in areas of sensitive, personal issues. Consequently, it is usually much easier to perform well one-on-one than it is to do the same job in a group setting. Unless one is willing to undertake some course work in group behavior, it may be better to use the individual consultant model.

Although forming groups of faculty at the same developmental level facilitates sharing and discussion because there is a common agenda and interest, it might be worth organizing groups where those present are at different levels and thus in a position to "advise" other group members, based on their experience. The idea here is that the older members of the group have experience of various developmental levels, some of which are yet to be experienced by other members of the group and, as a result, can offer some insights that would be lost in a group composed of equals. In a mixed group, it would potentially be easier to practice advising skills by the very nature of the discussion, so that group members would be able to look at the processes occurring in the group itself and evaluate successful strategies. For example, it would be possible for one of the senior members of the group to give a "presentation" on a typical level of faculty development and then "advise" another junior member of the group, with the rest of the group acting as observers, identifying and analyzing the advising strategies and their varying degrees of success. One of the advantages of this approach is the opportunity it would give senior faculty to discuss their feelings about the "role" of advising other faculty members and thereby offer analogies with numerous advising situations.

Value of Follow-Up Work. No matter which model is adopted, it is important to recognize that some sort of follow-up program is critical to the overall design. Although faculty development training programs can dispense information and stimulate thought, at some point this effort has to be supported with a follow-up that operates at the individual or small-group level. Such activities must represent the intersection of the faculty development/developmental advising activities by incorporating both elements for the individual; dwelling on faculty development or advising alone is insufficient. The drawback is that models for individual change cannot readily be publicized in the institution and usually are not described in the literature; the way to proceed is to examine the literature on adult development that is relevant and then draw parallels from the volume of work that has been completed on student development. The best approach is to view developmental advising as a continuum, with student development being a process that continues into adulthood and is shaped by the role faculty members play. Faculty are far more sensitive to the issues of student development when they become familiar with the issues surrounding their own development. Moreover, the peer-group model facilitates faculty understanding of developmental advising by having them come to grips with the issues of faculty development in an advising session.

Before undertaking follow-up work, it is worth the time to think seriously about the depth of effort one wishes to expend. Follow-up requires a large amount of time by all involved, and that time will be wasted if the skills and knowledge gained do not make individuals more valuable, in terms of the reward structure, to the institution. Although there can be little doubt that faculty involvement will make faculty members better advisors and that they will be more valuable to the institution, it does not follow that the reward structure will recognize this value. If, in fact, the reward structure recognizes those who are proficient at research or teaching and this is the primary basis for promotion and tenure, then facilitation of other valuable faculty skills through the advising program is a dubious, long-term effort since it will not be reflected in either salary or tenure. Unlike training programs, which have substantive face value and unquestioned administrative support, follow-up programs require everyone to take things seriously and get down to business. As Bess (1982a) has noted, excessive institutional ineffectiveness cannot continue indefinitely (especially in light of current budget stringencies in higher education). Equally important, patterns of activity that are not producing high levels of personal satisfaction can hardly be considered tolerable in a system whose central concerns are with human growth and development.

Evaluating Faculty Development

The role of evaluation in the overall faculty development effort is important, but formative and summative evaluation should not be mixed. Though theoretically possible, in practice mixing the two very different evaluation formats results in confusion and chaos for all involved. For the purposes of this chapter, discussion will be confined to formative evaluation—that is, evaluation designed to aid the individual advisor. If the feedback system is used to integrate people into the advising system by involving them in the process of setting goals, identifying problems, developing solutions, and monitoring their effectiveness, then the feedback system can increase the faculty member's commitment to the advising program and intrinsic motivation to perform well. Useful feedback serves to help faculty members reveal to themselves the competencies in advising that are important. As noted by Cammann (1982), the feedback system must consider the professor as primary recipient and must use the person's own definition of effectiveness in providing timely, appropriate information.

Within this framework, feedback provides information that triggers the level of intrinsic reward the person associates with advising. Hackman and Oldham (1980) note that there are at least three pleasurable psychological states that may be associated with increases in positive affect as a result of the faculty member's advising experience. They are a person's experience of the meaningfulness of work attempted, responsibility for work outcomes, and knowledge of results obtained.

During the planning, orientation, training, follow-up, and assessment activities, the faculty development objective is to surface, discuss, and establish the extent to which the advising program provides advisors with information pertaining to these three psychological states. The early discussions, continued use, and assessments of the evaluation efforts provide several benefits. The discussions about evaluation early in the orientation and planning stages both signal the importance of advising and force participants to clarify what they and the advising program wish to accomplish.

The continuing use of evaluation or feedback mechanisms throughout the program provides participants with information about the degree to which several important objectives are being accomplished. First, evaluation of the evaluation and feedback process allows the institution to monitor the faculty development effort and the extent that individuals' needs are being met. Colleges and universities, as well as individual faculty, must pay greater attention to the characteristics and concerns of each phase of the academic career (Baldwin and Blackburn, 1981). Ideally, services and support within the advising program would be available to aid faculty at different career benchmarks.

Second, evaluating the evaluation process aids the institution in maintaining the flexibility in the faculty development program necessary to encourage professional growth. If one believes that each student is a unique individual, one must also apply that logic to conceptions of faculty and develop procedures of challenge and support that recognize the uniqueness that each faculty member possesses. Thus, the monolithic, single-dimensional, information-laden, late-afternoon meeting for all advisors cannot carry the day. A variety of in-service development opportunities may be necessary to generate optimal faculty growth. For instance, advising involvement may be seen as one means for working through the career questioning that is a normal occurrence for faculty. Programs that focus on career planning can assist professors to be better prepared to help students with these concerns. More importantly, perhaps, the program can also assist professors in adapting consciously and systematically to personal and institutional change (Baldwin and Blackburn, 1981). This assistance to the professor is not without significance, since we may expect that the greater the faculty member's development, the greater his or her potential for helping students increase their growth.

Summary

Gaff (1978) commented that "anyone embarking on the road to teaching improvement should anticipate resistance not only from his colleagues and his institution, but from his fellow reformers and himself as well" (p. 47). Advising reformers should expect no less. The dedicated advising coordinator will experience firsthand the distinction Hodgson, Levinson, and Zaleznik (1965) make between role tasks and role task work. *Role task* denotes the linkage between one's assessment of personality, the here-and-now conception of oneself, and an assessment of the requirements of one's position in the organization. *Role task work*, on the other hand, is the sustained and directed effort of mind in which a person seeks to synthesize the organizational requirements of a position with his or her individual needs, interests, and aspirations.

The first element of the coordinator's role task work is to carry the banner for advising in the institution. The presence of the position itself epitomizes the institution's tacit recognition of the importance of advising. All the coordinator has to do is make the institution's commitment both real and effective! To do this, the coordinator, as well as many others, must strive to establish a faculty development program that alters organizational norms and cultivates faculty development and advising as a desirable, rather than merely acceptable, activity. The coordinator's intention to provide the right relationship to foster the capabilities of members of the academic community will be continually tested, both from the psychological and political perspectives. The coordinator is invited to be intrusive or to be neglectful of critical matters, or to take over formulation and direction. Only after passing these tests continually can the conditions for in-depth collaboration turn a promising program into a successful one.

Second, the coordinator must carry out the assignment of managing advising so as to provide the conditions under which individuals in collaboration can acquire new understanding of their environment, explore potentially adaptive alternatives to existing social designs in the institution, and plan to pursue new directions in advising by redesigning the organizations and more extended domains in which they participate. Understanding, as described by

Williams (1982), is regarded as a product of learning by which individuals discover how changes in environments are affecting the prospects for attaining desired outcomes by familiar means and as an outcome, seek new courses of action that are more effective in the changed conditions. The advisor training program becomes, then, an avenue for the institutional issues of faculty development and student development to be combined in new and creative ways.

The advising program and the attendant faculty development effort that accompanies it are not solely for the benefit of students. Faculty development programs are being asked not only to help faculty members improve the quality of their teaching or their advising but also to give them a better understanding of and capacity to actively participate in the management of a larger learning community (Gaff and Justice, 1978). The qualities that faculty and students will require in the future include (1) an openness to unfamiliar experiences and an active interest in discovering new responses to novel situations by experimenting and learning from experience; (2) awareness that complex, changing problems and issues cannot be understood adequately from the perspectives of particular established disciplines; (3) a willingness to help and learn from others through acquiring and sharing different kinds of knowledge; and (4) the ability to participate in determining the objectives of their own education, making decisions about achieving them and accepting much greater responsibility for their own learning (Williams, 1982).

The basic aim of the advising program, for coordinator, advisor, and student alike, is to enable those individuals involved to learn how to address the issues of change affecting them, to discover and pursue positive new directions, and to learn how to do this continuously for themselves. At stake are the evolution and growth of the individual participants, the advising program, and the institution. It is agreed that the task is to create conditions where faculty see teaching (and advising) as an opportunity for effort and achievement, as a channel for productivity, and as an avenue for experiencing meaningfulness and responsibility (Bess, 1982b). It should be added that this is a task that not only has its share of challenge but a hefty portion of merit.

References

Baldwin, R. G., and Blackburn, R. T. "The Academic Career as a Developmental Process." *Journal of Higher Education*, 1981, 52, 598-614.

Bess, J. L. "The Motivation to Teach: Meanings, Messages, and Morals." In J. L. Bess (Ed.), *New Directions for Teaching and Learning: Motivating Professors to Teach Effectively*, no. 10. San Francisco: Jossey-Bass, 1982a.

Bess, J. L. *University Organization: A Matrix Analysis of the Academic Professions*. New York: Human Sciences Press, 1982b.

Buhler-Miko, M. "Futures Planning and the Sense of Community in Universities." In A. E. Guskin (Ed.), *New Directions for Teaching and Learning: The Administrator's Role in Effective Teaching*, no. 5. San Francisco: Jossey-Bass, 1981.

Cammann, C. "Feedback Systems for Teachers." In J. L. Bess (Ed.), *New Directions for Teaching and Learning: Motivating Professors to Teach Effectively*, no. 10. San Francisco: Jossey-Bass, 1982.

Dornbush, S. M. "Perspectives from Sociology: Organizational Evaluation of Faculty Performance." In D. R. Lewis and W. E. Becker, Jr. (Eds.), *Academic Rewards in Higher Education*. Cambridge, Mass.: Ballinger, 1979.

Freedman, M., and others. *Academic Culture and Faculty Development*. Berkeley, Calif.: Montaigne Press, 1979.

Gaff, J. G. "Overcoming Faculty Resistance." In J. G. Gaff (Ed.), *New Directions for Higher Education: Institutional Renewal Through the Improvement of Teaching*, no. 24. San Francisco: Jossey-Bass, 1978.

Gaff, J. G., and Justice, D. O. "Faculty Development Yesterday, Today, and Tomorrow." In J. G. Gaff (Ed.), *New Directions for Higher Education: Institutional Renewal Through the Improvement of Teaching*, no. 24. San Francisco: Jossey-Bass, 1978.

Hackman, J. R., and Oldham, G. R. *Work Redesign*. Reading, Mass.: Addison-Wesley, 1980.

Havelock, R. *Training for Change Agents*. Ann Arbor: Institute for Social Research, University of Michigan, 1973.

Hodgson, R. C., Levinson, D. J., and Zaleznik, A. *The Executive Role Constellation*. Boston: Harvard University Press, 1965.

Lewin, K. *Field Theory in Social Science.* New York: Harper & Row, 1951.

Lewis, D. R., and Becker, W. E., Jr. (Eds.). *Academic Rewards in Higher Education.* Cambridge, Mass.: Ballinger, 1979.

McKeachie, W. J. "Perspectives from Psychology: Financial Incentives Are Ineffective for Faculty." In D. R. Lewis and W. E. Becker, Jr. (Eds.), *Academic Rewards in Higher Education.* Cambridge, Mass.: Ballinger, 1979.

McKeachie, W. J. "The Rewards of Teaching." In J. L. Bess (Ed.), *New Directions for Teaching and Learning: Motivating Professors to Teach Effectively*, no. 10. San Francisco: Jossey-Bass, 1982.

Metz, T. "Advisor Characteristics Resulting from Selection and Training." In D. Crockett (Ed.), *Academic Advising.* Iowa City, Iowa: American College Testing Program, 1978.

Newton, P. M. "Periods in the Adult Development of the Faculty Member." *Human Relations*, 1983, *36*, 441–458.

Nisbet, R. *The Social Philosophers: Community and Conflict in Western Thought.* New York: Crowell, 1973.

Nord, W. R. "Behavioral Modification in a Loosely Coupled System: Thoughts About Motivating Teaching Performance." In J. L. Bess (Ed.), *New Directions for Teaching and Learning: Motivating Professors to Teach Effectively*, no. 10. San Francisco: Jossey-Bass, 1982.

Perry, W. G., Jr. *Forms of Intellectual and Ethical Development in the College Years: A Scheme.* New York: Holt, Rinehart & Winston, 1970.

Sanford, N. "Social Psychology: Its Place in Personology." *American Psychologist*, 1982, *37*, 896–903.

Schneider, B., and Zalesny, M. D. "Human Needs and Faculty Motivation." In J. L. Bess (Ed.), *New Directions for Teaching and Learning: Motivating Professors to Teach Effectively*, no. 10. San Francisco: Jossey-Bass, 1982.

Williams, T. A. *Learning to Manage our Futures: The Participative Redesign of Societies in Turbulent Transition.* New York: Wiley, 1982.

16

Training Professional and Paraprofessional Advisors

Virginia N. Gordon

Previous chapters have described the processes, strategies, and clienteles that are part of academic advising. The multidimensional nature of advising is reflected in the many types of individuals it serves and in the diversity of its functions. This makes the need for comprehensive and ongoing staff development essential. Advising was once viewed by many as a simple exchange of procedural information between advisor and student. While this personal contact is still at the heart of the process, the types of students and the complexity and breadth of information have changed. This makes training critically important if advising programs are to be responsive to evolving advisor and student needs.

Training programs must be tailored to the many different types of professionals who are involved in academic advising today. Advising actually starts with the first student contact with the admissions office. Admissions professionals discuss major programs with students and must be prepared to answer many academically related questions. Most orientation programs are built around curricular information and scheduling. Faculty advisors and full-time professional advisors are often involved in orientation programs. Entering students' first concerns and questions are generally about the academic offerings of a college. Admissions counselors, orientation personnel, faculty advisors, and other professionals associated directly or peripherally with a comprehensive advising program have training needs unique to their roles and responsibilities. This chapter, however, focuses on the training of full-time professional advisors and paraprofessional advisors. While the needs of different professional groups must be acknowledged, it is important to note that there are basic advising functions that apply to all individuals engaged in this important activity.

Full-time professional advisors come from many types of institutions and disciplines. Even though trained for the helping professions (for example, educational counseling and student affairs), some may have had limited experience with academic advising techniques, knowledge, and skills. Advisors from subject matter disciplines, on the other hand, while knowledgeable about academic content, may have little background in communication or counseling skills, career planning, or decision making.

This chapter discusses the steps needed for developing an effective advisor training program (see Figure 1). These include:

1. determining the need for training
2. obtaining administrative support
3. setting training objectives
4. identifying training program topics and content
5. selecting appropriate strategies or methods
6. evaluating the program
7. reassessment and future planning

The final section of this chapter focuses on training programs for student and other paraprofessional advisors and discusses how training efforts might be tailored to these particular groups.

Figure 1. Steps in Planning an Advisor Training Program.

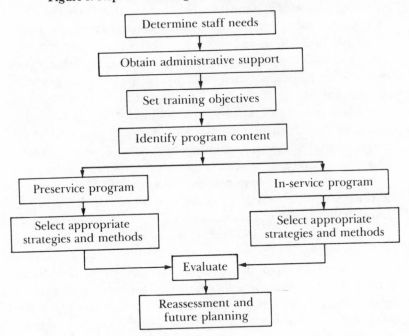

Developmental Approach to Training

An important component of any training program is a philosophy that views advising in a student development framework. This philosophy can provide direction and continuity to all advising efforts. This advising philosophy encompasses the whole student and is based on an understanding of how students develop—personally and socially as well as intellectually. Students are viewed as unique individuals with different needs, rates of growth, and maturity. Ender, Winston, and Miller (1982) define developmental advising as a process that is concerned with human growth, is goal related, and requires the establishment of a caring relationship. Advisors serve as role models and mentors in this relationship. Developmental advising incorporates all resources on campus, particularly in integrating academic and student affairs.

Advisor training programs using a developmental approach will offer knowledge and skill acquisition from a student-centered perspective. When curricular information or institutional procedures are learned in a training session, for example, they will be learned as vehicles for helping students solve problems rather than as *rules* to be followed. Advisors who understand student development concepts will be more likely to appreciate the uniqueness of each student and be able to relate each advising exchange to an overall educational plan rather than as an isolated incident.

Advisors' needs are also considered in a developmental training approach. As advisors clarify their own roles and responsibilities, they will acquire self-understanding that will enhance the quality of their interactions with students.

Organizing a Training Program

Advisor training on many campuses is often initiated ad hoc with little thought or planning given to an ongoing, coordinated effort. Effective training programs demand the services of a training coordinator who is responsible for identifying needs, pulling resources together, and implementing and evaluating the program. This role is often assumed by the director of advising or by the administrative dean responsible for advising.

Since academic advising functions are performed by many different types of personnel, it is essential that the initial approach to establishing a training program reflects these diverse backgrounds and needs. Selecting a training or staff development team should be the first step in initiating a training program. The team approach not only ensures that many perspectives will be represented but also encourages a sense of ownership for what transpires. The actual makeup of the training team will vary from campus to campus but could include representation from the faculty, full-time professional advising staff, administrators, student affairs staff, and students.

Administrative support is an essential prerequisite for an effective training program. If the members of the training team know they have the functional and financial support of the administration, they will feel confident that their efforts are recognized and will be implemented. The training coordinator may relay this support by (1) asking the responsible administrator to send a letter of appointment to each team member outlining the rationale for and the charge to the committee, (2) inviting the administrator to address the training committee at its introductory meeting, and (3) relaying the committee's plans as they progress to the administrator for immediate feedback and comment. The articulation of the training program's objectives and content to a supportive administrator will ensure that communication lines are open and that everyone understands that this is a cooperative, important function.

Training programs can be organized into two types, preservice and in-service. The former implies little prior knowledge or experience with advising and will be more comprehensive and basic in nature. In-service programs generally focus on specific topics as the need for more information or expertise in certain areas is identified.

Training Objectives

The first important task of the training committee is to determine training needs so that objectives may be formulated. What precisely needs to be accomplished? Very often training programs are put together quickly and informally as a reaction to a specific problem or when a deficiency in the system surfaces. An effective staff development program should be carefully conceived, well coordinated, and continuous.

Determining Training Needs. Surveying experienced advisors for suggested training content will serve several purposes. It will involve them in the process and create a cooperative climate for the training function in general. Advisors may be asked, for example, to prioritize the importance of advising tasks so more concentrated effort may be allotted during training. They may also have suggestions regarding the type of theoretical frameworks or background they have integrated into their advising approach. Surveying advisors will generate many other advising topics and will identify needs that are unique to that particular setting. Suggestions or issues that are used need to be acknowledged and feedback given to the appropriate individuals concerning their implementation.

It is often helpful to survey the advisors to be trained for their ideas about training topics. Including new advisors in establishing training objectives ensures more personally relevant content. A combination of written surveys and informal interviews can provide objectives that are particularly important to the group or individual being trained.

Learner Outcomes. Training goals may be categorized as knowledge based and skill based. Advisors not only need to learn *what* they are supposed to do and *why* they are doing it but *how* to do it. All three are equally important. When training is organized around knowledge and skill acquisition, advisors-in-training understand the information they need to acquire and can feel confident that they know how to use the knowledge in a practical way once it is learned.

Content goals might include, for example, the acquisition of knowledge about such diverse topics as curricular requirements and student development theory. Process goals might involve communication techniques and advising strategies for helping students select a major.

Bonar (1976) formulated instructional goals for a computer training approach by talking to administrators and faculty who were experienced advisors. A common concern was the lack of preservice training that seemed to be responsible for considerable experimentation on the part of new advisors at the students' expense. Setting training goals for new advisors consisted of instruction in content (that is, rules and regulations, programs, and resources) and process (the "how-to") of academic advising. These two instructional goals were then developed into eight goals and subgoals. These included understanding the advisor role, the advising relationship, specific information needed to help students formulate schedules and educational plans, and information about program resources and advising strategies. Advising skills were also programmed as training goals.

Learner outcomes associated with performance goals are more difficult to identify and implement. Acquiring knowledge about academic requirements is a far easier objective to attain than such skill-based objectives as teaching advisors to feel empathy toward a student. Most traditional advisor training programs are cognitive in their approach. Behavioral or skill-acquisition components are just as important as information dissemination, if the "how-to" needs of new advisors are to be met.

Institutional attitudes and needs will greatly influence the goals and objectives of a training program. If there is strong institutional commitment to advising, training programs assume an importance and priority commensurate with this attitude. Unfortunately, a few institutions still view advising as "information giving" and obtaining support for preservice and in-service advisor training beyond this limited scope may require strategies unique to that setting.

When virtually no training has been initiated on a campus, a more comprehensive approach may be indicated. An extensive preservice training program may be needed, followed by short-term in-service offerings. On campuses where advising has been viewed as important and where regular training has taken place, brief in-service sessions on specific topics may be sufficient. The number and comprehensiveness of previous training efforts will influence the training goals and objectives for a specific campus.

Preservice and In-Service Objectives. Objectives for a preservice program will be more general and comprehensive than will in-service objectives, which may encompass only one topic or a narrowly defined area of advising. Preservice objectives will generally include both knowledge- and skill-based competencies. Although a preservice training program may occur over an extended period of time, learner objectives will include a more general approach to the process of advising and the role of the advisor in this process. Skill development could include, for example, basic communication techniques and the "how-to" skills involved in a one-to-one advising interview. When the advisor completes the preservice training program, it is assumed that all basic knowledge and skills needed to be a competent advisor have been learned.

The learner outcomes for a particular in-service session may be to acquire information about a certain topic or skill. One training session, for example, may teach student development theory as well as specific techniques for incorporating this knowledge into interactions with students. Since most campuses use in-service training more than preservice training, most in-service training objectives will be narrower in scope.

Trainer Goals. A critical aspect of training is the goals set by trainers for themselves. Too often trainers do not identify objectives for their own behavior. For instance, the principles of andragogy should be incorporated into any training effort. Andragogy, the art and science of helping adults learn (Knowles, 1970), implies that adults are self-directed learners, want immediate application of what they learn, and bring to the learning situation a rich reservoir of experiences from which to draw. Cross (1981) points out that adult learners are problem centered rather than subject oriented in their learning. Since professional advisors are adult learners, the principles of andragogy are quite relevant here.

How the trainer presents material is as important as the content itself. Different learning styles will be represented within a group of participants. The way information is organized and presented must be varied so that every trainee will be able to learn in a personalized way. Kolb (1976) posited that individuals learn by experiencing, observing, conceptualizing, and doing. All four of these learning styles should be incorporated into the methods for gathering and processing the information provided in a training session. Setting goals for their own behavior is as important for trainers as formulating outcomes for the program itself.

Training Program Content

The diversity of training needs among different professional groups will dictate the content of a training program. There is, however, basic knowledge associated with the advising process that all types of advisors must acquire. For example, all advisors need to be conversant with how academic programs are structured, the rationale for basic and upper-level requirements, and the sequencing of courses for obtaining a degree. A common method for knowledge acquisition would include either preservice sessions on curricular information or an in-service update on curricular changes.

Regardless of the institution or the type of participants, certain basic topics are appropriate in a preservice program (Gordon, 1980; Ender and Winston, 1982).

Procedural Information. Knowing the institution's policies and procedures is necessary for many advising transactions. A student's problem can sometimes be resolved through a procedural approach. While many advisors-to-be are handed a book of faculty rules to learn, a more effective method might be to teach them through case studies or role playing how to use the rules. Knowing *how* and *when* to use procedures is just as important as knowing the rules themselves.

Course and Program Identification. Another central requisite for advising is a knowledge of the courses and programs that the institution offers. Many students expect the advisor to help them select (if not tell them) what courses to take. Freshmen, especially, need to learn about basic requirements, major possibilities, and how degree programs are organized. Often this knowledge is taken for granted and there is a "they can read it in the catalogue" attitude. While much of this information is learned through experience, a training program must cover this important information in such a way that new advisors during their first few weeks can feel confident in this area. Training materials should include an advising manual developed for this purpose that contains current information about each major and a list of faculty members to whom the student may be referred. Curriculum sheets or checklists are also helpful since advisor and student alike can learn the requirements for a degree at a glance.

Advisors working with undecided students will need additional training sessions on this subject, since they will be working with a broad spectrum of student interests and goals. Helping students explore and test their ideas through course work can be a very important advising activity. Careful course identification and selection is an important advising tool. Course selection and scheduling must reflect the student's abilities and needs. Both advisor and student have equal responsibility in this process.

Academic Planning. Students need an academic plan that reflects their personal interests and abilities and that helps them set goals. While students must take ownership of the plan, the advisor has an important responsibility in making sure the plan meets the institution's requirements in addition to the student's preferences (see Chapter Five).

A training session in how to help students set short- and long-term goals will provide advisors with the skills to teach students this important task. Advisors need to acquire the techniques for helping students initiate, implement, and monitor an educational plan. They also need to be sensitive to individual differences so that each plan reflects the student's unique values and aspirations.

Career Advising. An important part of advising, and one often neglected in training, is learning the relationships between academic and occupational choices. While career advising may be considered informational in nature, many advisors feel uninformed and therefore inadequate in this area. A training program can help advisors learn the factors in career self-assessment, information about occupations, and systems for classifying occupations. They also need the skills to help students recognize how they approach the career decision-making process (see Chapter Six). It is important to learn about the resources on campus for referral for more in-depth career counseling or placement.

Training programs can teach advisors the career development process, techniques for helping students explore alternatives, or how to help others confirm a choice they have already made. Academic, vocational, and life planning are so closely related in most students' minds that an advisor must be prepared to help students integrate them. In a training program, advisors may learn many of these techniques by experiencing them. They may take certain vocational inventories, learn to use the resources in the career library, or role play career advising with colleagues or students. Training programs can have great impact on advisor skills in this area and can help them feel more comfortable and confident in this important advising task.

Decision-Making Skills. A significant part of many advising transactions is problem solving, as was noted in Chapter Five. Students rarely consider how they personally approach the academic or career decision-making process. Advisors need to be able to recognize the different styles and strategies that students use when making decisions. In some cases, advisors may need to teach the decision-making process to students, especially as it relates to academic and career selection.

Training sessions focusing on value clarification, goal setting, and the decision-making process itself will help advisors become more sensitive to the problems students may be encountering. Advisors need to understand their own strategies for approaching decisions since they may have a very different perspective and style than the student they are seeking to help. Training programs can help advisors become more aware of their responsibilities for helping students formulate goals and make choices.

Communication Skills. The need for effective communication skills in advising is primary. Many advisor training programs incorporate a session on communication techniques, both verbal and nonverbal. Communication is basic to every advisor-advisee exchange. Ender and Winston (1982) describe the breadth of concerns and problems that students present in an advising exchange and categorize them as developmental or remedial in nature.

Appropriate communication skills will facilitate the development of a good working relationship. Training advisors to recognize the different levels and complexity of problems will help them decide later which can be dealt with by them and which need to be referred. Effective advising will take place only when advisor and student are discussing the same topic at the same level.

Kramer and Gardner (1983) outline the various roles advisors play and the importance of responding to students' questions and concerns from the role that is appropriate for that occasion. Faculty advisors, for example, play many roles (teacher, friend, committee member, mentor) and sometimes do not communicate effectively with a student because they are responding to a concern from a different or conflicting role from what the student expects.

There are many models available for teaching basic communication and counseling skills (Carkhuff, 1973; Egan, 1975; Loughary and Ripley, 1979). Helping every advisor learn and practice basic communication and counseling skills may be one of the important components of a training program.

Campus Resources. Another important advisor function is to be a knowledgeable and effective referral agent. Advisors need to be familiar with such academic resources as study skills or tutoring opportunities. They need a wide breadth of knowledge about student affairs programs such as counseling or financial aid.

During a training program it is not only important to identify the resources and the people to whom referrals may be made but also *how* and *when* to refer. Advisors sometimes refer too quickly in an attempt to "solve" the student's dilemma. Problems are sometimes complex and it takes a trained listener to untangle the obvious from the underlying complications that are sometimes involved. Students may view a quick referral as the "runaround," even though it may not be the advisor's intent. In other situations the advisor may be able to clarify a confusing situation with a phone call. The *why, how,* and *when* of a referral are as important as the *where.* Training programs often neglect this aspect of the referral process.

Student Development Theory and Practice. An important topic in any advisor training program is to provide a solid base of knowledge and understanding about student development concepts and how to use them in an advising relationship. This particular area may require an outside resource person if none is available on campus.

Developmental advising stresses the role of the advisor as mentor and friend to the student. Ender, Winston, and Miller (1982) describe developmental advising as helping students (1) develop a sense of self-responsibility, (2) become self-directed, and (3) develop a recognition of relevant developmental tasks and their achievement. Developmental advising places a responsibility that goes far beyond many advisors' expectations. On the other hand, many experienced advisors have been developmentally oriented for years without being conscious of it.

A training session introducing advisors to student development theory would provide the important background information needed to understand what developmental tasks students face and how these tasks are differentiated and integrated during the college years. Erikson (1968), Chickering (1969), Perry (1970), Kohlberg (1981), and Gilligan (1982) are a few theorists who offer many insights into cognitive, moral, and ego development. (An excellent summary of theorists can be found in Chapter Four.) Advisors also need background in career development theory (Super, 1957; Holland, 1973; Osipow, 1983) since they are involved in helping students identify and explore career options (also see Chapter Six).

Advisors working from these conceptual frameworks will feel more confident when advising students with diverse backgrounds and levels of maturity. They will be more aware of the individual differences among their advisees and will be able to tailor their advising approaches to the specific needs of particular students.

Special Topics. In-service training can focus on specific topics, such as advising special students (for example, the underprepared, adult, minority, or honors student) (see Chapter Ten). Advisors benefit from regular updates on career opportunities and job placement information. Other special topics can address the *advisor's* concerns, such as legal issues in advising (see Chapter Fourteen), stress and time management, or burnout. In-service training can provide a much-needed opportunity to listen to other advisors' concerns and to share ideas and successful advising techniques with colleagues.

Training Manuals. Some institutions develop a training manual to organize the materials used during the training experience. Not only can advisors look ahead to see the content of the total program while they are in training, but they have a handy reference for use when the training is over. Advisors often complain of overload when a training program is of any extensive length or when it is intensive, as vast amounts of information are given quickly. A training manual can help advisors discern the whole picture and how the parts are integrated. Training manuals can be an important tool for helping advisors assimilate a great deal of information and organize this for future use.

Selecting a Strategy

There are many methods for presenting training content. In some cases a new advisor may need an individual approach to training. While this may be necessary, it is not the most efficient use of staff time and energy. The advisor-in-training is deprived of the valuable interaction and sharing of a group that can deepen awareness and extend the knowledge base.

Group training is a common strategy for presenting advising information and for building skills. A systems approach has been tried with great success, but the cost-effectiveness of putting a training program in a computer-based format has been questioned (Bonar, 1976).

A particularly desirable strategy for training is the preservice graduate-level course on advising for students who will someday be faculty or student affairs professionals (Gordon, 1982). A graduate course on academic advising for credit can be an excellent vehicle for preparing *future* advisors. There are many general principles and basic advising functions inherent in every advising position. These can be incorporated and taught very effectively in an academic course. An advising course can also foster positive attitudes and enthusiasm for advising as a possible future profession among graduate students in guidance and counseling, student personnel, and related programs. Future faculty advisors will also benefit from this type of preservice approach.

Training Formats. Training can take place before, during, or after advisors assume their responsibilities. Ender and Winston (1982) argue convincingly that advisors be trained *before* their duties begin. A preservice program will help advisors feel more confident as they begin the complicated task of advising students. Workshops prior to the beginning of classes or regularly scheduled training sessions the term before their service are two ways of providing extensive preservice training. Continued training during or after advising duties are assumed is valuable in that the advising experience itself will help advisors recognize their need for training and identify specific areas where they need more in-depth help.

The length of a training program will depend on whether it is preservice for advisors with no prior experience or in-service for advisors who need an information update or refinement of certain advising skills. The training objectives that have been previously established will often dictate the length and timing of a program.

Training Methods. The delivery method for training will depend on what needs to be accomplished. Assigning preworkshop reading, for example, can bring all participants to the same level of knowledge as training begins. Varying the methods of presenting materials will create a better learning environment. A combination of lecture, discussion, observation, experiencing, and practice will provide an opportunity for different kinds of learners to participate in a way most effective for their own learning style. Training topics will often dictate a certain form of presentation. Learning student development theory may be approached through lecture and discussion, for example, while communication skills might be learned most effectively through observation and practice. Some advisors may prefer to learn through reading. Others may prefer a visually oriented presentation. The instructional form may vary considerably given a certain topic or audience.

The type of materials used in training should be relevant, concise, and easy to use. Training notebooks can be helpful in organizing information for immediate and future reference. A well-organized advisors' manual can serve as an outline for what will transpire during a preservice program. The annual updating of an advisor's notebook can provide the basis for future in-service programs.

Training workshops can take place on campus or at off-campus retreats. Each has its advantages and disadvantages. Attendance is usually better on campus but can be disrupted frequently by advisors needing to tend to job-related problems. The time involved traveling to an off-campus location may make it difficult for some to attend. An off-campus program does encourage full attention to the training objectives and activities, however. Administrative support can help to place a high priority on advisor training. When training is perceived as an important and necessary function for the success of an advising program, the length of time and location will be based on need rather than an accommodation to other factors.

Evaluation

Evaluation is a critical activity within an advisor training program since the effectiveness of the learning experience needs to be determined. Evaluation is not an activity that happens only at the end of a training program. A single session or activity or the entire training experience may be evaluated. Evaluation methods and process must be considered at the beginning of the planning phase since it must be recognized as an ongoing function. The evaluation process can be a learning experience for both the trainer and the trainee.

Formative evaluation methods may be used while the training program is in progress to determine what the trainee is learning. Methods for this type of evaluation might include a short verbal or written test for knowledge about academic major information or a trainee demonstration of a specific advising technique or procedure through role playing. Formative evaluation can provide immediate feedback about the progress that is being made in learning specific, measurable knowledge or skills. This type of evaluation can be used to make adjustment in training procedures when needed and will provide feedback to the participants while training is in progress.

An example of an outcome statement for a segment of a training program as it is evolving is as follows:

At the end of this session on course and program identification, the advisor will:

1. be familiar with all the majors on this campus and be able to identify the basic education requirements that relate to them
2. be able to explain to the student how a baccalaureate degree is structured and give the rationale for this organization
3. know the person or place on campus to refer students for more detailed information for each academic area

Evaluating the effectiveness of the overall training program may be based on the objectives that were initially stated before the program began. This summative evaluation may be performed immediately after the completion of the program or several weeks after the advisors have an opportunity to use the information and skills they have learned. Surveying or interviewing advisors on a regular basis after a preservice program will provide information about their progress and solicit their ideas for future in-service training programs based on their evolving needs.

Examples of outcomes for an overall training program may include:

1. Advisors will be able to demonstrate knowledge of career development theory by describing three theories and how they can be used in advising students.
2. Advisors will be able to demonstrate various communication techniques and how they may be used during advisor-advisee interaction.

3. Advisors will be able to list three campus resources for helping
    students in academic difficulty and how or when to refer
    students to them.

Using both formal and informal methods for evaluating a
training experience will provide the trainer with the affective as
well as the cognitive effect of the program on the participants. In
either case, the trainees need to know at the outset of the training
program what the experience is attempting to accomplish so that
their expectations are in harmony with the objectives stated by the
trainer.

Training Paraprofessional Advisors

Many institutions use student advisors to augment their
advising services (Carstensen and Silberhorn, 1979). Some institutions use student paraprofessionals as a regular part of their overall
delivery system while others use them as additional resource personnel during peak advising periods, such as registration. The effectiveness of upper-division students as curriculum advisors has been
well documented (Upcraft, 1971; Murry, 1972; Brown and Myers,
1975; Levinson, 1976).

When faculty and peer advisors are compared for effectiveness, few differences in advisees' grade point averages, attrition
rates, or attitudes toward college have been shown (Murry, 1972;
Brown and Myers, 1975). Zultowski and Catron (1976) found that
student advisors provided their advisees with more subjective,
experiential advice than objective advice. Faculty advisors were
found to be better at providing factual academic information. These
findings and others regarding peer advising effectiveness have
important implications for training.

Ender and McFadden (1980) outline these aspects of training
that help students integrate what they learn with the skills needed
in advising. First, they must learn a significant amount of information from which they can react, share, and develop a personal
understanding. Students-in-training must take this knowledge and
apply it to their own personal characteristics and growth. The third

step is to help them integrate these concepts into the helping skills they will use with others.

Habley (1979) suggests that a disadvantage of peer advisors is their tendency to use subjective observations rather than to objectively provide information about courses and professors. Habley encourages a strong training component to stress the value of objectivity in presenting information to students and to help them understand that personal value judgments do not belong in advising.

Objectives. While the objectives for a peer-advisor training program might be similar to those used in other training efforts, there will be many differences as well. The administrative structure and responsibility for training and supervision of peer advisors will be determined by institutions initiating peer advising programs. Peer advisors may work in a variety of settings (for example, orientation, academic advising centers, residence halls, academic departments, or developmental studies offices). Specific training objectives will depend on the tasks involved and the depth of knowledge student advisors are expected to possess.

The following common objectives can be found in many peer advising training programs (Stein and Spille, 1974; Friedman, 1979; Habley, 1979; Ender and McFadden, 1980).

1. to teach peer advisors procedural tasks, such as how to drop or add a course, register for classes, or declare a major
2. to teach peer advisors how and where to refer students for additional or specialized help, including various areas of the institutional bureaucracy or student affairs programs
3. to train peer advisors in basic communication skills so that they can communicate clearly as "friendly intervenors" rather than trained counselors (Stein and Spille, 1974)
4. to teach self-assessment and goal-setting techniques
5. to teach problem-solving skills so that student advisors do not solve the problems of their advisees but help them take responsibility for making their own choices
6. to teach peer advisors how to avoid personal stress and burnout by including time-management, interview-termination, and referral techniques (Habley, 1979)

Format. Peer advisor training may be offered in a variety of formats. A commonly used vehicle is the training workshop that can last one day or be offered at regularly scheduled intervals during the academic year. On-the-job or experiential training may be included in a regular training module or may be used as a separate approach. Actually working in the environment in which they will advise can provide realistic training for peer advisors who need to learn firsthand what is expected of them in that setting. Close supervision is essential in this type of training.

A more desirable training approach is the credit course that can be used to teach students advising skills and knowledge (Stein and Spille, 1974; Friedman, 1979; Ender and McFadden, 1980). Credit courses for training offer the opportunity for student development concepts to be incorporated in the teaching functions (Crookston, 1973). A student development approach to teaching offers students both the knowledge and the opportunity to apply what they learn. Developmental teaching acknowledges that students learn in a variety of ways. A training course for peer advisors can be an excellent opportunity for human development instruction (Miller and Prince, 1976). Training courses are usually considered preservice types of programs since the student who wants to be an advisor takes the course prior to applying for an advising assignment.

Teachers of training courses must be experts in student development concepts and communication and counseling skills. They must also have an intimate understanding of campus resources. They must be able to impress upon students the importance and seriousness of the course content. Readings, assignments, and testing will be of the same level and difficulty of any standard academic offering.

Stein and Spille (1974) broadened their course content so that in addition to training student paraprofessional advisors, it was an appropriate course for students interested in enhancing their own ability to be a helper in the college setting or in later life. This type of course is also relevant for students who are considering future careers in the helping professions.

If not enrolled in a course, student advisors will need frequent training meetings since peer advisors need to interact with professional trainers on a regular basis. Students are more open to schoollike training sessions than other types of advisors and usually consider this ongoing contact as helpful and reinforcing.

Training Program Content. Since students do not have the maturity or experience to work with other students in certain personal and academic situations, their training should incorporate the advising tasks that fit their abilities and purpose. Although the content of a training program will reflect the objectives for the entire peer advising program, there are a few basic areas usually included—academic information, interpersonal communication, student development concepts, and resources and referrals.

Peer advisors are usually trained in a specific area of academic expertise. They are usually not expected to learn vast amounts of information or advise in the intricacies of formulating educational plans. This will influence the level of information provided by most training programs since peer advisors are often cautioned to refer students with complex problems or questions to professional advisors or counselors. The content of courses, class size, required assignments, and the teaching style of the instructor are typical of the type of information they can offer effectively to another student.

Interpersonal communication is an area that requires training for most students since this is so basic to the advising relationship. Students need good listening skills and need to acquire the simple techniques of reflection and clarification. In order to teach students these techniques, a lecture describing these skills and laboratory practice sessions using case studies are necessary. Students need to be monitored during their first contacts with real clients so that they may receive feedback on their personal communication styles in advising transactions. This may be accomplished through the use of tape recordings that can be analyzed by peer advisor and supervisor.

Learning student development concepts will provide peer advisors with a more personal understanding of their advisees as well as providing insights into their own growth and development. Ender and McFadden (1980) suggest that the major themes of human development be incorporated in a training program. The themes of autonomy, interpersonal relationships, and life purpose are presented to the student as well as activities to assess their own personal growth and development in relation to the college experience. The Student Developmental Task Inventory (SDTI-2) (Winston, Miller, and Prince, 1979) would be a useful tool to give trainees since it will help them assess their own development, thus helping them recognize the levels of growth and development they will encounter in their advisees.

Perhaps the most important skill to teach in a training program for paraprofessionals is that of accurate and timely referral. Peer advisors need to know the resources on campus to help students academically, personally, and socially. Habley (1979) suggests that a good peer advising program will generate many referrals. Inviting the personnel to whom advisors will refer into the training program to discuss their area will help to provide accurate knowledge and build confidence in the referral process.

Other content areas may include information of a personal nature for the students themselves, such as time management and activities to foster self-confidence. Decision-making skills are often taught in a training program since many students may expect their student advisor to make decisions for them and this can lead to a complicated relationship.

Providing a peer-advising handbook during training can help to ensure that student advisors have a quick reference to information when it is needed in the future. Handbooks often contain academic policies, such as academic standards and course loads; institutional procedures, such as add-drop or withdrawal deadlines; major program information; listings of campus resources and their descriptions; career advising information, such as referral for career counseling and placement services; and copies of the various materials used during the training program. Handbooks can provide an organized, structured way for presenting information for either a workshop or classroom setting.

Training Graduate Students. While the discussion thus far has been focused on training undergraduates as advisors, graduate students also perform the advising function on many campuses. A training program geared to this population will generally be more comprehensive and complex in nature. Graduate students are considered as professional advisors on most campuses and their training will typically be organized and presented in the same manner as that used with other professionals.

Training Nonstudent Paraprofessionals. Some institutions use part-time paraprofessional advisors who are often alumni or have teaching or counseling backgrounds (King, 1979; Kerr, 1983). This type of paraprofessional is often used for economic reasons.

An advantage of nonstudent paraprofessional advisors is that they can provide continuity, stability, and a professional commitment to advising. Many paraprofessionals help with orientation, registration, small-group, and individual advising.

Nonstudent paraprofessionals may have associate or baccalaureate degrees. Since this type of paraprofessional is often a mature adult with professional experience, some aspects of training will resemble that of full-time advisors. The common elements in a training program for these individuals may include basic advising knowledge and skills, communication techniques, resources identification and referral, and problem-solving skills.

Whether a campus uses full-time professionals, faculty advisors, undergraduate or graduate student advisors, or other paraprofessionals, training is one of the most important ingredients of an effective advising program. The real challenge is to offer the type of training that responds to the unique needs of each of these types in the very special environment that each campus provides. Advising programs will reflect the quality of their training efforts.

Summary

A successful advising program will always incorporate a strong training component. Preservice training helps to ensure that basic knowledge and skills are acquired by all advisors. Periodic inservice training provides advisors with an update on changes that occur in academic and procedural information or offer the opportunity for more in-depth study of particular advising issues or topics.

When developing advisor training programs, it must be acknowledged that academic advisors comprise a heterogeneous group. The design, content, and implementation of a training program must reflect advisors' unique needs as well as institutional priorities. While there are many common elements that may be included in program content, different professional and student groups will require additional or more in-depth information about certain procedures and tasks.

A successful training program will contain several ingredients. Determining training objectives is an important first step. Administrative support for training will reflect the priorities that are placed on this critical function. Basic content may include institutional policies and procedures, academic information, communication skills, campus resources, referral skills, and career information and placement. Additional topics may be generated from the trainees themselves. Evaluation of the training program must be an integral part of the overall planning process.

While training programs for paraprofessional advisors may be similar in some aspects to those for professional advisors, many important differences do exist. The scope and level of advising tasks will be limited. Student advisors do not have the maturity or experience to assume responsibilities beyond information giving and shared experiences. Training for peer advisors must include topics that deal with objectivity in communicating information and personal concerns of the student as advisor, such as time and stress management. The ideal vehicle for training peer advisors is the credit course.

A developmental approach to advisor training implies that a philosophy of student centeredness permeates all aspects of planning and implementation. Advisors are taught student development concepts and this view of students is incorporated into the acquisition of knowledge and skills. Advisors who are trained to understand and use a student development approach will embrace a philosophy of student centeredness that will provide direction and continuity to the advising program.

References

Bonar, J. R. "Developing and Implementing a Systems-Design Training Program for Academic Advisors." *Journal of College Student Personnel,* 1976, *17,* 190–198.

Brown, C. R., and Myers, R. "Student vs. Faculty Curriculum Advising." *Journal of College Student Personnel,* 1975, *16,* 226–231.

Carkhuff, R. *The Art of Helping: A Guide for Developing Helping Skills for Parents, Teachers and Counselors.* Amherst, Mass: Human Resource Development Press, 1973.

Carstensen, D. J., and Silberhorn, C. *A National Survey of Academic Advising.* Iowa City, Iowa: American College Testing Program, 1979.

Chickering, A. W. *Education and Identity.* San Francisco: Jossey-Bass, 1969.

Crookston, B. B. "Education for Human Development." In C. F. Warnath and Associates, *New Directions for College Counselors: A Handbook for Redesigning Professional Roles.* San Francisco: Jossey-Bass, 1973.

Cross, K. P. *Adults as Learners: Increasing Participation and Facilitating Learning.* San Francisco: Jossey-Bass, 1981.

Egan, G. *The Skilled Helper.* Belmont, Calif.: Wadsworth, 1975.

Ender, S. C., and McFadden, R. "Training the Student Paraprofessional Helper." In F. B. Newton and K. L. Ender (Eds.), *Student Development Practices: Strategies for Making a Difference.* Springfield, Ill.: Thomas, 1980.

Ender, S. C., and Winston, R. B., Jr. "Training Allied Professional Academic Advisors." In R. B. Winston, Jr., S. C. Ender, and T. K. Miller (Eds.), *New Directions for Student Services: Developmental Approaches to Academic Advising,* no. 17. San Francisco: Jossey-Bass, 1982.

Ender, S. C., Winston, R. B., Jr., and Miller, T. K. "Academic Advising as Student Development." In R. B. Winston, Jr., S. C. Ender, and T. K. Miller (Eds.), *New Directions for Student Services: Developmental Approaches to Academic Advising,* no. 17. San Francisco: Jossey-Bass, 1982.

Erikson, E. H. *Identity: Youth and Crises.* New York: Norton, 1968.

Friedman, R. E. "The Advising Structure of McMicken College of Arts and Sciences of the University of Cincinnati and the Institution of Peer Advising Structure: Some Encounters and Observations." In D. S. Crockett (Ed.), *Academic Advising: A Resource Document (1979 Supplement).* Iowa City, Iowa: American College Testing Program, 1979.

Gilligan, C. *In a Different Voice.* Cambridge, Mass.: Harvard University Press, 1982.

Gordon, V. N. "Training Academic Advisors: Content and Method." *Journal of College Student Personnel,* 1980, *21,* 334–340.

Gordon, V. N. "Training Future Academic Advisors: One Model of a Pre-Service Approach." *National Academic Advising Association (NACADA) Journal,* 1982, *2,* 35–40.

Habley, W. R. "The Advantages and Disadvantages of Using Students as Academic Advisors." *National Association of Student Personnel Administrators (NASPA) Journal,* 1979, *17,* 46–51.

Holland, J. L. *Making Vocational Choices: A Theory of Careers.* Englewood Cliffs, N.J.: Prentice-Hall, 1973.

Kerr, B. "Alumni as Peer Advisors in a Community College." *Journal of College Student Personnel,* 1983, *24,* 366–367.

King, M. "Utilizing Part-Time Paraprofessionals as Academic Advisors: A Model." In D. S. Crockett (Ed.), *Academic Advising: A Resource Document (1979 Supplement).* Iowa City, Iowa: American College Testing Program, 1979.

Knowles, M. S. *The Modern Practice of Adult Education: Andragogy Versus Pedagogy.* New York: Association Press, 1970.

Kohlberg, L. *The Philosophy of Moral Development.* San Francisco: Harper & Row, 1981.

Kolb, D. *Learning Style Inventory Technical Manual.* Boston: McBer and Company, 1976.

Kramer, H. C., and Gardner, R. E. *Advising by Faculty.* (2nd ed.) Washington, D.C.: National Education Association, 1983.

Levinson, J. H. *Peer Academic Advisement: The Use of Students as Peer Paraprofessional Support Staff.* Paper presented at the annual conference of the National Association of Women Deans, Administrators, and Counselors, New Orleans, La., March 1976. (ED 136 159)

Loughary, J. W., and Ripley, T. M. *Helping Others Help Themselves.* New York: McGraw-Hill, 1979.

Miller, T. K., and Prince, J. S. *The Future of Student Affairs: A Guide to Student Development for Tomorrow's Higher Education.* San Francisco: Jossey-Bass, 1976.

Murry, J. P. "The Comparative Effectiveness of Student-to-Student and Faculty Advising Programs." *Journal of College Student Personnel,* 1972, *13,* 562–566.

Osipow, S. W. *Theories of Career Development.* (3rd ed.) Engle-wood Cliffs, N.J.: Prentice-Hall, 1983.

Perry, W. G., Jr. *Forms of Intellectual and Ethical Development in the College Years: A Scheme.* New York: Holt, Rinehart & Winston, 1970.

Stein, G. B., and Spille, H. A. "Academic Advising Reaches Out." *Personnel and Guidance Journal,* 1974, *53,* 61–64.

Super, D. E. *The Psychology of Careers.* New York: Harper & Row, 1957.

Upcraft, M. L. "Undergraduate Students as Academic Advisors." *Personnel and Guidance Journal,* 1971, *49,* 827–831.

Winston, R. B., Jr., Miller, T. K., and Prince, J. S. *Student Developmental Task Inventory.* (2nd ed.) Athens. Ga.: Student Development Associates, 1979.

Zultowski, W. H., and Catron, D. W. "Students as Curriculum Advisors: Revisited." *Journal of College Student Personnel,* 1976, *17,* 199–204.

Part Four

Translating Theory
into Practice

❧❧❧ ❧❧❧ ❧❧❧ ❧❧❧ ❧❧❧ ❧❧❧ ❧❧❧ ❧❧❧

Part Four concludes the book by presenting examples of academic advising programs that have addressed the goals of developmental academic advising with some success. These examples vividly illustrate that the assumptions and concepts of developmental academic advising have utility and that the goals of developmental academic advising are realizable. Recommendations are offered as well for those who wish to begin the process of re-evaluating their advising systems and introducing developmental advising concepts.

In Chapter Seventeen, Thomas J. Grites has collected examples of "Noteworthy Academic Advising Programs" in the context of four distinctly different service delivery approaches—decentralized advising programs, structured peer advising programs, centralized advising center programs, and advising programs offered as part of a formal course—at widely different sizes and types of colleges. Each institution's program is described in terms of its historical development, specific activities, evaluated outcomes, and utility for implementation at other colleges.

467

Roger B. Winston, Jr., Thomas J. Grites, Theodore K. Miller, and Steven C. Ender (Chapter Eighteen) conclude the book with the epilogue entitled "Improving Academic Advising." They propose viewing academic advising as educational quality control, emphasizing advising's vital importance to the overall health and vitality of the institution, and assert that developmental academic advising is an idea whose time has come. Challenges and opportunities for academic advising to make a difference in higher education in the next decade are identified.

17

Noteworthy
Academic Advising Programs

Thomas J. Grites

Many institutions across the country have developed excellent advising programs. Obviously not all of them can be recognized in a single publication, but this chapter will describe a variety of successful, noteworthy programs. These programs exemplify four basic delivery systems: the *centralized advising approach (advising center)*, the *decentralized approach*, the *peer advising approach*, and a *formal course approach*. Each program is reviewed for its development, specific activities, results, and utility, and readers should examine each program for its adaptability to their own institutions. Although an entire program may not be adaptable, some specific aspects may well be.

In addition to the program descriptions, an analysis of the advantages of each type of system that suggests recommendations for potential use by other institutions is provided. Implications for future considerations in the improvement of advising programs are also included.

Centralized Advising

In response to rapidly increasing enrollments, coupled with lessened faculty interest in academic advising, during the late 1950s and 1960s the concept of the advising center was established (Baxter, 1971). Since that time Crockett and Levitz (Chapter Two) found that approximately 30 percent of the 754 institutions they surveyed had established advising centers, which has become the primary, but not the only, centralized advising approach.

As illustrated in the programs described herein, most campus-wide advising centers are staffed by full-time professional staff advisors who are often supported by selected faculty advisors, counselors, and peer or paraprofessional advisors. The center is a readily accessible repository of information, a significant referral agency, and most recently an academic "home" for many types of students. In fact, Crockett and Levitz found that *the* primary responsibility of advising centers was to advise undecided/undeclared/exploratory students. Other major responsibilities include advising all students on general education requirements, conducting freshman orientation, developing advising handbooks, and maintaining advising records.

The effectiveness of the advising center concept has been shown by Shelton (1972), Pino (1975), and Bonar and Mahler (1976). These authors have reported improved perceptions of the advising process, more positive attitudes toward advisors, more accuracy in registration activities, and better-informed course selections and career plans made by students.

The following institutional programs exemplify the advising center concept.

University of Maryland

History and Development. Prior to the fall of 1972, there were no officially designated "undecided" students at the College Park campus. Recognizing that a student's premature choice of major could be causally related to academic difficulty, the campus senate adopted the 1972 report of its Adjunct Committee on Academic Advising, thus giving students the privilege of remaining "undecided" and creating an office where they would have special advisors until they selected a more definite program. That office became the General Undergraduate Advisement Office, now renamed the Undergraduate Advising Center.

Operating costs remained essentially identical. However, the tone and style of advising required some adjustment to deal with the specific first-year needs of more freshmen and to accommodate a larger number of students who now could officially call themselves "undecided." Staff changes included the appointment of a new director and the addition of a full-time staff member to coordinate advising programs for special student groups, such as handicapped students and honors students.

An organizational change that had considerable impact on the academic "legitimacy" of the office was its movement from student affairs to academic affairs under the direction of the newly appointed dean for undergraduate studies.

Goals and Objectives. In its report to the Board of Regents, the College Park Task Force on Academic Advising issued this statement of objectives for academic advising:

1. helping students understand the nature and purposes of higher education
2. increasing students' awareness of academic programs and course offerings
3. developing insights into personal behavior that promote improved adjustment to the campus setting
4. helping students to clarify their aspirations, interests, and goals
5. providing information about opportunities outside the classroom for intellectual and cultural development
6. identifying institutional resources that will serve each student's educational needs
7. assisting students in acquiring decision-making skills that will enhance academic and career planning

Description of Activities. The advising center has approximately 6,000 advising contacts annually. Two of the most significant annual activities are the preparation of the *Advising Handbook* for duplication and distribution and the coordination of a campus program to select the outstanding advisor from each of the five major academic units on campus. The handbook gives the advising center heightened visibility among all campus agencies that provide services for students. In the same manner, the selection of outstanding advisors provides an annual opportunity to review criteria for excellence in advising with each academic department at the College Park campus.

Other notable activities that, although not offered on a regular or continuing basis, have strengthened the center's coordinating position within the advising system include:

1. a "mentor program" in which new freshman students were paired with members of the campus faculty and staff in a helping relationship
2. the development of a "resident aide" program designed to make advising and informational services available to resident students at hours when regular offices were closed
3. a staff development program for campus advisors designed to introduce a new set of general education requirements
4. a joint effort with the Career Development Center to develop a "structured" approach to educational and career planning for undecided students
5. a joint effort with the Office of Minority Student Education to enlist parents as part of the student's educational and career decision making (the program is called FAST—Family as an Academic Support Team)
6. active and vigorous involvement in preparing a new retention plan for the College Park campus

Evaluation Procedures. For six of its eleven years the Undergraduate Advising Center has conducted annual surveys of academic advising, garnering student perceptions of their advising experiences. Return rates of questionnaires have ranged from a disappointing 9 percent to an astounding 100 percent from individual academic departments. Results have been distributed to the departments with accompanying suggestions and interpretations.

These results have been used as the basis for reprimanding the chief advisor in a major college program, for replacing an "arrogant" and "ineffective" advisor, and, more positively, for creating the criteria by which "outstanding advisors" are annually selected.

Results/Outcomes. The Report of the Adjunct Committee on Academic Advising was a landmark document. It helped transform advising at College Park from a "check-the-catalogue" and "get-your-dean's-stamp" procedure into a planning activity of professional quality.

Results from campus-wide advising surveys showed that students were satisfied with the overall quality of advising within the system and with the system itself.

The Undergraduate Advising Center sets the tone for and develops expectations for effective advising at a campus level. In turn, major academic units and their individual academic departments adopt these expectations and, consequently, students are able to perceive a reassuring "connectedness" within the system.

Limitations/Changes. Some areas that require or required alterations within the system include:

1. *Territoriality or "turf":* Even with a central coordinating office the system is, nonetheless, an intricate network of advisors and advising programs. Responding to unique personal preferences in a way that rewards constructive local initiative while discouraging activity that contravenes the purposes of a centralized system has required timely, sensitive negotiation.
2. *Criteria for advisor evaluation:* The various advising styles and approaches do not allow the use of a single set of criteria by which effective advising can be evaluated.
3. *Dependency:* The tendency in a centralized system may be to overcentralize. The resultant dependency on the central office to know all and provide all adds little professional vibrancy to the system.
4. *Budget diffusion:* A long-standing problem for the advising center has been having too small a budget to fulfill its assigned responsibilities. The money exists but in someone else's budget. The funds allocated to a central coordinating office must be in direct proportion to the kind and extent of respon-

sibilities it is expected to fulfill, and that office must control the expenditure of those funds. Both encourage planned use of resources, as well as planned responses to the many needs of the advising system.

Pennsylvania State University

History and Development. Pennsylvania State University has long been committed to providing an enrollment structure that accommodates students' indecision regarding curricular choice.

Following World War II the Division of Intermediate Registration (DIR) was established to provide advising and counseling for veterans returning to the college campus. In 1957 the function of DIR was integrated with the Student Advisory Service to create the Division of Counseling. During the 1960s highly competitive job placement activities evolved, student unrest characterized campus life, and students' indecision about major choices became more typical. Partly in response to these factors, the integrated Division of Counseling was dissolved in 1972, and three new functional units—the Career Development and Placement Center, the Mental Health Center, and the Division of Undergraduate Studies—were created.

Upon the recommendation of the University Faculty Senate, and with the approval of the university administration and Board of Trustees, the Division of Undergraduate Studies (DUS) was established in 1973 as an undergraduate academic unit. Currently, the DUS staff includes the full-time equivalent of ten academic advising staff members, which yields an average ratio of one advisor for 125–175 students. Four clerical support staff complete the personnel.

Goals and Objectives. Pennsylvania State University has recognized the importance of providing opportunities for freshman and sophomore students to explore a variety of educational and career options in order to meet their developmental needs and choose major programs. In the DUS Enrollment Program, students work with professional academic advisors who: (1) provide regular, systematic evaluations of their advisees' educational plans with respect to their abilities, academic performance, and changing interests and (2) provide advice regarding the appropriateness of their advisees' course choices.

Description of Activities. Entering freshman degree candidates may request direct admission to the Division of Undergraduate Studies (one of eleven possible enrollment units). Students matriculating in any other enrollment unit may request a transfer to DUS. Any student is eligible for enrollment in DUS for a maximum time period of one academic year, in addition to the freshman year.

Total student enrollment in DUS in 1984 numbers over 2,800. For freshman students alone, DUS is the second largest enrollment unit, surpassed only by the College of Engineering.

In addition to serving matriculated degree candidates, DUS is responsible for providing advising support to undergraduates not yet admitted to degree status (2,300 students in 1984). This group of "provisional" students includes individuals who must demonstrate their abilities to succeed in college-level course work in order to gain admission to degree candidacy. Included in this group are those students typically classified as nontraditional, for example, students who are older, in part-time attendance, or unsure about their commitment to complete a baccalaureate degree.

DUS maintains a staff of professional advisors whose full-time responsibilities are to provide academic advising assistance to undergraduate students. Personnel are selected, in part, based on their commitment to providing quality academic advising, as well as upon their skills. DUS advisors are trained to:

1. assist students with their academic decisions and plans by applying an understanding of individual differences in student interests, motivations, values, and educational and career aspirations
2. interpret results of tests of academic ability, aptitude, and achievement as well as vocational interest inventories and educational planning questionnaires
3. keep appropriate records of contacts with students
4. understand the academic policies and procedures of the university
5. understand the academic structure of the university including

the colleges, and the departments and majors that are part of each college

6. serve as an academic advising and information resource for faculty, professional support staff, and administration

7. be knowledgeable about current research and developments in the fields of testing, advising, and counseling

DUS is responsible for two additional programs that support the total advising effort of the university—the Freshman Testing, Counseling, and Advising Program (FTCAP) and the Academic Information Support Program (AISP). The purpose of the FTCAP is to assist freshman and provisional students, before their initial registration, in evaluating their educational plans by providing each student with a comprehensive program of testing and individualized counseling and advising. This program is the first stage of academic advising for all entering freshmen and provides students with an understanding of their scholastic preparation, academic abilities, and educational and occupational interests.

AISP's purpose is to support the academic advising activities of the university. This support is provided through a network of formally designated consultants assigned to each academic college and Penn State's branch campuses and through systematic dissemination of academic information, such as policy, procedure, and program changes.

Evaluation Procedures. Program efforts and individual staff performance are evaluated using a variety of approaches. Individual staff performance is evaluated through a mailed student evaluation survey and through evaluation conferences with supervisors.

Evaluation of the overall program is achieved through:

1. Academic Advising Analysis 1982 (student feedback and administrative review)

2. Intake Feedback Form (survey of students receiving advising assistance through the DUS intake service)

3. FTCAP Evaluation (separate written survey forms for students and families attending this pre-enrollment program)

4. Student Interview Record (quantitative analyses of numbers of students advised, class standings and enrollment units of

students advised, content of advising sessions, types of referrals made, and curricular goals of students advised)

Results/Outcomes. The major outcomes of the DUS program are as follows:

1. Students transfer to a program of study that is consistent with their interests and academic abilities.
2. Students who use DUS enrollment as a mechanism for curricular exploration change programs less frequently than students never enrolled in DUS.
3. Students who enroll in DUS initially as new freshmen graduate with higher grade point averages (GPAs) than students who enroll in other units as new freshmen.
4. One out of six students graduating from the university had been enrolled in DUS for at least one academic term.

Limitations/Changes. The DUS Enrollment Program could function much more effectively if it were expanded into a "University College." Such a concept would permit *all* university freshmen to enroll in the same unit, to work with full-time academic advising specialists, and to have the opportunity to explore curricular options and thus avoid being pressured into making premature and uninformed curricular choices.

University of Utah

History and Development. Prior to 1972, the responsibilities for academic counseling at the University of Utah were assigned to selected faculty members who were asked to provide assistance to students in program planning, registration, academic standards counseling, and adjustment to the university. Students who had not selected a major prior to entering the university were assigned to the faculty group designated as the general education counselors. When the major academic field was chosen, the students were assigned to a departmental faculty advisor and remained with this advisor until they graduated or transferred to another major.

During the period of the Vietnam conflict, the central administration asked an external market survey and organizational consulting firm to do a study of the student body and assess the potential levels and sources of unrest. The primary area of discomfort identified by the students was poor academic counseling. A parallel internal study was done by the counseling center staff to assess the counseling needs of the student body. This study also found that the primary area of complaint was related to poor academic advising.

After considerable planning, it was felt that an integrated advising "system" with a centralized office that would receive, monitor, and guide students to the appropriate departments and majors, supplemented by a supporting system of college satellite centers and departmental faculty advisors, would meet most of the student and institutional needs. Thus, in 1973, the deans of general education, admissions, and student affairs pooled their budgets and staff resources to create a new Center for Academic Advising.

Initially, the staffing for the agency resulted from combining an existing unit of registration advisors and the staff from the Office for Scholastic Standards. The associate director of the counseling center served as the new agency director.

A second major problem was the availability of space. If the agency was to be effective, it would also have to be centralized geographically. An existing "record listening" room in the student center was converted to house the office. The new office configuration had few walls and an "open landscape"-type office design that would more readily facilitate easy access to advisors by the students. Music, partial walls with special sound baffling materials, and the attention of students and advisors to their own tasks very easily provided the private atmosphere required for academic advising.

This new agency also allowed the creation of a matrix organizational model where tasks could be shared. The agency was able to go to the central administration for increased financial support after the first year. Over a three-year period there was incremental support of approximately 20 percent of the base budget per year. The 1983 budget was approximately $350,000.

The administrative model adopted for the center suggested the use of professional advising staff in the colleges. These "satellite" centers were located near the offices of the academic deans in order to make professional advising services more accessible and to facilitate intercollegiate transfer of students. Satellite center advisors were to provide record keeping, faculty training, and "backup" professional counseling for the faculty advisors. They also assisted the dean's office in establishing policy relative to advising, assigning students to faculty advisors, and providing information about advisor effectiveness. The advisor was always responsible to the advising center rather than the college dean. This administrative condition was to ensure that the advisor would not become an administrative assistant to the dean and would continue to be a student advocate rather than an agent of policy.

The third unit of this integrated advising system was faculty or departmental advisors. The selection process for faculty advisors was the same as it had been previous to the establishment of the integrated system; however, the attention paid to advising created greater interest by the academic deans in selecting good advisors.

Finally, a faculty advisor committee was established for the institution as a whole. This committee developed faculty advising training materials and workshops.

Goals and Objectives. The goals of the center and the integrated advising system included (1) providing students with accurate, accessible, and easily interpreted information about the various academic elements of the university; (2) assisting students with the integration of this information into their career and life plans; and (3) helping them make effective major choices and curriculum plans on the basis of this information.

Description of Activities. The following activities make up a large part of the center's work:

1. *New student academic conferences:* These conferences include information about the liberal education requirements, academic majors, and the registration process. They are designed to help students make appropriate course selections and to teach decision making through the choice of classes.

2. *Registration advising:* This service is available to help continuing students plan their programs of study to meet graduation

requirements or select courses that meet their own interests and
needs.

3. *General education/liberal education advising:* This includes
   monitoring, reviewing, and auditing a student's liberal education program.

4. *Scholastic standards advising:* This activity monitors the standards established by the Academic Evaluations and Standards
   Committee.

5. *Guided studies advising:* This function is designed to facilitate
   the placement of "predicted low-achieving students" into appropriate student support systems for the development of
   college academic achievement skills.

6. *Veteran and military affairs:* This office facilitates the entry of
   veterans by providing academic advising and certification for
   educational benefits.

7. *Ethnic tutorial services:* This service facilitates improved academic success among minority students by procuring and
   coordinating tutoring services.

8. *Learning and educational alternative programs:* This program
   offers students general information and counseling on the
   enrichment of their education via interdisciplinary degrees,
   work credit, campus exchanges, and study/travel abroad.

Evaluation Procedures. The procedures for evaluating the
advising system included five activities. The first related to student
traffic and was compiled by the secretarial staff as students entered
the various offices. A second activity was the completion of a brief
form by the advisor, describing the nature of the contact. A third set
of evaluations of the program was gathered during random time
periods to assess both advisors' and advisees' performances. A fourth
evaluation strategy included random sampling of members of the
student body, who were asked to respond to open-ended questionnaires on the use and effectiveness of the service. A fifth piece of
evaluative information was a one-time survey that was conducted
for the Student Affairs Division by an outside consultant.

Results/Outcomes. The following positive outcomes have
resulted from the program:

1. At the end of the first five-year period, there were over 30,000 advising contacts per year representing a 20 percent growth per year. An equal number of contacts that were not defined as advising but as simple information seeking occurred in the same time period.
2. Studies to evaluate student perceptions of counseling and advising effectiveness resulted in evaluations that were above national norms and above the norms for other institutions' professional counseling staffs. They were at the national norms for the faculty advisors in three of five studies completed, and in two of five they were above the national averages.
3. Two studies were conducted to evaluate the student needs so that further program planning and development could occur. A group program for probationary students and a parent advising program for the parents of incoming students resulted from these.
4. A business college consultant did an organizational diagnosis and analysis of the staff of the centralized offices. This led to the development of a staff workshop for upgrading of training and the basis for the creation of a management-by-objective worksheet for each advisor and the organization as a whole.
5. An evaluation was made of services for probationary students and found that they performed better in their academic work by nearly one-half grade point average (GPA).

Limitations/Changes. The limitations that must be addressed in a model such as the University of Utah's are as follows:

1. A model of this type demands a very high commitment on the part of the institution for effective academic advising. The corollary of this is that it also requires a significant budget base.
2. An integrated system requires an academically knowledgeable, credible facilitator as the director. The combined experience of a professional background, knowledge about student affairs, and the helping skills of counseling are important in making an integrated system work.
3. A system that has "outreach" offices with single advisors is

particularly vulnerable to "raids" from college deans or department chairs during periods of economic cutbacks.

4. For the staff members in the centralized and satellite center
    positions, considerable training and experience are necessary.
    It also takes considerable effort to prepare and train faculty for
    their role in the integrated system.

5. One of the real problems with the system at the University of
    Utah is not having sufficient incentives for the faculty.

6. The final and perhaps most critical aspect of establishing an
    integrated system of this type is having strong political allies
    and supporters among the deans and central administration
    staff. If these are not available, implementation of the program
    will be difficult.

Des Moines Area Community College

History and Development. As most institutions have experienced financial limitations, Des Moines Area Community College
also was challenged to adjust its 1978–79 resource allocations. In
order to accommodate this adjustment, the vice-president of student
life mandated improvements in the overall effectiveness of the
operations of the college. One method recommended to achieve this
was a centralized form of group guidance that would maximize
advisor time, institutional monies, and physical facilities.

A task force of counseling, admissions, adult education, and
placement personnel was formed. Its goals were to create a more
effective use of existing personnel, to coordinate various college
services, and to assist students in developing the skills and abilities
to "do for themselves."

With the assistance of an Advanced Institutional Development Program (AIDP) grant (Title III), the "Planning for College
Success Program" was begun. The grant provided for four to five
educational advisors, who were beyond the twelve currently funded
college counselors. Together the advisors and counselors constituted a central advising staff for new students.

Goals and Objectives. The two major goals of the program
are to assist new applicants in assessing their college readiness in
the areas of mathematics, reading, and writing and to assist new

applicants in developing a plan for achieving their college goals. These goals may be achieved through a self-assessment exercise, knowledge gained from other college facilities and resources (such as the Learning Center), or individual goals realized through advisor intervention and discussion.

A practical goal of the institution is to ensure participation in the program within the first four weeks after the student has applied. As an open admissions institution, new students range from those still in high school to those typically described as nontraditional, that is, older returning adults. It is critical, therefore, to orient this diverse student population prior to their first registration at the college.

Description of Activities. The program is required for all first-time, full-time students, and includes a sequential variety of advising activities. These activities are designed to be fairly uniform among advisors and counselors.

The first activity is a group discussion, led by an advisor or counselor, that centers on the academic program into which the students plan to enter.

The students next complete the *Planning for College Success Workbook.* This involves a series of exercises, ranging from skills assessment to the "College Success Survey." Discussions among students and facilitators occur throughout this activity.

Students then tour the campus with the advisor and end the tour in their academic department. Here the program chairperson or a faculty member describes specific aspects of that major and reviews core requirements. Requirement sheets for potential transfer institutions and articulation agreements are also reviewed for those students who plan to pursue bachelor's degrees.

Evaluation Procedures. Individual student evaluation is achieved by completing the workbook. Program evaluation is conducted via a questionnaire that is administered immediately after the program is completed. Results from this instrument are analyzed and evaluated by the Research, Planning, and Reporting Department.

Results/Outcomes. The Research, Planning, and Reporting Department found that students who participated in the program were (1) better able to assess their college goals; (2) better able to describe their test results as they applied to placement in developmental courses; (3) better informed about college resources; (4) less likely to change programs since they had made better course choices initially; and (5) less likely to seek personal, crisis-type counseling.

In addition, the following results have been observed:

1. an increased use of educational advisors; consequently, more will be employed
2. counselors are used more efficiently and effectively; although there are now fewer, they are better able to respond to the personal and emotional concerns of students, as well as to be able to teach human potential courses in the regular curriculum
3. an increased use of the Learning Center
4. students schedule classes that are more consistent with their abilities and needs; this is especially evidenced in their own choices to enroll in adaptor (developmental) courses

Limitations/Changes. For the future, the following recommendations have been made:

1. The workshop should be mandatory for *all* students, full-time and part-time.
2. The workshop should be extended to two days in order to include the actual registration for the next term.
3. The workshop might be offered as a separate short course for academic credit.
4. Additional training of group facilitators must be designed to include elements of student development theory and the management of time in presenting materials.

Summary

The advantages to centralized advising are clearly demonstrated in the programs just described. Crockett (1982) lists some of these as accessibility to students, well-trained advisors, a wide range of available services, more efficient record maintenance, and ease of administration, training, supervision, and evaluation.

In all these programs the institutional recognition of need and its commitment to improvement of the advising program are obvious. Without such commitment, no program will succeed to its fullest potential. The specific activities of each program are varied and also designed to meet certain needs, such as Maryland's resident aide and FAST programs and Utah's "guided studies" effort.

The most significant features of these programs are in the results shown. Student satisfaction with advising and better student decision-making skills seem to be the major outcomes of these programs, and these are not easy ones to achieve in any system. In addition, positive results have also been shown in the areas of student retention, student achievement (GPA), and student use of other campus resources.

Many diverse activities are included in the centralized advising approaches described here. The reader should carefully examine each activity for its conceptual base and its practical application in a new setting. Many can be modified to help ensure success in one's own program even if it is not centralized.

Although the direct cost of establishing an advising center may be prohibitive, institutions might still be wise to consider some alternative form of centralized advising, as Des Moines Area Community College has done. If for no other reason than to provide a controlled, timely, and consistent flow of information (to advisors and to students), some centralized effort needs to be maintained. Often this is accomplished by the identification of a director or coordinator of advising whose *primary* responsibility is the coordination of all aspects of the campus advising effort. Without such coordination, the flow of information becomes fragmented, inconsistent, or even absent.

Decentralized Advising

Until the advent of the advising center, academic advising was provided in a single mode, namely, faculty advising. Faculty members always had been considered the most appropriate persons to guide students in course selection and the most knowledgeable persons to provide academic information. Students were assigned to, or sought, faculty members in their academic majors and rarely extended themselves beyond these departmental confines. Thus, a decentralized approach to academic advising characterized most institutions.

Although academic advising has grown well beyond simple course selection to a total student development process, Crockett and Levitz (Chapter Two) reported that advising by faculty continues to be the predominant advising delivery mode at all types of institutions. Some faculty members are used in advising centers, but the majority still advise in the decentralized, usually departmentally based, arrangement. The potential problems with such an arrangement were summarized by Crockett (1982). He indicated that faculty advisors tend to be discipline oriented, have competing priorities of teaching and research, and generally lack the interest, skills, and rewards necessary for effective advising.

In recent years the advising center concept has been extended to the college, school, and department levels to offset these potential difficulties (Polson and Jurich, 1979; Hickerson, 1982; Spencer, Peterson, and Kramer, 1982). Periodic advising activities have also been employed successfully in hallways, other college centers, residence halls, and even off the campus. These decentralized approaches have resulted in more positive student attitudes toward advising, fewer major changes, reduced attrition, increased course registrations, and increased academic performance (Stein and Spille, 1974; Glennen, 1976; Brown and Twedt, 1981).

Though decentralized advising, in the form of faculty advising, has often been criticized, it should not be eliminated. As Grites (1979) noted, faculty advising should be considered for its potential effectiveness rather than for its problems. Faculty members are generally more knowledgeable about specific course content, subtle interpretations of major requirements, and graduate school and career opportunities within their disciplines.

The following programs provide examples of effective advising using various decentralized administrative approaches.

State University of New York, College at Oswego (SUNY-Oswego)

History and Development. The concept of shared responsibility for academic advising was initiated when an ad hoc group of academic and student affairs administrators began to discuss student attrition in 1976. The work of this group resulted in the identification of two high-risk, attrition-prone groups: students who started college without a major and those who have academic difficulty early in their college experience.

A pilot program of mentoring, based on an intrusive advising approach, was established for the academic year 1977–78. This was the first of many steps that led to the "differentiated delivery system" for academic advising at Oswego.

Following the success of the mentoring project, the Student Advisement Center was established as an expansion of the former Dean of Students' Office. This action represented the first time that the Division of Student Services was formally involved in the academic advising on the Oswego campus. The coordination of advisor assignments, advisor training, and academic advisor responsibilities were new functions added to the traditional ones for the dean of students' staff.

Delivery of these services depended on volunteer faculty and staff; thus, the costs involved in better serving this attrition-prone group were limited to materials. In the first year, trained volunteer advisors represented academic divisions of the college, student services, the library, and the administration.

Goals and Objectives. Initially, the intrusive advising approach was designed: (1) to serve better the attrition-prone students; (2) to support the effort with printed material; and (3) to inform better both students and advisors of policies, resources, and options. Subsequently, it became obvious that there were several groups of students who would benefit from specialized advising attention.

Because the academic deans' offices and the Student Advisement Center serve a broad cross-section of "walk-in" students, staff in these offices have continued to identify *patterns* of advising needs that have resulted in the identification of student groups to be served by a decentralized and differentiated delivery system. Currently the target groups include:

1. declared majors who receive advising from faculty in their major fields (Each academic department has identified an advisement coordinator; the coordinators meet at least once

each semester to be updated by both associate deans, the associate provost, the advisement center coordinator, and others.)

2. transfer students who must declare a major upon entrance and whose advising is coordinated by a system of transfer advisement coordinators in academic departments

3. undeclared majors who receive academic advising services through the Student Advisement Center

4. students on academic warning who are targeted for special attention (The Mandatory Readvisement Form must be completed with their assigned advisor before their final registration for the subsequent semester, and a prescribed follow-up contact with the advisor is scheduled.)

5. Office of Special Program students who receive intrusive advising services that are further supported by a system of math and writing clinics and tutorial services

6. reinstated students who continue contact with their assigned major advisors but must also follow a set of academic program conditions mandated by their respective deans

The traditional faculty-based advising system, which emphasizes expertise in a major field and depends on student initiative to "ask a question when you need something," continues to be adequate for many students. However, certain groups of students are better served by the more carefully tailored advising attention provided by an intrusive approach.

Description of Activities. The ongoing activities of the program reflect responses to the needs of the targeted student groups. Specifically, new undeclared students receive advisor assignments by mail prior to arriving on campus. The advisor is expected to initiate a minimum of three contacts with each new advisee over the first semester, ensuring that the initial contact occurs early in the fall semester. In addition, lower-division students who entered the college with a declared major may choose to become "undecided" and are reassigned to a volunteer advisor.

The orientation program for transfer students is primarily focused on delivering accurate and supportive academic information to the students who enter the college with declared majors.

Where possible, this initial contact with a major advisor becomes the continuing advisor contact for the entering transfer student.

Students who are placed on academic warning are obligated to "mandatory readvisement." This process includes a checklist to guide the discussion and culminates in a written Mandatory Readvisement Form. The conditions set forth on this form convey clear academic expectations for the student and leave little doubt about the seriousness of the academic situation.

Students who fail to meet the minimum scholarship standards are disqualified. Approximately one half of those students request permission to return to the college in the subsequent semester. After a formal hearing process, approximately 30 percent of these students are reinstated for a second chance to achieve academic success. Each of these reinstated students receives an individualized set of conditions governing reinstatement.

Evaluation Procedures. In addition to student retention at Oswego through the 1981–82 academic year, which was achieved in large part because of the increased attention to advising, there are other specific evaluation efforts.

The Student Advisement Center has been evaluated each year with an instrument distributed to a sample of students served by the center. The center is also evaluated more broadly in an annual effort to assess the effectiveness of the Division of Student Services for the general student body.

Evaluation of the mandatory readvisement process remains fairly subjective, but the success rate of reinstated students is reviewed annually.

Results/Outcomes. Evaluations of the center have typically indicated that (1) students were generally satisfied with the services; (2) there was little discrepancy between the level of service desired and service received; (3) there was a definite relationship between the level of student satisfaction and the "grade" they awarded their advisor; and (4) students served by the center staff throughout the entire year experienced the highest levels of satisfaction.

In the general student services evaluation, 84 percent of the students surveyed in 1981–82 indicated that they "have enough confidence to return to this (center) office," and an equal percentage responded that "the staff seemed to know their jobs."

The mandatory readvisement process seems to have diminished the disastrous patterns of course selection, failures to repeat courses, and/or misunderstandings of academic policies previously in evidence. Reinstated students succeeded at a rate of 65.1 percent, as compared to less than 50 percent prior to the program's initiation.

The program was designed to develop an approach that capitalizes on basic ability but also gives the student the insight, structure, and support necessary for academic success. In a sense, the differentiated delivery system for advising allows for "teaching the college" to groups of students who might not otherwise have been able to survive in the college setting.

Limitations/Changes. An inherent weakness in not hiring professional advisors is that inconsistencies in quality and time commitment of individual advisors are often apparent. In spite of better materials and more training and attention to good advising, some faculty members continue to regard academic advising as a very low priority in their workday. Those who volunteer to serve through the Student Advisement Center are usually positively motivated but, when burdened with other responsibilities, their "volunteer" activities are often compromised.

Finally, there is the terrible truth that those who provide quality academic advising are usually "rewarded" by increased student demands and heavier advising loads. Since additional staff resources or reduced teaching loads appear to be out of the question, the use of receptions and certificates and the institutional leadership's commitment to consider "service to students" for merit/promotion decisions must maintain staff/faculty commitment to quality academic advising services.

California State University, Chico (CSU-Chico)

History and Development. Through the mid-1960s faculty advising was coordinated through the counseling program under student affairs. In 1967, during a period of rapid university growth, the director of counseling created the position of coordinator of advising from a newly allocated counseling position. It was the responsibility of the coordinator to strengthen academic department advising. In the summer of 1969 the office was administratively separated from the Counseling Center and expanded to include the academic counseling of students who were subject to academic disqualification, new student orientation, and the coordination of draft counseling in liaison with draft boards.

Through the early 1970s the Advising Office experienced considerable growth in function, space, and personnel, largely because of increased student use, changing requirements, and the recognized value of combining academic advising and career counseling. Thus was laid the structure of a comprehensive advising center functioning within what remained a basically decentralized faculty advising system. Academic departments retained advising responsibility for their major, minor, and teaching credential candidates.

In subsequent years the office increased its emphasis on retention, established programs and services for re-entry students, conducted exit interviews for withdrawing students, and developed a summer orientation program. A significant effort has been the increased involvement with academic departments to prepare campus publications, notably the recent computerized catalogue. Improved accuracy and consistency have resulted.

Program costs for 1982–83, excluding professional and clerical salaries, total approximately $31,800. In addition, the largely self-supporting summer orientation program has an operating budget of about $60,000.

The most recent significant change affecting the office has been its reassignment. Since 1983, the Advising and Orientation and the Admissions and Records Offices report to the vice-president for academic affairs. The intent, in part, is to increase the visibility and communication between these offices and the academic leadership of the university, where responsibility for much of academic advising lies in the decentralized structure.

Goals and Objectives. The 1973 Advising and Orientation Office master plan contained the following statement of goals, which basically remain the same today:

1. to foster the educational development of students by
    a. helping them cope with institutional policies and proce-

dures, so that they may focus on educational goals more
completely

b. developing their awareness and creative use of educational
    programs and resources

c. enhancing the learning environment within the limits of
    our resources

d. "legitimizing" for them educational and developmental
    goals in light of competing peer groups and other
    influences

2. to develop and maintain quality academic advising and new
    student orientation programs in cooperation with several other
    offices and, thereby, contribute to the "humanity of the
    University"

3. to achieve consistency, clarity, and humanity in campus edu-
    cational policy and advising procedures

4. to provide specialized advising and educational counseling
    services

   In 1975 the office worked closely with the Faculty Senate
toward the development of a university advising policy, which has
since been revised. This process helped establish the concept of
advising coordinators for each academic program; increase attention paid to advising in retention, tenure, and promotion deliber-
ations; and clarify the various roles of those offices that have
responsibilities for advising and career planning. The policy describes the functions of academic advising as (1) providing students
with information on policies, procedures, and programs of the
university; (2) assisting students in choosing educational and career
objectives commensurate with their interests and abilities; (3) assisting students in exploring the possible short- and long-range consequences of their choices; and (4) making students aware of the
wide range of services and educational opportunities that may be
pertinent to their educational objectives.

   Description of Activities. The major activities of the office
include:

1. *Publications:* These include *A Guide to General Studies;*
    academic and student affairs program planning guides; sec-

tions of the *University Catalogue and Class Schedule; Last Minute Notes,* a newsletter highlighting general information and updates for prospective students; and occasional newsletters to faculty describing new and revised policies, procedures, and programs.

2. *New student orientation:* These activities include overnight sessions using fifteen paid peer advisors, faculty advising sessions, extensive campus tours, student and staff panels, and detailed explanations of requirements and procedures.

3. *Undeclared student advising:* For about 30 percent of the freshmen and sophomores, interest testing and other career planning tools are used as appropriate.

4. *Coordination of faculty advising:* Through the assignment of professional staff as liaisons to one or more of the academic schools of the university, the staff conducts workshops for academic departments and serves as a resource to faculty on student problems and academic policy and procedure. Each department/program has one or more advising coordinators who serve as communication links, but department approaches to advising vary widely. The office also distributes various reports to departments and schools, including information pertaining to their majors' grade summaries, academic standing, and change of major. In general, the office provides and administers the general framework in which departmental advising occurs and serves as a resource to the university community in that regard.

5. *Academic standing reviews:* Staff act as nonvoting members on each school's academic standing committee. Students who have been or may be academically disqualified are invited to meet with a staff member for academic counseling and to review records and consider alternatives.

6. *Drop-in advising:* Students bring to the office a wide variety of concerns including general education and other graduation requirements, changing major, use of elective credit, problems with instructors, and so on.

7. *Exit interviews:* These are conducted with students officially withdrawing from the university.

8. *Re-entry student advising:* This is primarily concerned with

coordinating special programs for older students returning to college.

9. *Staff and faculty training:* At one point the office directed a funded faculty advisor training program for three academic departments. The intent was to concentrate efforts on the three as a model for assisting other departments and for the development and application of various advising models, resources, and approaches. Faculty members participated in various advising workshops and elected other activities designed to assist them with each department's unique advising program.

Evaluation Procedures. The campus advising policy approved by the Faculty Senate specifies that advising be evaluated biannually. The Institution Research Office developed an instrument for this assessment that has now been incorporated into a five-year degree program review process. In 1983 the Faculty Senate conducted a survey of faculty attitudes.

The Advising and Orientation Office developed a second instrument for use by academic departments. The office also gathers data about academic standing of students and the performance of reinstated students, and tallies are kept on the numbers of students advised each semester and on participants in the summer orientation program. Students and parents attending summer orientation programs are also asked to complete evaluation forms, which are reviewed after each session.

Results/Outcomes. Verbal support for the office has remained high. The summer orientation program is very well regarded among the campus academic leadership. The number of students who use the office continues to increase. Financial support has remained relatively constant and adequate. The office has become the primary source of communication to the campus community about academic policy and procedure. Far fewer students are seen whose graduation is delayed as a result of poor advising; the numbers of students who seem to demonstrate effective use of the curriculum through the completion of double majors, minors, and in other ways has increased substantially; and the general reputation of the office among students seems relatively high as reflected in the various surveys. The office has been quite successful as a catalyst for changes in policy and procedure.

Perhaps most importantly, the advising approaches used in the office seem to work well in accomplishing its goals. A conscious effort is made to assess students' goals, self-awareness, and campus awareness. Staff are encouraged to be cognizant of the various developmental stages and states of readiness among students to make personal, academic, and career decisions. Students are taught to understand the overall structure of the degree program and how the various parts fit together so that they gain insight into relationships of the parts. The office seeks not to foster dependence among students but to teach effective problem-solving skills and to help students to take responsibility for the outcomes of their decisions.

Limitations/Changes. The scope of services rendered by the Advising and Orientation Office has been sufficiently broad, and the number of students who use it is at times overwhelming. Consequently, insufficient or at least inconsistent concern has been paid to strengthening the quality of faculty advising in the various academic departments. An administrative structure exists through the campus advising policy to facilitate interaction with the departments, but it has not been used to its full potential. For example, faculty contributions as advisors are not consistently considered in the retention, tenure, and promotion process.

Given the extensive interaction with undeclared students, staff recognize the need to increase their skills in the areas of career planning and development. However, the physical separation of the two units reduces the amount of interaction and sharing of such resources as the career library and staff.

Since many graduate students advise in the Advising and Orientation Office, a high rate of turnover is expected. Training and supervision of these advisors are high priorities, but adequate time and techniques for these functions are not always available. Consequently, a certain amount of risk and potential error exists.

Of deep concern is the discrepancy between the numbers of students gravitating toward high-tech and business programs, at the expense of the liberal arts, and the numbers who have adequate preparation for or lasting interests in such programs. The uncertainty of the need for "vocational" as opposed to "liberal" skills acquired in colleges in today's labor market and the difficulty in communicating the distinction between these to students present a major challenge to advisors.

Perhaps most importantly, the number of students who indicate some degree of dissatisfaction with advising remains higher than the staff desires. In a survey conducted in 1981, about 20 percent of the students expressed some degree of dissatisfaction. It requires a continued effort on several fronts to keep pace, to be responsive to current needs, and to improve the quality of advising in service to students.

Broome Community College

History and Development. Academic advising at Broome Community College has varied according to the types of students involved. Full-time day students have always been advised by the chairpersons and/or other department faculty members, although a few modifications have occurred. In 1974, when college enrollments grew and certain programs "capped" their enrollments, student development counselors in the counseling center began advising the undecided liberal arts students. In 1976, when the orientation program included academic and career testing, these counselors also began to work closely with those who tested poorly in math, reading, and/or writing. In 1979 the learning skills (remedial/developmental) staff began advising skills-deficient students.

Part-time day and evening students had been advised by specific program advisors in their respective areas of study since 1960. In 1973 four positions as assistant to the dean were created specifically to provide advising in the academic divisions of the college. In 1976 these positions were converted to three continuing education advisors, one each in business, technology, and liberal arts. This approach has continued, although since 1976 a somewhat more centralized approach was begun with designated hours, a coordinator of evening advising, and a concerted effort to encourage more of these part-time students to pursue a formal major.

Today Broome emphasizes a "one college" concept and is in the process of developing a Student Academic Advisement Center, primarily for part-time students and those on vocational education grants. Student development counselors and learning skills staff will continue to work with undecided and skills-deficient students, but the mainstay of advising will continue to rest with the academic departments.

Goals and Objectives. The following goals have been established for the program:

1. to recognize and understand that individuals go through a series of developmental stages and that all students are not at the same phase of any particular stage simultaneously
2. to develop group programs and individual efforts that communicate the academic options available and to assist students in developing their personal/professional goals and priorities
3. to facilitate the establishment of good rapport and relationships between advisors and advisees
4. to understand that each student derives a different meaning from each experience
5. to be familiar with student development theory and approach advisees in a manner that facilitates individual growth and development

To achieve these goals, advisors are encouraged to:

1. communicate information regarding degree/program requirements, scheduling of classes, and registration
2. collaborate with all other college personnel involved in the advising process as appropriate
3. refer students to appropriate college personnel when necessary ·
4. consult with students regarding academic progress toward degree/program, academic achievement, and instructional concerns
5. work with advisees regarding evaluation of college and noncollege transfer credit

Description of Activities. Advisors of part-time students, student development counselors, and department chairpersons all attempt to approach the advising process from the same perspective. This includes assessing students' interests and aptitudes for their academic or career goals; discussing specific program requirements and expectations; facilitating the administrative procedures necessary to meet these goals and requirements, including updating the information file; planning and implementing the new student orientation program; and monitoring academic progress, as part of an "early warning system."

Advisors attend various institutional training workshops, as well as state and regional ones, in order to improve their advising skills. Institutional training efforts have primarily focused on the appropriate use of materials throughout the advising process. These include the *Broome Community College Catalogue,* individual program worksheets, registration tallies, the *Liberal Arts Advising Handbook,* test scores, and transfer reports (to four-year institutions).

Evaluation Procedures. At each graduation period a Likert-type scale questionnaire is administered to each graduate. Part-time and evening students are asked to complete similar questionnaires each time they receive advising. These surveys of student satisfaction with advising have provided the basis for evaluation of the program.

As part of a current New York State vocational education grant, Broome is developing a new common evaluation form for all students.

Results/Outcomes. Graduates have consistently indicated that they are generally satisfied with the advising received. Knowing that students are satisfied has resulted in efforts to ensure more advisor availability, to develop a better advisor access to student records, and to create a more direct communication link between the academic departments and the centralized advising personnel.

Evaluations from the part-time students have resulted in a more concerted advising effort for dismissed and reinstated students, especially by making advisors more available and providing them better access to student records. Also, these data have provided favorable support for receipt of the vocational education grant.

Limitations/Changes. The flow of information among all offices and individuals involved in the advising process is not always as complete and efficient as it needs to be, and the system is still too passive. Although various brochures have been developed to assist students in such areas as determining academic status and choosing a major, additional publicity about advising is necessary, particularly in the area of early academic warning.

Summary

Though each of the programs just described includes central-ized offices or components, decentralized faculty advising plays a significant role in their overall success. At SUNY-Oswego, for example, the coordination between the areas of student affairs and academic affairs is especially exemplary; at CSU-Chico the advising coordinators provide a critical link between the central office and the faculty; and at Broome Community College the attempt to provide advising services according to the various types of student needs has appeal.

Not all institutions are able (or desire) to centralize their advising functions; therefore, the decentralized approach should be reviewed for its effectiveness. Besides those advantages listed earlier for faculty advisors, a decentralized approach can provide more of a sense of personalization to students, can be supervised more directly, and can usually be provided with currently existing personnel, space, and budgetary support. The programs described in this section have shown positive results in the students' academic planning, satisfaction with advising, and academic success. These advantages and outcomes are certainly worthy of consideration by all institutions as they seek to improve their own advising pro-grams. Furthermore, the activities described to achieve these results are generally adaptable at most institutions, whether the advising program is decentralized or not.

Peer Advising

Students influencing other students is not a new phenom-enon in higher education. Except in residence halls, however, institutions did not really capitalize on this influence until the 1960s. Since that time, formal peer assistance programs have been developed in counseling, orientation, tutoring, academic advising, and other areas. Most recently, such efforts have been directed toward specific student populations—for example, returning adults, minorities, veterans, and handicapped students.

Crockett and Levitz (Chapter Two) found 42 percent of the institutions surveyed had established some form of peer advising program, an increase from 31 percent found by Carstensen and Silberhorn (1979). The primary reason for using this supplemental advising effort is that it is effective. Peer advisors are usually rated higher than faculty advisors regarding their concern for advisees, and they have been effective in improving student retention, study skills, and grades (Abel and Alberts, 1978–1979; Brown and Myers, 1975; Murry, 1972; Upcraft, 1971).

Habley (1979) detailed several other advantages of peer advising. It is economical as compared to professional staff or faculty salaries; students are generally more available and accessible; they have a strong identification with "clients" so their expressed concerns can result in improvements in the total system; and their efforts allow more time for staff and faculty advisors to provide more in-depth advising. Furthermore, such involvement provides students with an opportunity to gain meaningful work and learning experiences.

Although outweighed by the above, Habley (1979) also pointed out certain difficulties with a peer advising program. Continuity of personnel is probably the greatest difficulty, mostly because of the nearly constant efforts to select, train, supervise, and evaluate peer advisors. Other difficulties include a perceived lack of objectivity about courses and faculty, as well as limited background and experience to be able to resolve complex educational issues.

The programs outlined in this section demonstrate how peer advisors have been used effectively to supplement faculty advising programs.

Marymount Manhattan College

History and Development. The Advisement Office at Marymount Manhattan College was formed in 1975 in order to help students choose well-rounded courses of study in an open-choice curriculum with only major requirements. Faculty had already served as informal advisors to students, but they now became part of a formalized process under the administrative supervision of the director of advisement. The attention thus given each student remained individualized and flexible but under the centralized control of an office responsible for record keeping and monitoring. The office also began to organize a way in which advisors could better reach students to help them more fully understand the need for careful and balanced program selections. In September 1976, a faculty advisors' workshop was held where students conducted a panel on their positive and negative reactions to advising experiences and attempted to define the ideal faculty advisor from the student's point of view. Their enthusiasm and interest provided impetus for development of the peer advisors' program.

From about a dozen students in 1976, the peer advisors' program has grown to approximately forty-five students in 1983. Peer advisors have clearly added an important dimension to the advising process. They provide opportunities for students to learn directly from the experience of other students about courses and the styles and expectations of teachers, and they convey information that faculty would sometimes be unable or unwilling to provide. Peer advising is not seen as replacing faculty advising—a faculty advisor still must approve students' programs—but rather as supplementing and enriching students' decision making. In addition, the responsibilities assumed by the peer advisors strengthen their ties to the institution and form a nucleus of students loyal to and knowledgeable about its programs and goals. Peer advisors are selected by the director of advisement upon faculty recommendations and division chairperson approval. Each must be at least a sophomore in good academic standing and must demonstrate interpersonal skills, a willingness to volunteer time for advising, and knowledge of the college and curriculum requirements.

The peer advisors program has grown in the number of participants and in the ways peer advisors contribute to the activities of the Advisement Office. The basic concept and direction of the program have not changed but rather have been expanded and refined. Peers volunteer their time and receive no compensation. The costs of the program, thus, are in the form of supervisory time from the director and her staff and in the materials developed for peer advisor training.

Goals and Objectives. The goals and objectives of Marymount Manhattan's peer advisor program stem from the very

reasons for its initiation—the need for a stronger and more comprehensive advising process and the desire to bond students more
firmly to the college.

The overall objective of the program is to reach students and
help them make the "right" decisions in their higher education in
order to achieve appropriate career paths and personal development. The insights into the institution that students have, and their
open and honest dialogue, supplement those of the faculty. The
primary goal of the program is to train peers in advising skills so
that they may listen, understand, communicate, and guide other
students into appropriate decisions and strategies for action. Other
goals are to provide a variety of experiences that will add value to
their resumés and to develop a closer relationship with the college
so that they will act as ambassadors and become supportive
alumnae.

Description of Activities. Peer advisors work in their own
academic divisions and are appointed in numbers proportionate to
the number of students in each division. Divisional chairpersons
define the assignments within the division. Peers are also available
at a special booth before and during registration to assist any and
all students who need it.

Peer advisors assist in conducting advising seminars for
incoming students each term. The seminars cover such topics as
faculty and peer advising, evaluating courses, and the advantages of
advising during course selection and registration. The peer advisors
prepare a handout on registration for students attending the
seminars.

In the fall of 1981 Marymount Manhattan initiated an
extended student orientation program of freshman seminars with
peer advisors chosen as cofacilitators. The nature and objectives of
these seminars were to make students feel at home at Marymount
Manhattan College and to prepare them for success.

The "Idea Fair for Deciding Majors," begun in 1979, also
relies on the help of peer advisors. Along with faculty from each
division, peer advisors staff booths in an informal and cheerful
setting that encourages discussing courses and career options. For
future fairs, peer advisors are contacting faculty in their depart-

ments and making short tapes in which faculty members describe the content and teaching methods of their courses.

The office conducts annual fall and spring workshops for faculty and peer advisors on such issues as advising the undeclared students and the adult learner, evaluating life experience credit, and helping students realize success. Special workshops on advising skills are also held for peers on a regular basis. The workshops include role playing to acquire and practice advising skills, video-taping the role-playing exercises of all participants to judge effectiveness, discussing actual situations that have arisen during advising, and learning new information about the college and its divisions. Advising staff, administrators, and faculty lead sessions at the workshops. The workshops also provide a rewarding opportunity for peers to meet faculty outside of their division and help them to use the information and forms in the *Faculty and Peer Advisors Handbook*. Off-campus training workshop weekends are also held, where peer advisors explore their listening and questioning skills and complete exercises that master knowledge of the catalogue.

Basically, the peer advisors' program is aimed at the full-time student population. Thus, the targeted and typical student served is a full-time day student under the age of twenty-five who is in need of advising because his/her interests and options are still being formulated. However, many of the older students feel comfortable in talking with and learning from younger peer advisors and are increasingly seeking a dialogue with them.

Evaluation Procedures. The divisional chairperson (or delegate) completes an evaluation form for each peer advisor on an annual basis. In addition, peer advisors are required to complete a self-evaluation form. The director provides ongoing supervision and evaluation.

Results/Outcomes. While the ultimate results of the program are difficult to measure in any tangible way since they hinge on the academic performance of each student, several other results have been described. The peer advisors report growth in their own self-awareness and ability to relate to others. They gain in judgment, self-control, and sensitivity. The advisees verbally report an appreciation for the contact, interest, and advice of their fellow students.

Limitations/Changes. Since students choose to consult peer advisors on a voluntary basis, the extent to which they are used is often dependent on students' awareness of their availability and services. Every attempt is made to publicize the program throughout the college—through distributed fliers, newspaper announcements, letters, bulletin boards, and the centrality of the peer advisors' booth. In an urban institution, however, where students commute and are often also employed, the pressures of time frequently work against a nonrequired activity. As a result, a weakness of the program is its limitation to achieve widespread use of the many contributions that peer advisors can make to a student's collegiate career.

University of Northern Iowa

History and Development. The University of Northern Iowa has traditionally placed a high value on student participation and involvement. The mission statement of the university to "develop the life of the university community itself as an effective education force" serves as a basis for the development of an array of student activities and creates a supportive environment for student development. For many years the student orientation staff had been involved in the initial advising and orientation of new freshmen but had not been a part of the ongoing advising freshmen receive throughout the year.

Several developments in the university moved peer advising from just being a good idea to implementation. First, it was recognized that support services for provisionally admitted students needed to be expanded. At the same time a reorganization combined advising and orientation responsibilities with examination programs. This reorganization formed the basis for establishing the Advising Center with special focus on freshmen and students who are undecided about their majors.

The feasibility of peer advising was first introduced by interested students from the student government in spring semester 1977. Contacts were made to gain support from the academic community, goals were developed, and peer advisor responsibilities were identified. In June 1977, a grant proposal was submitted to the Exxon Education Foundation. The grant was received and these funds, along with a workshop presented by William F. Brown of Southwest Texas State University (whom many people consider the modern father of student skills instruction), provided further direction and content for the program to be established in fall 1978.

The director of academic advising services is responsible for administration of the program. A counselor in the Counseling Center is codirector and has responsibilities for the selection, training, and implementation of the program.

The peer advising program involves three components: Impact, a structured continuing orientation program for selected new freshmen; ongoing Advising Center advising; and the evaluation and selection of new peer advisors. Peer advisors meet their responsibilities through three major roles: support for new freshmen, a resource for academic skill development, and a liaison to faculty, staff, and general university services.

Goals and Objectives. The major goal of the peer advising program is to increase the probability of academic success for freshmen. Ultimately, the goal is to provide a setting that is conducive to the growth and development of each student on the basis of individual abilities, interests, and personal characteristics. A second important goal is to provide significant growth experiences for peer advisors themselves. The specific objectives of the program are as follows:

1. to help freshmen become more self-confident and comfortable in the university environment
2. to provide freshmen with an immediate support person on campus
3. to provide freshmen with an opportunity to gain study skills necessary for academic success
4. to provide freshmen with information about academic requirements and university services

Description of Activities. The first major peer advising activity is in the Impact program. Each year those freshmen who rank in the lower half of their graduating class and/or have an American College Testing Program (ACT) composite score of 17 or below are invited to participate. During summer orientation those who wish to participate sign a contract agreeing to attend the meetings and apply the skills they learn.

The Impact program involves two major activities: a two-day workshop prior to the beginning of fall classes and group meetings throughout the semester. Each peer advisor is assigned a group of approximately fifteen Impact participants with whom they work throughout the semester.

The two-day workshop includes survival and time-management and note-taking skills, mostly planned and conducted by the peer advisors. Each peer also invites a favorite professor to meet informally with the group. A second faculty involvement, which has been highly successful, is the session on effective note taking.

Peer advisors meet with their groups throughout the first semester. The scheduled group meetings are held weekly for the first three weeks of the semester and monthly thereafter.

This schedule coincides with events of the semester such as preregistration and final exams. Part of the meeting time is structured on topics such as reading a textbook or taking tests, while a large portion of time is devoted to discussion of concerns and situations of group members. Many of the groups plan informal social activities throughout the year.

The second major activity for peer advisors is to spend two hours per week in the Advising Center. Most of this time is spent with freshmen who are seeking scheduling assistance, information on curriculum requirements, or examination opportunities.

The third activity involves the selection of new peer advisors and participation in training programs. During the selection process, a general meeting is scheduled where a panel of peer advisors explain the program, how they became involved, and some of the experiences they have had. Next, each peer advisor discusses typical situations with a small group of applicants and writes an evaluation of each participant.

The fourth phase involves two days of interviewing in which peer advisors and professional staff members interview as a team. The final phase of the selection process usually involves a Saturday morning session during which the directors and peer advisors work together to make final selections.

In-service development for peer advisors is implemented through spring in-service activities, a fall retreat, weekly staff meetings during the academic year, and individual conferences. Spring in-service programs focus on activities that will help peer advisors become acquainted with each other, share expectations for the program, and define their roles.

The most intensive portion of the in-service development is implemented through the fall retreat. The peer advising staff spends an extended period of uninterrupted time during which the development and preparation of content, skills, and methods for use in the Impact workshop are interlaced with building team cohesiveness, development of effective helping skills, and group leadership skills. A unique feature of the process is that the training modules are conducted in the same sequence as the individual sessions of the Impact workshop.

Peer advising staff meet weekly throughout the academic year to plan group meetings, share ideas and strategies for working with the groups, and share frustrations and problems. They also have a one-hour conference with the program codirector to evaluate the progress of their group, to discuss problems of individuals and ways of helping them, and to review their own goals in the program.

For their efforts, Impact advisors are paid a $200 stipend, while those in the Advising Center are paid a $600 annual stipend. Although the peers appreciate the money, their commitment is primarily for the personal development and satisfaction they receive from the program.

Evaluation Procedures. Evaluation of the Impact program includes written evaluations of the program and peer advisors by Impact participants, a review of grade point averages, and persistence at the university of students who participated in the program. While grade point averages and persistence of the various Impact groups have been compiled, comparative statistics are not available. Evaluation of the 1978 Impact group did involve a comparison of attrition rates among Impact participants and various nonparticipants who had similar ACT scores and high school class ranks.

Evaluation of peer advisors in the Advising Center is incorporated into the annual evaluation of the center. Peer advisors write their expectations of the program at the beginning of the year and are asked periodically to assess their progress toward these goals and expectations. This process, along with evaluation of their skills in relationship to their group activities, provide the foci for peer self-evaluation and assessment.

Results/Outcomes. Based on comparative research findings, surveys, and personal observations, the outcomes of the peer advising program may be summarized as follows:

1. Impact participants, as reflected in the 1978 group findings, earned better first-semester grade point averages than their matched nonparticipating group members.
2. The evidence further indicates that although they tend to persist through their first semester at a higher level than nonparticipants, higher grade point averages and higher retentions are not necessarily sustained as the Impact participants continue in college.
3. Impact freshmen are very positive about their involvement in the program.
4. Impact participants view the peer advisor as an important support person during the first year.
5. Impact participants view the program as helping them gain academic skills and better understanding of what will be expected of them in college.
6. Peer advisors indicate that their experience is a positive force in their educational growth.

The peer advising program, therefore, involves a developmental process both for the Impact freshmen and the peer advisors. Over the years, peer advising can and does fulfill important advising and student development goals.

Limitations/Changes. The major limitation of the Impact program was that it had not been available to large numbers of freshmen, but in 1984-85 the program will make a transition to accommodate all undecided freshmen. In order to remain a student development program, it is essential that the supervisor-peer advisor-group size ratio be maintained. It is a program that provides a growth experience for a relatively small number of freshmen while requiring considerable resources and energies from the professional staff.

Ongoing evaluation and change will continue to be a part of the advising program. The Impact program and the team of ten peer advisors will remain the same, but one or two peer advisors will be brought into the advising center for eight to ten hours per week for assistance in helping students select their majors.

Over the years, the benefit of this kind of program to the peer advisors themselves has become more evident; therefore, plans are being made to do a follow-up study of peer advisors. This follow-up would ask the peer advisors to evaluate their experience as it relates to activities, community involvement, and/or job experiences they have had following their peer advising role.

University of Montana

History and Development. In 1976 the University of Montana, in anticipation of projected national enrollment declines, began to look seriously for strategies that would help students remain in school. It was clearly evident that sound academic advising was to be a critical component of that effort. Historically, departmental faculty members served as academic advisors, but a large and growing group of undeclared students did not have ready access to advisors with a generalist perspective; therefore, a group of faculty members representing departments within the College of Arts and Sciences were recruited to work with the general studies student.

After a ten-year lapse, mandatory advising was reinstated in 1979, and the university made a concerted effort to enforce it. Since only a few general studies advisors were available to serve about 1,300 undergraduates, the need for more generalists was obvious. Students who left general studies moved into all of the other majors on campus, so they needed early access to general advisors who had familiarity with all programs. The professional schools were unable to designate individuals to work with undeclareds. Thus, peer advising was initiated by the advising coordinator in the spring of 1980 in order to broaden the General Studies Advising Program.

Each spring a new cycle of the peer advising program begins. In the 1983–84 school year, thirty advisors made up approximately half of the total General Studies advisor complement.

Goals and Objectives. The goals of the peer advising program have been twofold. The first goal is to provide students who are uncertain about their major with an academic advising experience that facilitates personal development. The second is to teach peer advisors skills that not only will be utilized in their work with advisees but also will generalize to other situations. A prime objective of this program is to assist in the personal growth of each peer.

Altruism is not an uncommon characteristic among the peers. They are reimbursed with one credit of independent study in education for every thirty hours they work in advising. Transcript notations indicate that they were selected into the Peer Advising Program. They understand they will learn to interact with others in a paraprofessional capacity and they will gain experience working in a professional setting. These incentives and future letters of recommendation are the only rewards offered to prospective peer advisors. Every effort is made to help the peer advisors recognize the skills they are building and to seek ways of applying what they learn to new situations.

Description of Activities. The keys to success of this program are the peers themselves; therefore, recruitment, selection, and training activities are significant. Initial recruitment is by direct mail to upper-division students with a 3.0 or higher GPA, and approximately 40 percent of these request interviews.

The interviews are structured by the program supervisors but are actually conducted by the outgoing peers. They obtain impressions of the peer candidates as well as further educate them about the program. Final selections are made by the coordinator, with heavy emphasis placed on the written evaluations of the peers.

New peer advisor training begins with a two-hour orientation meeting at the end of spring quarter, and they are given various resources to read over the summer. In the fall they return for two six-hour sessions just prior to registration week. The first session pertains to the logistics of the program's calendar for a typical quarter, the development of their advising schedules, and a review of their contractual obligations.

The second session focuses on advising skills and includes instructions on the use of various university publications, an exploration into the characteristics of the undecided student with special emphasis on the developmental approach to academic advising, proper use and interpretation of standard test scores and transcript evaluations, and instruction in communication skills. Students also observe and respond to videotaped vignettes of good and bad advising sessions and themselves engage in mock advising interviews.

Regularly scheduled in-service or "group" meetings are conducted by two graduate students from the counseling and guidance program who are selected to serve Advising Office internships. These supervisors meet with the academic advising coordinator to determine in-service topics, but it is their responsibility to teach the material, introduce guest speakers, and otherwise facilitate group learning and interaction.

Topics presented to the peers during a two-hour group meeting have included exit interview and study skills advice, referrals, postregistration advising follow-up techniques, methods for overcoming defense mechanisms, assessing student potential, counseling skills, teaching decision making, resumé writing, vocational development, evaluation of program and supervisors, and assessment of recent personal growth.

Guest speakers are often invited to describe specific campus resources that are available to advisees, including health service, counseling center, reading laboratory, financial aid, and foreign student and disabled student advisors. Group meetings always conclude with case studies raised by the peers themselves.

The major activities conducted by these highly skilled peer advisors are registration advising and daily advising in the Advising Office. During registration each peer advisor is assigned an average of twelve advisees, mostly new students to the university. They conduct their advising sessions in a laboratory classroom that has a number of adjacent rooms around its perimeter. This location permits privacy for advising but with access to other peers and close staff supervision.

Throughout the year the peers staff their own office in the Advising Office during regular university hours. They advise walk-in students on a variety of academic and other concerns. Because of their careful training, they are especially able to determine accurate resources and to make appropriate referrals when necessary.

Evaluation Procedures. At the conclusion of each quarter, the supervisors conduct individual interviews with the peers. They are asked to set personal objectives for the upcoming quarter and to contemplate methods for achieving them. In June they are asked to summarize their personal growth and development over the preceding nine months and to share insights they have gained. It is during these evaluation interviews that the supervisors and the academic advising coordinator gain information that may inspire alterations in the program.

Students are routinely asked to complete surveys about their peer advisors. These results are used solely for feedback to the peer advisors, not for evaluation purposes. The evaluation occurs through the interviews just described.

Information evaluations from the deans have been favorable and supportive, although they were skeptical of the program at first. This informal procedure will continue.

Results/Outcomes. The outcomes of this program have been gratifying. Each year, the peer advisors deliver a high caliber of academic advising to as many as 700 students. They have enabled the Advising Office to operate many outreach programs that, due to budgetary limitations, could not otherwise be staffed. These have included assistance in choosing a major for those students who are no longer eligible for general studies advising, advising Native-American students who are on probation, and contacting students with low midterm grades to prescribe study skills assistance. Additionally, the peer advisors have been able to effect several changes within the university because of their keen awareness of inappropriate policies and procedures.

Several features of this program account for its success. First, the University of Montana is committed to providing its enrolled and prospective students with academic advising that focuses on the student as a developing individual, and it supports programs that endeavor toward that end. Second, the program strives to translate student development theory into practice. The conscientious application of theory into the small-group learning environment by counselors-in-training effectively assists the peers and their advisees in the personal growth process. They begin to reflect and self-disclose their changing attitudes toward the role of the advisor, the university, other students, and themselves. Finally, the counseling interns maximize the effectiveness of group work while minimizing costs of supervision.

Apart from the extensive commitment of human efforts, this program is astonishingly inexpensive to operate. It initially required the organizational energies of the academic advising coordinator, whose office still provides clerical assistance and who determines the prospective candidates each spring. The graduate student supervisors have very responsible roles, and much is delegated to them throughout the year.

Limitations/Changes. One area that has continued to be a source of frustration is the awarding of the quarterly letter grade for the independent study credit. At the beginning of the school year, the peers sign a contract to earn an A for the quarter. The problem arises when students only partially fulfill the requirements, since no criteria for grades other than A had been prepared. Consequently, when the occasional student did not meet the contract criteria, uniform and equitable grading proved to be a great challenge, especially since deviations were never uniform.

Two alternative approaches to grading are being tested. In 1983–84 the quarterly grades are N or "work in progress." Informally, students are provided with a letter grade descriptive of the work they have performed to date; it is hoped that the N will encourage them to continue to improve and to strive for an A. The following year it is intended to have them sign the same contract but for a letter grade of B. This might encourage some to exceed the minimal expectations and will certainly permit the supervisors to draw an adequate distinction between those who merely do the job and those who excel.

In the future, the Advising Office hopes to develop peer advisors in most of the schools, thereby providing more "professional" advising time and expertise for special efforts, such as advising student athletes.

Summary

The peer advising programs described in this section clearly demonstrate the effective use of students helping students, and three observations seem to stand out among them. First, peer advising is not designed to lessen student-faculty interaction but rather to make it more meaningful. Second, intensive selection and training efforts ensure the success of the program; these efforts for peer advisors far exceed similar ones for faculty advisors. Finally, various forms of compensation are available for peer advisors—as shown by the totally volunteer program at Marymount Manhattan, paid stipends at Northern Iowa, and academic credit at the University of Montana. These common elements of peer advising programs exist in all institutions. The variety of compensation forms mentioned here would seem possible at most institutions; therefore, any combination of elements from these peer advising programs should be readily adaptable.

Since college students always attempt to provide assistance to other students, institutions should regularly consider ways to harness this infinite energy source and direct it into a variety of productive efforts. Academic advising performed by highly skilled peers has proven effective and is operable on many campuses. Along with tutoring, counseling, and residence hall programs, peer advising provides a means to enrich student experiences and to improve the general quality of student life on the campus.

Advising Through Courses

The final format for providing academic advising described herein is that of the academic course. Many of the changes in American higher education during the past three decades—such as increased enrollments, flexible curricula, and a focus on retention—demonstrated the need for a better orientation of students into the higher-education environment. Summer and various other early orientation programs flourished during these years, and the concept of an extended, ongoing orientation program for entering students became evident. This concept has been implemented through a variety of "freshman year" programs, many of which include a course that provides a complete approach to developmental academic advising.

Cohen and Jody (1978) described three goals of an ongoing orientation program: (1) to assist new students to become active participants, rather than passive recipients, in the learning process; (2) to help them gain information about resources of the institution and the appropriate use of information in the postcollege world; and (3) to help them acquire the scholastic skills necessary for achieving success in college and beyond. These goals have most often been achieved through such courses as "Advising Seminar," "Introduction to College," and the most popular "Freshman Seminar." The specific content of such courses varies widely, but, from a developmental perspective, should include academic planning, personal and social growth, and career development activities (Gordon and Grites, 1984).

Research on the outcomes of such courses is overwhelmingly positive. Lower attrition rates, more intellectual growth, greater satisfaction with college, more cultural sophistication, increased student participation, and additional student-faculty interaction have resulted (Robinson, 1972; Dwyer, 1981; Gardner, 1982).

The following programs provide developmental academic advising through the formal course structure. Each has distinctive features that have potential for adaptability.

Brenau College

History and Development. Prior to 1977, freshmen and transfer students were advised at registration by faculty selected by the academic dean. Orientation to the college occurred in large group sessions. There was no training for advisors, no delivery of information prior to advising conferences, no continuity in advising over time, no recognition for advisors, and no systematic evaluation.

By 1977–78 the college had realized a 50 percent freshman attrition rate, and approximately 70 percent transferred to other schools by the end of the sophomore year. In the fall of 1977, freshmen were grouped by major into orientation units of twenty students each, with one faculty and one peer advisor. A one and one-half day workshop on college-student rules and regulations and an orientation critique were also added.

In 1978-79 a coordinator for the Lower-Division Academic Advisement Program was appointed. The coordinator requested faculty to participate as advisors, selected twenty-five peer advisors, divided the orientation units by residence hall, and conducted a three-day staff training workshop prior to orientation week. The advising process became goal oriented, support materials were made available, and faculty and peer advisors were recognized with workshops, retreats, letters, and faculty stipends.

In 1979-80 the faculty advisors assumed responsibility for the program under the supervision of the coordinator and "Act I," a required one-quarter-hour academic course, was initiated. Topics such as time management, study skills, values clarification, self-exploration, decision making, assertiveness training, and career exploration were studied in the twice weekly classes. Act I advisors were given released time, and peer advisors received five hours of academic credit for their participation. Acts II, III, and IV were later developed to correspond with the sophomore, junior, and senior years respectively. Thus Acts I to IV became the student development model for the college with Act II emphasizing academic/career exploration, Act III career internship experiences, and Act IV senior opportunity seminars.

Since that time, refinements have been made in the areas of training materials, a training program, and evaluation. Although original funding (1978-81) came from a Title III grant, the program has since been funded by the college in an amount not to exceed $13,500 per year, the equivalent of tuition for three students. From 210 to 280 students are served directly by the Act I sequences.

Goals and Objectives. The required Act I one-hour class serves as the foundation for Brenau College's four-year student development model. This model is designed to offer a learning experience essential to "cope with a pluralistic and contemporary world." All incoming freshmen are required to enroll in Act I. Acts II, III, and IV are optional credit courses open to students who may choose to enter the developmental sequence as needed or advised.

ACT I is a course of survival skills essential to a successful college experience and for personal growth. The goals of the course are to improve study skills, goal setting, decision making, determining measurable objectives, and the evaluation of subsequent progress in personal growth. Specific objectives are developed in each of these areas. Additional seminars dealing with contemporary issues important to today's woman are also offered.

ACT II is an optional course intended to emphasize self-awareness, academic/career exploration and investigation, and thorough research of specific fields of interest. ACT III is an optional course intended to provide an internship experience in areas of career interest. The course objectives are to recognize the value of on-the-job training, to reinforce interest in the field of choice, to apply theory to practice, and to provide valuable work experience for future job searches.

ACT IV, the Senior Opportunity Seminar, is an optional course designed to identify and develop necessary job search skills, to emphasize goal setting, decision making, and assertiveness training in preparation for the job search, to initiate that search for fulfillment of lifelong career goals, and to prepare the senior to make a smooth transition from college to the work environment.

A paraprofessional training program supports Acts I to IV. Selected students enroll in the paraprofessional training course to qualify as peer advisors, campus officers, office assistants, and resident advisors. Leadership-training workshops and seminars reinforce the paraprofessional training course.

Description of Activities. The more notable features of the overall program include:

1. Faculty from all disciplines are trained to teach the various developmental skills and topics. Approximately half of the faculty is rotated in and out of the program every two years.
2. Student peer advisors are trained to assist faculty advisors in the program.
3. A ten-week paraprofessional training program is required of all faculty and peer advisors and is available to other students who serve the college. The program is offered in the spring preceding service as an advisor. Faculty and peer advisors with several years' experience serve as trainers and facilitators in this program.

4. Three days of in-service training are required of all faculty and peer advisors during the fall quarter, and classes meet twice weekly during Act I.
5. Orientation units have between twenty and twenty-five students for each faculty advisor, assisted by two or three peer advisors. The orientation units are organized by residence hall areas to enhance group cohesiveness.
6. All freshman students and transfer students who have not completed the sophomore year are required to take Act I for graduation.
7. The student development staff supports the entire Lower-Division Academic Advisement Program through advising, training, and facilitation in the program and its training components.
8. Support manuals and materials are revised annually based on critiques by faculty and peer advisors.

Evaluation Procedures. The Lower-Division Academic Advisement Program of Brenau has been evaluated in several ways. The orientation workshop, orientation week for fall quarter, and the registration process are evaluated through an internal instrument completed by all new freshmen and transfer students, all faculty and peer advisors, and the administration.

External evaluation was conducted by members of the Washington staff of the Small College Consortium (Title III) from 1977 to 1980, by an external evaluator from 1980 to 1982, and by the administrative staff of Brenau College. A summative evaluation of the support materials was conducted by the faculty and peer advisors, and the paraprofessional training course was critiqued by the prospective faculty and peer advisors who took the course and by two external consultants.

The Act I course is evaluated in two ways. Internal evaluations are conducted by students in the Act I class, which provides a summative evaluation according to student satisfaction with each topic presented and a formative evaluation from groups of students who construct their own Act I class. In addition, pretests and posttests are given on each topic to determine the degree to which the topics were understood and internalized, and the peer advisors provide both written and oral summative critiques of the training and the class.

Results/Outcomes. Positive outcomes of the program have been achieved in four areas:

1. *Student satisfaction:* The level of satisfaction with the educational experience at Brenau improved markedly with the implementation of the developmental advising program and four-year student development model. Retention of students during the freshman year rose from 50 to 65 percent. The general educational milieu was affected in a positive manner, and, for many students, setting goals and writing objectives became a way of life.

2. *Cooperation:* The involvement of faculty and student affairs personnel in a joint education process helped to develop strong links between the groups. The unifying concept was the concern for the welfare of the student, and the outcomes were increased cooperation, understanding, and support.

3. *Faculty development:* Faculty from many disciplines were involved in the program. Training in various skill areas allowed faculty to grow and develop. An increased awareness of and cooperation with other colleagues and a sensitivity to the unique learning characteristics of students indirectly affected teaching in the classroom. An understanding of the mentor concept made faculty more aware of their roles and responsibilities as growth facilitators of students, and a better understanding of the college made them more valuable members of the college community as a whole.

4. *Recognition:* Representatives were invited to participate in regional meetings, where the Brenau College model was presented as a functional developmental advising program.

Limitations/Changes. During 1982–83 there was some regression in the overall system, primarily in the faculty training components of the program. The regression was due, in part, to a change in coordinators for the program and to a general misunderstanding of the philosophy of developmental advising on the part of some of the administrative staff. Ongoing faculty training is essential to guarantee understanding and conscious support of the developmental process and the role of the advisor in that process.

University of South Carolina

History and Development. University 101 is an academic program consisting of a three-credit freshman orientation course and a mandatory forty-hour faculty development training program. The University 101 program is administratively structured as a "department" with a director who holds a dual faculty/administrative appointment. Initially, University 101 reported directly to the president, but since 1974 it has reported to the Office of Executive Vice-President for Academic Affairs and Provost.

University 101 is administered by a half-time director and one full-time administrative/secretarial person. It has a constantly changing faculty drawn from all academic and administrative units of the university. Up to one third of the University 101 teaching staff in any semester teaches the course as part of their regular duties. The remaining instructors teach for a modest overload payment, considerably below the overload stipend paid at this university.

University 101 was begun as an educational experiment in 1972 as a result of faculty efforts and presidential support to revitalize the freshman year at the University of South Carolina. The president requested that a group of faculty and some staff from the Social Problems Research Institute design a unique course for freshmen that would simultaneously increase student retention, promote faculty development, and humanize the university environment.

The resulting University 101 program was initially funded by the Ford Foundation Venture Fund grant to the University of South Carolina. The course was first operated as an experimental course and approved as a permanent course offering in 1973 by the Faculty Senate with the following description: "University 101— The Student in the University. The purposes of higher education, and the potential roles of an individual student within the university and other learning environments, open to freshmen only."

The course has been subsequently funded by regular state monies (approximately $85,000 annually). These monies have provided instruction for over 12,000 freshmen on the Columbia campus and hundreds more on the other eight campuses of the university system.

Students for University 101 are recruited through freshman orientation, through the encouragement of faculty advisors, and by direct mail brochures sent to incoming freshman students and their parents. Most students who take University 101 do so in the fall semester, but sections are offered in the spring and summer as well. Other sections have been offered specifically for special, uniquely identifiable populations of freshman students, such as returning adults, undecided majors, handicapped students, and students in specific majors.

It is in the University 101 sections for undecided students (101-U) that an academic advising function rests. Since the fall of 1982, the University 101-U concept has provided these undecided students with a more comprehensive approach to making career/major decisions.

Goals and Objectives. The goals and objectives of University 101 are as follows:

1. to provide an extensive introduction to the purposes of higher education
2. to provide extensive, continuing orientation at this university
3. to help freshmen adjust to the university and to deal with the normal developmental problems associated with adjustment to a major university
4. to develop more positive attitudes toward the university
5. to develop more positive attitudes toward the learning process and toward faculty
6. to increase the involvement of freshmen in the extracurricular life of the university
7. to make students aware of and to force them to use student support services
8. to introduce students to the many cultural opportunities afforded by a major university
9. to teach freshmen "survival skills"
10. to provide a "support group" during the critical first semester and first year of higher education in which they can examine common problems and develop a friendship network

11.   to introduce the students to a college official as a thinking, reasoning, and caring person
12.   to improve the retention rate of freshmen
13.   to give faculty and staff special preparation to teach the course
14.   to make faculty more knowledgeable about their own university and its services and resources to assist student development

The goal of University 101-U can be defined more specifically as an attempt to provide a structured approach to the decision-making process involved in the choice of an academic major and career direction. Through the study of the purposes of higher education and the potential roles of an individual student within the university and in other learning environments, students learn to make better choices.

Description of Activities. The content of the 101-U course is divided into four major parts: the foundation component, the academic orientation component, the career planning/major decision-making component, and the student development/campus resources component. Each instructor has the flexibility to present additional topics as desired. Individual topics are sequenced so that the four components are woven together to culminate in actual decision making and planning for the future.

The foundation component includes a course overview, a study of young adults in higher education, and individual conferences with the instructor. The academic component introduces the student to the mechanics of the institution, faculty expectations, necessary study skills, and student responsibility in academic advising. The career component explores the total career choice process from values and expectations through interest and skill assessment to resumé writing and interviews. The resources component exposes students to student development and leadership activities in which they can become involved.

Faculty who teach University 101-U are all veteran University 101 instructors who have also completed an additional forty-hour faculty training workshop designed to enable them to better understand the special characteristics and needs of undecided freshmen. These participants are also introduced to various theoretical approaches to student development, career development, and decision making, as well as critical academic information.

Evaluation Procedures. Independent research has been conducted on the University 101 program since 1974. The data collected on the program trace the impact of the program on students from 1972 through 1982. For University 101-U, in particular, a questionnaire is administered to the students enrolled to evaluate whether or not the course objectives have been met. In general they have, but a more precise evaluation will be done in the future to assess persistence toward a degree and satisfaction with initial choice of major.

Results/Outcomes. This research has found that participation in University 101 is positively correlated with a significantly higher retention rate of freshmen even when the freshmen taking the course have a lower predicted potential for survival. This research has also demonstrated that University 101 students have an increased knowledge and utilization of student support services and have become much more involved in the extracurricular activities of the university than have non-University 101 freshmen. In summary, all results have been favorable for University 101 students.

Limitations/Changes. University 101 is an extremely well institutionalized program in its eleventh year. The University 101-U concept is relatively new, but it is consistent with the evolutionary and dynamic nature of University 101. It is anticipated that both versions of the concept will continue to make necessary changes to accommodate the changing student and institutional needs and priorities, but no specific ones are projected for the immediate future.

University of Puget Sound

History and Development. The University of Puget Sound, under a new university dean, authorized and developed its Freshman Advising Program during the 1973-74 academic year and introduced it in 1974. The purpose of this program was to place students in relatively small classes taught by their faculty advisors. The class setting assured that advisors and advisees had regular, frequent contact and that they became more personally acquainted.

Since that time the program has experienced several minor changes:

1. A freshman advising assistant (peer advisor) was added to help new freshmen become familiar with campus resources, facilities, and their first registration.
2. A training program was developed in 1979.
3. Materials sent to entering students have improved since 1979, including a preadvising questionnaire.
4. A series of computerized reports for tracking entering freshmen through the sophomore year was developed for the fall 1981 class.

Several other modifications have been made to articulate the program better to entering students, to prepare freshman advisors for their duties, to make the program work more smoothly, and to provide better management information.

Goals and Objectives. The primary goal for the Freshman Advising Program at the University of Puget Sound is to help ensure each student's academic adaptation to and success in college. The program posits centrality of the advising relationship to this process. The program *guarantees* that each student will have regular and frequent contact with an advisor throughout the first term, and it is assumed, that an ongoing advising relationship is maintained throughout the sophomore year.

This program is based on the assumption that freshman have academic needs that range beyond new registration forms and procedures, namely, certain academic skills that may have to be improved or developed. Advisors are unlikely to identify these critical concerns unless they also know the advisee as a student. To achieve these goals, students are placed in small classes or science labs with instructors who are also their advisors. By having the advisee as a student in class, the advisor is able to gain firsthand information about the advisee's academic habits. Skills such as written and oral communication can also be assessed, and the advisor can ask about skills such as taking lecture notes or outlining texts in a context that is supportive and nonthreatening.

Once the basic survival concerns are alleviated, the advisor guides the student toward longer-range academic exploration and planning. The final expectation of the program is that the advisee will develop a long-range plan of study, declare an academic major, and change to a departmental advisor by the spring term of the sophomore year.

Description of Activities. Preparations for the arrival of freshmen begin ten months earlier with the selection of freshman advisors by the director of academic advising in consultation with the dean and department chairs. Students are actually able to select their advisors by identifying preferred "Freshmen Advising Classes," once they have declared their intent to enroll. The director of academic advising assigns students to the classes after reading the admissions file, preadvising questionnaire, and list of preferred advising groups.

In the spring advisors select the advising assistants (student peer advisors) who will assist them during orientation, and two separate training programs are conducted by the director. One program is for the advising assistants and includes an outline of the content and purpose of the materials to be mailed over the summer. The other is a series of luncheons for advisors. First-time freshman advisors are expected to attend all sessions; experienced advisors are invited to attend as they wish. Topics include the expectations of advisors, interpretation and use of admissions materials and test results, support services, and a review of student development theories.

Orientation in the fall begins with a general reception where parents meet freshman advisors and university officers. Over one half of the freshman parents attend this function, which has proven valuable for subsequent contact about the progress of students.

Each freshman advisor and assistant then meets with the advising group to explain the week's activities and to schedule individual appointments. During these individual sessions, students' test results, strengths, weaknesses, and interests are surveyed, and the fall schedule is arranged. The advising group registers as a unit, accompanied by the freshman advisor and advising assistant.

Once classes begin, advisees and advisors see each other as students and professors for three or four hours each week in class. Very little class time is used specifically for advising purposes, but the option is available.

Each advisor has the option to invite advisees home for dinner. To encourage this, advisors are offered $3.50 per student to defray expenses. The original idea was to add an informal dimension to the advising relationship, but this option has been broadened. Some advisors use it as a reunion during the sophomore year; others host dinners at the faculty club preceding the group's attendance at a cultural event.

Each advising class is tracked for enrollment from orientation through the fifth semester. Advisors are asked to report any important concerns about retention to the director.

Even though advisees have the option to change advisors, freshman advisors are expected to remain informed about their advisees through the end of the sophomore year.

Evaluation Procedures. At the University of Puget Sound, academic advising is one of the criteria for faculty advancement and tenure; however, no agreement has been reached on a standard for evaluation that can be applied consistently throughout the university.

The Freshman Advising Program has been evaluated by means of a student survey executed by the director of institutional research. This evaluation helped identify certain needs, such as more clearly notifying students about advisors' responsibilities. Internal analysis of the data has also directed attention to gaps in information for advisees and advisors on procedural matters.

Results/Outcomes. In 1973-74, with the arrival of a new president and dean who both believed in the importance of academic advising, the Freshman Advising Program was created. One of the most important results of the changes made is the dramatic improvement in student retention. For the freshman class entering in 1972, only 39 percent graduated within five years. At least 50 percent of the fall 1977 class graduated by May 1983, and the retention rates for the classes currently enrolled show continuing improvement.

Additionally, each year more advisors become sensitive to student development and more concerned about providing good advising for students. Specifically, probation and dismissal rates have leveled although tougher academic standards have been implemented, and there has been a dramatic increase in the use of the Learning Skills Center.

At the same time, each succeeding freshman class expresses greater satisfaction with the institution generally and relations with faculty in particular. The results of the student survey have also provided a behavior pattern for "very effective" freshman advisors. Though the pattern is what one might expect, these results have been useful in training new advisors.

Limitations/Changes. The model of freshman advising used at the University of Puget Sound poses some problems and limitations that should be considered:

1. The system excludes use of faculty who do not teach freshman-level classes.
2. The system may require the use of some faculty members who are not very effective as advisors.
3. The system may overuse some faculty members.
4. Schedule conflicts must always be considered.

Expectations with respect to the sophomore year have not been realized. Only a fraction of the students actually develop a formal long-range plan of study, and it appears that both advisors and students are content to accept the programs of study outlined in the college catalogue as sufficient. More disturbing, however, is that the groups do not meet as frequently for substantive discussion as desired. This may help explain why the sophomore-to-junior retention rate has not improved as much as the freshman-to-sophomore rate.

Recently, the Student Life Committee created a set of task forces to study these problems. It appears that at least two relevant proposals are likely to be adopted. For freshmen, there will be a peer advisor program in the residence units designed for groups of about ten freshmen each to provide academic support services. The problems of the sophomore year will be addressed in several ways. A general model of student development will be adopted to help sharpen the focus and structure of programming in the area that is the concern of the dean of students. The expectations of advisor behavior with sophomores will also be modified. Regular contact and the development of a long-range plan of study will still be expected, but advisors will be given much more support and assistance. This will include more specific training, a revised and expanded advising manual, and a more structured program of academic/career planning support services.

Heidelberg College

History and Development. The program began in 1977 when the college community became dissatisfied with the traditional academic counseling process. Attempts to improve the system during the previous three years had proved disappointing, Although advising had focused exclusively on academic matters, studies revealed that student knowledge of academic requirements was sparse and that many were not utilizing the campus resources to best advantage. These concerns, and a commitment to the goals of a liberal arts education, led to the development of Total Student Development (TSD).

The program was researched, planned, and developed by a faculty-staff-student committee in the spring and summer of 1977 and was adopted by the faculty in May. Several faculty and staff members wrote the *TSD Manual* and *TSD Handbook* during the summer months; faculty and upperclass students who were to serve as facilitators attended workshops in May and August; the first students participated in the program in August 1977. Since then, the program has been reviewed and changed yearly by the faculty-staff-student TSD Committee.

The original budget for administrative costs, materials, and workshop consultants was $4,700; the current operating budget is $4,500. No new personnel have been hired to participate in or administer the program, but a part-time coordinator was named in the office of the dean of students. Facilitators receive no compensation for participation in the program, but the college has recognized their commitment with annual appreciation dinners and certificates or small gifts. Faculty facilitators have usually been assigned fewer departmental tasks in order to allow them time for participation, and peer advisors serve in a totally volunteer capacity.

Goals and Objectives. The TSD program has carefully established the following goals:

1.˙ to encourage students to see themselves as developing, complex persons by providing necessary information and support for their initial adjustment to college and enabling them to understand better their personal strengths and weaknesses

2. to develop goal-setting skills useful both during the collegiate period and throughout a lifetime by integrating the social, personal, cultural, career, and academic areas of the collegiate experience

3. to make the student aware of all the college resources available for reaching goals and to encourage students to view college activities, programs, and courses as strategies for meeting individual goals

4. to enhance the student's ability to achieve self-determined goals and to control change rather than merely adapt to future pressures

5. to create a support group of peers, faculty members, and upperclass students for the new student

Description of Activities. Since 1977 all new freshmen have participated in the program, and most transfer students have experienced some of the activities.

Two sets of materials have been developed to ensure breadth of content and consistency in the experience. The *TSD Manual* for facilitators includes lists of necessary supplies, directions for each activity, and copies of all materials used by students. The *TSD Handbook* contains information about all academic departments and special programs of the college and supplements the college catalogue as a resource for academic advising. Both resources are updated each year by a faculty committee.

The program is designed and developed by a faculty committee appointed by the president and administered through the dean of student life. It is presented to the new students by a team of facilitators, including one faculty member and one or two upperclass students, who share responsibility for the group and the program. Although consultants have been used, most of the advisor training sessions have been conducted by members of the TSD Committee.

TSD at Heidelberg has several unique features. First, the advising program is conducted both in small groups and individually, and parents are included in the early group process. Second, faculty and peer facilitators serve as equal members of a team, and equal assistance and cooperation exist between the faculty and the dean of student life. Third, students learn to set future goals based upon their past experiences and personal assessments. A fourth feature is that faculty facilitators serve without compensation and that they have advising responsibilities outside their academic disciplines, since groups are assigned somewhat randomly. Finally, parents have been very receptive to the program and often contact the facilitator when a problem arises.

Evaluation Procedures. The program was evaluated at its inception by an outside evaluator who provided a very positive reaction and encouraged further development of the program.

The TSD program has administered surveys to both facilitators and new students. In 1980 an expanded new student survey attempted to measure knowledge of college resources and policies, the extent of participation in cultural, social, and governance activities at the college, and attitudes concerning the effectiveness of the student's facilitator and the TSD program. In addition, nonparticipant faculty have been asked twice to submit evaluations of the program. Their comments have led to some of the proposed changes listed in the next few paragraphs.

Results/Outcomes. The surveys have shown that the students who attend regularly demonstrate greater participation in such campus activities as departmental organizations and honoraries, artistic productions, and student government. There is also a perceived increase in the use of career-planning services.

Pre- and postresults of the *Student Developmental Task Inventory* (Winston, Miller, and Prince, 1979) in 1979 indicated that TSD students do increase their goal-setting behavior and have a greater awareness of campus resources. Long-range goal setting is also reflected in the increased number of students who are selecting a second major.

Other incidental, but not insignificant, results include a 6 percent increase in the four-year retention rate, the opportunity to train faculty in small group teaching and discussion techniques, a strong peer support system throughout the campus, and an impressive recruitment device.

Limitations/Changes. In 1982–83 the TSD Committee began to revise the program. General concerns and corresponding changes that are currently being implemented by the committee include:

1. increased flexibility for facilitators to incorporate their own varied interests, attributes, and expertise into their roles— achieved by providing several alternate procedures to meet the general objectives and permitting facilitators to select the topic of certain sessions from a group of alternatives according to the specific needs of their students
2. reordering of topics to be more consistent with the students' motivation and/or preparation
3. additional emphasis on community building/support group development through several new small group exercises and some monetary support for off-campus activities
4. making TSD a graduation requirement to legitimatize it for all faculty and students

In 1983–84 the flexibility in topics and procedures has been extremely well received by faculty, and TSD participation has become a graduation requirement. One nonacademic credit hour is now awarded upon completion.

Summary

The course approach to providing academic advising is especially effective, and the variety of ways in which these courses exist is appealing. The opportunity to provide a truly developmental academic advising service cannot be found in a better setting than the classroom. This physical environment establishes a climate for learning as students expect in all other classroom situations. The only differences they experience from classroom to classroom are the content, the instructional process, the teachers, and the other students in the class.

The programs described have all been developed on sound educational grounds, and they have reached all expectations, although through very different approaches. The Act I program at Brenau has evolved into Acts II, III, and IV; University 101 at South Carolina is completely elective and for academic credit, while Total Student Development at Heidelberg is for nonacademic credit but required; and the University of Puget Sound has uniquely used existing academic courses to achieve the same goals.

Whatever the format or conditions under which such courses are offered, it is obvious that they achieve significant, positive educational outcomes. Elements of these approaches are adaptable in most institutions, since courses are the standard instructional mode in higher education.

Summary and Conclusions

This chapter has provided descriptions of successful advising programs that are delivered in four basic modes. Although some overlap occurs, each has its own particular strengths. As institutions seek to improve their advising programs, they should review those included here to consider elements that could be adapted.

The centralized approach usually provides a comprehensive array of advising services by well-trained professionals to large numbers of students. Decentralized advising offers the personalized assistance that traditional faculty advising was intended to provide. Peer advising captures the confidence and trust already generated among students and channels those into productive educational experiences. Advising through courses parallels both the expectations and format of most of American higher education, that is, learning in the classroom. Results from each of these advising approaches have been favorable. Higher retention rates, increased use of campus resources, better academic planning, and greater satisfaction are all in evidence.

It appears that some combination of the above approaches might provide the "ideal" advising program. Using faculty and peer advisors in a centralized unit and requiring all new freshmen to complete an advising course would seem to encompass all the goals and achieve all the results an advising program could be expected to provide. As institutions develop these combinations, a new set of exemplary programs will come into existence. For now, the fourteen programs herein described provide a solid foundation of characteristics upon which to build for the future, and each one welcomes inquiries for assistance in reviewing and/or developing other advising programs.

Further Program Information

For additional information about programs described in this chapter, contact the following offices.

Centralized Advising

Undergraduate Advising Center
University of Maryland
College Park, MD 20742

Division of Undergraduate Studies
The Pennsylvania State University
University Park, PA 16802

Center for Academic Advising
University of Utah
Salt Lake City, UT 84112

Office of Career Development
Des Moines Area Community College
2006 S. Ankeny Blvd.
Ankeny, IA 50021

Decentralized Advising

Student Advisement Center
State University of New York at Oswego
Oswego, NY 13126

Office of Advising and Orientation
California State University - Chico
Chico, CA 95929

Office of Dean of Academic Services
Broome Community College
Binghamton, NY 13902

Peer Advising

Office of Advisement and Retention
Marymount Manhattan College
221 East Seventy First Street
New York, NY 10021

Office of Academic Advising Services
University of Northern Iowa
Cedar Falls, IA 50614

Offices of Advising and Retention
University of Montana
Missoula, MT 59801

Advising Through Courses

Dean of Student Development
Brenau College
Gainsville, GA 30501

University 101 Office
University of South Carolina
Columbia, SC 29208

· Office of Academic Advising
University of Puget Sound
Tacoma, WA 98416

Dean of Student Life
Heidelberg College
Tiffin, OH 44883

Acknowledgments

The author acknowledges the following persons for preparing descriptions of the advising programs included in this chapter. Appreciation is expressed to them for their cooperation and assistance.

Janice Abel, University of Northern Iowa
Ronald V. Adkins, University of Puget Sound
Joyce Alberts, University of Northern Iowa
Francis L. Battisti, Broome Community College
Kitty Corak, University of Montana
John N. Gardner, University of South Carolina
Linda C. Higginson, Pennsylvania State University
Mary Stuart Hunter, University of South Carolina
David W. King, State University of New York at Oswego
Margaret A. Landry, Marymount Manhattan College
Harry M. Langley, Brenau College
Joseph F. Metz, Jr., University of Maryland
James Pappas, University of Utah
Bryan D. Smith, Broome Community College
G. Robert Standing, California State University at Chico
Linda A. Syrell, State University of New York at Oswego
Sharon Van Tuyl, Des Moines Area Community College
Kathryn O. Venema, Heidelberg College
Eric R. White, Pennsylvania State University
Leanne Wolff, Heidelberg College

References

Abel, J., and Alberts, J. "Peer Advising Report." Cedar Falls, Iowa: University of Northern Iowa, 1978-1979.

Baxter, R. P. "A Study of the Emergence and Functioning of Academic Advising Centers Within Academic Units of Major Universities." *Dissertation Abstracts International,* 1971, *32,* 731A.

Bonar, J. R., and Mahler, L. R. "A Center for 'Undecided' College Students." *Personnel and Guidance Journal,* 1976 , *54,* 481-484.

Brown, C. R., and Myers, R. "Student vs. Faculty Curriculum Advising." *Journal of College Student Personnel,* 1975, *16* (3), 226-231.

Brown, G., and Twedt, A. "Continuing Education for Workers: Meeting the Needs of Unions and Their Membership." Paper presented at annual meeting of the American College Personnel Association, Cincinnati, Ohio, March 1981.

Carstensen, D. J., and Silberhorn, C. A. *A National Survey of Academic Advising, Final Report.* Iowa City, Iowa: American College Testing Program, 1979.

Cohen, R. D., and Jody, R. *Freshman Seminar: A New Orientation.* Boulder, Colo.: Westview Press, 1978.

Crockett, D. S. (Ed.). *Academic Advising: A Resource Document.* Iowa City, Iowa: American College Testing Program, 1978.

Crockett, D. S. "Academic Advising Delivery Systems." In R. B. Winston, Jr., S. C. Ender, and T. K. Miller (Eds.), *New Directions for Student Services: Developmental Approaches to Academic Advising,* no. 17. San Francisco: Jossey-Bass, 1982.

Dwyer, J. O. "As Freshmen First." In P. Brown, *The Forum for Liberal Education.* Vol. IV (2). Washington, D.C.: Association of American Colleges, 1981.

Gardner, J. N. *Proceedings of the National Conference on the Freshmen Orientation Course/Freshman Seminar Concept.* Columbia, S.C.: University of South Carolina, 1982.

Glennen, R. E. "Intrusive College Counseling." *School Counselor,* 1976, *24,* 48-50.

Gordon, V. N., and Grites, T. J. "The Freshman Seminar Course: Helping Students Succeed." *Journal of College Student Personnel,* 1984, *25,* 315-320.

Grites, T. J. *Academic Advising: Getting Us Through the Eighties.* American Association for Higher Education-Educational Resources Information Center (AAHE-ERIC)/Higher Education Research Report No. 7. Washington D.C.: American Association for Higher Education, 1979.

Habley, W. R. "The Advantages and Disadvantages of Using Students as Academic Advisors." *National Association of Student Personnel Administrators (NASPA) Journal,* 1979, *17* (1), 46-51.

Hickerson, J. H. "A Model for Advising in an Individualized

Undergraduate College." *National Academic Advising Association (NACADA) Journal*, 1982, 2 (2), 90–96.

Murry, J. P. "The Comparative Effectiveness of Student-to-Student and Faculty Advising Programs." *Journal of College Student Personnel*, 1972, 13 (6), 562–566.

Pino, J. A. "The Organization, Structure, Functions, and Student Perceptions of Effectiveness of Undergraduate Academic Advisement Centers." *Dissertation Abstracts International*, 1975, 35, 4205A–4206A.

Polson, C. J., and Jurich, A. P. "The Departmental Academic Advising Center: An Alternative to Faculty Advising." *Journal of College Student Personnel*, 1979, 20 (3), 249–253.

Robinson, L. H. "Renovating the Freshman Year." In ERIC Higher Education *Research Currents*. Washington, D.C.: American Association for Higher Education, 1972. (ED 068 075)

Shelton, J. B. "A Comparison of Faculty Academic Advising and Academic Advising by Professional Counselors: Final Report." Shawnee Mission, Kans.: Johnson County Community College, 1972. (ED 065 088)

Spencer, R. W., Peterson, E. D., and Kramer, G. L. "Utilizing College Advising Centers to Facilitate and Revitalize Academic Advising." *National Academic Advising Association (NACADA) Journal*, 1982, 2 (1), 13–23.

Stein, G. B., and Spille, H. A. "Academic Advising Reaches Out." *Personnel and Guidance Journal*, 1974, 53, 61–64.

Upcraft, M. L. "Undergraduate Students as Academic Advisers." *Personnel and Guidance Journal*, 1971, 49, 827–831.

Winston, R. B., Jr., Miller, T. K., and Prince, J. S. *Assessing Student Development: A Preliminary Manual for the Student Developmental Task Inventory (Second Edition) and the Student Developmental Profile and Planning Record*. Athens, Ga.: Student Development Associates, 1979.

Epilogue:
Improving
Academic Advising

Roger B. Winston, Jr., Thomas J. Grites,
Theodore K. Miller, Steven C. Ender

In a wide variety of ways, it has been asserted throughout this book that there is a need to reconceptualize both the content and process of academic advising, if it is to realize its potential for improving the quality of students' educational experiences. The definition of developmental academic advising proffered in Chapter One lays a conceptual foundation for a regeneration of academic advising's potential. This definition states, "Developmental academic advising is . . . a systematic process based on a close student-advisor relationship intended to aid students in achieving educational, career, and personal goals through the utilization of the full range of institutional and community resources. It both stimulates and supports students in their quest for an enriched quality of life." If academic advising practice is to meet the test of this definition, much needs to be done on most college campuses.

This chapter is designed to synthesize much of what has been presented in earlier chapters. Specifically, it is suggested that the concept of quality control, borrowed from industry, may serve as a useful paradigm of academic advising's role in higher education. Drawing on personal experience as academic advisors and interaction with the experts who have written the chapters herein, a series of proposals are advanced for improving the quality of advising programs on many campuses. Finally, projections are made concerning challenges and opportunities for academic advising in the next decade.

Educational Quality Control

Academic advising can be conceived as the institution's quality control mechanism. "Quality control," as defined in industry, "is the overall operations aimed at producing quality of product that will meet meaningful specifications" (Foster, 1963, p. 797).

Applying this concept to higher education, what are the specifications or outcomes one should expect as a result of the higher-education experience? Many would support Bowen (1977) who contends that higher education has three important purposes or missions: "It embraces both the formal academic program and the extracurricular life of an academic community, [and] is intended to help students develop as persons in three respects: cognitive learning by expanding their knowledge and intellectual powers; affective development, by enhancing their moral, religious, and emotional interests and sensibilities; and practical competence, by improving their performance in citizenship, work, family, consumer choice, health, and other practical affairs. . . . insofar as these three goals are achieved, they are the ingredients for the flowering of the total personality. . . . They define the ideal personalities to which many educators aspire for their students" (p. 39).

As Japanese auto manufacturers have demonstrated, quality control is most effective when practiced on the plant floor by those who are involved directly in production and assembly. In effect, academic advisors are on the "plant floor" and potentially can be in positions to ensure educational quality. In their multiple roles (see Chapters Five, Six, and Seven), they can help maintain rigorous intellectual and academic standards, while also assisting students in translating experiences from the classroom, laboratory, library, student organization, residence hall, and their families into a personally meaningful whole.

The formation of relationships that assure that at least one educator has close enough contact with each student to assess and influence the quality of that student's educational experience is realistic only through a systematic process, such as an academic advising program. Advisors can help students form comprehensive pictures of their present lives and articulate and plan for accomplishment of reasonable and attainable life goals. They also can encourage students to take advantage of the programs and services already offered on the campus. Unless someone takes this task as a responsibility, it is unlikely to be attended to systematically by anyone. In other words, everyone's business is no one's business! In most colleges no one is assigned this important responsibility of quality control on the most fundamental level, the individual student's level.

Whose responsibility should it be? In most institutions it is unrealistic to expect each instructor, even with small classes, to form personal relationships of sufficient duration and depth with each student in his or her class to accomplish this. It does occur with some students each term, however, but seldom with more than two or three per class. If it is unrealistic to expect the establishment of such close relationships between teachers and students in every class, then it is also unrealistic to assume that such a relationship will be formed between *any* institutional representative—faculty member, staff member, or administrator—and individual students, unless carefully planned. Some may argue that it is the student affairs division's responsibility to attend to the affective and emotional development of students, while faculty attend to their minds. Such a dichotomization of responsibility is unrealistic for three reasons: (1) A very small number of student affairs professionals, when compared to faculty and academic administrators, would be expected to influence 80 percent of students' lives. (Most students spend only about 20 percent of the day in the classroom and laboratory.) (2) There are no mechanisms on most campuses that can ensure systematic contact between student affairs staff members and all students. (On some campuses where the student affairs division has proposed a required, systematic personal development program, there has been great resistance, generally led by faculties who argue that this is not appropriate.) Quality academic advising requires frequent, purposeful, and planned contact. (3) If it were possible to assure such systematic contact between student affairs professionals and all students, a dramatic increase in the number of student affairs staff would be required, which is not a financially viable solution on most campuses. Active collaboration between academic affairs and student affairs, as noted in Chapter Three, seems both desirable and necessary, provided attention can be focused on students' educational experience, rather than protection of traditional turf.

Academic advisors are the most appropriate ones to assume the responsibility of educational quality control and can thereby enhance the quality of the educational experience of *every* student. An advising system that attends to such goals is possible only if there is commitment from the institutional leadership, an adequate reward system for advising, and active collaboration between the faculty and a strong, well-educated student affairs staff.

A comprehensive, systematic academic advising program structured to foster sustained, close relationships between students and advisors is the most practical vehicle for meeting the goals of higher education specified by Bowen (1977). Advisors in such a system (see Chapters Twelve and Thirteen) are in the best position to assure that rigorous academic standards are maintained and at the same time that students are able to use the resources available on the campus to accomplish their goals and to personalize their educational experience.

Academic Advising Revisited

The following propositions are offered for examination by those interested in improving the quality of students' educational experiences through academic advising.

1. *The first step in changing the structure and nature of academic advising is to reconceptualize its purpose.* Academic advising should be first a teaching-learning activity, second an active attempt to stimulate personal and intellectual growth, third a psychological and social support function, and finally an administrative record-keeping function.

    Through advising, when functioning at its full potential, students learn how to use resources and take advantage of a wide range of learning opportunities in order to realize their goals and aspirations and to further their intellectual development, academic competence, and personal effectiveness. It involves not only teaching students what is there but also helping students expand their visions of what "educated citizen" means. If advisors are pursuing this teaching goal, then students will be challenged or stimulated to become active participants in the learning enterprise. Developmental academic advising intentionally seeks to provide stimulation. However, psychological and social support are also necessary; otherwise, students will become overstimulated or feel threatened and will either psychologically withdraw from active involvement in the environment or will seek to leave it altogether (see Chapter Four). Lastly, academic advising must assure that accurate records are maintained and that students understand and satisfy the academic prescriptions established for graduation. Advising programs, however, that emphasize registration and record keeping, while neglecting attention to students' educational and personal experiences in the institution, are missing an excellent opportunity to influence directly and immediately the quality of students' education and are also highly inefficient, since they are most likely employing highly educated (expensive) personnel who are performing essentially clerical tasks.

2. *Academic advising must be viewed as a total institutional concern, not the sole province of any single constituency.* If institutional leaders make a commitment to developmental academic advising as a worthy institutional goal, then they also must be willing to focus institution-wide attention on it and allocate scarce funds to support it. Faculty must be given the

opportunity to elect to expend their time in academic advising, with the assurance they will be recognized and rewarded. Student affairs staff members should be expected to contribute to the advising program through expertise in designing and administering student-oriented programs and services, understanding human development processes and principles and their applications, and knowledge about career decision-making processes. Many student affairs staff members also should serve as academic advisors for limited numbers of students, thereby assuring that they do not lose contact with the breadth of student interests and concerns. Effective academic advising is most likely to result when both academic and student affairs personnel collaborate in designing, staffing, and administering the program.

Class scheduling and registration, in fact, can probably best be accomplished by student paraprofessionals who are closer to the process than most advisors can or desire to be. Student paraprofessionals and support staff are more likely to master more completely the mechanics and nuances of the registration process than are advisors who have other higher priorities to attend to, such as administrative tasks, class preparation, or research.

3. *Academic advising can be understood best and more easily reconceptualized if the process of academic advising and the scheduling of classes and registration are separated.* For many years, class scheduling has masqueraded as academic advising, which explains in part why many in higher education view academic advising as simply an administrative chore that requires little in terms of skill or knowledge. Class scheduling (Do I take English in the morning or afternoon?) should not be confused with educational planning (What sequence of courses better prepares me for a major in physics?) or course selection (Do I take a biology sequence or a chemistry sequence to satisfy the science requirement?). Developmental academic advising becomes a more realistic goal when separated from class scheduling because advising can then go on all during the academic year, not just during the few weeks prior to registration each new term.

4. *The creation of undergraduate advising centers—staffed by professional, student paraprofessional, allied professional (faculty and student affairs staff) advisors, and adequate support personnel—offers the best prospect for achieving the goals of developmental academic advising.* Developmental academic advising appears to offer promise as a sound conceptual foundation. Advising centers, when coupled with a comprehensive view of advising, have several important advantages: (1) By having all personnel in a central location, it is possible to determine better whether contacts are made regularly with students and whether appropriate records are kept and deadlines met. (2) If advisors who also have other major institutional responsibilities are used, a center in a location away from their other offices helps them separate advising activities from other responsibilities, such as class preparation, program administration, or research. (3) Assignment to an advising center signifies that academic advising is an important responsibility, performance in which can be evaluated. (4) Centralization allows for better use of specialized training and skills and easier referrals.

    The establishment of centralized advising centers, however, is no panacea. As Hines (Chapter Twelve) notes, the effectiveness of advising depends as much on the conceptual soundness of goals and approaches as on the specific organizational structure. Advising centers that primarily concentrate on registration signify the adoption of an assembly line approach to students. To accomplish the goals of developmental academic advising requires a reconceptualization of the traditional purposes and roles of academic advising, support from institutional leaders, reallocation of resources, intensively trained personnel, tangible rewards for good performance, and congenial organizational relationships.

5. *Every student deserves at least three hours a year of individual attention that focuses on personal assessment, academic and personal growth goal identification, and strategies for accomplishing those goals.* Although counseling, career planning, and learning centers meet some of the students' needs in the mentioned areas, students also deserve a single designated per-

son who is willing to assist them with overcoming adjustment problems associated with the college environment and who is knowledgeable about services, programs, and other resources. (Advisors do not have to be experts in all these areas. When issues are encountered for which they are unprepared to deal confidently, referrals can be made to appropriate professionals. Advisors should be viewed by students as *the* person with whom to begin when uncertain about appropriate action.) If higher education is to be something other than a "knowledge assembly line," then there must be direct, personalized methods of communicating the institution's concern for the welfare of each student and her or his educational experience. Any college arguing that it cannot organize its personnel and budget to accomplish this modest proposal of at least three hours a year of individual attention is suspect as a viable educational institution.

6. *Graduate programs need to address academic advising.* Attention needs to be focused at two separate levels: (1) Graduate programs that seek to prepare students for careers as faculty members or administrators should assure that their students have exposure to at least one course about academic advising similar to the one described by Gordon (1982). (2) Graduate programs in higher education and college student development/student personnel should introduce the concept of developmental academic advising and assure that students seeking careers as professional advisors acquire the skills and knowledge necessary to meet the demands of conceptualizing and administering advising centers and programs. Minimum necessary skills, experience, or knowledge for professional advisors include:

- knowledge of organizational and governance structures in higher education
- knowledge of psychosocial, intellectual, and career development theories as applied to college students
- experience in administering collegiate organizations
- knowledge of management and organization development techniques and strategies

- experience in teaching and training in small group formats
- knowledge of student needs assessment, research design and execution, and program evaluation techniques
- computer literacy
- experience in using and teaching effective interpersonal communication skills and counseling techniques
- knowledge of effective personnel management practices and staff evaluation approaches

Academic Advising in the Next Decade

The next decade portends both challenge and opportunity for academic advising.

Challenges. The time has come for institutions and their administrators to take academic advising seriously in terms of research and evaluation. There is a need to develop psychometrically proven instruments that can be used to assess the quality and impact of different approaches to academic advising. Most attempts at research on academic advising have been handicapped by narrowness of purpose and parochial orientations. The lack of instrumentation that is generic enough to apply across institutions and that addresses issues beyond student satisfaction has been a major limitation.

Two instruments that are trans-institutional, thus allowing comparisons between and among colleges, seem to hold some promise. Winston and Sandor (1984) have developed the *Academic Advising Inventory,* which measures developmental advising process dimensions based on Crookston's (1972) theorization, documents student-reported content of advising sessions, and assesses student satisfaction in a global sense.

Trombley (1984) piloted the *Student Evaluation of Faculty Advisors Inventory* and has confirmed a model that suggests that a range of advising tasks can be differentiated by type and complexity. Student ratings are used to identify three primary advisor domains— providing information, developing academic and educational goals, and providing personal support. This instrument has been used at the University of Vermont to provide one component of the individual Faculty Advisor Evaluation Profile; the profile also contains descriptive characteristics, faculty self-reports, and student self-reports about the context in which the advising variables exist.

Polson and Cashin (1981) suggested another research challenge, that is, to develop an "advising needs inventory." Though other college student needs inventories exist, this instrument would be specific to the developmental advising role and would include academic decision making and identifying potential academic and personal problems. They argued that until such needs are differentiated, it may be too difficult to assess the relative effectiveness of different advising approaches.

In the future, academic advising will be called upon to be more accountable for the quality of its services, especially if institutions elect to make major investments of financial and staff resources. Academic advising administrators also are going to be called upon to substantiate the claimed link between quality of academic advising services and student retention and student development. Controlled experimental studies that compare different advising techniques or interventions and delivery systems are necessary in order to establish advising's credibility and impact on students' academic and personal lives.

Another dimension of challenge for academic advising may be in the area of actual service delivery. Though faculty members have traditionally provided the bulk of the services, Teague and Grites (1980) found that half of the faculty contracts and collective bargaining agreements made absolutely no mention of advising as a specified faculty responsibility. They warned that without such specificity, the faculty role in this activity could eventually disappear. (It is not recommended that advising responsibility automatically be written into every faculty member's contract; not all faculty are interested in or possess the temperament and skills required to be an effective advisor. Preferably, academic advising should be sought as an assignment, just as research time is sought on many university campuses.) Coupled with rapidly advancing educational technologies, such as computer-assisted career guidance and academic planning programs as well as televised and at-home instruction, the faculty member may become even more removed from the advising role. Those responsible for advising programs will need to balance these conditions with the effective, desirable, and necessary use of faculty members as academic advisors.

Opportunities. A number of developments asseverate promise for academic advising as an effective, potent educational intervention. The National Academic Advising Association's (NACADA) membership continues to grow, giving persons interested in improving academic advising additional opportunities to obtain support, share ideas, confer about concerns and problems, and discover new options and approaches. NACADA has also established a Consultants' Bureau that acts as a referral agency and resource for institutions that desire assistance in evaluating, reconceptualizing, or organizing their advising programs. (Additional information about the NACADA Consultants' Bureau can be obtained by contacting Dr. Gary L. Kramer, Director of Academic Advising, Brigham Young University.)

To stimulate research in advising, NACADA has granted annual research awards to both professionals and graduate students and was responsible for "academic advising" being designated as a descriptor in the Educational Resources Information Center (ERIC) information retrieval system.

The American College Testing Program (ACT) has conducted seminars on academic advising around the country since 1978 and has conducted several studies that have direct implications for advising programs. Most recently, ACT and NACADA jointly have sponsored a National Recognition Program for Academic Advising through which seven Outstanding Advisors and seven Outstanding Institutional Advising Program's Awards are presented annually.

As of early 1984, the Council for the Advancement of Standards for Student Services/Development Programs (CAS) is in the process of developing professional practice standards for a wide range of academic and student affairs areas, of which academic advising is one. These standards are designed to assist institutional leaders who have responsibility for initiating and administering academic advising programs by providing guidance in program development and, eventually, criteria by which programs can be evaluated for accreditation purposes as well. This marks a great opportunity to keep the institution's attention focused on the quality of advising programs and provides an external source of support for efforts to improve and/or maintain quality services for students. For the first time, advising programs can be compared against a set of minimum standards.

Students will continue to press for their "consumer rights" in the next decade, including an expectation of support and concern for each individual from an identified college representative. This press brings renewed energy into the system of higher education, fueling the push for innovation and change. This impetus for change assures that academic advising will remain in the spotlight during the next decade. The advising system offers a vehicle to re-establish meaning and quality within higher education. Astute administrators will begin, in consultation with a broad institutional constituency, the process of reconceptualizing their institution's goals for academic advising and reorganizing the delivery systems.

References

Bowen, H. R. *Investment in Learning: The Individual and Social Values of American Higher Education.* San Francisco: Jossey-Bass, 1977.

Crookston, B. B. "A Developmental View of Academic Advising as Teaching." *Journal of College Student Personnel,* 1972, *13,* 12–17.

Foster, G. R. "Quality Control." In C. Heyel (Ed.), *Encyclopedia of Management.* New York: Reinhold, 1963.

Gordon, V. N. "Training Future Academic Advisors: One Model of a Pre-Service Approach." *National Academic Advising Association (NACADA) Journal,* 1982, *2* (2), 35–40.

Polson, C. J., and Cashin, W. E. "Research Priorities for Academic Advising: Results of a Survey of NACADA Membership." *National Academic Advising Association (NACADA) Journal,* 1981, *1* (1), 34–43.

Teague, G. V., and Grites, T. J. "Faculty Contracts and Academic

Advising." *Journal of College Student Personnel,* 1980, *21,* 40-44.

Trombley, T. B. "Analysis of the Complexity of Academic Advising Tasks." *Journal of College Student Personnel,* 1984, *25,* 234-239.

Winston, R. B., Jr., and Sandor, J. A. *Academic Advising Inventory.* Athens, Ga.: Student Development Associates, 1984.

Name Index

Schuette, C. G., 7, 33
Schuh, J. H., 330, 341–342
Scott, R. A., 319, 341
Sedlacek, W. E., 248, 373, 379
Seibert, A., 285
Shane, D., 17–18, 34, 336, 345–346
Shatkin, L., 226, 249
Sheehy, G., 94, 100, 118
Shelton, J. B., 470, 537
Shipton, J., 89–90, 118
Silberhorn, C. A., 13, 31, 35–36, 63, 348, 354, 371, 373, 374, 377, 456, 463, 500, 536
Simon, H., 322, 346
Singletory, L. A., 249
Slaney, R., 139, 146
Smith, B. D., xii, 535
Smith, E. J., 270, 272, 273, 284
Smith, J., 26, 34
Smith, S. H., 175, 195
Snow, J. J., 257, 284
Sorenson, G., 297, 314
Spaulding, S., 308, 314
Speizer, J. J., 295, 314
Spencer, R. W., 120, 226–249, 333, 346, 486, 537
Spille, H. A., 457, 458, 465, 486, 537
Sprandel, H. Z., 264, 267, 284
Sprandel, K., 333, 344, 348, 378
Standing, G. R., xii, 192, 196, 535
Starr, E. A., 335, 344–345
Stein, G. B., 457, 458, 465, 486, 537
Stelling, J. G., 295, 312
Steltenpohl, E. H., 89–90, 118
Steppanen, L. J., 341, 346
Stern, G. G., 175, 196
Sturgis, J. T., 262, 282
Sue, D., 272, 274, 279, 284
Sue, D. W., 274, 284
Sue, S., 273, 285
Suen, H. K., 272, 285
Super, D. E., 101–102, 118, 150, 159, 172, 451, 465
Syrell, L. A., xii, 535

T

Taylor, A. R., 288, 314
Teague, G. V., 547, 549–550

Terenzini, P. T., 66, 87–88, 252, 285
Theodorson, A. G., 106, 118
Theodorson, G. A., 106, 118
Thielens, W., Jr., 328, 344
Thomas, R. E., 2, 89–118
Thompson, J. D., 319, 346
Thompson, M. J., 82, 87
Thoresen, C. E., 124, 146
Tiedeman, D. V., 125–126, 130, 146
Titley, B. S., 130, 139, 146
Titley, R. W., 130, 139, 146
Toffler, A., 149, 172
Tolbert, E. L., 301, 312
Tollefson, A. L., 226, 248
Trombley, T. B., 13, 34, 273, 280, 546, 550
Trow, M., 148, 172
Trudeau, G. B., 11n
Twedt, A., 486, 536

U

Underwood, J., 260, 285
Upcraft, M. L., 338, 346, 456, 465, 500, 537

V

Valdez, R., 293, 314
Vandecreek, L., 400, 411
Van Tuyl, S., xii, 535
Venema, K. O., xiii, 535
Villeme, M. G., 371, 380

W

Wagner, C. S., 285
Walker, C., 268, 269, 270, 285
Walsh, E. M., 18, 34, 65, 88, 371, 380
Walter, T., 285
Waters, W., 260, 285–286
Watkins, B. T., 327, 346
Wedemeyer, R. H., 226, 249
Weick, K. E., 321n, 323, 346
Weissberg, M., 65–66, 88
White, B. J., 192, 194
White, E. R., xiii, 335, 344, 535
White, M. T., 335, 344, 349, 379
Widick, C., 175, 196

Subject Index

Students (continued)
146; experiences and perceptions of, 7–8, 28; faculty in interaction with, 10–12, 13, 65–66; in graduate and professional schools, 287–314; handbook for, 199; honors or gifted, and educational planning, 141–143; individual attention to, 544–545; intellectual development of, 425–427; life-cycle status of, 113–114; new, and as undeclared majors, 33; as prefreshmen, 334–335; preprofessional, 333; professional college changes by, 141; as resource, 219–220; right to access and privacy of records of, 397–399; special advising needs of, 250–286; special planning needs of, 135–144; stage and age variations of, 112–113; undecided, and planning, 135–139; variables in matching with advisors, 112–114. *See also* Peer advising
System of Interactive Guidance and Information (SIGI), 170, 247

T

Tanner v. *Board of Trustees of University of Illinois*, and contract change, 390, 411
Teaching, advising linked with, 413–414. *See also* Faculty entries
Technology, growth of, and higher education, 149–150
Tedeschi v. *Wagner College*, and contract change, 391, 411
Texas, University of, Health Professions Office at, 277
Third Circuit Court of Appeals, 384
Timing, in life cycle theory, 100
Tinker v. *Des Moines Independent Community School District*, and constitutional relationships, 383 385, 411
Training program: academic planning in, 448–449; analysis of, 440–465; background on, 440–442;

career advising in, 449; communication skills in, 450, 459; content of, 447–452, 459–460; course and program identification in, 448; decision making in, 449–450; and developmental theory, 442–443, 451–452, 459–460; evaluation of, 454–456; formats for, 453, 458–459; as intervention method, 180, 186, 190–191, 192–193; manuals for, 452; methods for, 453–454; needs survey for, 444–445; objectives for, 444–447, 457; organizing, 443–444; outcomes for, 445–446, 455–456; for paraprofessional advisors, 456–461; preservice and in-service objectives of, 446; procedural information in, 448; recommended, 545–546; for referral, 450–451, 460; special topics in, 452; steps in, 441–442; strategies for, 452–454; summary on, 461–462; and trainer goals, 447
Trans World Airlines, Inc. v. *Hardison*, and religious discrimination, 396, 411
Transcripts: as resource, 209–211; student development, 80, 210–211

U

Underprepared students: advising needs of, 253, 256–259; characteristics of, 253, 256; strategies for, 256–259
U.S. Constitution, 381–384
U.S. Department of Labor, 229, 249
U.S. Department of Labor Statistics, 261, 285
U.S. Merchant Marine Academy, verbal contract at, 387
U.S. Supreme Court, 382, 385, 395
Universal ethical principle orientation, in moral reasoning, 107
University of Texas Health Science Center v. *Babb*, and contractual issues, 385, 391, 411